Rear Admiral Stephen B. Luce, 1827-1917, founder and first president of the Naval War College. Painting by Frederic P. Vinton, 1900, in the Naval War College.

SAILORS AND SCHOLARS

THE CENTENNIAL HISTORY OF THE U.S. NAVAL WAR COLLEGE

by
John B. Hattendorf
B. Mitchell Simpson, III
John R. Wadleigh

NAVAL WAR COLLEGE PRESS - Newport, Rhode Island

For sale by the Superintendent of Documents, U.S. Government Printing Office, Washington, D.C. 20402
Stock No. 008-047-00364-1

Library of Congress Cataloging in Publication Data

Hattendorf, John B., 1941-
    Sailors and scholars: a centennial history of the U.S. naval war
college.

    Bibliography: pp. 354.
    Includes index.
    1. Naval War College (U.S.)—History. I. Wadleigh, John R., 1915-
    . II. Simpson, B. Mitchell III, 1937-   . III. Title.
V420.H37   1984   359.4′07′1173   84-8257

CONTENTS

ILLUSTRATIONS

PRESIDENT'S FOREWORD

One spring day in 1978 at a long forgotten meeting in Conolly Hall the idea of a centennial history was discussed. The Naval War College would be 100 years old in 1984 and its inception, growth and contribution spanned a period of incredible expansion in the history of the United States. The Navy's participation and that of its War College were inextricably woven into the fabric of those times and plainly deserved to be told. What better way than with a Centennial History? ·

Vice Admiral James Stockdale, then President of the Naval War College, lent his prestige and support to the project and discussed it frequently and enthusiastically at meetings that followed in spring and summer of that year. It was no secret that preparation of a credible history took great patience, talent and time. A start in the near term, by qualified authors and researchers, was absolutely necessary if the work was to be finished in time for the Centennial celebration in 1984. In August, Jim Stockdale received his first serious proposal. Retired Rear Admiral John R. Wadleigh wrote that, "such a history can be of benefit to the Navy and the War College and can serve as a worthwhile addition to naval and academic history." Jack Wadleigh proposed to team up with retired LCDR B. Mitchell (Tony) Simpson, III and compile "a volume which will suitably commemorate the first century of service of the world's oldest senior military educational institution."

Wadleigh and Simpson's proposal was everything it needed to be—detailed, logical and doable. In due course it was approved and the project was launched. By the time I arrived in Newport in the fall of 1982, the lion's share of the research was finished and drafts for many chapters had been prepared for comment. Fred Hartmann, my Academic Advisor and an experienced, accomplished author in his own right, became the project manager. Publishing a book, I was to learn, was not an uncomplicated effort and I needed a solid professional to navigate around the currents and shoals of the publishing world. Professor John Hattendorf, newly returned from the University of Singapore, joined the team next as the deadline loomed ever larger. John's expertise as an author and historian were invaluable ingredients that added to the already high quality of the research and assured us of success—on time. It was a collaboration that was close and continuous and one in which I took immense personal pride.

Other principal members of the Naval War College team have contributed substantially to the production of this book. Mr. Frank Uhlig contributed wise counsel, sound editorial advice, and consistent guidance on style. Mr. Robert Laske handled printing arrangements for Library of Congress cataloging and provided a priority listing for distribution of the finished work. Mr. Roger Levesque handled the difficult and complex problem of the production of print-ready copy. Mr. Anthony Nicolosi made the initial selection of pictures and wrote the captions. Mr. Tony Sarro, with his usual flair, coordinated the design for the covers and the Centennial insignia.

Special thanks go to Mrs. Carole Boiani for her outstanding work of phototypesetting, and to Barbara Atkins, Rose Lundy, and Rachelle Lapre of the Word Processing Branch, who made the initial inputs of the entire text. The demanding requirements of the final layout and pasteup of camera-ready copy were efficiently handled by Mrs. Eleanor Silvia, Mrs. Margaret Corr, and Mrs. Jackie Audet Cayer of the Editorial/Copyright Branch. My appreciation also extends to Ian Oliver, John Ramos, and Gerard Lamothe in the Graphics Arts Department. Photography was handled by James Deffet, William Arnold, and Thomas Cookinham.

The Naval War College Foundation generously provided the financial backing which assured production of a book whose quality would in every way reflect the prestige and academic excellence of the Naval War College.

It is my great personal pleasure to commend this history to you. It has been a rewarding professional opportunity for me, as 41st President, to direct the activities of the Naval War College in the last two years. The College continues to grow in importance and to justify the expectations of the Naval Establishment and the nation.

I am sure that, as you read this history of the College, you will come away with some real sense of the human dramas which have marked the institution's evolution during a period which is almost exactly the second century of the national existence of the United States of America.

James E. Service
Rear Admiral, U.S. Navy
President

AUTHORS' PREFACE

The Naval War College was founded in October 1884 at a time when the U.S. Navy was a minor force among the world's naval powers. In the century since, extraordinary changes have taken place in the life of the nation, the role and size of its Navy, and the role and size of the Naval War College.

This account of the life of the college in its first century is intended to present an overview of the major events and developments the college has experienced. It is not an "institutional history," narrowly confined to events at the War College—a dry-as-dust recital of curricula changes. Since the Naval War College is the professional intellectual extension of the U.S. Navy, we thought it would be practical and useful to link the development and changes at the War College to the events affecting its parent and sponsor. And in portraying the Navy's development as a continuous background theme, we have also shown the gradual expansion of national policy. We believe that the history of the War College is made both more meaningful and certainly more interesting through this effort.

Previously published accounts of the college's history have concentrated on one period or another, or on a single aspect of concern. But there has been no reasonably concise history of the entire first century of the Naval War College for the informed reader. This volume seeks to fill that gap.

Achieving a well balanced account is always challenging. The later history of the War College has its share of controversies (just as in the early decades) but with the difference that many participants in recent events are still alive to comment! We made it a rule to show all later sections of the manuscript to every principal participant. In some cases we had the demanding responsibility of deciding between directly opposing viewpoints.

In writing this centennial history we had the considerable college archives at our disposal, which we have used and relied upon extensively. Unfortunately, for the early period of the college's history, up to about 1920, there was no deliberate and orderly collection or preservation of administrative documents. Valuable material remains from other aspects and other periods of the college's history. All the remaining records have been brought together and arranged in the Naval Historical Collection of the Naval War College in a readily accessible way for scholarly research through the dedicated effort of Anthony S. Nicolosi. Little of value could have been achieved without his preliminary work, and that of his assistant, Dr. Evelyn Cherpak. As archivists and manuscript curators their contribution is significant.

We have gratefully utilized the valuable research on various periods carried out by scholars such as Rear Admiral John D. Hayes on Luce, Doris Maguire on Mahan and Chadwick, Dr. Robert Seager on Mahan, Dr. Ronald Spector on the early years of the college, Commander Thomas Buell on Spruance, King and *Sound Military Decision*, Dr. Gerald J. Kennedy on the inter-war years, and Commander Nepier Smith on the post war years. In addition we are deeply in debt to earlier college historians who blazed the trail for us with unpublished, typescript histories. We are particularly grateful for the work of Rear Admiral Austin Knight and Captain W. D. Puleston who prepared a draft history in 1916, and to the many college staff members who endeavored to up-date it in the years up to 1937. In the late 1950s and early 1960s, officers such as Captain Paul R. Schratz and his successors recorded useful data in their efforts to meet the requirement for the annual command history.

The work of Dr. John T. Mason with the Naval Institute's Oral History Program has proved very useful and the copies of the growing collection of transcripts deposited in the college's Naval Historical Collection provided a valuable source.

In preparing this history for publication, the detailed, candid and constructive editorial criticism of Frank Uhlig, Jr., quickly established high standards. We have gratefully followed his sound advice.

We are particularly grateful to Frederick H. Hartmann, the college's Special Academic Advisor since 1966, for his patient and sustained advice, comments and suggestions. As our "project manager," he piloted this project through all its phases. As a knowledgeable witness to many of the events since 1966, he provided valuable insights.

Numerous participants and witnesses to recent War College history kindly read and commented upon the relevant chapters. They also freely shared their own observations with us. They were: VADM

Frederick Bennett, Capt. David G. Clark, Prof. Philip A. Crowl, RADM
Henry E. Eccles, Dr. William R. Emerson, Capt. Clarence O. Fiske, Prof.
Philip Gamble, Capt. Robert S. Guy, Prof. Frederick H. Hartmann, VADM
John T. Hayward, Col. John B. Keeley, Cdr. Robert M. Laske, Dr. J. Kenneth
McDonald, Capt. James F. McNulty, Prof. Richard Megagee, Capt. Arthur
F. Newell, Anthony S. Nicolosi, Capt. Hugh G. Nott, Capt. Jack Q. Quinn,
Capt. William C. Rae, Prof. Warren Rogers, VADM F. S. H. Schneider, Prof.
Earl R. Schwass, VADM Benedict J. Semmes, Capt. Paul R. Schratz, VADM
James B. Stockdale, Prof. William E. Turcotte, ADM Stansfield Turner,
VADM Thomas R. Weschler, Prof. Robert S. Wood and RADM Joseph C.
Wylie.

We alone are responsible for the contents of this volume.

John B. Hattendorf
B. Mitchell Simpson, III
John R. Wadleigh

CHAPTER 1

THE NAVY THAT THE WAR COLLEGE JOINED

A navy and its institutions reflect the nation they serve. In 1884, the year the Naval War College was founded, the United States felt no great or imminent danger from the sea. Since the Civil War, the Navy's strength and capability had withered away because there had seemed no immediate need for a large navy. Writing in 1880, Chief Engineer J.W. King noted that epochs of exceptional naval activity alternated with periods of decay during the first century of American naval history. "The several great national emergencies have each called forth most remarkable displays of maritime capabilities and powers," King wrote, "to be followed, when the crisis is past, by a reversion to the other extreme of inefficiency and neglect."[1]

By comparison to Britain's Royal Navy, the largest in the world, the U.S. Navy with 92 ships, 32 of them in commission, and 8,000 officers and men, was small indeed. Britain had 359 ships with 63,598 officers and men, followed closely by France with 329 ships and 47,950 officers and men. There was then a large gap in relative numbers to the level of the Russian, Spanish, Italian, and German navies. After them ranked the navies of Brazil, Chile, and Argentina.[2] Some people argued that its total numbers placed the U.S. Navy in the middle group. Others said it ranked only among the other navies of the western hemisphere, considering its poor equipment and training. A U.S. Senator from South Carolina declared that in battle with a "vessel of any other power in the civilized world our guns would compare with theirs almost as a popgun with a long range rifle." Going further, he told the Senate

> I venture to say that the most insignificant, the least valuable ship of the Italian Navy is better than the best one in the American Navy.[3]

In 1884, the only vessel classified as a first-rate ship on the U.S. Navy list was the wooden, steam frigate *Tennessee*, flagship of the North Atlantic Squadron. When the ship was sold in 1887, Secretary of the Navy William Whitney commented in his annual report for that year, "She had a short life, but as a consumer of money, a brilliant one."[4] Earlier the Secretary had reported to the President, "It is questionable whether we have a single naval vessel finished and at sea at the present time that could be trusted to encounter the ships of any important power—a single vessel that has either the necessary armor for protection, speed for escape, or weapons for defense."[5]

In Washington, the Secretary directed the U.S. Navy from his office in the State-War-Navy building overlooking the west side of the White House. He was the only central figure in a cumbersome, decentralized administrative scheme that spawned bureaucratic competition. Since 1842, Secretaries had administered the Navy through eight independent Bureaus, each headed by a senior officer and each competing for prestige, power, and money. Often the lines of responsibility among the Bureaus were indistinct, and sometimes they overlapped. The Secretary personally sent all operational instructions, by mail or cable, to the five squadrons in the North and South Atlantic, Eastern Pacific, East Asian, and European waters.[6]

The most important of these petty principalities in 1884 was the Bureau of Navigation, headed by Commodore John G. Walker. Although the Secretary made all decisions on fleet operations, Walker's Bureau served as the means of implementing instructions. In the absence of the Secretary, the Chief of that Bureau became Acting Secretary. In addition, the Bureau of Navigation was responsible for officer assignments, for the Naval Academy, for the Office of Naval Intelligence, and for the Office of Naval Records and Library. When the Naval War College was established in 1884, it was added to the Bureau's responsibilities. In Newport, Rhode Island, two other Bureaus had interests. The Bureau of Ordnance, under Commodore Montgomery Sicard, controlled the Naval Torpedo Station and its school on Goat Island, and the Bureau of Equipment and Recruiting, under Commodore Earl English, was responsible for recruit training at the Naval Training Station, which shared Coasters Harbor Island with the College.

Each head of a Bureau was equal to the heads of all the others. In the administrative structure, there was no single naval officer senior to any one of them. However, there was an Admiral of the Navy, the most senior officer on active duty. Although he held a position of great prestige and status, he had little authority or power. Since 1870, Admiral David Dixon Porter had held this position. Although his attempts to bring power and authority to his exalted rank ended in frustration, Porter remained an influential figure in naval affairs.[7]

To the casual observer, the U.S. Navy appears to have been at a low point in its history. Its ships were outmoded, it had little financial support from Congress, and it had a confused and overlapping system of administration. Yet beneath that superficial impression, deeper streams of development pointed toward a dramatic resurgence of American naval power over the next quarter century.

Spur to World Naval Revival

In international terms, 1884 was a turning point for navies. In England, the year marked the end of public complacency toward the Royal Navy. "The Dark Ages of the Admiralty" began to give way to the era of naval revival. Relations among the great powers had been generally calm for several years, but in 1884 the situation changed. Russian moves in Central Asia seemed to menace British India. Britain's refusal to evacuate Egypt irritated France, and German relations with England grew tense as Chancellor Bismarck encouraged German colonial expansion in Africa and the Pacific. To make matters worse, good relations between France and Germany created rumors that a continental maritime league was about to be formed against England.

In September 1884, the *Pall Mall Gazette* published a series of anonymous articles which exposed the need for naval improvements at a time of growing crisis. Even the First Sea Lord joined the critics, asking for increased naval expenditure to keep pace with France, Germany, and the other great powers.[8] The public outcry in 1884 forced the British government to increase dramatically its expenditures for warships, naval ordnance, and coaling stations.[9] This political discussion was reported widely, bringing to the attention of the reading public in America the intensive naval building programs that were under way in Europe. By following the English political situation, readers learned of naval developments in France, Italy, Germany, and other countries and began to realize that the American Navy lagged far behind.[10]

In the United States, professional naval officers knew of these developments long before the public became aware of them. In 1877 and 1878, Chief Engineer J. W. King, USN, had been ordered to investigate European naval construction. He published his findings in 1880 in his book, *The Warships and Navies of the World*. American perceptions of these naval developments abroad helped to form criteria by which both the public and the professional naval officer judged the capabilities of the U.S. Navy. These perceptions were as important as those which correlated the Navy to American foreign policy.

In 1884, the principal concern of American naval men was the U.S. Navy's traditionally defensive posture. Responsible American officials focused entirely on two primary roles for the Navy, the defense of overseas trade and coast defense. It would be several years before imperialism and ideas of overseas expansion began to have a serious influence on naval policy and development. There were, however, a number of forces already at work that were turning American interests outward and that made possible future use of the Navy as an effective tool in seeking political goals beyond American waters.[11]

At the close of the American Civil War, the United States had the most numerous and innovative fleet of ironclad warships in the world. John Ericsson's monitor designs had provided the seed for future battleship design, but it was not developed in America after 1863. The decline from this far-reaching pinnacle down to a motley collection of obsolete and unarmored, steam-sailing vessels, armed largely with smooth bore ordnance, gave pause for reflection. One Secretary of the Navy reported that the accumulation of old hulls, machinery, and stores in the navy yards "presents an unsightly appearance sometimes ghostly and discouraging to those whose labors are to be performed near it."[12] The situation suggested, without any other factors, that a cleanup was necessary. It encouraged officers to seek a variety of ways to build up the Navy at a time when the prospects for future advancement, and even employment, in the Navy caused a great deal of anxiety.[13]

While the U.S. Navy had seriously declined in strength and capability, it was not moribund. Its ships cruised worldwide. Although there were few ships in the fleet, perhaps insufficient for their limited purposes, they represented an established pattern of wide-ranging activity. Beginning with USS *Ticonderoga*'s world cruise in 1878, the Navy Department was preoccupied with the Navy's role in protecting American overseas commerce. Naval officers commonly based their strategic views on the belief that a growing industrial nation, like the United States, must export its products in order to maintain harmony and prosperity at home.[14]

Several events in the 1870s and 1880s forced American naval men to think clearly and sensibly about the Navy's ability to carry out its traditional role in a period of decline. The first event was the *Virginius* affair in 1872-1873. This incident in the Cuban Revolution of 1868-1878 had a profound effect by creating a situation which could have been dealt with by combined fleet action and amphibious operations. The inability of the U.S. Navy to act effectively raised a series of questions for American naval men about tactics, training, ship types, roles and the direction of the Navy in wartime. Although a minor incident in overall terms, the situation illuminated important and basic issues which were continually discussed by professionals over the next two decades.[15] The importance of these same issues was underscored for American naval officers by the victory of Chile's new navy in the War of the Pacific, the threats to American interests created by French plans for a canal across the Isthmus of Panama, and German moves in Samoa.[16] The means by which these various incidents were translated into impulses for a revived American Navy were complex, but the ideas that this process engendered were also those that contributed to the foundation of the Naval War College.

Several subsequent developments that occurred in the 1870s created the means of progress. First, the relationship between the Navy and Congress underwent a subtle transition. A change in the relative continuity of duties for congressmen, senators, and naval officers played an important part. In the early years, the Chiefs of Naval Bureaus remained in office for many years. Rear Admiral Joseph Smith, for example, headed the Bureau of Yards and Docks for a record 23 years between 1846 and 1869. On the other hand, there was a fairly rapid turnover in the memberships of the congressional committees dealing with naval affairs. By 1875, the situation had reversed so that Chiefs of Bureaus, and even Secretaries of the Navy, changed rapidly, while the average length of service on the congressional committees became much longer. In this way, men such as Eugene Hale could dominate the Senate Naval Affairs Committee from 1883 to 1911, and Washington C. Whitthorne and Benjamin Harris could serve important and continuing roles on the House committee which outlasted institutional conservatism within the Navy and changes in the White House.

Second, the means to reform the Navy were facilitated by growing professionalization within the Navy. During the last decades of the 19th century, many occupations in America began to develop a sense of group identity, which was expressed by the formation of professional associations and journals that promoted the development of a specialized and theoretical knowledge relating to the occupation. In America, no occupational group had fully developed this status, but lawyers, doctors, educators, and engineers were each moving in this direction. Within the armed forces, the same developments were discernible. Since 1845, the Naval Academy had provided a basis for the naval profession by creating a standard system of education and a means of officer selection. About the same time, naval lyceums were established at several navy yards as a means to promote discussion on naval issues. The New York Naval Lyceum published the first, but short-lived, professional journal, *The Naval Magazine*.[18]

A more effective and lasting professional organization, the U.S. Naval Institute, appeared in 1873. Organized by Stephen B. Luce, Foxhall Parker, and David Dixon Porter, the organization and its *Proceedings* became a primary vehicle for the advancement of professional and scientific knowledge among American naval officers. It became the organization which was needed to elevate the naval officer's occupation to professional status.[19] By providing a means for officers to publish their professional thoughts, the Naval Institute cultivated a sense of mental determination and self-discipline among its members, which provided guidance and constructive thought for the naval revival in the United States. By 1884, the Naval Institute had served this function for more than 10 years and had made a great contribution by providing a basis for the formulation of a theoretical and comprehensive maritime philosophy in the future as well as helping to define the need for professional education.[20]

Professional Development

The professional development in the Navy took two forms which were, at the same time, complementary and competing. On one hand, officers saw the need to develop technical and scientific expertise which would allow full use of modern armaments. The establishment of the Torpedo Station on Goat Island in 1869 is an example of this approach. On the other hand, they also saw the need to develop the critical and analytical skills which would facilitate a full examination of the purposes, functions, and limitations of naval power and allow officers to formulate effective strategy, tactics, and logistics. These two lines of development were complementary in their purpose, but they were built on quite different intellectual foundations that required different sets of academic values and different approaches in solving problems.

Some, but not many, naval officers have excelled in both lines of professional development. This has created tensions and rivalries between those officers who favored one side of the professional outlook and those who chose the other. Members of each group supported the establishment of institutions that fostered and promoted their own professional outlook. Not uncommonly, some individuals believed that one or the other outlook should be not only preeminent but the exclusive basis of development. The tension between the two groups is readily discernible in the pages of the Naval Institute's *Proceedings* in the 1880s.[21] In origins, however, one must go back to the controversy between the line and the staff which broke out following the establishment of the engineer corps in 1842. The wide-ranging and entangled debate was complicated by the fact that both groups were struggling for professional standards without clear-cut or fully developed concepts. It was an intellectual contest blurred by issues of status, authority, pay, and promotion.[22]

While the Naval Institute *Proceedings* provided the jousting ground for these debates, it, like other professional publications such as the

Army-Navy Journal, was not an official journal and was not formally backed by any official organization. The first important, official organizational change within the Navy Department that reflected the new thinking was the establishment in 1882 of the Office of Naval Intelligence (ONI) within the Bureau of Navigation. In its early work, the Office of Naval Intelligence concentrated on collecting technical data about foreign naval construction, organization, and equipment. The information was useful and welcomed by Bureau Chiefs involved in planning the new American steel warships. Less welcome to such technical specialists was the tendency among officers in ONI to be distracted by broader war problems, higher strategy, and naval history.[23]

Link Between Historical Study and Naval Intelligence

Naval history was a new area of inquiry. It was part of the development of the serious academic study of history that was only just beginning to be accepted. The first doctorates in history were awarded by Harvard University in 1876, and in 1881 the first academic chair in history was established at Cornell. In both America and England, the study of history was growing up outside the universities and then "crashed the conservative academic portals" to secure a permanent place. The early practitioners of naval history, such as John Knox Laughton, John Colomb, and A. T. Mahan, became more perceptive and accurate as they carried on with their pioneer work in the 1870s and 1880s. The impulse which set naval men reading about the past was clearly a growing dissatisfaction with the increasing narrowness of the technical viewpoint within the naval service.[24] Increasing emphasis on naval improvement, material change, and industrial development was so readily accepted that little thought was given to the purpose and the use of the new machines. The newly forming school of history offered a means to consider naval issues in broad perspective unencumbered by the distractions of either contemporary political passion or rapidly advancing technology.

Several American officers had already demonstrated a keen interest in naval history and had written historical articles for the Naval Institute's *Proceedings* during the 1870s. One of the leaders in this endeavor was Professor James R. Soley, a prolific writer, Naval Academy instructor, and international lawyer. In 1882, he was appointed Librarian of the Navy Department Library, in the Bureau of Navigation. Immediately upon taking up his duties, Soley consolidated the rare books scattered throughout Navy Department offices, established a collection of historical naval prints and photographs, and began to build the 7,000 volume collection. He also made the first serious attempt to collect and preserve American naval records. In 1884,

Congress encouraged Soley's efforts further by appropriating funds for the publication of the documents on naval operations in the Civil War. Although this series did not begin to appear in print until 1894, Soley began the initial work and research to gather and use these historical records as a means of "ensuring the efficiency of the naval service."[25]

As a matter of administrative convenience during their early years, the newly established Office of Naval Intelligence and the Office of Naval Records and Library shared the same rooms in the State-War-Navy Building. The location of this early historical work close to the work of intelligence compilation created a link in the approach and concerns of both enterprises. Intelligence officers seemed to become increasingly interested in historical insight while the historical work was kept specifically on the professional and service aspects of the topic.

The development of professionalism within the United States Navy, engendering both technological and analytical progress, was the hallmark of the naval revival in the 1880s. Numerous obstacles stood in the path, deflecting and slowing growth. Party rivalry in Congress, inexperience, defective administrative organization, lack of manufacturing facilities, prejudices from the earlier period, as well as geographical and political isolation were all obstacles to be overcome but the work of naval reconstruction was clearly under way. In 1882, Congress had limited the amount of money that could be spent for repairing the old wooden ships, as a means to phase out the old ships. In the following year, Congress took the first step in replacing the old ships by authorizing four steel vessels, the nucleus of the "New Navy." These were tentative steps which signified further change to come but required great effort in the future. By the end of 1884, Congress had compelled the retirement of many outmoded ships, but provision for an adequate number of new ships to replace them was still needed along with clear ideas for their design and use.

In 1884, the United States Navy was in a period of transition which reflected the broad developments in American intellectual perceptions, the growth of industrial power, technological progress, and general professional development. The undercurrents that created a new navy were already discernible even while the old appearances remained. Change was in the air, and suggestions for future development were heard in many different areas. In Newport, Rhode Island, *The Mercury* reported in the spring of 1884 that Coasters Harbor Island in Narragansett Bay might be the site of either a school for the advanced instruction of naval officers, or perhaps it would become the site of a naval asylum.

Notes

1. J. W. King, *The Warships and Navies of the World, 1880* (Annapolis, Naval Institute Press, 1982), p. 377. Reprint of 1880 edition.

2. Quoted in Benjamin Franklin Cooling, *Gray Steel and Blue Water Navy* (Hamden, Conn.: Archon Books, 1979), p. 49, from U.S. Congress 48th, 1st and 2nd Sess., *Congressional Record*, 15, pt. 2, p. 1391.

3. Ibid.

4. Quoted in Frank M. Bennett, *The Steam Navy of the United States* (Pittsburgh: Nicholson, 1896), p. 544.

5. U.S. Department of the Navy, *Annual Report of the Secretary of the Navy, 1885*, (Washington: Govt. Print. Off.), p. xxxiii.

6. For general history of administration, see C. O. Paullin, *Paullin's History of Naval Administration, 1775-1911: A Collection of Articles from the U.S. Naval Institute Proceedings* (Annapolis: Naval Institute Press, 1968).

7. Kenneth J. Hagan, *American Gunboat Diplomacy and the Old Navy 1877-1889* (Westport: Greenwood Press, 1973), pp. 14-28, and "Admiral David Dixon Porter: Strategist for a Navy in Transition," USNI *Proceedings* 94 (July 1968), pp. 140-43; James R. Soley, *Admiral Porter* (New York: Appleton, 1903).

8. Arthur J. Marder, *The Anatomy of British Sea Power: A History of British Naval Policy in the Pre-Dreadnought Era, 1880-1905* (New York: Knopf, 1940), pp. 119-121, and N. A. M. Rodger, "The Dark Ages of The Admiralty, 1869-85," *Mariner's Mirror*, Vol. 61 (1975), pp. 331-334; Vol. 62 (1976), pp. 33-46, and pp. 121-128.

9. Paul M. Kennedy, *The Rise and Fall of British Naval Mastery* (New York: Scribners, 1976), p. 178.

10. Marder, op.cit. For a summary of general naval developments at the time, see J. W. King, *The Warships and Navies of the World, 1880*.

11. Russell F. Weigley, *The American Way of War: A History of United States Military Strategy and Policy* (Bloomington: Indiana University Press, 1973), p. 169-70.

12. U.S. Department of the Navy, *Annual Report of the Secretary, 1881-82*, p. 25. Quoted in Sandler, see footnote 13.

13. Stanley Sandler, "A Navy in Decay: Some Strategic Technological Results of Disarmament, 1865-69 in the U.S. Navy," *Military Affairs*, XXXV (December 1971), pp. 138-142; Peter Karsten, *The Naval Aristocracy* (New York: Free Press, 1972), pp. 277-325.

14. Kenneth J. Hagan, *American Gunboat Diplomacy and the Old Navy 1877-1889*, pp. 188-191.

15. Lawrence Carroll Allin, *The United States Naval Institute Intellectual Forum of the New Navy: 1873-1889* (Manhattan, Kansas: Military Affairs, 1978), pp. 45-49.

16. Walter R. Herrick, Jr., *The American Naval Revolution* (Baton Rouge: Louisiana State University Press, 1966), p. 23.

17. Robert G. Albion, "The Naval Affairs Committee, 1816-1947," U.S. Naval Institute *Proceedings*, 78 (1952), pp. 1227-37, and *Makers of Naval Policy 1798-1947* (Annapolis: Naval Institute Press, 1980), p. 206, pp. 634-38.

18. S. de Christofar, "The Naval Lyceum," U.S. Naval Institute *Proceedings*, 78 (1951), pp. 869-870.

19. L. C. Allin, op.cit., pp. 21-24; Ronald Spector, *Professors of War: The Naval War College and the Development of the Naval Profession* (Newport: Naval War College Press, 1977), pp. 3-4.

20. Allin, op.cit., pp. 71-120, 219-23, 343.

21. See, for example, Ibid., p. 219-23.

22. See F. M. Bennett, *Steam Navy of the United States*, pp. 75-88, 177-192, 603-21, 732-43, 750-56; Lance C. Buhl, "Mariners and Machines: Resistance to Technological Change in the American Navy, 1865-1869," *Journal of American History*, Vol. 61, No. 3 (1974), pp. 703-27.

23. Jeffery M. Dorwart, *The Office of Naval Intelligence: The Birth of America's First Intelligence Agency 1865-1918* (Annapolis: Naval Institute Press, 1979), pp. 24-25.

24 D. M. Schurman, *The Education of A Navy: The Development of British Naval Strategic Thought 1867-1914* (Chicago: University of Chicago Press, 1965), pp. 5-6. See also Allin, *United States Naval Institute*, pp. 223-235.

25. U.S. Department of the Navy, *Official Records of the Union and Confederate Navies in the War of the Rebellion* (Washington: Govt. Print. Off., 1894), I, p. viii. For a history of the Navy Department Library, see John McElroy's unpublished manuscript in the Navy Department Library, "Office of Naval Records and Library 1882-1946," p. 1, and W. J. Morgan and Joye L. Leonhart, *A History of the Dudley Knox Center for Naval History* (Washington: Govt. Print. Off., 1981), pp. 1-4.

26. Harold and Margaret Sprout, *The Rise of American Naval Power 1776-1918* (Annapolis: Naval Institute Press, 1980), pp. 190-197; George T. Davis, *A Navy Second to None* (Westport, Conn.: Greenwood Press, 1971), pp. 37-43.

27. *The Mercury*, 22 March 1884.

CHAPTER 2

A STRUGGLE FOR EXISTENCE: THE ERA OF LUCE AND MAHAN, 1884-1893

The idea of the Naval War College was conceived in the mind of Stephen B. Luce. Through Luce's outspoken leadership, the institution formed on his concept was both an expression and a part of the forces that were leading toward America's naval revival. All the reformers met many of the same obstacles, but the college represented a new element in the reform movement. Luce always saw the requirement for a practical testing of ideas, but his college clearly emphasized the analytical line of professional development and, by its very intellectual foundations, differed from the technological approach. This different outlook created tension, and the War College became fair game in the endemic rivalry among the Bureaus in Washington.

In July 1884, Stephen B. Luce was appointed Acting Rear Admiral, in command of the North Atlantic Station. Having served more than 40 years on active duty, he had attained the senior and most prestigious flag assignment at sea. Luce was widely recognized as one of the most capable officers in the Navy at that time. He had served at sea in a variety of capacities, including the command of seven different ships under sail and steam. In 1863, Luce had commanded one of the Navy's most modern warships, the Ericsson-designed monitor *Nantucket*. Promoted to commodore in 1881, he gained further practical experience for fleet work when he commanded the squadron of ships devoted to sea training for apprentice seamen.[1]

Training, administration, organization, and education were the principal underlying themes of Luce's career. These were unusual types of activity for a naval man at the time, but Luce devoted his life to improving the Navy in these areas. Much of his experience and practical achievement and most of his published works were related to these professional subjects.

From his earliest days in the Navy, he expressed an interest in naval administration and education. As a lieutenant and instructor at the Naval Academy in 1861, Luce complained of the Navy's weakness in intellectual pursuits. "Compared to the Army with their wealth of professional literature," he wrote, we in the Navy "may be likened to the nomadic tribes of the East who are content with the vague tradition of the past."[2] Even then, Luce was determined to do something about it. He started with practical textbooks. His first publication was a revised and updated gunnery manual. In the same year, he compiled the first seamanship textbook for the Naval Academy, a volume which would become, through later revision, the standard American work on the subject for nearly 30 years.[3]

Luce's association with the Naval Academy in 1860-1863 was important not only for his contributions to professional literature at that time but for his first close acquaintance with Newport, Rhode Island, where he would later choose to establish both a Naval Training Station and the Naval War College. Soon after the beginning of the Civil War in 1861, the Naval Academy was moved north to Newport where it could continue its work more safely.[4] There Luce saw that Newport offered some great advantages in education for naval officers. In Annapolis, "it is always the battalion, the musket, a banner, and a drum and fife!" But at Newport "it was different; there in a seaport town the youngsters inhaled the sea breezes by day and at night were lulled to rest by the roar of the Atlantic surf." Above all, Newport offered a location where students "can come in daily contact with seamen fresh from the ocean."[5]

It was not only Newport, but Coasters Harbor Island in Narragansett Bay, which struck Luce as an ideal place for a naval school. Remembering his days as a lieutenant commander at the Naval Academy in Newport, Luce recalled that in 1863 "Commodore Blake, the superintendent of the Naval Academy, at that time in the Atlantic Hotel, Touro Park, Newport, R.I. invited me to accompany him on a drive to look at a site at Coasters Harbor Island for a new building for the Naval Academy. Mr. George Mason, an architect of Newport, made one of the party. Mr. Mason was then engaged in preparing plans under the Commodore's direction for the building; for there was good reason then for thinking that the Naval Academy would remain in Newport permanently . . . . The proposed site was on Coasters Harbor Island. As we stood on the highest point of the Island . . . and looked upon the broad expanse of the waters of Narragansett Bay, the Commodore grew very eloquent upon the many advantages of the harbor and bay as a naval station, and the perfect adaptability of the site where we stood for a Naval Academy. The very favorable impression made upon my mind at that time was never effaced."[6] Despite Commodore Blake's plans, the

Academy returned to Annapolis, but even before that Luce was ordered to command the monitor *Nantucket* in the South Atlantic Blockading Squadron.

While in command of *Nantucket*, Luce began to write his first series of articles which suggested plans for improving naval apprentice training and creating a parallel program for the merchant marine. With these articles, the young naval officer began a long connection with W. C. Church's *Army and Navy Journal* and publicly laid the foundation for his lifetime campaign to improve nautical education and training. Luce's first success came in the campaign for merchant marine schools. His active work directly resulted in the Marine Schools Act passed by Congress in 1874 and the establishment of what later became the State University of New York Maritime College at Fort Schuyler.[7]

Luce's campaign for the improvement of professional naval education and training proved to be a far more complicated affair. He had in mind a complete view which included the training of apprentice seamen, chiefly in gunnery, engineering, and practical seamanship. Luce added both religious and naval instruction and stressed the value for apprentice training in old Navy ballads and songs as well as in naval history. Luce's plans came to fruition with congressional authorization in 1875 for the enlistment of 750 sixteen to eighteen-year-old boys into the Navy. The USS *Minnesota* was made the naval apprentice training ship.[8]

At the same time, Luce approached the president of the Massachusetts Institute of Technology and pointed out that the new Marine Schools Act of 1874 authorized the establishment of a branch, in an already established institution, for instruction in naval architecture and marine engineering. Although the MIT president encouraged Luce and others to join in the effort, a school of naval architecture was not established at MIT until 18 years later.[9]

In 1877, Luce took command of the *Minnesota* and devoted himself to developing an enlisted training program on a permanent and uniform basis. The acrimonious debate that ensued centered on such issues as the value of sail training, the control of training by a Bureau that would support it, and the location of a base for enlisted training.[10] By the 1890s Luce's position on sail training had been soundly defeated, and young apprentices were moved ashore where close order drill replaced the discipline of handling yard, sail, and sheet. Despite this setback to his ideas, Luce remained a major force in developing the enlisted training program.[11] In the process, he achieved one success which later found a place in his plans for advanced officer education. Luce believed that the apprentice training program could reach its potential quickly if the various elements of training were united in one place, under one man.

In November 1880, the Secretary of the Navy appointed Luce to a board of officers to select a location for the headquarters of the apprentice training squadron. After careful consideration of both New London, Connecticut, and a site near Newport, Rhode Island, the board chose Coasters Harbor Island in Narragansett Bay. Luce had already prepared the way for this decision by encouraging in 1878 the establishment of a committee of the Rhode Island General Assembly to select a suitable site in Narragansett Bay for a training station and, at the same time, encouraging the city fathers of Newport to give to the Navy Coasters Harbor Island where the city poorhouse was located.

"The object and sole object," Luce wrote, "in getting possession of the Island was to have a place where the boys might land occasionally for drills under arms and recreation." The apprentices lived on board the anchored ship-of-the-line *New Hampshire*, swinging to the wind and tide just to the south of Coasters Harbor, where the apprentices could become accustomed to shipboard life. On 16 December 1880, the Secretary of the Navy designated the island a temporary training station. Following this, on 9 February 1881, the State Assembly of Rhode Island ordered the island to be ceded to the federal government by a deed dated 2 March 1881. The station was made a permanent one on 4 June 1883 after Congress formally accepted the gift.[12]

With this work done, Luce wrote to his son-in-law in July 1883:

> My great hobby now—now that the Training System is fairly established—is to erect a "War School" for officers, the prime object being to teach officers the science of their own profession, the Science of War . . . I have the plan roughly mapped out and the Alms House on this Island is to be the College . . . Whether it will end in smoke or not I cannot say . . . . [13]

The Concept of the War College

The idea of a college for professional naval officers to study the science of warfare was a much more complex and intellectual problem than Luce had faced in his plans for merchant marine or apprentice training. Those had required training in specific, practical skills. The War College, in Luce's mind, went far beyond that to educating the mind for perception and analysis.

Luce, a self-educated man, was well read and sensitive to the new intellectual trends of his day. Following Herbert Spencer, the English philosopher, who applied the principles of evolutionary progress to all branches of knowledge, Luce believed that education was a process through which each individual discovered for himself the nature of the world around him. To Luce, truth and understanding were found through the discernment of basic and immutable laws in nature. As scientists had demonstrated that there were basic physical laws of the universe, Luce and many others believed that similar laws could be found in human affairs. These, however, were to be discovered by individual reading and research in a cooperative effort by a wide variety of people.

Luce thought that laws of human nature could be found through two complementary methods of reasoning, the comparative and the inductive. The comparative method was reasoning by analogy. Here Luce saw great relevance in examining the recent developments in studies of law, history, literature, science, technology, and education. In this he was profoundly influenced by his reading of the historian Thomas Buckle and the philologist Friedrich Max Müller, both of whom were great exponents of comparative study. Luce drew from them his conviction that the comparative method was essential to establishing a science of naval warfare. Going a step further, he saw that the study of naval warfare must be coordinated with military science and art. The complementary approach to the comparative method was through inductive reasoning, by which a person proceeded from thinking about specific events to making broad generalizations. The generalizations, however, were conceived at a level of understanding that was thoroughly steeped in theoretical developments in a wide variety of fields.

In all of this, the study of history was important. Luce thoroughly agreed with the historian Macaulay that "no past event has any intrinsic importance; the knowledge of it is valuable only as it leads to form just calculations for the future." Like Lord Bolingbroke, Luce firmly believed that "History is philosophy teaching by example."[14] The value in historical study was to be found in its effects on individual thinking, on the process which comes from dealing with a range of specific examples and developing generalizations from them.

Luce believed that a theoretical basis could be developed for the naval profession. He saw the technological revolution that was about to transform the Navy, and he proposed an intellectual method by which professional officers could effectively deal with the technological conundrums of the new Navy. Luce believed that first one must understand what a Navy does and why it exists, before one can effectively select the means, the tactics, and the weapons by which it is to be employed.

Luce developed his ideas largely through his wide reading and extensive professional experience, but he was also influenced by several individuals in the process. He believed that the seed of his thinking was planted in January 1865, when he met General William T. Sherman during the siege of Charleston, South Carolina. Sherman explained the Navy's strategic failures in a few sentences and declared that he would make the city fall without a battle. "I will cut her communications and Charleston will fall into your hands like a ripe pear" Sherman said, "and that is just exactly what came to pass," Luce related.[15] This demonstration of military thinking was a revelation for Luce and opened his eyes to the proposition that certain fundamental ideas underlay operations. "In other words," Luce wrote later, "the Civil War demonstrated conclusively the necessity of a War College and a general staff."[16] In Luce's mind, the War College was the essential prerequisite for the establishment of proper military direction of the armed forces, so it was on education that he concentrated first.

Establishing a College

About 1877, Luce encountered a second Army officer who stimulated his thought further along this line. This was Brigadier General Emory Upton, then commanding the Artillery School at Fort Monroe, Hampton Roads, Virginia. Based on ideas that had come out of American military experience in the Civil War and were merged with the new trends in thought revealed by German success in the Franco-Prussian War, the Army's Artillery School had become America's model institution of higher military learning. Like the Navy, the U.S. Army was passing through a period of decline, neglect, and struggle for professional identity. Upton was one of the Army's leaders who fostered the cultivation of professional study and encouraged others along the same lines.[17] It is not surprising that two like minded men found much to share. While in command of a ship at Norfolk, Luce had met Upton and had an opportunity to examine the curriculum of Upton's school. On 8 August 1877, Luce wrote to the Secretary of the Navy, forwarding a copy of the "Programme of Instruction" at the Artillery School and recommending that a similar school be established for the Navy. "The leading feature of the postgraduate course would be the carrying of the young officers through a course of instruction in the Art of War," Luce wrote, adding

> Extraordinary as it may appear, the naval officer whose principal business is to fight is not taught the higher branches of his profession. The U.S. is not singular in this respect. The defect is common to nearly all navies and is an inheritance of a past and less enlightened age. But with the recent revolution in naval warfare comes a demand for a higher order of talent in the conduct of naval operation . . . . [18]

Luce shared his ideas with Upton who supported and encouraged them. After reading one of Luce's articles, Upton wrote to him, "It gave me quite new ideas as to the similarity between land and naval tactics, and I can now fully comprehend your scheme in relation to a postgraduate course as a means of educating the officers of the Navy in the strategy and tactics of their profession."[19]

Although the Secretary of the Navy seemed to receive Luce's proposal favorably, no action was taken to establish a new school. In April 1883, Luce again took the initiative. In a lecture before the recently formed Newport Chapter of the United States Naval Institute, he described the various "War Schools" that the Army had established, and focused primarily on the Artillery School at Fort Monroe. Luce emphasized the Army's precedent and stressed that naval officers, as well as army officers, should have the basic knowledge of the art and practice of war "so far as it can be acquired from books." In addition, the naval officer "should be led into a philosophic study of naval history" so that he might see the manner in which theory has been illustrated and where a disregard of it had led to disaster.[20]

During 1883, Luce found another means of getting his ideas across to the people who could implement them. In the summer of 1882, he had been appointed senior member of a commission to investigate Navy yards. The Commission's final report was completed in December 1883, and gave Luce the additional opportunity to present to the Secretary of the Navy and senior officers his ideas on naval education, strategy and administration. At the same time, he encouraged the editor of the *Army and Navy Journal* to publish articles on the subject, and "thus start a controversy and a BOOM."[21]

On 6 November 1882, Luce wrote a formal letter to Secretary of the Navy W. E. Chandler recommending a naval school for "the higher branches of the naval profession: the science of war, naval tactics, military and naval history, international law, military and naval law, modern languages, and such elective branches as might be found desirable."[22] Citing the Artillery School at Fort Monroe and the Infantry and Cavalry School at Fort Leavenworth "as examples worthy of imitation," Luce went on to point out that with the land and buildings on Coasters Harbor Island readily available, the plan could be put into effect immediately with no congressional action required "and but trifling expense."[23]

Following conversations with Chandler and Admiral of the Navy D. D. Porter in early 1884, Luce submitted a draft General Order for the Secretary to issue.[24] In response to this letter, Chandler ordered on 30 May 1884 that Luce be president of a board to consider and report on the subject. Lieutenant Commander Caspar F. Goodrich and Captain William T. Sampson were ordered as members of the board. Before meeting, Luce wrote to both younger officers, suggesting that they read his article on "War Schools" and consider his opinion "that we should have for the Navy what the Army has in the schools at Fort Monroe and at Fort Leavenworth."[25] They were also asked to review, as a possible model, the organization of the Royal Naval College at Greenwich, which was described in Professor Soley's book on *Naval Education*.[26] Greenwich and its predecessor at Portsmouth had offered higher technical training to officers since 1839. It was at Greenwich that John Knox Laughton began the modern study of naval history in 1874, although the subject played little role in its curriculum.

The purpose of this board was to discuss the proposal and to draw up a plan of organization for the proposed college. It was not a forum for discussion of opposing views. Luce had already raised strong opposition by his published article. Notable among the opponents was Captain F. M. Ramsey, the Superintendent of the Naval Academy, who believed that the War College would detract from the Academy's course of instruction by creating a rival academy.[27] Others wanted to amalgamate it with the Torpedo Station School on Goat Island, but Luce, with Sampson and Goodrich, set out to define the character of the new college. In a report written on board the flagship of the Training Squadron, USS *New Hampshire*, then moored at South Point on Coasters Harbor Island, the three agreed that naval officers are "too apt to lose sight of the ultimate object of all" and become devoted to the application of electricity to torpedoes, chemistry to explosives, or metallurgy to ordnance instead of the central issue, "success in war."[28]

The board of officers declared that the United States Navy should have

> a place where our officers will not only be encouraged, but *required*, to study their profession proper—war—in a far more thorough manner than has ever heretofore been attempted, and to bring to the investigation of the various problems of modern naval warfare the scientific methods adopted in other professions.[29]

The fact that the United States had no adequate naval force at the time made it even more difficult for officers to gain professional knowledge. Luce, Goodrich, and Sampson believed that a War College was an absolute necessity in that situation. Like other professions, the Navy was beginning to form specialties of knowledge among its officers, and the board believed that in this process, warfare, "the one subject *par excellence* of the naval profession" was being ignored. "Failing to produce specialists in this one branch, we fail utterly in our whole system of naval education, for all others are but subordinate or accessory."

The board also outlined a proposed course for the college. To appease the opposition, the board suggested that the course could be linked with and supplement the technical course in ordnance at the Torpedo Station on Goat Island by offering an additional six months' study in the science and art of war, law, and history. The courses in war would include study of strategy, tactics, and campaigns, from the military, naval, and joint standpoints. "As the principles underlying all hostile movements are at bottom the same, whatever be the nature of the field of action, the board is of the opinion that an intimate knowledge of military operations is essential to the naval strategist."[30]

The war course would also be paralleled by a study of modern political history and general naval history. In addition, international law was added as a subject "of the utmost importance in its bearing upon action taken by our naval commanders abroad."

The board recognized that the college would eventually need to provide additional courses that would accommodate "the increased complexity of certain branches of the profession," but these should be offered as electives in a way that did not detract from the main thrust of the study of warfare.

For all the college's academic work, the board recommended that no one should be permitted to engage in the courses who could not pass a satisfactory examination. Additionally, those who finished the instruction with credit were to receive certificates of proficiency and a signifying letter or mark would be placed by their names in the Navy Register as a means of denoting their professional attainment.

The board, however, did not conceive only of academic and library study. Luce, in particular, believed that practical tactical exercises were an important part of the curriculum. The board suggested that "the North Atlantic Squadron affords the nearest approach to be found to a proper course in naval tactics." It also suggested that at a stated time, once a year, the squadron should demonstrate the whole range of its operation for the college class.

That factor made Newport the best choice among the other locations contending for the school: Washington, Annapolis, New York, and Boston. Among them, only Boston and Newport had buildings and ground readily available. Boston had the eminent professors and excellent libraries available, but they were also within reach of Newport. As a seaport with ready access to the fleet, Newport offered "exceptional advantages," as Luce had seen many years before. In addition to an excellent anchorage for the fleet, the Torpedo School could readily extend its technical instruction in sciences in a way that would complement the War College's course of study. War College students could also avail themselves of special courses at "the great institutions of learning at Boston."

When the report was submitted in mid-June 1884, Luce was still Commander of the Training Squadron. A month later he was ordered to command the North Atlantic Squadron with the rank of acting rear admiral. With approval for his fledgling Naval War College imminent, Luce preferred to continue his work for the college rather than accept permanent appointment as rear admiral in command of the squadron.

Before relinquishing his command, and resuming the rank of commodore, Luce welcomed home from the Arctic the Greely Relief Expedition, entertained President Chester A. Arthur when he visited the squadron, and conducted one of the Navy's first amphibious exercises at Gardiners Island, near the eastern end of Long Island.

As early as February 1884, Luce had begun to cast about for possible faculty members. He first approached Caspar Goodrich to take up the position in naval strategy and tactics, which later was given to Mahan.[31] Among others, he requested Richard Wainwright and Professor J. R. Soley and began to search for an Army officer as well.[32]

Even before the War College was formally established, Luce was detached from command of the squadron and ordered to assume the duties as "Superintendent of the College at Coasters Harbor Island." Reporting the changes of command which took place on board USS *Tennessee* in Newport Harbor, the *Army and Navy Journal* noted

> Commodore Luce is expected to come to Washington shortly for the purpose of consulting with Secretary Chandler regarding the establishment of the postgraduate school. He has not been communicated with on the subject, but his coming is regarded as a matter of course. He was relieved from the command of the North Atlantic Station by Commodore Jouett on the 20th of September, with the usual ceremonies, with the addition of a salute from the Torpedo Station. The two officers made brief addresses to the officers and crew. Immediately after being relieved of the command of the squadron, Commodore Luce proceeded in his barge to Coasters Harbor Island to carry out his orders. He was accompanied by Captain Yates and Lieutenant Symonds, of the *New Hampshire*, and by the members of his late staff, Lieutenants Very, Tilley, and Mulligan, Ensign Everett, and Midshipman Wells. Arriving at the building on the island, he put his hand on the door and said: "Know all men by these presents, and in the name of the Father, Son, and Holy Ghost, I christen this building the War College of the American Navy."[33]

Three weeks later the same journal reported, "the new college . . . has been dubbed by naval officers at the Navy Department, the 'Trinity College,' a name they have derived from the manner in which the institution was christened."[34] On 6 October, Secretary of the Navy Chandler signed General Order 325 which formally established the Naval War College as "an advanced course of professional study." The principal building on the island with the surrounding structures and immediately adjacent grounds was thereby transferred from the Bureau of Equipment and Recruiting to the Bureau of Navigation. At the same time, the War College was placed in charge of a president, not to be below the rank of commander. He, with the faculty, constituted a board that was given authority to arrange the course of instruction. The course was to be opened to all officers above the grade of naval cadet.[35]

With its formal establishment, the Naval War College entered the endless bureaucratic struggle within the Navy. From the outset, the placement side by side on the same island of two separate entities, belonging to two different bureaus, created difficulty. Even though both were the product of Luce's effort, the Bureau of Equipment and Recruiting saw the War College as an intruder from the Bureau of Navigation on an island that rightly belonged to the Training Station. At the same time, officers at the Naval Academy in Annapolis feared that the War College was a kind of academic postgraduate school that would become a rival.

Despite the orders given to establish the Naval War College, no immediate action was taken to carry them out. Only Luce was on the scene. In order to draw attention to the new enterprise, he wrote an article for the *United Service Magazine*, clearly pointing out the rationale behind it, and simultaneously persuaded the *Army and Navy Journal* to publicize the college. Luce was also in close contact with Rhode Island Senator Nelson Aldrich in making plans for the college.

By early February 1885, still no action had been taken for the college. To inquire into this matter, the U.S. Senate adopted a resolution directing the Secretary of the Navy to report to the Senate on the steps that were being taken. The report was made, but no funds were allotted to the college. Eventually, naval officers were ordered to the college as students. In the first class there would be four lieutenant commanders and five lieutenants.

The First Course

At the opening ceremony of the War College, on 4 September 1885, Rear Admiral Daniel Ammen, a distinguished officer and author of a naval history of the Civil War, gave the main address. Aware that he was dedicating a new enterprise, he told the students that it was a matter of prime necessity for the nation to have officers who understood the nature of war. A school such as Annapolis provided a basis of understanding the special appliances required for war. But here, in Newport, he said, the "economy of war" should be a specialty, "that we may not sacrifice ourselves and those under us unnecessarily."[36] With those thoughts in the minds of the small audience, Luce brought attention to the fact that it was an inauspicious beginning for such a serious and important purpose. With no money for books, furniture, heat, or light, Luce reminded the audience that the building offered little but shelter from the winds of Narragansett Bay. The cornerstone for the building had been laid on 25 June 1819 to be Newport's poorhouse and deaf and dumb asylum. Luce declared the college open by saying, "poor little Poorhouse, I christen thee the United States Naval War College."[37]

The class that convened for the next four weeks made do with borrowed furniture and could hear only the visiting lecturers who were willing to spend their own time and money to come to the college. The first course was hardly what Luce had hoped to have, but it was the best he could get. Professor James Soley temporarily left his duties as librarian in the Navy Department to lecture on international law. The Army sent Lieutenant Tasker Bliss to lecture on military affairs, and Luce gave several lectures.[38]

Less than a week after the opening of the first class, Admiral Luce participated in the dedication ceremony of a statue to one of Newport's naval heroes, Oliver Hazard Perry. Ironically, the ceremony brought Luce together with another important figure in naval education, the Newport summer resident and historian George Bancroft, who as Secretary of the Navy in 1845 had established the Naval Academy.

Luce took the opportunity to point out the difference between the two institutions. The War College was designed, he said, to take the academy graduate, only after an interval of sea service, into the highest realm of professional thought: war. "That particular name has been given to the college in order that its special mission may be kept steadily in view—that it may never be lost sight of," he said. "War and its cognate branches constitute the college curriculum. It is only by a close study of the science and art of war that we can be prepared for war, and thus go very far toward securing peace."[39] Luce explained that the college was not an ordinary course of instruction, "not teaching war," but giving the student the opportunity of understanding it.[40]

Many years later, he explained his idea further when he declared that "there are no professors competent to teach" warfare. "All that the College can do," he said, "all that it professes to do, is to invite officers to come to it; and to offer them every facility for pursuing the study . . . All here, faculty and class alike, occupy the same plane, without distinction of age, rank, or assumption of superior attainments . . . In the beginning I, myself, . . . announced myself as one of the class in attendance . . . ."[41] The War College, Luce believed, "is a place of original research on all questions relating to war and to statesmanship connected with war, or the prevention of war."[42]

The concept that lay behind the college was not widely understood. Critics poked fun at the Navy for having as its only full-time staff member an Army lieutenant. Despite the criticism, Luce was generally pleased by the first experiment and set about plans for the next session to open in the following year. In January 1886, however, Luce was promoted to the permanent grade of rear admiral and ordered again to sea in command of the North Atlantic Squadron.

Mahan's Arrival

In September 1885, Luce had arranged for Captain Alfred T. Mahan to be ordered to the college to be lecturer in naval strategy and tactics. Enroute from command of a ship on the South American station, Mahan was ordered home to New York to pursue studies at the Astor Library and the New York Public Library in preparation for the Naval War College course beginning in September 1886. Meeting Mahan at Newport on 20 October 1885 to discuss plans, Luce directed Mahan to work in two areas, fleet battle tactics and history. In Luce's mind, these two subjects were directly related. He stressed to Mahan that he should employ the comparative method, avoid the purely naval point of view, and consider the interrelationships among naval and military tactics, strategy, diplomacy, and national power. As Mahan wrote to his old friend and Academy classmate, Samuel Ashe,

> I want if I can to wrest something out of the old wooden sides and 24-pounders that will throw some light on the combinations to be used with ironclads, rifled guns, and torpedoes; and to raise the profession in the eyes of its members by a clearer comprehension of the great part it has played in the world than I myself have hitherto had.[43]

This work became his lectures in the following year and resulted five years later in Mahan's first famous book, *The Influence of Sea Power Upon History 1660-1783*. Although he would become the most famous member of the college in its early years, Mahan's work was only part of the concept that Luce had in mind. Luce had been able to win, at least temporarily, the favor of the Bureaus in Washington, gain an $8,000 appropriation for its maintenance, accumulate a small library through gifts, and arrange for the main lecturers. Tasker Bliss of the Army was still the only permanently assigned officer, other than the president of the college. With Luce's departure in June and Mahan's arrival delayed until August, there was no activity at the college that summer.

When Mahan arrived to take up residence in the college building, he discovered that he was its sole occupant, Bliss having accommodations in town. "As I walked around the lonely halls and stairways," Mahan wrote, "I might have parodied Louis XIV, and said, "Le College, c'est moi." Although there was a steward who made his meals and his bed, Mahan commented,

> There was but one lamp available, which I had to carry with me when I went from room to room by night; and indeed, except for the roof over my head, I might be said to be 'camping out.'[44]

When the class convened on 6 September for the two-and-a-half-month course, 21 officers attended, including two commanders, eleven lieutenants, six ensigns, and two Marine Corps officers. The course was more successfully modeled on Luce's plan than the first year had been. Sixteen lectures were on the tactics of naval gunnery, by Lieutenant William B. Hoff, the author of a recent book on the subject. Professor Soley returned again from Washington with a series of 20 lectures on international law dealing with the relations of states, in both peace and war. Lieutenant Bliss gave 18 lectures on military tactics, minor military operations, and the principles of modern strategy. Additional lectures were given on subjects of general interest such as coastal defense, hygiene, and Civil War history. During the first 10 days of the course, Rear Admiral Luce was present with his flagship, USS *Tennessee*, which he allowed the college students to use for practical exercises.[45]

In general, its friends praised the small beginnings of the college and were heartened by the progress of its second year. The Admiral of the Navy, David Dixon Porter, wrote in his annual report, "The War College has had a struggle for existence owing to the prejudice existing against it in the Navy, although none of those who have antagonized the institution can give a single good reason why it should not be fostered."[46]

A retired lieutenant, William McCarty Little, was one of the enthusiastic supporters of the War College. Forced to leave active duty following an eye injury, McCarty Little volunteered his services to Luce at the opening of the college. He continued to work with Mahan by drawing some of the maps that Mahan used in his lectures and that later appeared in his books. At the same time, Mahan and McCarty Little, working together, devised a system to examine and to explain the tactics of historic battles by using cardboard vessels of different colors for the contending navies moved over a sheet of drawing paper. When satisfied that the graphic representation corresponded with the facts and the technical conditions, Mahan then fastened the cardboard in place. Through this method, Mahan and Little were able to apply their technical knowledge of ships and begin to work out with care the principles of naval tactics. This was the beginning of war gaming at the college. McCarty Little began to develop the idea further and suggested some broader uses of war gaming in his lecture on "Colomb's Naval Duel Game," delivered to the 1886 class.[47]

As the second year of the War College drew to a close, Mahan reflected his thoughts and his new situation when he wrote to a friend,

> Our position entirely out of Newport, indeed in the very opposite direction from the fashionable quarter, has advantages of view and air over the latter. The island which is connected by causeway with

the main is windswept and almost treeless, but the old house (formerly an almshouse) faces the seabreeze and looks straight down the narrow entrance through which, over a hundred years ago, D'Estaing sailed in with the French fleet under the fire of the English batteries . . . . [48]

By the end of the course, Mahan was pleased that the college had managed to stay clear of the kind of postgraduate course that might be considered a follow-on to instruction at Annapolis. As Luce had planned, the War College devoted itself to the much needed, broadly based study of warfare. "The want had been proved, and a means of filling it offered," Mahan wrote, and "the listeners had been persuaded."[49]

Mahan's optimism stemmed from his academic success, but at the same time a serious threat was brewing in Washington. In the autumn of 1886, Mahan suddenly realized that there was strong opposition to the War College in Congress. Hilary Herbert, Chairman of the House Naval Affairs Committee, considered the college a postgraduate school, and therefore, better placed in Annapolis where the laboratories and equipment already existed. He let it be known that he would prevent any appropriation to support the college. Mahan began immediately to develop a campaign to protect the college. He believed that if technical subjects were allowed into the curriculum, inevitably they would predominate over the study of warfare. The college would then decline into an instrumentality merely to promote mechanical perfection. He decided to avoid any discussion of materiel, thus removing grounds for the argument that the college was a postgraduate school. At the same time, influential officers such as Francis M. Ramsay and Winfield Scott Schley criticized the college for its emphasis on the comparative approach as a means of developing naval theory. Mahan pled his case before congressional leaders. He failed. About Herbert, Mahan later wrote, "In vain did I try to divert his thoughts . . . He stopped his ears like Ulysses, and kept his eyes fixed on the necessity of strangling vipers in their cradle."[50]

Despite the support of many others, the War College received no money for 1887. In writing to Senator Nelson Aldrich of Rhode Island, Mahan apologized for the appearance of his letter, "The poverty of the college does not admit of my having a clerk—and the typewriting is done by the kindness of my aide, who is not yet very expert."[51] As winter came on, there was no fuel to heat the building. Mahan submitted a request through the routine channels, and coal was delivered before Washington noticed that there was no appropriation to pay for it. Finding that the delivery had already been made, officials in Washington eventually decided not to freeze the college out literally, but paid for the coal through the Bureau to which the Training Station belonged. A fact "which would not nullify its feelings," Mahan commented. Mahan searched through the refuse left over from converting the poorhouse into a school and dwelling. He collected, sorted, and sold the bits and pieces to support the college, using some of it to purchase books for the college's small library.

Later, Mahan looked back with pleasure on his two years living in the old building. In so isolated and exposed a location, the thick walls and small windows of the building proved to be a great advantage. After the first repairs were completed, Mahan and his family never suffered from cold in the winter or heat in the summer. The rooms on the front, or south side, were both warmer in winter and airy in the summer, and Mahan nearly always kept his office window open. Although it was not large, the building housed not only Mahan's quarters but also rooms for teaching, offices, library, and a lecture room. Mahan tried to separate home and school, but visiting lecturers slept, sometimes for weeks, in the college part of the building and dined with Mahan and his family.

Despite all efforts the building was not well suited for teaching. The lecture room was not high enough to display properly the necessary large maps. There were too few rooms for student offices and too little space to use as a lounge between lectures. Makeshift arrangements were necessary for meals when the college remained in session during an entire day. Fortunately, the library was sufficient, but only because the collection of books was small. Toilets and washing facilities were available only in a run-down out building.[52]

Despite the strength of his feelings on the issue, Mahan assuaged the critics by modifying the course in 1887 to emphasize current naval issues. Nonetheless, he kept the substance of the course as it had been maturing over the previous two years. In reporting on the activities for the now lengthened three-and-a-half-month course, Mahan stressed that new material had been introduced, "all bearing upon the practical question of carrying on naval war to the best advantage." In particular, the students considered the naval problems arising in the Caribbean and Gulf of Mexico out of French interest in an isthmian canal.

That autumn Lieutenant Charles C. Rogers of the USS *Galena* delivered four lectures on duties of a general staff. This was the first presentation on a subject that would grow in importance for the War College in later years. In the same course, William McCarty Little gave the first series of six lectures on war gaming, reflecting the work he was doing to develop a system of naval war games.

To emphasize the practical aspect of studies, Mahan reported that Admiral Luce had brought the North Atlantic Squadron into Narragansett Bay, and its exercises were arranged specifically "to illustrate and give point to teaching given orally in the lecture room, as well as diffuse information connected with the new materiel of the Navy."[53] These maneuvers were a major innovation by Luce. They were part of his plan to have a squadron of evolution that would test and put into practice the theories of sea warfare worked out by the college. The maneuvers, comprising one of the first fleet exercises of the U.S. Navy, involved the passage of five ships, including two of the new steel ships and four torpedo boats, through a minefield, under the opposing guns of Fort Adams at the entrance to Narragansett Bay, and a landing, repulse, and reembarkation of nearly 400 men, with artillery, at Coddington Point.[54]

Mahan was greatly pleased with the general program of the college and the success of his own series of lectures with the students. The opponents of the War College, however, were not to be silenced. Mahan commented privately, "their ignorance and my success alike testify to the want of the college."[55] After the course was over, Mahan returned to Washington to lobby for the college in 1888. Initially, it appeared as though 10 of the 13 members of the House Naval Affairs Committee would vote for a separate budget to sustain the War College. The Secretary of the Navy told Mahan that he would not oppose the college, but neither would he allow Mahan to report he approved of it. Mahan's plea for the War College was on the grounds that it was the world's only institution devoted to military and naval theory that was not dominated by reference to technological development. It was a plea that only a few in Congress understood or supported, but the initial appropriation measure supporting the college managed to pass the House and was referred to the Senate. Secretary of the Navy Whitney appeared before the Senate Appropriations Committee and suggested, unexpectedly, that the House legislation be amended. He suggested that, for reasons of economy and administrative efficiency, the War College be consolidated with the Torpedo School on Goat Island. The combined forces could then use the facilities on Goat Island under the control of the Bureau of Ordnance. The building on Coaster's Harbor Island could then be returned to the apprentice training station administered by the Bureau of Equipment and Training. With this change, Secretary Whitney recommended that the Senate approve the $10,000 budget for the college. This was approved by Congress.

To make matters worse, Secretary of the Navy Whitney ordered on 1 August that the four month course of instruction that had been scheduled to begin in less than a week was to be shortened by a month. "In view of the fact," the Secretary announced, "that during the last year's course less than an average of two lectures per day were delivered, including Saturday and Sunday, the Department feels that the interest attached to the course will not be impaired by condensing the course into a shorter period."[56]

Both Mahan and Luce were livid with anger. Not only did the Secretary of the Navy fail to understand the educational approach of the War College but he threatened its very existence. The college curriculum required large blocks of time for the students to read and to think actively about the abstract problems presented. It was not a course in which data was poured into the ears of the students by a series of lectures. The lectures were only a stimulus to the main thrust of the college. Mahan pointed out that the two schools could be joined in several ways, "but if by consolidation is meant the merging of two lines of thought radically distinct and in temper of mind opposed, under a single directing intellect, the result will be the destruction of one or the other."[57]

Luce joined the protest with a formal letter to the Secretary of the Navy, signed by his ally, Admiral of the Navy David Dixon Porter, and six other officers. They suggested that consideration would best be carried out through the appointment of a high ranking officer to command all the activities on Narragansett Bay, but allowing each a separate and healthful growth. "The subjects treated by the War College, though of the highest importance, have been and are neglected by naval officers generally, in favor of material," they wrote, adding "the merging of the college will stifle at birth a movement which gives the highest promise of future usefulness . . . . "[58]

In the midst of these protests, the course of 1888 was in session. The course opened for only 14 officers with nearly the same staff offering lectures to cover a more fully developed version of the previous year's course. Among the additional lecturers for 1888, Admiral Luce had been able to obtain thirty-year-old Theodore Roosevelt, whom Luce had known since Roosevelt's days as a member of the New York State legislature in 1882-1884. In 1882, Roosevelt published his book *The Naval War of 1812*. Having recently reread the book, Luce wrote to Roosevelt in February 1888, from his flagship at Barbados, to explain the purposes of the Naval War College. "We are now giving some attention to the subject of naval history, or what may be called a philosophical study of naval history; and on the part relating to the War of 1812 your work must be our textbook."[59] Luce encouraged Roosevelt to contact Mahan to learn more about the college in the hope that Roosevelt's work in naval history would lead him to take an active interest in the college. It resulted in Roosevelt's first lecture at the college and the beginning of Mahan's association with the future Assistant Secretary of the Navy and President.

Upon completion of the 1888 course, Mahan was ordered to head a commission that was to select a site for a navy yard on the northwest coast. Thus exiled, Mahan was no longer in a position to carry on the fight. Any hope for the college lay in procrastination and the hope that the newly elected administration of Benjamin Harrison would be more friendly to the aims of the college. Mahan felt frustrated and defeated by the turn of events. "I have determined not to move a hand with reference to any attempt to reestablish the college," he wrote Luce. "I should feel that I was fighting in the dark and might at anytime be blown up in the rear."[60]

Fight for Survival

Luce took up the standard without hesitation and led the battle to reestablish the college. "The triumph of the enemies of the Navy will be but temporary," he wrote David Dixon Porter.[61] In Washington, however, the lines had been laid for a plan to kill the college and let it be overwhelmed by technical instruction at the Torpedo School. When the 1889 class convened at the War College on Goat Island, only 12 officers enrolled after completing the torpedo course, and of that tiny group only six stayed to complete the eleven week War College course.

The course remained true to the general outlines that Luce and Mahan had envisaged. The lecture topics and many of the lectures themselves, remained familiar. Among the visitors during the course was Major William R. Livermore, then stationed at Fort Adams, but who was the foremost American authority on Army war gaming. Livermore's ideas and the German Kriegspiele, an example of which had been purchased for the college by Commander French E. Chadwick, the U.S. naval attaché in London, were important in the development of the naval war gaming system in Newport.[62] The practical application of tactical study, however, proved impossible. Luce was not allowed to arrange fleet maneuvers for the class, although the students were able to witness some of the trials of the new cruiser USS *Chicago*.

In March 1889, Congress provided $100,000 for constructing a new building on Goat Island for the combined use of the Torpedo School and War College. This allocation, made in the last days of the outgoing administration, was the first target which Luce chose to attack in his battle to restore the War College to Coasters Harbor Island. "The placing of a $100,000 building on Goat Island . . . is a rank absurdity," he wrote, " . . . before any steps are taken the further wishes of Congress should be known."[63] This argument was the means by which Luce and Porter opened up to the new administration the full question of the nature and site for the Naval War College.

In the meantime, the college was finding supporters. The move to Goat Island might well have meant the instant end of the War College, but quite by chance the ordnance specialist in charge happened to be Commander Caspar F. Goodrich, an old friend whom Luce had chosen six years earlier to sit on the board that had selected Coasters Harbor Island for the college and laid down its original curriculum. Reminiscing about the situation years later, Goodrich recalled, "The evident purpose in this move was to kill the college. It happened, however, that the latter fell into friendly hands, and I made a point of honor of keeping it alive."

Goodrich claimed that the appropriation was made by Secretary Whitney as an especial and personal favor to him, quoting Whitney:

> I am doing this merely because Goodrich wants it, and because I am fond of Goodrich; but why Goodrich wants it, I am blessed if I can understand.[64]

While a friend had been found in Goodrich at the local level, Luce continued to work for favor in Washington. Encouraged by Senator Aldrich, the new Secretary of the Navy, B. F. Tracy, became interested in the college. Five days after the inauguration of the new administration, Tracy wrote to Luce, "I can assure you that I consider no matter of greater importance than the education of our officers in the subjects which have been introduced at this college."[65]

Tracy took immediate action and wrote in his annual report for 1889 that the legislation which had authorized the construction of the $100,000 building on Goat Island should not be undertaken until Congress expressed itself more definitely on the issue. He went further, however, in recommending specifically that the War College be returned to Coasters Harbor Island and that the new building be built on that island with the money for it appropriated to the Bureau of Navigation. "The present condition of things, in which the college is made a sort of appendage to the Torpedo Station, under the Bureau of Ordnance, should be corrected. It is attaching the greater to the less." The Naval War College, Tracy declared, "is of the highest importance . . . nothing should be done that will in any way interfere with its efficiency."[66]

The return to Coasters Harbor Island was approved by Congress in the Appropriation Act of 30 June 1890, and the Torpedo School was discontinued, although the name, Naval War College and Torpedo School was retained in the Act and officially used until 1898.

In July 1890, the college gained even greater support when Professor James R. Soley was appointed Assistant Secretary of the Navy under Tracy. Having attended every session of the War College course and delivered all its international law lectures, Soley was the most knowledgeable person in Washington on the work of the college. With Luce's retirement from active duty in 1889 at the statutory age of 62, Soley was its most important spokesman. The only cloud in this bright sky was the appointment of the college's old opponent, Commodore Ramsay, to replace the friendly John Walker as Chief of the Bureau of Navigation.

Because of the administrative changes taking place and the move from Goat Island, no classes were offered at the War College in 1890 or

1891 and there was no staff or faculty assigned. The future seemed bright, however, as construction of the new building was begun on Coasters Harbor Island on 14 September 1891, under the supervision of Lieutenant Commander Charles H. Stockton, who had been ordered to Newport for that purpose, reporting to Captain F. M. Bunce, then acting as officer in charge of the War College and Torpedo School as well as Commandant of the Training Station.

Although detached from the War College in January 1889, Mahan played an important role in selecting the site for the new building and designing it through his reports and letters to the bureau chiefs. The original college building had the best site on the island, and it was far too substantial to be removed. The next best location in Mahan's view was just to the west of the old building where the ground was a uniform grade until the bluffs were reached at the shoreline. Placed there, the new building would leave six acres for the Training Station's ballfield and drill grounds to the south and a meadow of ten acres to the north, where a naval hospital was then located. That site offered the best location in terms of space, sewerage, and sea breeze, but not unexpectedly, the Training Station objected. The expansion of the War College, Training Station officers argued, would interfere with apprentice drills.[67]

In mid-1889, Admiral Luce published his article, "Our Future Navy," in both the widely read *North American Review* and the Naval Institute *Proceedings*. It deeply influenced the new Secretary of the Navy. Based on historical example, Luce argued that a balanced fleet should be built around battleships and its primary duty should be offensive. In May 1890, Mahan's *Influence of Sea Power Upon History* appeared and provided the detailed historical argument from which Luce's thinking was derived. These two published works provided concrete evidence of the War College's work and helped to sustain the effort for its revival. Secretary Tracy saw that Mahan could provide the codification and clarity of expression necessary for public under-standing of his plans for the new Navy.[68]

Mahan had returned to his home in New York "on special duty" upon completion of his work in the northwest, during which he had helped select Puget Sound as a site for a navy yard. Expecting that a course would be held at the college in 1890 and 1891, Mahan devoted his time to continuing his research and writing, taking advantage of the fact that he had no administrative responsibilities. From Mahan's point of view, it was an excellent situation. "The college slumbered and I worked," he recalled.[69]

Mahan was ordered to resume the presidency of the War College, but he was allowed to remain at his home in New York until the new quarters were ready in Newport. On 10 May 1892, the political situation was eased temporarily by the removal of the college from the direct administrative control of the Bureau of Navigation and placement under the direction of the Assistant Secretary of the Navy. During the spring of 1892, Mahan completed the draft of his course of lectures and, on 21 July, relieved Captain F. M. Bunce of command of the joint War College and Torpedo School, the Training Station remaining under Captain Bunce. In arranging for the new course, Mahan made a special point in requesting permission to revert to what "was formerly the practice," that "officers connected with the college not be required to wear uniforms within its limits, except on special occasions." In obtaining this, Mahan emphasized the academic character of the War College and differentiated it from the Training Station.[70]

The new college building was completed by the contractor on 28 May 1892 to the designs drawn by George C. Mason & Sons. Flemish in style, it had three stepped gables on its facade, which faced Narragansett Bay and the open sea beyond Newport harbor. The structure cost only $82,875 to construct and the remainder of the $100,000 appropriation was used to install heating and other equipment. The college lecture rooms, library, and offices were located in the center of the building, and each of the four corners of the building contained separate, two-floor apartments to be used as quarters for the officers of the staff. This arrangement had been particularly pressed by Mahan. He argued that the essence of the college was the close association of the students with capable instructors and a good library. A college building that provided living quarters for the staff as well as a library and lecture room would provide the staff with "the most favorable condition for their work," Mahan argued.[71]

In opening the new building and launching the revived course of study on 7 September, Mahan devoted his remarks to a carefully thought out defense of the War College. The difficulties the college had experienced and the criticism it had endured led Mahan to stress "the Practical Character of the Naval War College." The new and revived American Navy was clearly in preparation. The Navy Act of 1892 had authorized the armored cruiser *Brooklyn* and the battleship *Iowa* with the heaviest armor, most powerful ordnance, and highest practicable speed. Improvements were rapidly being made to armor and ordnance.[72] While the material was being readied, "there is time yet for study; there is time to imbibe the experience of the past, to become imbued, steeped in the eternal principles of war, by the study of its history and the maxims of its masters," Mahan declared. "Use the time of preparation for preparation . . . ; to postpone preparation to the time of action is not practical."[73]

The course for 1892 was short, lasting only seven weeks with 24 students. The new course was designed to follow the basic ideas used in the earlier courses, but in order to meet the opposition, all lectures dealt directly with naval subjects; no lectures were devoted to international law or military affairs. Mahan delivered a series of lectures on naval history which, after the course was completed, were published under the title, *The Influence of Sea Power Upon the French Revolution and Empire, 1793-1812.* In the preface to the book Mahan paid tribute to the Naval War College. Whatever success his books had is due, he wrote, "wholly and exclusively to the Naval War College, which was instituted to promote such studies." Equally as important, he paid tribute to the influence of Admiral Luce who had given Mahan the guidance "into a path he would not himself have found."[74]

By the end of the year, friends of the college were pleased with its success and gratified by Secretary Tracy's report that

> The Department is deeply impressed with the importance of the college to the Navy, as a means of insuring the development of the science of naval warfare as distinguished from the development of the naval material.[75]

The glow of success was short lived. In November 1892, the anti-expansionist Grover Cleveland was returned to the White House. The college had not fared well during his first administration, and there seemed little hope for any different treatment in the new term of office, particularly with the hostile Commodore Ramsay as Chief of the Bureau of Navigation. Although the Bureau no longer controlled the college, it was still responsible for assigning officers to their duty stations. Ramsay continued to believe that the college was in the wrong location and teaching the wrong things. "I am strongly in favor of the higher education of officers and am ready to assist in it in every way in my power," Ramsay wrote, "but I do think that the present War College system has very much the appearance of a farce." Ramsay insisted that the only proper type of higher education for officers was a direct continuation of the Naval Academy curriculum at a higher plane. "We have the means of furnishing officers with excellent postgraduate courses," he declared, "and we can do it in a much better manner than has been done at the War College."[76]

It was difficult enough to have the Chief of Bureau hold such views, but to make the outlook worse, Cleveland appointed the hostile Hilary Herbert as his Secretary of the Navy. The new Assistant Secretary was William McAdoo, a former representative from New Jersey and once a member of Herbert's Naval Committee. It was he who charged, "There is a well founded suspicion that this so-called munificent gift on the part of Rhode Island to the United States Government was given for the purpose of enhancing the charm of her well-known watering place, The City of Newport." Wealthy hotel owners would profit, he suggested, and while doing a little study, naval officers will "find some time to devote to the festive dance; and the giddy maidens, who disport themselves on the rocks in sunbonnets." The alleged War College is "but really a dancing school" for those who "find quite a romantic charm in sometimes strolling on the shining beach with the epauleted, embryonic Admirals of our decaying and dilapidated Navy."[77]

Within two months after the new administration came to power, Mahan was ordered away from the college to take command of the new cruiser *Chicago*. Although long overdue for a sea assignment after eight years ashore, Mahan preferred to stay to continue his historical research and to carry on his study into the *The War of 1812*. Contemptuous of Mahan's predilection, Ramsay told one of Mahan's advocates, "It is not the business of a naval officer to write books."[78] Mahan was detached on 10 May 1893, leaving the college in the charge of Commander Charles H. Stockton. If not bleak, the future was uncertain. There were only two staff members in addition to Stockton, and the Navy Department authorized no course to be given in 1893. Undaunted, Stockton and his two colleagues prepared for their lectures, but no students were ordered. The newspapers reported that the old arguments had been raised again, but with a new twist. After Mahan had left, the new Assistant Secretary of the Navy, William McAdoo, came to Newport, reportedly to look over a suitable site for a marine barracks and the feasibility of combining the Naval War College with the Torpedo Station again. The *New York Times* commented that the War College building was occupied only part of the year while the apprentices lived in crowded conditions and the marine guard had to live in tents, even in the winter. By July, Washington gossip suggested that the War College might most economically be transferred to Annapolis where there was already a library of 30,000 volumes.[79]

In August, Secretary Herbert embarked in USS *Dolphin* to inspect the naval activities at Newport. He left Washington with every intention of closing down the War College. Rumors were widespread that the end of the college was near. Earlier in the summer, Bowman McCalla, the former assistant to Commodore Walker as Chief of the Bureau of Navigation, called on Commander Stockton in Newport and learned the seriousness of the situation from him. McCalla was disturbed for he had long seconded Walker's friendly attitude toward the college and saw the college as a means of improving the Navy's direction. Not knowing what to do, McCalla wrote to his old friend, Lieutenant Benjamin H. Buckingham, then commanding *Dolphin*. Buckingham had served with McCalla in 1885 on a board which had recommended reorganization of the Navy. At that time, both were convinced of the role that the Naval War College could play in educating officers to reform the Navy's administration. When Secretary Herbert boarded the dispatch boat for the trip to Newport, Buckingham suggested he read on the trip a copy of Mahan's new book, *The Influence of Sea Power Upon the French Revolution.* Upon returning to Washington, Herbert sent for Buckingham to return Mahan's book to him. "This book alone is worth all the money that has been spent on the Naval War College," Herbert told him. "When I embarked on this cruise, I had fully intended to abolish the college; I now intend to do all in my power to sustain it."[80] Thus the War College earned a reprieve at the last minute. Born in the mind of Stephen B. Luce, it earned its justification in the fruit of the historical research which Luce dreamed it would engender. The work of Alfred Thayer Mahan was both the result and the saviour of the college in its first decade.

Notes

1. For biographical studies of Luce, see Albert Gleaves, *Life and Letters of Rear Admiral Stephen B. Luce, U.S. Navy, Founder of the Naval War College* (New York: Putnam, 1925); John D. Hayes and John B. Hattendorf, *The Writings of Stephen B. Luce* (Newport: Naval War College Press, 1975), "Introduction," pp. 3-35 and "Chronology," pp. 237-249.

2. Quoted in Hayes and Hattendorf, *Writings*, p. 8.

3. Ibid., pp. 164-65, 218-19.

4. For a general history of the Navy's connection with Narragansett Bay, see Anthony S. Nicolosi, "Foundation of the Naval Presence in Narragansett Bay: An Overview," *Newport History*, vol. 52, (1979), pp. 61-82. A description of the Navy's 1832 survey of Narragansett Bay is in William J. Morgan, et al., *Autobiography of Rear Admiral Charles Wilkes, USN, 1798-1877* (Washington: Govt. Print. Off., 1979), pp. 286-93. A history of the Naval Academy's years in Newport may be found in J. Sweetman, *The U.S. Naval Academy, An Illustrated History* (Annapolis: Naval Institute Press, 1979), pp. 62-83.

5. Quotes from Gleaves, op. cit., p. 94.

6. NWC Archives, RG 14, S.B. Luce, "A Talk on the History of the Naval War College," 20 August 1906.

7. Hayes and Hattendorf, op. cit., pp. 9, 166-67.

8. Gleaves, p. 146.

9. Ibid., pp. 330-336.

10. Ibid., pp. 154-160.

11. Frederick S. Harrod, *Manning the New Navy: The Development of a Modern Naval Enlisted Force, 1899-1940* (Westport: Greenwood Press, 1978), pp. 18-21, 75-76.

12. Ibid., p. 20; Nicolosi, op. cit., p. 70; quote from Gleaves, op. cit., p. 158.

13. Luce to Boutelle Noyes, 19 July 1883. Quoted in Gleaves, op. cit., pp. 162-64.

14. Hayes and Hattendorf, op. cit., pp. 27-28, 45-46. See also Luce's best expression of these concepts in his article, "On the Study of Naval Warfare as a Science," annotated in Ibid., pp. 47-68. Quotes from Ibid., pp. 27, 74n.

15. Luce, "Naval Administration, III" U.S.N.I. *Proceedings*, vol. XXIX, no. 4 (1903) 1-13.

16. Ibid.

17. For a study of Upton, see Stephen E. Ambrose, *Upton and the Army* (Baton Rouge: Louisiana State University Press, 1964).

18. Quoted in Gleaves, op. cit., p. 169.

19. Ibid., p. 170.

20. S. B. Luce, "War Schools," U.S.N.I. *Proceedings*, vol. XIX, no. 5 (1883), pp. 633-57.

21. John D. Hayes, transcripts of S. B. Luce letters: Luce to W. C. Church, 2 Nov 1882.

22. Ibid., Luce to Chandler, 6 Nov 1882.

23. Ibid.

24. Ibid., Luce to Chandler, 8 March 1884.

25. Ibid., Luce to Goodrich, 6 May 1884.

26. James R. Soley, *Report on Foreign Systems of Naval Education* (Washington, 1880) [46th Congress 2nd Session, Senate Executive Document 51].

27. Gleaves, op. cit., pp. 174-75.

28. "Report of Board on a Post-Graduate Course" 13 June 1883. In 48th Congress, 2d Session, Senate Ex. Doc. No. 68. *Letter from the Secretary of the Navy Reporting . . . Steps taken by him to establish an advanced course of instruction for Naval officers at Coaster's Harbor Island . . . 1885*, p. 4.

29. Ibid., p. 3.

30. Ibid., pp. 4-6.

31. Robert Seager II and Davis Maguire, eds. *Letters and Papers of Alfred Thayer Mahan* (Annapolis: Naval Institute Press, 1975) I, p. 577.

32. Hayes transcripts, Luce to Walker, 29 Aug 1884.

33. *Army and Navy Journal*, 27 September 1984, p. 168.

34. *Army and Navy Journal*, 18 October 1884, p. 225.

35. "Letter from the Secretary . . . ," op. cit., pp. 6-7.

36. Naval War College Archives, RG16, "Addresses" Box 1.

37. Gleaves, op. cit., p. 179.

38. Two of the lectures are printed in Hayes and Hattendorf, op. cit., Chapters III and IV.

39. *Inauguration of the Perry Statue, September 10 1885 with Addresses . . . .* (Newport, 1885), p. 42.

40. Ibid., p. 43.

41. Hayes and Hattendorf, op. cit., p. 38.

42. Ibid., pp. 39-40.

43. R. Seager II, *Alfred Thayer Mahan: The Man and His Letters*, (Annapolis: Naval Institute Press, 1977), pp. 165-66; Seager and Maguire, eds., *Letters*, I, pp. 603, 606-07, 610, 612, 614, 616-24. Quote from Mahan to Ashe, 2 Feb 1886, p. 625.

44. Mahan, *From Sail to Steam*, (New York: 1907), p. 293.

45. Seager and Maguire, *Letters*, I, pp. 636-8; Austin M. Knight and William D. Puleston, "History of the United States Naval War College," unpublished typescript, 1916, in Naval War College Library, Chapter: 1886.

46. Mahan, *From Sail to Steam*, p. 294.

47. John B. Hattendorf, compiler, *Register of The William McCarty Little Papers* (Newport: Naval Historical Collection, NWC, 1981), pp. 1-2.

48. Seager and Maguire, Letters, I, p. 636.

49. Mahan, op. cit., p. 296.

50. Ibid., p. 297.

51. Seager and Maguire, op. cit., p. 639.

52. Mahan, *From Sail to Steam*, p. 297; Letters, II, pp. 3-7.

53. Seager and Maguire, *Letters*, I, pp. 642-44;

54. Hayes and Hattendorf, op. cit., pp. 197-99 and references noted therein.

55. Seager and Maguire, *Letters*, I, p. 646.

56. Seager, *Alfred Thayer Mahan*, pp. 180-183.

57. Seager and Maguire, op. cit., p. 661.

58. Hayes transcripts: Porter, Luce, et al., to Secretary Whitney, 18 August 1888.

59. Ibid., Luce to T. Roosevelt, 13 Feb 1888.

60. Seager and Maguire, op. cit., p. 677.

61. Hayes transcripts: Luce to Porter, 9 March 1889.

62. Spector, pp. 77-78; Seager and Maguire, op. cit., p. 689; P. Coletta, *French E. Chadwick* (Lanham, Md: University Press of America, 1980) p. 110.

63. Hayes transcripts: Luce to Porter, 9 March 1889.

64. NWC Archives, RG 1: Goodrich to Sperry, 5 March 1906.

65. Quoted in B. F. Cooling, *Benjamin Franklin Tracy* (Hamden, Ct: Archon, 1973), p. 72.

66. U.S. Navy Department, *Report of the Secretary of the Navy . . . 1889*, p. 37.

67. Seager and Maguire, *Letters* II, pp. 4-5, 25.

68. Hayes and Hattendorf, op. cit., pp. 203-05; Cooling, *Tracy*, pp. 72-74.

69. Mahan, *From Sail to Steam*, p. 303.

70. Seager and Maguire, op. cit., pp. 72-75, 81, note discrepancies in dates; Seager, *Mahan*, pp. 242-43.

71. Knight and Puleston, op. cit, 1892, p. 1; Seager and Maguire, op. cit., p. 25.

72. W. R. Herrick, Jr. *The American Naval Revolution* (Baton Rouge: Louisiana State University Press, 1966), pp. 142-45.

73. A. T. Mahan, "The Practical Character of the Naval War College," U.S. Naval Institute *Proceedings*, Vol. 19, 66 (1892), p. 165.

74 A. T. Mahan, *The Influence of Sea Power Upon the French Revolution and Empire, 1793-1812* (Boston: Little Brown, 1892), pp. v, vi.

75. U.S. Navy Department, *Annual Report of the Secretary of the Navy . . .*, 1892, p. 57.

76. Ramsay to H. C. Taylor, quoted in Gleaves, op. cit., p. 187.

77. Quoted in J. A. S. Grenville and G. B. Young, *Politics, Strategy, and American Diplomacy* (New Haven: Yale University Press, 1966), p. 21.

78. Mahan, *From Sail to Steam*, p. 311. See also Seager, *Mahan*, p. 242, and footnote 22, p. 649.

79. "Mr. McAdoo at Newport, *New York Times*, 24 May 1893, p. 4:6; "Uncle Sam's Naval Schools; All within sight of each other in Newport Harbor, *New York Times*, 29 May 1893, p. 9:1; "Summer Talk in the Capital," *New York Times*, 9 July 1893, p. 2:5.

80. P. E. Coletta, *Bowman Henry McCalla: A Fighting Sailor* (Washington: University Press of America, 1979), p. 37; Seager and Maguire, *Letters*, II, pp. 142, 144-45; Doris Maguire, ed. *French Ensor Chadwick: Selected Letters and Papers* (Washington: University Press of America, 1981), pp. 178-79.

CHAPTER 3

FROM EDUCATION TO APPLICATION, 1893-1909

Secretary Herbert's recognition of Mahan's work in 1893 was a great victory for the War College and provided a new impetus for its work. The battle for the college's survival was by no means won, but the tide had turned in its favor, and with it came the practical application of the theories that were being worked out in Newport.

By and large, naval officers were not convinced that the War College had an important role to play. In its first decade, the college had taught barely 200 students, and only a few intellectually minded officers outside the college understood its purpose. The technically minded men agreed with Captain Richard Meade's 1888 criticism that naval officers should study "modern war," not the useless and boring historical studies carried on by the advocates of "naval conservation" in the War College's "Department of Ancient History."[1] In 1892, the Chief of Naval Engineers complained that contemporary historians, such as Mahan, ignored "the immense influence upon modern history by the steam engine. They follow in the same well-worn ruts, giving dubious descriptions of battles, names of monarchs . . . and the whole array of puppets who seem to push the car of time, while they are only flies upon its wheels."[2] Such critics were unconvinced that the college could make a practical contribution to future naval development. One naval engineer even suggested that it was merely a line officer's scheme to expand the number of their shore billets.[3]

To continue the work of the college, Secretary Herbert chose Captain Henry C. Taylor to be the new president of the Naval War College. Having commanded one of the ships in Luce's training squadron in 1880-1884, Taylor was well known to Luce and understood his ideas. In 1885, Taylor had given a lecture to the opening class. A firm believer in the college, Taylor had not incurred the direct hostility that other college advocates had. Generally considered in the service to be a very capable officer and excellent tactician, he combined both sympathy for its purpose and widespread respect.[4]

Taylor relieved Commander Stockton on 15 November 1893 and immediately faced the long standing hostility of the Training Station. The issue Taylor faced was a plan of the Station's commanding officer, Captain F. M. Bunce, to gain control of the college's new building. As a first step in December, Bunce succeeded in getting the quarters at the northeastern corner of the new college building assigned to Commander F. W. Dickens of the Training Station, and boasted that within six months his apprentice boys "would be eating their grub in the lecture room."[5]

On 14 March 1894, the Secretary of the Navy removed the War College from the direct responsibility of the Assistant Secretary of the Navy and agreed to carry out the earlier recommendations of Porter and Luce by consolidating the various naval activities in Narragansett Bay under one senior officer. Unlike the earlier attempt at consolidation, this plan provided for the separate development of the War College, Training Station, and Torpedo Station, but improved overall military administration by removing the duplication of offices. The only problem with the new arrangement was that Captain Bunce was the senior officer present and, therefore, was named Commandant of the new U.S. Naval Station, Newport. His personal hostility to the college did no permanent harm, but Taylor's position was a difficult one. He privately confessed, "I find the work here interesting . . . ,but we prosecute the work with the unpleasant dread of ugly personal attacks."[6]

A Model Course in 1894

Under Taylor, the college curriculum took a revised form, which was largely unchanged for the next 15 years and provided the basis for the course for another 10 years, up to 1919. In previous years, the course had been offered in the autumn or late summer. Beginning in 1894, the standard course was offered over a four-month period in the summer, from June to September.

In opening the new session in June, Assistant Secretary of the Navy William McAdoo substantiated the official approval of the college as a means to foster professionalism in the naval service. It is anomalous, he said, that in a season of profound peace the study of war as a profession should be inaugurated, but he pointed out "our Achilles' heel is at the water's edge." Noting that the nation's wealth and population were on the seaboard, he alluded to the danger of possible invasion, and he discussed the future interoceanic canal to be built in Central America.

He concluded that "in these days of wonderful modern implements of warfare, more than ever depends upon skill and ability to use them well."[7]

The revised course of instruction was divided into seven parts: (1) lectures on professional subjects, including international law; (2) the war problem for the course; (3) war charts and defense plans; (4) war games; (5) steam launch exercises; (6) torpedo instruction; and (7) reading. The lectures were similar to those offered in previous years, but modified slightly to focus attention on the course's war problem. Taylor's basic purpose was to establish a unified course and to stimulate active thinking in students whose training and experiences tended to establish a set routine. "The idea of this summer's course," Taylor declared, "has been primarily based upon the desire to promote professionally a mental activity, and to dispel a certain passive condition of the brain which receives and passes in review all questions that are brought before it, but which does not of its own accord seek for such questions."[8] The annual war problem was designed to create a concrete situation for the students so they would have a common practical basis on which to concentrate while the lectures provided new perspectives and raised theoretical debate.

The problem for 1894 was placed before the students at the outset. It supposed a Red (British) fleet off New York harbor with six battleships and ten cruisers about to be joined by an invasion force from Halifax with 100 transports, 10 battleships, 20 cruisers, and other smaller vessels. The opposing Blue (U.S.) force had only 5 battleships, 15 cruisers, and other small vessels. The students were asked to prepare a plan for the best disposition of Blue forces to meet Red.

This naturally led to a consideration of defensive measures and the study of tactical defense plans. That in turn led directly to a consideration of the part of the course which dealt with the preparation of war charts, defense plans, and war gaming. The exercises with steam launches illustrated the practical problem of various formations developed on the war game board and raised by the technical training given at the Torpedo Station.

In addition to the stimulation of lectures and participation in problems, all the students were obliged to complete a reading course that paralleled the lectures. Although reading had always been an important part of the course, this was the first time in which a set list of books was recommended for individual reading. It ranged from Jomini, Mahan, Hamley, and Colomb on strategy and the art of war, to Barrow and Clarke on naval history, and Wheaton and Snow on international law.

In addition, two other important innovations were made in the course. Both stressed the traditional method of inductive reasoning which the college employed in its teaching. Individual and special cases were used not only in the problem but also in war gaming, naval history, and international law as a means of stimulating broad, original thinking about naval warfare.[9]

In the study of international law, Dr. Freeman Snow of Harvard University gave a series of 22 lectures which paralleled the student's consideration of hypothetical cases in naval application of international law. The case method of teaching international law had been introduced at the Harvard Law School and soon became the accepted method of teaching the subject in America. Snow was one of the pioneers of this method but at the time there was no American book adaptable to the method. Following Dr. Snow's death at the midst of the 1894 course, Taylor directed Commander Stockton to edit Snow's War College lectures and to expand them, where necessary, from Snow's notes. Published in 1895, this was the college's first publication in international law. Together with Snow's 1893 book, *Cases on International Law*, it established an important part of the basic nucleus of American textbooks on the subject. For the Naval War College, the emphasis on the case method in international law, as in other areas of the curriculum, was to foster an active interest "in the principles of the science" by looking at specific issues.[10]

The 1894 session of the college also saw a new use of war gaming as a means of linking broad principles to specific issues. Previously, war games had been used for occasional demonstrations and examination of particular problems, but in 1894 they became an integral part of instruction. Three different types of games were employed. Admiral Colomb's dual game, revised by a staff member, Lieutenant (j.g.) Henry B. Wilson, used two ships. A tactical game had been prepared by Commander Bowman McCalla and modified by the experience of Austrian and German games. It was played on a board or table and represented a fleet action. Third was the strategic game that had been developed over the years at the college, based in part on a study of *Kriegspiel* and other foreign games. The strategic game was played upon charts with players in separate rooms, in order to represent an entire war. It proved to be invaluable in teaching strategy and strategic geography.[11] William McCarty Little, although only a volunteer on the college staff, was the driving force behind the development of these games. He believed that in the games the college played, "It is a matter of small moment who is adjudged the winner, while on the other hand it is of great importance to ascertain as nearly as possible what conditions make for success or failure." In carrying out its function, Captain Taylor believed that "the war game has been useful to a degree far beyond my most sanguine anticipation."[12]

For the students who came to the Naval War College in 1894, the results of the course were more than a brush with theory. The 18 regular members of the course were joined by officers of the U.S. Revenue Cutter Service, the Rhode Island Naval Militia, and the College's first foreign students—Commanders Carl-Gustaf Flach and Gösta af Ugglas of the Royal Swedish Navy. In 1895, an officer from the Royal Danish Navy, Captain Fritzer, attended the course. Later, as matters under discussion became increasingly more sensitive, foreign officers were no longer included. In addition to the other changes in 1894, the college added to its role as a school of theory the attributes of an organization that could test and plan future uses of the Navy. Taylor told the students at the end of the course, "Our plans will be formulated and ready for instant use." As the work continued in future years, it would develop, he said, into the naval equivalent of the planning that had successfully prepared Prussia for wars with Austria and France. In addition, while preparing these plans, Taylor suggested,

> in the study of the principles of warfare necessary to perfect them, of naval and military history in order to utilize past experience, and in the lectures of experts keeping us abreast of the latest developments of tactical forces and weapons, we shall learn the immutable laws that govern the Conduct of War.[13]

At the end of the 1894 course, the college published an abstract of its course as a means to publicize its accomplishments and to explain to its critics what was done at the college. Since assuming the presidency, Taylor was convinced that the best means of winning friends and support for the college was through an active public relations campaign. The invitations to officers of the naval militia and to foreign officers were part of that program. Taylor stressed the practical results the college achieved and, during the three years of his presidency, he published the various conclusions which the college had reached. In 1894, for example, he listed 11 tentative conclusions that had resulted from the course, the first six of which were:

1. Men-of-war of each class should be more alike in order that squadrons might be homogeneous.

2. The militarily useful limit in size and cost for ships seemed to have been reached and passed by modern navies.

3. U.S. fighting ships should draw less water than those at present in service in modern navies.

4. The Navy should not strive for extreme high speed in fighting ships.

5. Discussions as to thickness of armor were not conclusive.

6. The weight of guns and projectiles should not be allowed to increase unduly; rapidity of fire must be maintained.

In the practical problem for 1894, the students and staff concluded that the U.S. Navy could only deal with a superior naval force by effectively using bays, sounds, and interior waterways for engagements with the enemy. The United States, they believed, did not have the capacity to win a fleet battle in the open sea. This conclusion led to the additional conclusions that

7. Naval officers should navigate frequently and for long periods the channels, sounds, and bays of the coast.

8. Preparation should be made in peacetime for "a great flotilla of gunboats, torpedo boats, and rams" in Peconic Bay, to defend New York.

9. The system of lookouts, signaling, and transmission of information ashore should be perfected in peacetime.

10. Officers should improve their ability in shiphandling in squadron maneuvers in shallow waters.

11. A ship canal across Cape Cod would have important strategic value.[14]

In the courses for 1895 and 1896, these deductions were reaffirmed and, in addition, it was suggested that a standard classification of ship types be established, confidential sailing directions be issued for coastal areas, and that a suitable coaling port was needed in the Aleutian Island chain to defend the United States in the Pacific. Numerous questions in regard to submarine mines and torpedo boats were raised but could not be answered without further practical experience. The college recommended that preparations be made in these areas with a view toward joint maneuvers with the Army.[15]

A General Staff for the Navy

As this type of war gaming experience and general criticism accumulated at the Naval War College, it began to create a body of doctrine that could be used in the absence of a central strategic planning office in the Navy Department.[16] This was an important aspect in the line of thinking behind the development of a military staff that had come from Prussia. By the 1890s, military and naval writers no longer recommended a slavish imitation of Prussian organizational methods, but broader applications of it.[17] In American naval thinking, the recognition of the need for war planning in peacetime was part of the same perception that had created the Office of Naval Intelligence as a body to collect data and had created the Naval War College. The course at the War College stressed the advantage of a staff system for the U.S. Navy. The War College became the leading institution within the Navy which was pressing for the creation of what later became the Office of the Chief of Naval Operations. Not surprisingly, many of the War College presidents, as well as its students, became the leaders who developed and applied the staff system to the needs of the Navy.

From the beginning, Stephen B. Luce had seen the reform of naval administration and the creation of a naval staff as integral parts of a concept which embodied both improved training for enlisted men and officer education. Luce's published writings on naval administration date from 1864, and by 1911, he had written 16 articles on the subject. In 1888, he stated the issue directly:

> On looking into the constitution of the U.S. Navy Department, one is struck at the first glance with its utter incapacity for dealing with the problems of war, or with military questions in general.[18]

With the Naval War College on a surer footing after 1893, both Luce and Henry Taylor continued the campaign. Now retired from active service, Luce devoted his energies to writing articles and using his influence with individuals. Taylor ordered staff members to lecture on various types of administrative methods. Studies were made of business organization, the British Admiralty, and the German Army's General Staff. Taylor and others at the War College concluded that the German system was best, but it would have to be changed to suit American political conditions. Taylor explained the value of a general staff to the Governor of Rhode Island, using this argument:

> The events which procede and follow war progress too quickly to allow for general or special reconnaissance of the theater of operations, either at home or abroad. Hence this work which took place formerly in time of war should be made in time of peace . . . [The] measures taken upon the eve of war—a time of emergency and excitement—will naturally be imperfect, ill digested, and extravagant.[19]

In making this statement, Taylor expressed the pervasive attitude at the Naval War College that warfare was a logical and rational enterprise, conducted by professionals on the basis of principles deduced by reason, guided by international law, and limited in purpose to clearly defined objectives. Carefully planned preparations were a key part of this basic approach.[20]

Taylor and the War College discovered immediate and strong opposition to the establishment of any new organization which would carry out the tasks that were envisaged. The Bureau Chiefs objected to any measure which seemed to lessen their power, and the civilian Secretaries of the Navy opposed any plan which increased the policy making influence of naval officers. The lack of unanimity among officers and the nature of bureaucratic routine added to the burden of static inertia and prevented any reform.[21]

By 1896, Taylor reluctantly concluded that a naval staff would have to grow slowly. He and Luce agreed that the best way to do this was to create the methods and establish the procedures, using existing institutions to do what could be readily done. They would have to wait on later laws and regulations to create the necessary bureaucratic machinery. Luce hoped that if an evolutionary approach was the best method, it would occur at the War College and not within a bureau. Ramsay, at the Bureau of Navigation, opposed this.

With these ideas in mind, Taylor employed the War College curriculum as a means of not only educating naval officers in theory, but demonstrating to them, in both hypothetical and actual situations, the functions of a general staff.

The work that the students began in the summer course was carried on by the college staff and completed during the winter months.[23] The results were then summarized and sent to Washington where they were filed in the Office of Naval Intelligence and were available to be used by ONI in advising the Secretary of the Navy. In this way the first body of naval plans was developed for the defense of the East Coast. In addition, the general strategic situations of the Gulf of Mexico, the Caribbean Sea, and the Great Lakes were examined, along with the Japanese threat to Hawaii. As early as 1894, students were specifically assigned papers on "Strategy in the Event of War With Spain." In 1896 and 1897, the main problem was devoted to possible war with Spain and the need to refuel the U.S. Fleet in the Caribbean. One of the recommendations which resulted from the discussion was a proposal to burn oil, rather than coal, in ships. At that time the only known naval use of fuel oil was by the Russian Navy in the Black Sea.[24]

Planning for the War With Spain

In the years leading up to the Spanish-American War, the curriculum at the Naval War College played an initially modest but growing role in the perceptions of naval officers and national leaders, such as Theodore Roosevelt, as they began to think out possible courses of action in a war with Spain. Although three students had considered war with Spain in their 1894 essays, the issue was not a central one for the class of 20 officers. As the revolt in Cuba became more acute in international terms, both Admiral Luce and McCarty Little advocated a full-scale study of the possibility of American involvement in a conflict with Spain. McCarty Little approached Taylor with the idea, and Taylor directed that the 1895 class consider two problems, a general problem devoted to the defense of New England against Britain, and a "special problem" devoted to war with Spain. Taylor justified the double workload for the students by stressing the great importance of both issues "in the near future to the country."

In the earliest study of the problem, two different scenarios were considered. One considered Spain and Britain allied against France and the United States. A second considered a war between only the United States and Spain. In January 1896, following the previous classes' work, the War College developed a more advanced study in which three options were considered:

1. Direct attack on Spain.
2. Attack on Spain's Pacific colonies: Philippines and Guam.
3. Attack on Spain's American colonies: Cuba and Puerto Rico.

Of the three options, the War College concluded that the first was too expensive and risky; the second would be safe but not decisive; and the third would probably not be decisive, but would place the burden of continuing the war on Spain.

These early considerations in 1895 had some influence on thinking in Washington, but the next important step came with a consideration by Lieutenant W. W. Kimball in the Office of Naval Intelligence. His plan envisaged a purely naval war based upon a blockade of Cuba, which would allow the Cubans to establish their own nation, avoiding an American invasion and preventing Spanish interference in Cuba. Two secondary naval campaigns were proposed. One would hold the Spanish fleet in its home waters by an American naval attack on trade and coastal cities; the other would capture Manila in order to control Spanish commerce from the Philippines. Kimball postulated that the subsequent release of the Philippines back to Spain would induce her to accept peace and the liberation of Cuba.

The Naval War College staff and students were dissatisfied with the Kimball plan when it was examined during the 1896 course. Much influenced by Mahan's historical deductions and American Civil War experience, they concluded that a blockade of Cuba would not be decisive and, moreover, an effective blockade could not be established until the enemy's fleet had been defeated. In place of these plans, Taylor recommended, in November 1896, that the best course was to concentrate the main effort on a joint Army-Navy attack on Cuba, which would result in the capture of Havana by a force of up to 60,000 troops in a period of less than 30 days, the time that Spain would need to reinforce her troops. At the same time, American ships could attack and blockade the Cuban coast, obtaining Cienfuegos, Bahia Honda, or Matanzas as bases. A parallel operation was envisaged against the Philippines, but American naval operations in European waters were to be carefully avoided until the Cuban campaign was completed.

In December 1896, the Navy Department was not satisfied with either the War College or the ONI alternatives. Secretary Herbert convened a special board of officers to review the situation. The board was headed by the War College's old nemesis, Admiral Ramsay, and included Bunce, now a rear admiral in command of the North Atlantic Station, as well as Captain W. T. Sampson, Richard Wainwright, and

Taylor. Taylor was ordered to Washington for duty in connection with this board and was relieved as president of the Naval War College on 31 December 1896 by Commander Caspar F. Goodrich. Despite Taylor's objections, the new board explicitly rejected the War College plan and devised a new one that had broad similarities to Kimball's ideas.

In March 1897, the new administration of William McKinley took office. With it came a new Secretary of the Navy, John D. Long, and Assistant Secretary, Theodore Roosevelt. The new Secretary called the planning board into session, but its membership was altered by new officers having succeeded the older members in their billets. Goodrich carried on with an attempt to promote the War College view, but, like Taylor, he met with little success. The second board adopted a plan similar to the Kimball plan with some alterations. Despite that, the plan did not represent any consensus of view among political leaders in Washington, and no action was taken to prepare for war along the lines indicated by the naval officers' plan. Differences of opinion and contradictions remained. In July 1897, the War College staff was no longer convinced that war with Spain was certain and thought that other threats were equally important. Great Britain and Japan also appeared as threats, and Theodore Roosevelt directed the War College to consider as a "special" problem a possible clash with Japan over the Hawaiian Islands.

Although none of these plans and considerations turned out to have a direct bearing on the war that followed the sinking of the *Maine* in 1898, the basic point at issue was the War College's strong belief in advance planning, detailed preparation, and rational consideration coupled with rapid execution in the event of war. It was one of the specific points which Assistant Secretary Theodore Roosevelt took up in his thinking. And it was what he had in mind on 25 February 1898 when, left in temporary charge by the absence of the Secretary of the Navy, he gave orders to move ships and distribute supplies putting the Navy in a position to act in the event of war. Often considered the brainchild of Roosevelt and Henry Cabot Lodge, it was, in fact, the type of preparation that had been long advocated by a significant group of naval officers, particularly those associated with the Naval War College.[25]

The College Threatened Again

The antagonism between the Naval War College and the Naval Training Station continued quietly but unabated. In the 1890s, the Training Station changed its approach and moved further and further away from the shipboard training that Luce had envisaged when he established the Apprentice Training system. Up to 1889, the recruits

lived aboard the old ship-of-the-line *New Hampshire*, berthed alongside
the wharf at Coasters Harbor. In that year, however, the increasing
numbers of recruits along with the difficulty in maintaining proper
sewage forced the recruits to move ashore where the sailors in training
were housed in tents and temporary buildings on the island. From this
point on, the Training Station began to agitate for the construction of
buildings ashore and to expand its use of Coasters Harbor Island. Much
of the island had been leased for the use of local farmers, but in 1895,
the Training Station stopped this practice. In its expansion, the officers
in command of the Training Station failed to carry on the same
appreciation that Luce had shown for the two complementary organizations. Following Captain Bunce's promotion to rear admiral and his
departure from Newport in 1894, the Training Station came under the
command of another like-minded officer, Captain Francis W. Dickens,
the occupant of one of the War College's quarters. Early on he declared
his hostility to the college and, like Bunce, wished to remove it for the
advantage of the Training Station. In a conversation with McCarty
Little, Dickens declared that the use of the Training Station for "the
training of the man behind the gun" was the most important thing in
the Navy after the "education of officers at the Naval Academy."[26]
There was no place, in Dickens' view of the Navy, for a War College.

Officers of the War College had been worried about the Training
Station's intentions for several years, and by 1895 they sensed that a
strong and well planned move to construct barracks for the apprentices
would be used to mask an attempt to take over the college's buildings.
In an effort to stop the bickering on the island, the Secretary of the Navy
had explicitly told Henry Taylor that the Secretary's support for the
college was dependent on the college refraining from interference with
the Training Station's plans. "This would mean," as McCarty Little put
it, "that Johnny musn't cry out should Tommy see fit to beat him in the
head. It seems quite possible that the barracks will be placed as to be
very close to the north windows of the College and flank it, so that in
the course of time the college building will be in the very position for
the offices of the Training Station."

"Do you begin to perceive a slight mousy odor?" McCarty Little
asked.[27]

During the spring of 1896, there was an attempt by members of
Congress to amend the naval appropriation bill in that year by adding
an item of $100,000 for a barracks on Coasters Harbor Island. Luce
began a letter writing campaign which pointed out to Rhode Island's
congressional delegation that the purpose of this appropriation was
really part of a larger effort "to drive the college from the island and
secure its building for the Training Station."[28] The Training Station did
not receive authorization for its barracks in 1896, but it continued to

expand and built a handsome residence to house its commandant on the edge of the hill to the east of the old almshouse.

In 1896, Captain Dickens was ordered to Washington as an assistant to Rear Admiral Ramsay, Chief of the Bureau of Navigation. By August 1897, Dickens was Acting Chief of the Bureau and, in that capacity, he renewed his attack on the War College. This time, he exploited the tension between the Office of Naval Intelligence and the War College over war planning. The War College and ONI had sought to ease the difficulties that had arisen from their joint need to obtain and use intelligence information by promoting an exchange of junior officers. In January 1897, Ensign John V. Chase of the War College staff spent the month at ONI as a beginning step in this direction. In 1890, Assistant Secretary Soley had already taken the War College, ONI, and the Office of Naval Records and Library directly under his administration as a means of coordinating their related activities. Dickens, however, saw that the overlapping functions could be used to attack the college and he could, therefore, counteract the efforts that college officers were making to demonstrate the college's practical usefulness through its ability to examine actual war plans in the light of theory and through war gaming. As acting Bureau head, Dickens was responsible for detailing officers to their assignments. Under the guise of a recommendation to prevent duplication of effort, Dickens suggested to Assistant Secretary Roosevelt that ONI should be "augmented by officers of experience and all work now done at the War College by its staff removed to Washington and made part of the functions of the Office of Naval Intelligence." Acknowledging the value of the main problem as a worthwhile and useful study, Dickens took the line of those critics who valued only practical experience unaugmented by study and reflection. The main war problem, he said "could be sent out to the fleet, the country thus having a real War College where the art of war can only be practically learned, at sea."[29]

Caspar Goodrich, the college's president, was called upon once again to come to assist the college as he had in 1884 and again in 1889. In an impassioned letter to Assistant Secretary Roosevelt, Goodrich defended the college's independence of thought, academic integrity, and location away from the immediate pressure of Washington's political life. "To suggest or to appear, in even a remote way, to suggest that preliminary reading and study are unnecessary to success in naval warfare," Goodrich wrote, "is to ignore the essential facts in the lives of both Nelson and our great Farragut, who were earnest students of the history and literature of their profession and even noted for intellectual activity." Pressing the point further, Goodrich pointed out that Dickens clearly misunderstood the War College's curriculum. There was no other institution which offered the opportunity for the type of study undertaken at Newport. Moreover, "knowledge can be gained in the science of war in one way only—careful study in time of peace—and this study cannot be carried on amid the numerous distractions of life aboard ship. It is idle to claim the contrary."

Turning to Dickens' suggestion that the fleet undertake the main war problems instead of the college, Goodrich replied, "The college is now, as always heretofore, desirous of the cooperation of the fleet in solving tactical problems and it greets with ardor the proposal . . . to inaugurate practical exercises with the fleet as a measure of the highest importance to the Service, supplementing the work done here. 'Practical' work in strategy must, however, be done ashore." The War College could provide preparation and thinking that could make fleet exercises more productive. "The information obtained from one single strategic game in three hours could not be secured by the North Atlantic Fleet in as many weeks," Goodrich declared.

In concluding his argument, Goodrich suggested that the critics of the college were merely members of a dying breed.

> There is nothing new under the sun. The same spirit of opposition which combated the establishment of the Naval Academy and afterwards sought to cripple and deprecate it, still survives; but failing of its original purposes, now turns its criticisms against the later child of professional progress. Such things may be expected. Sidney Smith said he once knew a man to speak disrespectfully of the equator.[30]

A supporter of both ONI and the War College, Roosevelt urged Goodrich to publish a "moderately strong" defense. In November 1897, the correspondence between Goodrich and Roosevelt appeared in the *Army-Navy Register.* Its publication effectively quashed Dickens proposal and nothing more was done to carry it out. Although the proposal had been defeated, it was not the last attempt to destroy the college.

In March 1898, Goodrich was ordered by the Navy Department to carry out a previously worked out plan to establish signal stations along the Atlantic coast. Before that order could be carried out, however, war with Spain was declared on 19 April. On 23 April, Goodrich was ordered to command the USS *St. Louis,* a passenger liner converted to a cruiser, and plans for a summer course were suspended for the duration of the war. The War College building was placed in the custody of the Commandant of the Naval Training Station, Newport. Officers attached to the Training Station were also sent to sea, and by June all the quarters in the college building had been vacated by the Training Station. For the first time since 1894, the college was now in possession of everything under its own roof. There was little activity at the War College, but in early June Commander C. H. Stockton was ordered to duty there to prepare a new edition of

Professor Freeman Snow's War College lectures on *International Law.* The widely read book, which Stockton had edited in 1894, was now out of print and a new edition was in demand.

On 12 August, after only three months, the war came to an end, but no immediate moves were taken to revive the college. In September, Admiral Luce wrote an alarmed letter to Senator Henry Cabot Lodge,

> The days of the War College are few and short. It must soon cease to exist. The enemies of the college are now all powerful in the Navy Department and are so bent on its destruction, that the end is already in sight unless the Secretary of the Navy himself comes to its relief.[31]

Rumors were already rife that the new Chief of the Bureau of Navigation, Captain A. S. Crowninshield, wanted the War College removed from Newport. The first move in this campaign seemed to be Secretary of the Navy's General Order 496 which revoked the 1894 order consolidating the Training Station, Torpedo Station, and War College as separate and independent activities under the Commandant, Naval Station, Newport. The Training Station, thus, became the college's direct, administrative commander. When asked to resume the presidency of the college, Henry Taylor looked at the new situation and refused outright. "As president I would be practically subordinate to my junior in rank at the Training Station," he wrote.[32]

The War College had lost a knowledgeable advocate of its work when Theodore Roosevelt resigned his position of Assistant Secretary of the Navy to go off to join the Army as a "Rough Rider" in May 1898. His successor, Charles H. Allen, had no previous knowledge of the War College. His first visit there came on 14 October 1898 while on an inspection tour of various naval stations. No class was in session and there was little activity, and Allen received the false impression that the college was a graduate school built along university lines. With this in mind, he suggested that Annapolis was the best location. There it could complement the Naval Academy in the way the universities had patterned the relationship between undergraduate and graduate education. The existing Naval Academy could become the basis of a "great Naval University," he suggested. The libraries, laboratories, and instructors could be shared as they are in universities. Furthermore, the central location of Annapolis would allow naval officers to visit it more frequently and Senators and Congressmen could easily attend lectures. The more moderate climate of Annapolis allowed practical exercises the year around while in Newport they could only take place in the summer.[33] None of these arguments were new, although the direct parallel with recent developments in American higher education added a new twist to the arguments of those who saw the college as only a postgraduate course.

The supporters of the Naval War College quickly came to its defense and argued the essential errors in Allen's thinking. As Luce consistently pointed out, any move would destroy the distinctive characteristics of the college. Although the college took advantage of the best academic expertise it could obtain for its purpose, it was not designed to offer a set course of instruction that followed strictly the established lines of academic training in universities.[34] It was not a place where masters taught disciples, but where faculty and students formed "a sort of cooperative or joint-stock affair, where all work in unison for the common good."[35] In making this point, Luce stressed that the science of naval warfare was just in the process of development and had not yet reached a stage where there was any consensus about its basic character. The real work of the college, he said, was "the investigation and analysis of problems which represent conditions of modern warfare especially as would arise in defense of our own territory."[36] This essential characteristic would be lost if the War College were moved to Annapolis and made part of the more rigid, academic process of education there. Similarly, a move to Washington would force the college into the bureaucratic machinery of Washington. Luce believed that the ultimate purpose of the War College should be educational, but in a professional sense, not an academic one. Its separate and distinct location in a cool climate and at a deep sea port were key ingredients to ensure its essential characteristics.

Luce's views carried great weight, and his younger friends and followers, Mahan, Sampson, Taylor, Goodrich, Chadwick, and Stockton, had all earned a position from which they could carry on Luce's fight. The college remained without a president from the time of Goodrich's departure in April until 2 November 1898 when Stockton was ordered to assume the presidency. Immediately upon taking office, Stockton wrote a series of letters to Assistant Secretary Allen, pointing out the value of the college in terms of its international position:

> The War College is unique in its character, a prototype of the Berlin General Staff School, and it has been followed in its general lines by the schools since established in Russia, France, and to be established in Sweden and Japan. The establishment of these, copying our struggling institution, give testimony to its standing and worth, and place a grave responsibility upon those who would extinguish it by an affiliation with and absorption by a school for cadets.[37]

While the dispute simmered in the winter of 1898-1899, the Bureau of Navigation indicated to Stockton that the demand for officers at sea and other assignments was so great that no officers could be spared for student assignments at the War College. In March 1899, The *New York Times* reported that there would be no session because of the expected move to Annapolis, although many officers had indicated a keen interest in studying and critiquing the strategy and tactics of the recent war with Spain.[38] Stockton reacted to these threats, but with a more moderate tone than the extreme views of Luce. He thought that although the two institutions should be in touch mentally and professionally, but a move to Annapolis would be fatal. A move elsewhere was not nearly so serious a threat. The main arguments for Newport were that the facilities existed already and that a move to any location further south would require a winter course instead of a summer one. As Stockton wrote, Newport has "a climate much more congenial for mental work in summer. . . . "[39] The failure of the Bureau to assign any students on the grounds that they were engaged in more important duties was both a fallacious argument and a policy that would be fatal to the War College. "There is no more important duty on shore, except the absolutely essential professional administrative work, than the study of naval warfare," Stockton countered.[40] While the college defended itself along these lines, it became clear that it could not be removed from its location on Coasters Harbor Island without congressional authorization.[41] The War College had several influential friends in Congress, including Senator William E. Chandler of New Hampshire, the former Secretary of the Navy whose order had established the college, as well as Senator Nelson Aldrich of Rhode Island and Senator Henry Cabot Lodge of Massachusetts.

Thwarted by the college's supporters in Congress, the Bureau of Navigation continued to insist that no students were available. So Stockton turned to Rear Admiral William T. Sampson, Commander-in-Chief of the North Atlantic Fleet, an old friend of the college, and a member of the original board which had planned the college in 1884. He obtained the Secretary of the Navy's approval for the North Atlantic Fleet to rendezvous at Newport, thereby allowing fleet officers to attend the course. Stockton and Sampson arranged a course in which each day's work was as nearly complete as possible, thus allowing for shipboard duties and possible ship movements. On 29 May, the armored cruiser *New York*, and the battleships *Indiana, Massachusetts,* and *Texas* anchored in the bay off the college. They were followed by the cruisers *New Orleans* and *Brooklyn* and the old steam sloop *Lancaster*. The course was spread over several months, beginning on 31 May and ending in October, with an average daily attendance of about 18 students.[42]

Much of the study revolved around a group of guest lectures given by Captain Bowman McCalla on the lessons of the war with Spain. McCalla, one of the more colorful officers of the period, had been on the college staff in 1897 and at the outbreak of the war had taken command of the small cruiser *Marblehead*. As the senior naval officer in the capture of Guantanamo Bay from the Spanish, McCalla had found himself confronted with mines, happily old and inefficient, but new to U.S. Navy men. He pointed to health problems in tropical waters that became acute for the troops embarked in hastily commandeered transports.

McCalla pointed out that tactically the fleet had been unprepared for war. It had few torpedo boats and misused those it had. The evidence of the battle of Santiago demonstrated the need for torpedo boat destroyers. He severely criticized the sinking of the collier *Merrimac* in the channel at Santiago in an attempt to trap the Spanish squadron in port. Also he emphasized the demonstrated need for smokeless powder and for some way to reduce coal smoke from the boilers. In general, McCalla demonstrated the consequences of lack in doctrine and advance preparation.

Secretary Long's War Board, of which Mahan was a member, came in for severe criticism. McCalla, with many others, believed that the War Board had mistakenly endeavored to direct tactics from Washington. It was a makeshift affair which failed to perform effectively the function of a naval staff.

In the first discussion of convoying at the college, McCalla objected to the practice, used in moving American troops to the Philippines, Cuba, and Puerto Rico, of placing the escort ships under the operational command of the senior Army officer afloat. Believing that the Navy should control all aspects related directly to naval activities, McCalla further recommended that the Navy should control not only the ports but also the coastal artillery which defended them.[43]

McCalla's lectures raised a debate throughout the U.S. Navy on tactical issues and fueled the already bitter controversy between Rear Admirals W. T. Sampson and W. S. Schley over their respective roles in the war. Future classes at the Naval War College repeatedly returned to McCalla's controversial criticisms over the years as they re-examined those actual operations in the light of theory, exercises, and war gaming. Not all McCalla's ideas were adopted by the Navy, but they provided a new and innovative perspective which laid a foundation for the later evolution of American tactical thinking.[44] The McCalla lectures were only a portion of the 1899 course, but certainly they were its most memorable portion.

The Course and the College 1900-1909

By the opening of the new century, the foes of the college conceded defeat, at least temporarily. The four month summer course for 1900 opened with 30 students, 20 of them from the Navy. The others consisted of six Marine Corps officers, two Army officers, and two officers from the Revenue Cutter Service. One of these, Lieutenant H.

G. Hamlet, later became Commandant of the U.S. Coast Guard. In the years which followed, the classes included several other officers who later distinguished themselves. Among them were Austin M. Knight, Royal R. Ingersoll, Bradley Fiske, W. B. Caperton, Hugh Rodman, W. A. Moffett, and Louis McCarty Little of the Marine Corps, son of William McCarty Little. In 1901, E. M. Shepard was the first student to attend the course as a rear admiral.

The subject areas studied were the same as those examined in 1894, but in order to organize the larger number of students more effectively, the class was divided into four committees. Each committee prepared a solution to the main problem and discussed the obvious subjects at hand. To emphasize that the matters dealt with were of the utmost gravity to the naval profession, college president Captain C. S. Sperry stressed the professional character of the College over its function as a school. To do this, he ordered in 1904 that the words *course* and *class* were to be replaced, when describing the college, with the term *conference*.

The lectures were of two kinds, those directly related to the conference work and those of a more general academic interest. Among the latter were lectures by well known academics and visitors such as Brooks Adams, Albert Bushnell Hart, James F. Jameson, Frederick Jackson Turner, and A. C. McLaughlin, all of whom spoke on aspects of American history.[45]

In the study of international law, the college made several innovations. By direction of the Secretary of the Navy in 1899, Captain C. H. Stockton and Captain Asa Walker prepared a Code of the Law and Usages of War at Sea, elaborating on the legal conventions established by the recent Hague Conference. The Code, drawn up at the college, was approved by the Secretary of the Navy in June 1900 and established as a directive for American naval officers to follow. This was the beginning of the modern effort to codify maritime international law, following the U.S. Army's earlier initiative to codify the law of land warfare.[46]

Discussions at the college in 1903 concluded that the Code would restrict American naval forces in war without similarly restricting an enemy. In February 1904, the Secretary of the Navy approved the college's recommendation that it be withdrawn as a directive, although retained as a guideline.[47] The Code served, however, as a guide for the American negotiating position at the Second Hague Peace Conference in 1907 and the London Naval Conference of 1908-1909, in which the United States was represented by C. H. Stockton and two of his successors as president of the Naval War College, Rear Admirals C. S. Sperry and J. P. Merrell.

The study of international law followed the practice established by Stockton and Freeman Snow in 1894 by dealing with the subject in terms of specific situations likely to arise in modern conditions. In 1901, this approach was given renewed emphasis under the direction of Professor John Bassett Moore of Columbia University. An Assistant Secretary of State during the Spanish-American War, Moore later became a judge of the Permanent Court of International Justice. The discussions he led at the Naval War College in 1901, together with the students' reasoning and tentative solution, formed the first volume of the college's series of nearly 60 "blue books" on international law, which were published during its first century.

On Moore's suggestion,[48] the Naval War College appointed George Grafton Wilson, a professor of sociology and political science at Brown University, to be lecturer in international law. Wilson, like Moore and Freeman Snow, was one of the pioneer teachers of international law. He had begun teaching the subject as an undergraduate course at Brown in 1891. He had first lectured at the Naval War College in 1900 on the legal aspects of "insurgency." Moving from Brown in 1910 to become professor of international law at Harvard, Wilson retained his Naval War College lectureship until he retired in 1937. For that long period, he gave form and substance to the education of naval officers in international law. One of the founders of the American Society of International Law, Wilson's major contribution to the subject lies in the 7,000 pages of international law blue books which he edited at the college, "every one of which was intended to provide the naval officer at home and alone in foreign ports with precise answers to problems he might face."[49]

In the study of tactics, the college staff made several modifications to the previous arrangement. Tactical situations at sea were developed corresponding to the problems set by von Moltke for the Prussian Army. As a means to produce readiness of mind in naval emergencies, only half an hour was allocated for each student to give his solution to a problem. Reviving Admiral Luce's original ideas from the first years of the college, a series of small landing operations was undertaken by the students to give naval officers a soldier's point of view and to compare tactical problems afloat with those ashore. In a further development, battle problems were introduced into the course in 1901. Using the war gaming board, they were designed to examine an overall battle situation with emphasis on problems of attack, situation problems, and problems of unequal speed. The war games were continued and remained the main coordinating feature in the various elements of the conference. "The principles of strategy and tactics may be gleaned from history," Captain French Chadwick wrote,

> but the games afford the only practicable means known whereby these principles may be supplied. The strategic game teaches the admiral how to dispose his forces in a maritime campaign, the

tactical game how to handle his fleet in action, while the duel game
shows the commander how to best fight his ship.[50]

As the course settled into a mold, new orders from the Navy
Department returned several familiar figures to the college. In 1901,
Rear Admiral Stephen B. Luce was ordered back to active duty at the
college, having taken only an informal part in the work of the two
previous sessions. Luce remained on active duty at the college until
1910, when at the age of 83, congressional critics forced his
retirement. He wrote, lectured, and influenced the ideas of students
and staff alike. Bradley Fiske, who came to know Luce during this
period, later recalled that Luce, more than any other man, "taught the
Navy to think, to think about the Navy as a whole."[51] In December
1900, before his formal return to duty, Luce had been honored by the
college with a large portrait by Frederic Porter Vinton. The college
paid the artist $1,000.00 from a fund raised by subscription.[52]

In 1903, Lieutenant William McCarty Little was promoted to the
rank of captain by special Act of Congress and ordered to active duty
at the Naval War College in recognition of his nearly 20 years of
voluntary work, chiefly in war gaming. He continued to devote his
attention to this area until his retirement a dozen years later in 1915.

For many years, Little read to the students Mahan's lectures on
naval strategy. In 1906, Luce began a campaign to persuade Mahan to
revise and to update them to be what Luce termed "the capstone, as it
were, of the great monument you have reared."[53] Consenting after two
years of persuasion, Mahan began work on his last major book, *Naval
Strategy*. He argued with the War College and the Navy Department
as to whether he would be paid as a captain, or as a rear admiral, the
rank he had been promoted to on the retired list. But to Mahan's
displeasure, the law prevented pay at a higher level than for the grade
held before retirement. In October 1908, he reported for duty at the
War College, by letter from his home at Quogue, on Long Island. His
orders specifically directed him to prepare his lectures for
publication. He completed the book in 1911. His detachment in June
1912 marked the end of his long association with the Naval War
College.[54]

During these same years, the college began to expand its physical
plant. In June 1903, the president occupied for the first time Quarters B,
the house built for the Commandant of the Naval Training Station. Five
months later, when Chadwick left the college, the house reverted to the
Station, but in 1906 it was returned to presidents of the Naval War
College, who, with one exception, have occupied it since that time.[55]

In 1903, the college also obtained its first automobile, an electric
vehicle, which seemed to offer cheaper transportation than horses for
the occasional uses which the college had.[56]

At the same time work was in progress for a new library. Completed on 17 June 1904, the new building was reached from the main part of the college by a covered bridge, which led to a staircase ascending to the main reading room. The library's rotunda was supported by eight columns, each capped with ornamental capitals cast, apparently at Luce's suggestion, at the Washington Gun Factory from old bronze naval cannon.[57]

The ground floor of the new annex was designed to house the archives, which were the main source for intelligence and data used in conducting war games and evaluating war plans. Adjacent to the archives and chart rooms was a meeting room for the General Board. There was also an office designated for the Secretary to the General Board. When the board met in Washington during the winter months, these spaces were used as lecture rooms.[58]

The War College and the General Board

It was entirely appropriate for the General Board to have a meeting room in Newport, as the board was a direct outgrowth of the same movement which had created the War College. It was part of the War College's campaign to establish a naval version of the General Staff. The General Board was the creation of Henry C. Taylor more than of any other individual. As president of the Naval War College, 1893-1896 Taylor had hoped that the nucleus of a General Staff would evolve from the joint planning efforts of ONI and the War College. His efforts were at first strongly opposed by Secretary of the Navy John D. Long, who feared that a permanent naval chief of staff would usurp the power of the civilian Secretary. The experience of the Spanish-American War and the new, worldwide responsibilities of the United States Navy which followed the acquisition of colonies in the Pacific and the Caribbean, made a reorganization necessary. Even the experience of the Civil War had shown the old Bureau system was inadequate for the task.[59]

By 1900, Taylor's persistent effort paid off and Secretary Long agreed to establish a more effective staff organization. Taylor took the opportunity to propose an elaborate organization headed by a chief of staff. The proposed staff had three basic functions: to gather information on foreign powers; to prepare war plans; and to train officers in the art of war making and war planning. Taylor recognized that the Naval War College and ONI contained the basic structure for these functions, but that they needed to be coordinated by a common superior. He suggested that the board be headed by George Dewey, the hero of Manila Bay, who had been promoted by Act of Congress to the lifetime rank of "Admiral of the Navy."

Secretary of the Navy Long did not fully endorse Taylor's proposals, but he saw the advantage in creating the means to employ Dewey, whose high rank made him too senior for nearly any other position. With this in mind, Long tenuously approved a modified version of Taylor's proposal, establishing the General Board of the Navy on 13 March 1900 with the proviso that it was an experiment which could be dissolved the moment it was no longer useful.[60]

The General Board met for the first time in Washington at the State, War, and Navy Building on 16 April 1900. It consisted of six ex-officio members and five individual members. The ex-officio members were the Admiral of the Navy, the Chief of the Bureau of Navigation, the Chief of Office of Naval Intelligence, his principal assistant, and the president of the Naval War College with his principal assistant. Each member received one vote. The Chief of the Bureau of Navigation was to have custody of the war plans, direct the War College and ONI in furnishing the information required, and act as presiding officer in the absence of Admiral Dewey. Although he did not hinder its progress at the board's inception, the Chief of the Bureau of Navigation showed little interest in its success. He delayed until 16 December 1901 bringing the War College back under his direct administrative control.

The lackadasical attitude of the Bureau changed radically in April 1902, when Henry Taylor was promoted to rear admiral and assigned as Chief of the Bureau of Navigation. Taylor's vested interest in the board and active support for it expanded the board's influence. In promoting the board, Taylor used the War College as the intellectual reservoir from which it could draw. In the board's early period, few naval officers had any training in strategic problem solving, but the majority of those few were found at the War College and among its 200-odd graduates. Taylor encouraged the practice of submitting questions to the War College for study. This gave students practice in the solution of concrete issues and increased the value of their work in Newport. The college played a key role in the development of war plans by analyzing them critically and testing them on the college game board, then supporting or revising the plans in the light of the results obtained. With the War College president as a voting member of the General Board, the college's direct influence on war planning was firmly established and promoted.[61]

The creation of the General Board, as one officer put it, was "the first glimmerings of light on a true naval policy" for the United States. The full development of the strong General Staff, envisaged by Luce and other early reformers, did not materialize. The General Board never acquired the status or the authority to centralize control of the Navy Department, eliminate the autonomy of the Bureaus or relieve the Secretary of the Navy of his responsibilities for directing operations.[62] Taylor regarded the General Board as only an evolutionary step. In

February 1903, when the U.S. Army established the Army General Staff, the way was open to create the Joint Board in July 1903, with Dewey, Taylor and two other members of the Navy's General Board as members.[63] This was the first step toward the development of a national defense staff.

Through these means, the work of the Naval War College had a direct influence on naval policy, which was augmented by the General Board's practice of meeting at the War College during the summer months. The General Board's first summer meeting at Newport took place on 26 June 1900, but the practice was criticized by those who saw the duty with the board only as "a pleasant place for those who wish to winter in Washington and summer in Newport."[64] Dewey, made it a rule not to attend the summer sessions. The meetings scheduled to be held in Newport were cancelled in 1903, even though some of the members and the board's records were already there.

In the first decade of the century, the college participated deeply in war planning. Contingency plans for future wars were considered, ranging from the Venezuelan crisis of 1902-1903[65] to the Black Plan for war with Germany and Orange Plan for war with Japan.[66] In the process, the college did not always find itself in agreement with the General Board. Specifically, the Naval War College consistently supported the doctrine of naval concentration. In 1903, the college concluded, "The battle fleet should at all times be concentrated in the Atlantic . . . . Habitual concentration is Blue's [the United States] only safeguard unless the battle fleet is at least one and one-half times the strength of Black's."[67] This conclusion opposed the views of former college leaders such as Luce, Mahan, and Taylor who staunchly insisted on the presence of an American battle fleet in the Far East. The War College, however, persisted in its view, and after reviewing the experience of the Russo-Japanese War,[68] reaffirmed the opinion that "the battle fleet should at all times be concentrated in the North Atlantic. The policy of concentration is paramount. Concentration is the policy of all great powers."[69] In 1906, the college succeeded in making its point; the American battle fleet was ordered to be concentrated in the Atlantic. No sooner had this been done than War College analysts began to weigh the relative threats offered to the United States by Germany and Japan. By 1910, the War College again clashed with the General Board and developed a plan for the fleet to be based on the Pacific coast, equidistant from the Philippines and the main base at Guantanamo Bay.[70] This proposal was rejected by the Secretary of the Navy, and the president of the Naval War College was warned that there would be "no vote or conclusion . . . or any publicity" from the War College that would contradict the General Board's decision.[71]

While strategic employment of the battle fleet was a major concern for the Naval War College in its planning effort, the college also became embroiled in controversy over ships' design and characteristics. Beginning in October 1903, the General Board began to expand its area of concern, looking into questions of ships' speed, steaming radius, armament, armor, free board, and displacement. The board's consideration of these technical matters was controversial in itself and led to strong objections from the Bureaus, the traditional authorities in technical matters. The split in professional thinking between strategic analysis and technical development entered the issue as each group of professionals contended that their view was paramount. Naval constructors took affront at this challenge to their domain while the line strategists were infuriated at the failure of the constructors to take strategic and tactical factors into consideration.

The ship design controversy fragmented the naval officer corps to such a degree that the issue spilled out into the popular press just at the time that the Navy was enjoying great popularity at home.

The 1908 Battleship Conference

During the winter and spring of 1908 the operations of the American battle fleet, "Great White Fleet," in its round-the-world cruise were reported frequently in the press as the ships cruised south, visiting Brazil, skirting Argentine waters, and winding through the tortuous Strait of Magellan. Stops on the west coast of South America were followed by maneuvers in Mexican waters. Several correspondents embarked with the fleet and filed stories at each stop. Rarely had the peacetime Navy received such favorable publicity.

In contrast, the January issue of *McClure's* contained an article entitled, "The Needs of Our Navy," by Henry Reuterdahl, American editor of *Jane's Fighting Ships*. The article summarized many of the complaints made by the General Board and drew much of its inspiration from insurgents in the Navy such as Captain Bradley Fiske and Commander William S. Sims, who were ever more restless with the Bureau organization of the Navy Department. These and several others had written and spoken critically of ship designs, officer promotion rules, and departmental organization. Some of the insurgents were graduates of the War College, where they had the opportunity for thinking, reading, and discussing of these issues. Others were well known to the President, particularly Sims, his naval aide. Roosevelt publicly viewed the *McClure's* article as ill-timed and obnoxious, contrasting it with complimentary reports of the fleet cruise. He knew that Sims supported Reuterdahl's thesis and may even have assisted the author. Secretly agreeing with most of the shortcomings Reuterdahl described in the *McClure's* article, Roosevelt saw them also as politically unwelcome for his Administration.

In Congress, and particularly in the Senate Naval Affairs Committee, *McClure's* had waved a red flag in the bullring. The powerful chairman, Senator Eugene Hale of Maine, commenced a full investigation of Reuterdahl's criticisms, which became the subject for numerous press comments and editorials during that winter of 1908. Many of these were accusations against the Administration in Washington. The ensuing Senate investigation can at best be viewed as a draw in a contest between the Navy Department, represented by the bureau chiefs supported by Hale, and the insurgents, symbolized by Sims, the President's naval aide and Commander A. L. Key, a former naval aide to Roosevelt, acting ostensibly on their own, but with encouragement from the White House. Both Key and Sims testified at length before Hale's generally hostile committee. In return, Hale encouraged refutations from the various bureau chiefs. Rear Admiral Washington Capps, Chief of the Bureau of Construction and Repair, was most emphatic in opposing the criticisms of the battleships under construction. The investigation ended in late March and no specific changes in ship designs or other actions were taken as a result.

Key at this time was the prospective commanding officer of the scout cruiser *Salem*, under construction at the Fore River Shipyard in Quincy, Massachusetts. On a nearby slipway the new battleship *North Dakota* was being readied for launching. A *Dreadnought* type, she and the identical *Delaware* followed on from the first American all-big-gun battleships, *South Carolina* and *Michigan*. Reuterdahl's article was especially critical of the new ships. After a careful inspection of *North Dakota* and her plans, Key put Reuterdahl's and other criticisms into an official letter to the Navy Department. His letter reached Secretary of the Navy Truman Newberry early in June. Undoubtedly, the President, as well as Sims, had copies. Simultaneously, Newberry had already received a lengthy report from Rear Admiral Robley D. Evans concerning defects in the operating battleships uncovered during the long transit to the West Coast.

Roosevelt, in characteristic fashion, ordered the General Board to convene for a joint conference with the War College. With the college's staff and students as well as other officers from Washington, the conference, numbering 50 line and staff officers, was to study the Key letter and Evans report. Recommendations on what was required to correct deficiencies in the *North Dakota* class and what changes should be made in plans for the next class of battleships, the *Florida* and *Utah*, were to be made and forwarded to President Roosevelt.

The 1908 War College summer conference now turned into "the battleship conference." Rear Admiral John P. Merrell as War College president was chairman of the conference, which was divided into four committees, each studying a major item in the Key memorandum (for example, armor distribution, main battery arrangement, torpedo defense, and characteristics of the future battleships). The conference, representing the entire Navy, addressed problems heretofore exclusively in the hands of naval constructors. As the committees reported, it became apparent that many officers thought design changes were necessary but they were unwilling to vote for them at the risk of delays and extra costs in construction.[72]

President Roosevelt attended and served as chairman of the 22 July session of the conference. Arriving in Narragansett Bay on board the presidential yacht *Mayflower*, he was the guest of Admiral Merrell in the War College president's house. Roosevelt made the principal talk of the day with what a correspondent for the *Army and Navy Journal* reported as "an address which was primarily formal platitudes carefully framed for public consumption, while the real purpose of the meeting, behind closed doors and with double guards, was known to be specific discussion of controversial forms of construction and the safeguarding of the lives of officers and men of the American Navy."[73] The same writer noted that among naval officers the conference was regarded as one of the most important events in upgrading the fleet.

During the summer, Roosevelt kept up to date on the discussions in Newport. On 15 August he sent a memorandum to Admiral Merrell, spurring on the conferees and noting that he wanted to know defects and whether there would or would not be delay in construction. Six days later he received the final conference report recommending only some modifications in *North Dakota* and *Delaware*, but requesting a major change in the turret distribution of the next class of battleships. He studied the report at his summer home at Oyster Bay, Long Island, with the assistance of his former and current aides, Key and Sims. In announcing approval of the conference recommendations, he also replied to a reporter's question as to whether the plans of the *North Dakota* were unsatisfactory. "There is no question about the plans being unsatisfactory," he stated, "merely whether they can be made better. The *North Dakota* class is far better than any ships afloat. The conference is simply engaged in an effort to try and make them better."[74]

The battleship conference officially ended with the submission of the report to President Roosevelt. Both before and after the conference, the college attempted to carry on its regular course with 25 students in attendance. But this could not be done and little was accomplished beyond the international law discussions. However, the battleship conference was important to the Navy and for the War College. For the first time the President of the United States, acting as Commander in

Chief, had involved himself directly in the work of the War College and in the details of naval planning (in this case, for ship design) for the future. The conference had made decisions on new construction previously left entirely to the naval constructors. Although the conference had not accepted all of Commander Key's recommendations, enough were accepted to confirm that the ship designing process within the Navy was unsatisfactory. In this respect, one of the most important reasons of the conference was its resolution that called for future ship designs to be approved by a special board of officers. The implementation of this resolution marked the end of the Bureau of Construction's domination of warship design.[75]

The battleship conference and the publicity surrounding it created a momentum for administrative change within the Navy. In 1909, former Secretary of the Navy, W. H. Moody, now a Supreme Court Justice, was appointed to head a commission to study naval administration. Luce and Mahan were both appointed as members. This group recommended to President Roosevelt that the Navy Department gain tight control of the Bureaus and that it be divided into five functional areas, one of which would be headed by a chief of naval operations. This officer would be the Secretary's principal military advisor. The Moody Board's recommendations were far too radical to be accepted by Congress, but, following the recommendations of another board of officers under Rear Admiral William Swift, a modified version of the Moody Commission's recommendations was adopted.

Following the Swift Board's recommendations in October 1909, President William Howard Taft's Secretary of the Navy, George von Lengerke Meyer, appointed four rear admirals to be in charge of Navy Department activities. Using the simplified form of spelling fashionable at the time, he called them Aids. There were Aids for Fleet Operations, Material, Inspections, and Personnel, each of whom would coordinate the work of the Bureaus whose functions related to his areas of responsibility. Two of the Aids, those for Material and Operations, became ex-officio members of the General Board. The Aid for Operations and the General Board had an overlapping responsibility for fleet operations, although the Aid for Operations was the individual who issued orders to the fleet. Rear Admiral Richard Wainwright, a Spanish-American War hero and former War College lecturer, became the first Aid for Operations.

Two important changes for the Naval War College followed in the wake of this administrative reorganization. First, the Naval War College was removed from under the Bureau of Navigation and placed directly under the Aid for Operations. This tied the War College even more closely to the strategic planning process. The new arrangements in Washington also had given the General Board full responsibility for defining ship characteristics. With no additional staff to deal with the detailed and time consuming technical questions involved, the War College found that the General Board was moving away from its original role as a war planning agency. The increased burden of responsibility and the altered direction in General Board activity quickly threatened to overwhelm the teaching staff in Newport.[76] Time devoted to wide reading, teaching, reflection, and innovation was rapidly lost to Washington's demands for the college's advice on immediate problems and involvement in technical issues. By 1911, college president Raymond P. Rodgers formally requested that either the college staff be augmented or the college be relieved from the additional duty imposed by Washington. No new staff members were sent, but in October 1911, the Secretary of the Navy directed that the college's participation in the formulation of war plans be restricted only to areas that could be carried out as part of the college's educational mission.[77] Application had reached the point where it threatened proper education.

Notes

1. Quoted in Peter Karsten, *Naval Aristocracy* (New York: Free Press, 1972) p. 345.

2. Ibid.

3. Ibid.

4. Knight and Puleston, typescript "History of the Naval War College," chapter 1893, p. 3; Spector, *Professors of War* (Newport: NWC Press, 1977) p. 64.

5. Quoted in Spector, op. cit., p. 64.

6. Quoted in Knight and Puleston, Chapter 1894, p. 1.

7. Naval War College Archives: RG19: *Abstract of Course* (Washington, 1894), p. 4. Full address is in RG16: Addresses, 1894.

8. Naval War College Archives, RG16, Box 2, Addresses: H. C. Taylor, *Address delivered . . . Upon the Closing of the Session of 1894.*

9. *Abstract of Course 1894*, pp. 29-30.

10. Freeman Snow, *International Law: A Manual Based upon Lectures Delivered at the Naval War College* (Washington: Govt. Print Off., 1895); John M. Raymond and Barbara J. Frischholz, "Lawyers Who Established International Law in the United States, 1776-1914," *American Journal of International Law*, vol. 76, no. 4 (October 1982), pp. 816-18.

11. Taylor, *Closing Address*; Knight and Puleston, op. cit., 1893, p. 4.

12. *Abstract of Course 1895*, p. 37; Knight and Puleston, op. cit., p. 5.

13. Taylor, *Closing Address*.

14. *Abstract of Course 1894*, pp. 34-37.

15. *Abstract of Course 1895*, pp. 38-39; . . . 1896, p. 45-46.

16. Walter R. Herrick, *The American Naval Revolution*, (Baton Rouge: Louisiana University Press, 1966) pp. 171-72.

17. Jay Luvaas, "European Military Thought and Doctrine, 1870-1914," in M. Howard, ed. *The Theory and Practice of War* (Bloomington: U. of Indiana Press, 1975), p. 90.

18. S. B. Luce, "Naval Administration," U.S. Naval Institute *Proceedings*, vol. XIV, No. 3 (1888), p. 584. See also Hayes and Hattendorf, *The Writings of Stephen B. Luce* (Newport, Naval War College Press, 1975), pp. 199-200, 251.

19. Quoted in D. J. Costello, *Planning for War: A History of the General Board of the Navy 1900-1914* (Unpublished Ph.D. Thesis, Fletcher School, 1968), p. 13 and R.G. O'Connor, "Origins of the Navy General Staff" in O'Connor, ed., *American Defense Policy in Perspective* (New York: Wiley, 1965), pp. 140-141.

20. Spector, op. cit., p. 85-87.

21. O'Connor, op. cit.

22. Costello, op. cit., pp. 14-15.

23. P. A. Coletta, *Admiral Bradley H. Fiske and the American Navy* (Lawrence, 1979), p. 48.

24. Knight and Puleston, op. cit., 1896, p. 3.

25. Spector, op. cit., pp. 92-97; David F. Trask, *The War With Spain in 1898* (New York: MacMillan, 1981), pp. 72ff; J.A.S. Grenville and G. B. Young, *Politics, Strategy and American Foreign Policy*, (New Havan: Yale Univ. Press, 1966), pp. 267-73.

26. Library of Congress, Luce Papers: McCarty Little to Luce, 15 September 1895.

27. Ibid.

28. Quoted in A. Gleaves, *Life and Letters of Stephen B. Luce* (New York: Putnam, 1925), p. 189.

29. Dorwart, *The Office of Naval Intelligence* (Annapolis: Naval Institute Press, 1979), p. 54; Spector, op. cit., p. 97; Knight and Puleston, op. cit., 1897, p. 1.

30. "The Future of the Naval War College," *Army and Navy Register*, 20 November 1897, p. 332.

31. Quoted in Gleaves, op. cit., p. 190.

32. Spector, op. cit., p. 99.

33. U.S. Navy Department, *Annual Report of the Secretary, 1898*, vol. I, pp. 99-100.

34. Spector, op. cit.

35. Hayes and Hattendorf, op. cit., p. 39.

36. Quoted in Spector, op. cit., p. 99.

37. Naval Historical Collection, Naval War College, [Hereinafter NHC] Ms. Coll. 56, Box 2; C. H. Stockton papers; Letterbook as president, NWC, 1898-1900, p. 49: Stockton to Allen, 25 Nov 1898.

38. "The Naval War College: Removal to Annapolis Expected at Newport," *The New York Times*, 26 March 1899, p. 3:3.

39. NHC Stockton papers, loc. cit., p. 62; Stockton to A. M. Knight, 5 Dec 1898. See also p. 72 Stockton to Goodrich, 9 Dec 1898.

40. Loc. cit., Stockton papers, p. 124, Stockton to Goodrich, 23 Feb 1899.

41. Loc. cit., Stockton papers, p. 92, Stockton to Luce, 3 Jan 1899.

42. "Outline History of the Naval War College" in unpublished typescript in the Naval War College Library, *History of the Naval War College to 1937*.

43. See Paolo E. Coletta, *Bowman Hendry McCalla: A Fighting Sailor*, (Washington: University Press of America, 1979), pp. 73-102 and NWC Archives, RG15: B. H. McCalla guest lecture, 1899, "Lessons of the Spanish American War."

44. Doris Maguire, ed., *French Ensor Chadwick Selected Letters and Papers* (Washington: University Press of America, 1981) pp. 272-79: President, Naval War College to President General Board, 24 May 1902, Tactical Signal Book, 1897. Report by Capt. B. H. McCalla.

45. Knight and Puleston, op.cit., Chapters: 1900-1909.

46. L. Oppenheim, *International Law: A Treatise.* 8th ed. H. Lauterpacht, ed. (New York, 1955), p. 59 footnote 3.

47. Naval War College, *International Law Discussions 1903: The United States Naval War Code of 1900* (Washington, Govt. Print Off., 1904), pp. 90-97; Calvin De Armond David, *The U.S. and the Second Hague Peace Conference* (Durham, N.C.: Duke Univ. Press, 1975) pp. 144, 307.

48. See Doris Maguire, ed., *Chadwick Letters*, Chadwick to Moore, pp. 229, 262.

49. Denys P. Myers, "In Memoriam: George Grafton Wilson," *American Journal of International Law*, vol. 45 (1951), pp. 549-50.

50. Quoted in Knight and Puleston, op. cit; 1901, pp. 4-5.

51. B. A. Fiske, "Stephen B. Luce, An Appreciation," U.S. Naval Institute *Proceedings*, vol. XLIII, No. 9 (Sept. 1917) pp. 1935-40.

52. Doris Maguire, ed., *Chadwick Letters*, pp. 220-22.

53. Hayes and Hattendorf, op. cit, pp. 21-22.

54. Seager, *Mahan*, pp. 547-559; Seager and Maguire, eds., *Letters*, III, pp. 269,460, 464.

55. The exception was the presidency of W. L. Rodgers, Nov 1911 to Dec 1913, when the house was occupied by the senior officer at Newport, Captain Albert Gleaves, Commander, Training Station.

56. Maguire, ed. *Chadwick Letters*, pp. 286, 297.

57. Ibid., pp. 285-86, 300, 301, 303, 304, 308.

58. NWC Archives, RG 1, Box 3 File 22. Construction memoranda.

59. Ronald Spector, *Admiral of the New Empire: The Life and Career of George Dewey* (Baton Rouge: Louisiana State University Press, 1974), pp. 125-27.

60. Daniel J. Costello, *Planning for War: A History of the General Board of the Navy 1900-1914* (Unpublished Ph.D. Thesis, Fletcher School of Law and Diplomacy, 1968), pp. 19-22.

61. Ibid., pp. 37-38.

62. R. G. O'Connor, "Origins of the Navy 'General Staff'" op. cit., p. 143, with quote from Captain John Hood.

63. Costello, op. cit., p. 40.

64. Ibid., p. 56.

65. R. G. Albion, *Makers of Naval Policy* op. cit, pp. 332-33.

66. For detailed studies of these plans, see for example, Louis Morton, "War Plan Orange," "Evolution of a Strategy," *World Politics*, Vol. XI (January 1959), pp. 221-50; J. B. Hattendorf, "Technology and Strategy" in B. M. Simpson III, ed. *War Strategy and Maritime Power* (Rutgers, 1977); Michael Vlahos, "The Naval War College and the Origins of War Planning Against Japan," *Naval War College Review*, Vol. 33, (July-August 1980), pp. 23-41; John H. Maurer, "American Naval Concentration and the German Battle Fleet, 1900-1918," *The Journal of Strategic Studies*, Vol. 6, No. 2, (June 1983), pp. 147-179.

67. Maurer, op. cit., pp. 154. Quoted from NWC Archives, RG 12. "Solution to Problem, 1903."

68. Spector, op. cit., pp. 106-07; Maurer, p. 155.

69. Quoted in Maurer, p. 156.

70. Spector, op. cit., p. 107.

71. Maurer, op. cit., p. 163.

72. Costello, op. cit., p. 78.

73. *Army and Navy Journal*, 25 July 1908.

74. Ibid., 11 September 1908.

75. Costello, op. cit., pp. 87-89. See also Hattendorf, "Technology and Strategy" op. cit., Elting E. Morison, *Admiral Sims and the Modern American Navy* (Boston: Houghton Mifflin, 1942), pp. 201-15. NWC Archives, RG 27: Battleship Conference; *Report of the Board to Consider CDR A. L. Key's Comments on the Design of the Battleship North Dakota Decisions.*

76. Costello, op. cit., p. 97.

77. Ibid., pp. 117-118.

CHAPTER 4

THE END OF AN ERA AND THE INTRODUCTION OF NAVAL DOCTRINE, 1909-1918

The Aid system was associated with the Naval War College and with the views of prominent War College men who sought increased military control of naval operations along with improved naval administration. Although the Aids had no executive power, being only advisors, the four admirals met daily as a council in the office of the Aid for Operations to coordinate their work, to discuss major issues, and to pass upon proposed regulation changes, proposed general orders and legislation, recommendations to the General Board, as well as orders to captains and admirals ashore and afloat. The system improved management and direction, but left much to be desired.

In the process of their work, however, the Aids directly supported the Naval War College and sought to place War College graduates in responsible positions.[1] This emphasis by the Navy's most senior officers helped to increase the prestige of the Naval War College within the officer corps. As the Western world was experiencing the end of an era in the years preceding World War I, the Naval War College in its own way reached an end of an era. The struggle for survival was over, the founders were gradually disappearing from the scene, and the college was beginning to reassert its educational role as it withdrew from direct and active participation in the preparation of naval war plans. With this change came a new and different emphasis which grew from the adoption of the German "applicatory system," an approach that grew to dominate Naval War College thinking.

Estimate of the Situation

The applicatory system was known popularly among Naval War College students and staff as the "estimate of the situation." It was only the first of three fundamental steps in dealing with a military or naval problem: (1) analyzing or estimating the situation to determine the plan of action and decisions to be made; (2) translating the decisions to be made into orders; and (3) translating the orders into action.

The Naval War College's adoption of this method may be attributed to Commander W. L. Rodgers' assignment to the Army War College in Washington. The Army War College had begun its first year of systematic instruction in 1903 under Brigadier General Tasker Bliss as commandant. Bliss, one of the first staff members at the Naval War College who served as lecturer on military strategy in the college's first three academic years, 1885-1887, had a long time interest in the professional link between the Army and the Navy. As Army War College president, he established a link between the two colleges by arranging for joint studies of war problems. The study of these problems produced a set of rules for joint maneuvers and standard procedures for army transports to follow them under naval convoy. Bliss' successors carried on with further arrangements, and in 1906-1907 the first two naval students were sent to the Army War College. One of them, Commander H. S. Knapp, had been graduated from the Naval War College in 1897.[2]

In the autumn of 1907, W. L. Rodgers was sent to Washington to act as liaison officer between the two colleges and to be Naval Advisor to the Army College staff concerning naval matters. "The method of work of the Army War College was the applicatory system," Rodgers wrote.

> It used specific situations as a basis of study and passed from these to generalizations. Lectures, the preparation of monographs, and field exercises and studies all were employed as auxiliaries in the effort of the staff to teach. The college regarded it as a duty to instruct the class in sound methods of thought and to inculcate a common doctrine of war, so as to prepare graduates of the college for ready cooperation and mutual support through knowledge that the same principles of warfare were accepted throughout the Army in all its branches.[3]

During Rodgers' second year at the Army War College, 1908-1909, he continued to serve on its staff and helped to introduce new war gaming techniques that had been developed in Newport by Little. Instead of following the course a second time, Rodgers devoted his energy to applying Army methods to solving some of the naval problems that had been set in Newport in previous years and then comparing the analyses and solutions. "This work of a year convinced me that the Army method was not only practicable but desirable," Rodgers said, "and it was necessary if the [Naval] War College was to remain alive and progress and grow."[4]

Returning to Newport in May 1909, Rodgers submitted his views to William McCarty Little, who was deeply interested in them. When Rodgers thereupon suggested that adapting Army methods be formally proposed to the president of the Naval War College. "Captain Little advised me against this course," Rodgers recalled

> He said that Admiral Merrell would no doubt require some weeks to consider the proposal before formally adopting it, and then the session would be well advanced and the class would be annoyed by a change in procedure. On the other hand, if he and I were to start the class on this method as a matter of accepted administrative detail, they would never know anything had been "wished on" them and would go on cheerfully. This we did, and although we had to be easy with some points because we had no recognition by authority to back us, yet at the end of the session the results were good.[5]

At the end of the 1909 summer conference, Admiral Merrell was relieved as president by Rear Admiral R. P. Rodgers, a relative of Commander Rodgers. Admiral Rodgers, however, was also appointed Commandant of the Naval Station, and he left many of the details in developing the curriculum for the 1910 conference to Captain Little.

The introduction of the ideas behind the applicatory system in 1909 began to excite interest in the staff. The available literature on the applicatory system was not extensive, but several U.S. Army officers had been at work trying to apply the ideas and adapt them for American use. In 1906, Major C. H. Barth published his translation of Otto von Griepenkerl's *Letters on Applied Tactics*, which expounded the system. In the same year, Major Eban Swift published *Field Orders, Messages, and Reports*, and in 1909, Army Captain Roger S. Fitch wrote *Estimating Tactical Situations and Composing Orders*. These three works, in particular, became the standard sources of reference over the next few years as the Navy began to develop its version of the applicatory system.

In the autumn of 1909, after the summer conference had ended, there was time to reflect on the new ideas. Perhaps inspired by a reference in the 1909 lectures, Major John H. Russell, USMC, a future commandant of the Marine Corps, sought out a copy of Barth's translation of Griepenkerl. While he was reading it, McCarty Little stopped in his office and the two discussed the book. Russell was impressed with its soundness and potential utility in the work of the Naval War College, but he doubted it would be possible to interest other staff members in it; Russell was not aware of Rodgers' earlier interest. Little borrowed the book, read it, and discussed it with Admiral R. P. Rodgers. Thereupon

Rodgers appointed a committee consisting of McCarty Little, Lieutenant Commanders Frank Marble and Carl T. Vogelgesang, and Lieutenant Walter S. Turpin to report on the utility of the applicatory system for the Navy. The committee developed a plan to revise the curriculum, and the system was explained to the students at the summer conference of 1910. The following year, Vogelgesang elaborated on the subject in his lectures.[6]

The link between military and naval thinking was made even closer in November 1911, when W. L. Rodgers was ordered to duty as president of the Naval War College. Since his detachment from the Army War College, Rodgers had been promoted to captain and had commanded the battleship *Georgia*. Reinforced by these recent experiences Rodgers reformed the course of study at the Naval War College to include ideas from the Army. The "estimate of the situation," the "order form," and war gaming were brought together to provide a new direction for the Naval War College's course. As one contemporary writer noted, "A great white light broke on the service, especially in 1912 when the War College first laid emphasis on the importance of doctrine."[7]

From this point, for more than half a century, the Naval War College course stressed the doctrine and procedures of the applicatory system. This was an important expansion of Luce's conception of the college as a place of voluntary, original research in the creation of a naval science and Henry Taylor's use of the college as a direct part of the war planning process. The new approach embraced a system of procedures which in combination approximated the Jominian laws of warfare that Luce had sought and also stressed the German methods that Henry Taylor had advocated for war planning.

As it was explained to the students, the estimate of the situation was a "mental process which leads up to and expresses a decision." The estimate consisted of four steps that were to be covered in sequence: (1) a statement of the mission; (2) an assessment of enemy forces—their strength, disposition, and possible intentions; (3) an assessment of one's own forces—their strength and disposition, and (4) the courses of action open. It was a logical process of thought to be applied to concrete situations to enable a commander to reach a definite decision. It was by no means a prescriptive formula to be followed religiously; rather, it was an orderly method for analyzing a problem. Only after such a process, its advocates concluded, should orders be written and executed.

The faculty presented to the students specific fleet problems and required individual rather than group or committee solutions. The students were not only required to pursue the mental processes of the sstimate of the situation but were also required to draft the ensuing orders in a logical, clear, and coherent form. The orders were then executed in war games which gave as much realism as possible to the endeavor.

The drafting of orders to execute the commander's decision and its actual execution were obviously as important as the mental processes that gave rise to the decision. The faculty explained, "War is not simply fighting; it is fighting for the attainment of a definite purpose. Now since each act of war should be in harmony with the general purpose, it is evident that there must be a supreme control to direct the act of war."[8] The exercise of command required not only personal leadership and technical competence but also required—and still does—a disciplined habit of mind, the result of systematic self-training.

The introduction of the estimate of the situation thus represented the triumph of two ideas in a new and fruitful coordination. The first was that war could be studied in the same way that law or medicine could be studied. This was one of the major concepts upon which Luce had founded the college in 1884, but at that time he had lacked an effective intellectual vehicle for systematically utilizing that approach. Once a science of naval warfare was accepted and established, then it could be studied and learned. This meant that junior officers as well as their seniors could acquire by means of mental discipline the habit of mind from which action would flow by the exercise of reason. What before may have seemed higher mysteries were now no longer to be reserved for admirals. They could be known, shared, and understood by all officers.

The implications were profound. Where formerly seniors commanded and juniors obeyed without question, now the full range of what was involved in any given strategic or tactical situation could be known and understood by all. Juniors would still exhibit proper subordination, but instead of giving blind obedience, they would intelligently execute orders from their seniors, because they could be aware of the objectives sought and how they were to be achieved. Thus, they would be able to adapt to the fluid and ever-changing conditions of war while still pursuing the objective their seniors sought.

Development of Doctrine

The intelligent execution of orders should be a product of mutual understanding between junior and senior officers and a common body of procedures to be followed under more or less recurring circumstances and in similar conditions. In time, this common body of procedures came to be known as doctrine. Thus, if both juniors and seniors were familiar with and understood a duly authorized, widely promulgated, and commonly understood doctrine, there would be little doubt in anyone's mind about what actions ought to be taken at any level. With a doctrine established, officers would not find it necessary to write new orders (in varying degrees of detail) to cover a wide range of points. Specific directives would be necessary only for the really different or unique circumstances. Because such naval doctrine did not exist before 1910, it had become necessary to invent it. The senior officers at that time had been trained as midshipmen at sea in sailing ships, although they had received a certain degree of exposure to the physical sciences and their application at sea by way of steam engineering and electricity. Yet, the intangible service traditions were rooted in an earlier and very different age. The requirements of naval warfare in the early twentieth century, with new technology, increased mobility and firepower, demanded a much stricter intellectual dimension. The mental process of the estimate of the situation filled the need and was used as the basis for naval science.

The summer conference of 1911 opened on 2 June with Secretary of the Navy George von L. Meyer the principal speaker for the occasion. The college's founding father, the eighty-four-year-old Luce, was invited to speak as well. It was to be his last address to the college, but rather than reminisce, he seized the opportunity to make a strong and public plea for a two-year course.

Meyer spoke first, but he took some of the wind out of Luce's sails by stating that he intended to see to it that at least some officers would be detailed to the college for a longer period than the customary four months. Luce was delighted to hear Meyer state officially what he was about to urge. Nevertheless, when Meyer finished, Luce delivered his prepared remarks to provide added justification and to stress that the college should educate officers, not draft war plans for the General Board.

Luce reviewed the reasons for establishment of the War College, saying, "The object of this college is to enable officers *to fit themselves* to prepare war plans." He was frankly worried because there was so much interest in the Naval Post Graduate School of Engineering, recently established in Annapolis, and still so little support for the War College. Officers still seem to care little for understanding the main purpose of their profession. "Let officers who have completed their terms of sea service in their respective grades come here for a two-year course of study," Luce declared. Pointedly, he added:

> not for discussion, *but for study*. On the completion of such a course they will then be eligible as conferees to discuss intelligently questions relating to naval warfare—and not before.[10]

Instituting the Long Course

As college staff members developed the ideas of the applicatory system after 1910 and began to infuse them into the curriculum, the college continued to be concerned about the length of the course and the low numbers of students who attended it.

In 1910 and 1911, college president Rear Admiral Raymond Rodgers presided over summer conferences of four months in length, with the curriculum still built around a main problem. The brevity of these courses precluded examination in depth of the strategic and tactical issues involved and severely restricted the amount of time available to students for individual study and reading. After a quarter of a century the War College was firmly established as a part of the Navy, but responsible officials in the Department did not take it seriously enough to send students for a full year of study. As Rodgers' term began, there were nearly 800 officers in the Navy whose rank was suitable for assignment to the staff or student roster. However, with the Navy expanding rapidly in terms of men and ships, the Bureau of Navigation was unable to assign four on a regular basis to the faculty or even to find 20 or 30 more for students. Luce believed that it was high time the course was expanded to what he thought was its proper length. W. L. Rodgers and McCarty Little had urged in 1909 the establishment of a 16-month course lasting over two summer sessions for a small, selected group of officers. After the 1910 summer conference, McCarty Little, a good friend of Rear Admiral Nicholson, Chief of the Bureau of Navigation, was sent to Washington to try to get the Bureau to assign 20 student officers for such a course. Nicholson was outwardly unimpressed, stating that the War College still had lowest priority in the assignment of officers.

Citing the danger of crude views held by bright, but not fully trained minds that left the college after too short a period of study, Luce admonished the students,

> Your profession is the art of war and nature will be avenged if you violate one of its laws in undertaking to make a part greater than the whole.[11]

Although Luce's remarks might have seemed unnecessary following Secretary Meyers' address, they provided forceful statement from the college on its educational purpose and the need for a longer course.

The summer conference for 1911 continued, from its opening in June through September, to complete its usual four months. The conference was based on the model used in previous years, but now included lectures on the applicatory system and the formulation of orders which had begun in the previous year. At this early stage, the two approaches were used in a complementary fashion that stressed the study of individual situations as the means to develop general principles through inductive reasoning. In October 1911, four students from the summer conference were assigned to the newly established long course. A sixteen month long study, the course as established under R. P. Rodgers involved no new features but allowed greater time for the full treatment of the subjects in the existing summer course. The students assigned were Captains William S. Sims and Josiah McKean, Commander Yates Stirling, Jr., and Marine Captain Earl H. Ellis.

All of these new students distinguished themselves in later years. Sims, McKean, and Stirling reached flag rank, and Ellis, although he died mysteriously in 1923 as a lieutenant colonel, was a pioneer student of amphibious warfare in the Pacific. As a long course student in 1911-1912 and a staff member in 1913, Ellis wrote a series of papers on advanced base forces, the defense of the Pacific islands, and began to develop the idea of offensive amphibious operations, which were used so successfully 30 years later in the war against Japan.[12]

At the time, Sims was one of the best known officers in the Navy. As an advocate of improved naval gunnery, Inspector of Naval Ordnance, and naval aide to President Roosevelt, Sims had become an important and outspoken critic of naval policies. In 1906, he successfully attacked Mahan's interpretation of the Russo-Japanese War and proved him incorrect on several issues.[13] In 1910 as commanding officer of USS *Minnesota*, then visiting London, Sims replied to a welcoming speech by the Lord Mayor of London at Guildhall. In his reply, Sims declared his personal opinion that "if ever the integrity of the British Empire be seriously threatened by an external enemy, they might count upon the assistance of every man, every ship, and every dollar from their kinsmen across the sea." In concluding his remarks, Sims asked all the American naval officers and men to stand and proposed to the Lord Mayor three American cheers for three British things: the Sailor King, the British people, and the integrity of their Empire.[14]

Sims' speech was warmly received by the British press, but when reported in America it raised such violent public criticism that the incident was fully discussed at a cabinet meeting in Washington. The critics wanted Sims punished, but the Secretary of the Navy realized he was one of the Navy's most capable officers. There was still a chance that the incident might damage Sims' future career. Finally, in April of the following year, Sims' friends and supporters arranged for him to have orders to the War College, where it was hoped he would "tone down his ideas" to "make him proper stuff for an able Commander-in-Chief."[15]

Like many students in the early years, Sims came to the summer conference somewhat unwillingly. On receiving his orders, he wrote to his wife, "Soon I may get some duty I would like better—something in closer touch with practice and less on the theoretical side."[16] However, during the 16 months that Sims was a student in the first long course at the college, a close relationship grew between him and the senior instructor on the staff, Commander William Veazie Pratt. Pratt came to the staff in 1911 without having been a student and frankly admitted he had a hard time keeping ahead of those taking the course. Though nine years senior to Pratt, Sims took him as a friend and equal. As Pratt's biographer remarked, "Pratt was not the antithesis of Sims but quite different. . . . What Pratt was best at was logical analysis—his thought processes always started with an 'estimate of the situation.' One gets the impression that Sims sensed a solution to most problems and then drafted his 'estimate' to match his conclusions."[17]

In later years Pratt said that he could remember little of a factual nature learned at the college that would be of lasting importance, but he added, "I began to learn the intimate connection between the Fleet in being and the War College, the home of thought. Strange perhaps as it may seem, the deeper I became involved in complicated mass movements, the less their inherent value appealed to me, but more and more there appeared as a dominating factor . . . the inherent characteristic of the leader who used the material things which he held power over."[18]

Sims and the other students began the academic day at 9:30 a.m. There were three periods devoted to lectures, discussion, and individual work, two of which were scheduled before lunch. Classes were over at 3 p.m. Some students who lived with their families in Jamestown across the bay, commuted by War College boat, which left the Coasters Harbor Island daily at 3:15. Others living in Newport used the Newport Electric Railway trolley from Washington Square in downtown Newport to Training Station Road just outside the main gate. Classes were also held Saturday mornings from 9:30 until noon.

The 1911 summer conference, like its predecessors, was divided into student committees. The senior officer in each committee was in charge, and he was responsible for the attendance of the other students and for the timely submission of academic work. The college specifically instructed the students that "For the sake of uniformity, the solutions will be submitted in ink." Typing services were available upon request.

The course of instruction consisted of tactical games, introduced with a lecture by Commander Pratt; lectures on the estimate of the situation by Lieutenant Commander Carl T. Vogelgesang; a lecture on explanations of the strategic game by William McCarty Little; and five lectures on naval strategy by Alfred Thayer Mahan read by a staff member. Professor George Grafton Wilson delivered lectures on international law, after which the students were required to write solutions to five law problems that he had formulated on neutral vessels and contraband cargos. There was also instruction on recent aspects of technical innovation in the areas of engineering, wireless telegraph, battleship design, and mining operations, discussing their tactical and strategic meaning. The students were divided into two committees which were given specific problems to discuss and on which to prepare a committee response. One question was,

> Should well-established and accepted obligations in regard to foreign policies influence the naval policy of a country? Discuss the necessity of proper coordination between the State and Military authorities in arriving at a proper naval policy, and in the conduct of war.[19]

One student committee commenced its response, "The serious business of diplomacy is carried on by diplomatic notes, which are, in effect, promissory notes of war." Continuing in the same vein and with the same metaphor, the students concluded bizarrely, "The Navy and Army are diplomatic instruments. War is the political substitution for discounted and protested diplomatic notes and unavailing ultimatums."[20]

The college continued to concern itself with strategic planning, but limited its participation to aspects that could be accomplished within the course. In 1910 and 1911 the college completed work on a contingency plan for war with Orange (Japan). In this period, War College students saw Japan as a potential enemy for three reasons: (1) Japanese incursions into Manchuria were perceived as creating points of friction by violating the Open Door Policy and by creating trade rivalries with the west; (2) they suspected Japan of harboring aspirations to prevent American mastery of the Pacific by seizing both Guam and Hawaii as a means to choke American hold on the Philippines; and (3) they were aware that racial antagonisms toward Japanese then in the United States, particularly those in California, could lead to serious trouble. In their analysis, they commented, "The conditions which cause war are intimately connected with the object for which the war is waged; hence, by a study of those conditions, the ultimate objective of a possible war is brought into view, and on this the strategy of the war should be based."[21]

While Japan was a potential threat in the Pacific, Germany was seen as presenting a possible threat in the Atlantic. The summer conference of 1911 dealt with specific aspects of a German naval threat to the Western Hemisphere. The students were given a problem reminiscent of that caused by the Spanish fleet in 1898 in which the Black (German) fleet proceeded to the Caribbean by way of the Cape Verde Islands. They were directed to examine the logistics of the coal supply for such an operation and for the maintenance of this fleet in the Caribbean, while also considering possible Blue (American) reactions. These issues were considered further both by the long courses and the summer conferences in 1911, 1912, and 1913, culminating in a formal document on American strategic posture in the event of war with Germany—the Black Plan. As finally developed by the General Board with assistance from the Naval War College, the plan was based on the conclusion that if parity existed in battleship numbers between Blue and Black, "it would be suicidal for Black with a fleet only approximately equal to that of Blue . . . to attempt a descent upon . . . the Caribbean."[22] This view complemented War College reasoning which advocated an American naval building program that would match Germany's rather than Japan's. In War College opinion, the United States would soon match Japan, but Germany presented both a more immediate threat and a stronger force.[23]

The four-month summer conference of 1911 was excellent preparation for Sims and his three colleagues in the long course. At the end of September they commenced the year-long course in which they studied in greater depth what had been covered in the summer.

In November 1911, Captain W. L. Rodgers succeeded his kinsman as president of the Naval War College. He was pleased with the progress that had been made in developing the applicatory system and establishing the long course during his two and a half years' absence from the college. During the next two years he devoted his effort to broaden "the scope of the work to include studies of national policy as the foundation for laying out naval plans of expansion and also of logistics, organization, and administration of navies as the basis of strategy and tactics of battle."[24]

The students in the long course studied tactics, strategy, policy, and logistics, each for two months. Their time was more or less equally divided among reading, discussion, solution of problems, and testing the solutions in war games. The reading lists were impressive, thorough, and weighty. They included many European authorities on land and naval warfare, such as von Moltke, Griepenkerl, Jomini, Clausewitz, Daveluy, Darrieus, Clerk of Eldin, Corbett, Wilkinson, and Hamley. Mahan's works were appropriately included, and Thucydides' classic on the Peloponnesian War was also read.

The students were told to make notes "of tactical principles, gleaned from any of those sources, that may be considered to be applicable to present-day conditions in naval warfare." The purpose of this directive was to force students to derive general principles from their studies. Luce had insisted upon inductive reasoning as appropriate to the study of the art of war, and Mahan had used this method to reach his conclusions in his studies of the influence of seapower upon history.

Bismarck's *Reflections and Reminiscences* was prominently included in the reading list as an example of the relationship of national policy to war and the use of war to achieve national objectives.

For logistics, the readings were mainly in recent European and American military history. The college directed that the students, when writing their papers in this area, must deal with the subject "not only in the abstract, but illustrated by concrete historical examples of the bearing of logistics on the conduct of war."

Besides these essentially academic endeavors, the students received a naval problem fortnightly. They were required to provide an "estimate of the situation" and "formulation of orders." When these steps were accomplished, their solution was tested on the game board. Although this phase of the course was an exercise, its purpose was hardly academic. Students were expected to present a solution to some definite, concrete tactical or strategic situation "in which we may be directly interested." These exercises were preparation for the final four months of the year-long course, during which time the long course students worked on preparation of contingency plans for the General Board.

The final four months of the course included the summer conference of 1912. During these months, long course students commenced a major planning exercise in which they prepared and drafted a plan for a possible campaign.

At the end of the second long course on 1 October 1913, the college issued diplomas for the first time. They were awarded at that time to the members of both the first and second long course.

Three-Course Plan

The system of having both a four month summer conference and a 16-month long course continued from 1911 through 1913. During 1913, in the last year of his War College presidency, Captain W. L. Rodgers proposed a three course plan for the War College. This consisted of (1) the elementary course; (2) the preparatory course; and (3) the War College course.

In July 1913, on the personal initiative of Secretary of the Navy Josephus Daniels, 50 officers of the Atlantic Fleet were ordered to the two-week elementary course. As an introduction to the work of the Naval War College, they were given lectures on the applicatory system, were presented a strategic problem, with tactical war game, and were required to write a thesis on loyalty.[25] The four-month preparatory course was the summer conference renamed, and the long course was now renamed the War College course. Still, the college was concerned about the brevity of the courses it offered. As the Secretary of the Navy's report for 1913 indicated,[26] the 16 months that the long course students had was short when compared to the three years that the U.S. Army devoted to extraregimental work or to the two-year courses provided by war colleges in Berlin, Paris, and Rome.

The Secretary's report noted that a naval officer had two classes of duties to perform. The first was to perfect his command and to maintain it in efficient condition. The Naval Academy and its postgraduate school were created to furnish the education and training for this duty. The second, and equally important, duty for a naval officer was "to make himself an efficient leader, ably wise to use the warlike instrument which he has created." Education for that duty was the mission of the Naval War College. Moreover, the report stated

> The War College training is of the utmost importance to the development of the Navy, demanding the sole and entire time of officers taking it.[27]

The two-week elementary course and the four-month preparatory course created administrative difficulties. While the two-week course was successful, it created difficulty in finding short-term accommodation for so many officers, while, at the same time, officers commanding ships in the fleet found it difficult to carry on with their operations and resented the college's "unwarranted interference" with their work. Similarly, the Bureau of Navigation found it administratively difficult to maintain each year two small, four-month preparatory classes, six months apart.[28]

Rodgers sought to adjust the college course to meet these objections. He took the initiative in introducing correspondence courses to replace the two-week elementary course, giving fleet officers an introduction to War College work. Rear Admiral Austin M. Knight, commanding the Reserve Fleet, was one of the first to undertake these correspondence courses as a means to acquaint himself with the work of the college, knowing that he would soon relieve Rodgers as college president.[29]

Early in November 1913, Rodgers prepared for Secretary of the Navy Daniels a draft General Order which recognized the new course changes that Rodgers had made. The Aid for Operations, Rear Admiral Fiske, declined to approve the draft, noting that it might hinder Admiral Knight in developing the policy which he thought fit for the college. Relieving Rodgers in December 1913, Knight reviewed the plans which Rodgers had made and recommended their approval, with only minor amendments.

In January 1914, Secretary of the Navy Daniels issued a General Order which, in effect, abolished both the elementary and preparatory summer courses. The standard course was established as one of 12 months duration, with two groups in classes of no less than 15 each. One group assembled in January of each year, and the other in July.

Using the curriculum previously designed for the long course, the War College offered the new one-year course from January 1914 until 1917. Although some student writing had been required since 1912, under the new course of 1914 all students were required to write theses. They were required to write in five different areas: (1) strategy, in its principles and practice; (2) policy—its relation to war and preparation for war; (3) logistics; (4) tactics; and (5) the strategy of the Pacific.

On 1 April 1914 the Secretary of the Navy issued another General Order, on the college's recommendation, which established a correspondence course at the Naval War College designed for those naval officers who were not available for assignment to Newport. Two courses were made available to be sent out in a series of numbered installments. Extension Course A was designed for groups of officers to participate in jointly under the direction of one of the students in the group. Extension Course B was prepared for individual officers who were situated where they could not join a group. This General Order gave the Navy Department's approval to a long-standing War College effort in bringing the work of the college directly to the fleet. While it was not practical to bring the fleet to Newport as Luce and Sampson had done on occasion, the college could now reach officers at sea by correspondence.[30]

The Great War

As the July crisis gripped European diplomats in 1914, students and staff at the Naval War College watched the events with intense interest. Rear Admiral Bradley Fiske, Aid for Operations, asked permission from the Secretary of the Navy to spend the month of August in Newport with the General Board, instead of taking the customary summer leave offered to Navy Department officials at that time. Reaching Newport on 31 July, Fiske was aware that war in Europe was imminent. In Newport, Fiske found himself in an anomalous position. As the Navy's chief staff officer, he was equivalent to the senior officer of other armies and navies, and he felt that he could best perform his duty in direct consultation with the Navy's planning body, the General Board. The Naval War College was administratively under Fiske as Aid for Operations, yet the college's president, Austin M. Knight, was senior by date of rank, besides being additionally the Commandant of the Second Naval District, and the senior officer of the General Board after the 76-year-old Admiral Dewey.

Fiske's reading of the latest dispatches from Europe on 31 July convinced him that war was imminent and that he should act immediately to prepare the U.S. Navy for war. The United States, he felt, could not escape being dragged into the war. On the evening of 31 July, Fiske asked Admiral Knight to convene a meeting of the General Board at the Naval War College as early as possible the following morning and to urge the Navy Department "to take immediate steps to put the Navy on a war footing." Meeting on 1 August 1914, the Board sent an urgent letter to the Secretary of the Navy pointing out the possible causes of danger to America, especially in regard to American neutrality. In particular, the General Board recommended that all battleships, except those needed in Mexican and Caribbean waters, be sent to their home yards for immediate docking and repairs for war service. As Aid for Operations, Fiske sent a personal letter to the Secretary stressing the same points.

Fiske remained at the Naval War College throughout August 1914 for the meeting of the General Board. He reported, "Naturally, the subject of the war occupied our minds virtually all the time." Seeing ahead a situation of great peril, Fiske left Newport on the evening of 30 August and arrived at his office in Washington at nine o'clock the morning of 1 September. "I expected to find an atmosphere of tension and excitement," Fiske remembered, "but I found perfect calm. No one seemed to think that anything in particular had happened or was going to happen." No preparations had been made for war and no orders had been sent to the fleet. As Fiske wrote in his diary, "Sec. has created office of 'Aid for Education' and is much stuck on idea! Gosh!"[31]

Increasingly, Fiske found himself at odds with Secretary of the Navy Josephus Daniels. Daniels quietly allowed three of the Aid positions to fall vacant without refilling them and undoubtedly wished to be rid of Fiske. Fiske, a prickly and opinionated character in any circumstances, passionately fought for a strong, reorganized Navy with an effective General Staff. Daniels, however, saw Fiske's ideas as an attempt to copy German militarism. By the end of December 1914, a deep division had developed between Fiske and Daniels over a number of issues, including the development of naval aviation, increased fleet strength, fleet efficiency and, not least, naval administration. Voicing the attitude of many naval officers, Fiske took his campaign directly to Congress in early January 1915 without Daniels' knowledge. Working with Representative Richmond P. Hobson, a Spanish-American War naval hero, then a member of the House Naval Affairs Committee, Fiske was joined by several War College graduates including Captains H. S. Knapp, John Hood, Lieutenant Commanders W. P. Cronan and D. W. Knox, as well as Fiske's assistant and member of the July 1915 War College class, Lieutenant Commander Zachariah Madison. Working together, this group of officers provided Hobson with data and secretly drafted legislation to create an Office of Naval Operations whose chief would be "responsible for the readiness of the Navy for war and be charged with its general direction." Hobson took their draft and maneuvered to get it attached to the naval appropriations bill. On 26 January 1915, War College president Austin Knight was called out of a meeting of the General Board and reprimanded by Daniels at President

Woodrow Wilson's order. The day before, Knight had criticized Navy Department organization and supported the kind of staff that Fiske envisioned. Wilson indignantly told Daniels that Knight should confine his remarks to answering the direct questions asked by congressional committees.[32]

On 3 March 1915, Congress passed the Act which included provision for a Chief of Naval Operations and a staff of 15 who would constitute a General Staff. As passed, the Act of Congress modified Fiske's concept by retaining management of the Navy in civilian hands and leaving the Bureaus uncoordinated. It was, however, a further step in the evolutionary process. Taking the title from that proposed by the Moody Commission in 1909, the new Chief of Naval Operations was charged directly with operation of the fleet and with preparations and readiness of plans for use in war. This included the direction of the Naval War College.

Fiske's office of Aid for Operations was absorbed in the new office of Naval Operations headed by the first Chief of Naval Operations, William S. Benson. While he liked Benson and admired him in many ways, Fiske thought that Daniels' appointment of Benson was a mistake. "For the position, the first requirement was a clear apprehension of strategy and a fine mind," Fiske wrote.

> I had never heard that he had ever shown the slightest interest in strategy or been on the General Board, or even taken the summer course at the War College.[33]

Fiske's statement was unfair for, although Benson was not part of Fiske's group of reformers, he had qualifications for the position and his views were certainly attractive to Daniels. Benson had not completed the Naval War College course, but he did attend part of it in 1906, even if the Bureau of Navigation ordered him to it late and detached him early, leaving him less than a month in Newport.

Fiske had sacrificed his own naval future in the campaign for the Chief of Naval Operations. Having more than a year to go before reaching the statutory retirement age of 62, Fiske was soon rusticated to Newport where he was assigned to the Naval War College. Fiske had no duties at the college and was an obvious incongruity for the staff. Admiral Knight "gave me a desk in the delightful library of the War College" Fiske remembered,

> from the windows of which I would see in three directions most beautiful and inspiring views of Narragansett Bay and its green-covered shores and islands. The library is an excellent one, and is especially complete in books written on history, government, and the naval and military arts.[34]

Fiske mingled with the students and attended lectures, but the majority of his time was spent in the library reflecting on the role of armaments and navies in the future. His thoughts brought forth a series of articles, published in late 1915 and early 1916, which raised great public attention and stressed the need for preparedness. Secretary Daniels became so incensed over Fiske's writings that he ordered Fiske to make no public statements without prior approval from the Navy Department. Newspapers picked up Fiske's criticisms and began an investigation of his charges. Fiske once again aired his views in testimony before the House Naval Affairs Committee. He retired from active duty while assigned to the Naval War College on 13 June 1916.

A German U-Boat at Newport

At 2 p.m. on the afternoon of 7 October 1916, the American submarine *D-2* sent an urgent coded message to the Commandant, Naval Station, Newport, reporting that she had sighted a surfaced German submarine three miles east of Point Judith and standing in toward Newport. *D-2* approached the U-boat and paralleled her course in order to escort her into port. Flying the German man-of-war ensign, commission pennant, and armed with two deck guns, the German submarine requested permission from *D-2* to enter Newport harbor. As she approached the anchorage, the Germans signalled USS *Birmingham*, flagship of Rear Admiral Albert Gleaves, Commander, Destroyer Force, Atlantic Fleet, requesting a berth. She was assigned to berth one, a mooring buoy located southwest of the college. Rear Admiral Knight, president of the Naval War College and Naval District Commandant, ordered his aide, Lieutenant W. D. Puleston, to take a boat alongside and "to make the usual inquiries, but with instructions not to go on board, as no communications had yet been had with the health authorities."[35]

At 3 p.m., the commanding officer of the German submarine came ashore in a boat supplied by *Birmingham* to make a formal call on Admiral Knight. Identifying himself as Kapitänleutnant Hans Rose, Imperial German Navy, commanding *U-53*, he appeared in uniform, wearing the Iron Cross. He told Admiral Knight, "apparently with pride, that his vessel was a man-of-war, armed with guns and torpedoes. He stated that he had no object in entering the port except to pay his respects; that he needed no supplies or assistance, and that he proposed to go to sea at six o'clock."[36] Rose's call on Admiral Knight was returned by Lieutenant Puleston, and the German officer's call on Admiral Gleaves was returned by his aide, Lieutenant Mark Bristol. The officers and men of *U-53* politely showed their visitors, both naval and civilian, over their boat, generally answering a wide variety of questions. When the commanding officer of the destroyer tender *Melville*, Commander

H. B. Price, came on board, he asked the German engineer officer if he
spoke English. "No," the German replied, "I speak American." They
"spoke our tongue with careful correctness, though not fluently," Price
observed, "and answered all questions except when we asked their
names, which they obviously declined to give. We refrained from
seeming too inquisitive."[37]

The visitors were told that the 65-meter long submarine had been
built in 1916 and had traveled in 17 days from Wilhelmshaven,
touching at Heligoland, passing north of the Shetland Islands and along
the coast of Newfoundland. They were also told that the vessel had a
cruising range of 10,000 miles and could travel 450 miles on its
unrecharged batteries alone. She carried six weeks' provisions and
could theoretically remain on the bottom for four days, but two days
was the longest they had remained submerged.

Getting underway at 5:30 p.m., the German crew manned the rail,
facing several passing vessels. After passing and saluting USS *Melville*,
the officers and crew waved their caps to the last destroyer they passed.

The following day, *U-53* captured and sank three British ships, and
two neutrals, a Dutch and a Norwegian ship, all of about 3,000 to 5,000
gross tons in international waters off Nantucket Lightship.

The visit of the German submarine was the first direct contact which
the War College had with the war. Within six months the war not only
dominated the attention of the college, but caused suspension of its
operations.

America Enters the War

In the months before America entered World War I, the Navy made
little preparation for modern naval war in the Atlantic. The Navy of the
Wilson Administration was too busy in Mexican and Caribbean waters
to study carefully the implication of the growing German U-boat fleet.
At the Naval War College, students and staff were engaged in following
the standard course and writing their usual theses with only peripheral
study of current affairs. Reports on the war were followed in the press
and professional journals and since 1914, the college had the additional
advantage of receiving copies of American naval attache reports. These
were available for students and staff to read. Only a few guest lectures
for 1916 and early 1917 dealt directly with the war. In 1916, Captain
William S. Sims came as a visiting lecturer to speak on "Military
Character" to a group of civilian volunteers for a naval training cruise,
and Surgeon Archibald Fauntleroy spoke on "Politico-Military Aspects
of the European War" to resident students. In March 1917, International
Law Professor George G. Wilson lectured on "Armed Merchantmen," a
subject of intense interest as the Navy considered ways to protect its

commerce in wartime. In the study of tactics at the college, battleship operations and the use of destroyers to screen and protect them predominated. In general, Atlantic Fleet officers believed that submarines and aircraft were not capable of keeping up with the fleet, so no plans were laid for their use in engagements with an enemy fleet. Some War College staff members criticized this idea and suggested that such rigidity and single focus be avoided by examining additional means of employing all types of naval forces. In addition to German submarine operation, such as *U-53's* impressive, trans-Atlantic passage, the College showed interest in the general implications for moving submarines. This followed the towing of the American submarines *F-1*, *F-2*, and *F-3* from Hawaii to California during 1916.[38]

The Naval War College stressed, however, that it existed not to provide immediate answers to specific questions or to establish specific rules of warfare but, rather, to elucidate general principles and to develop a habit of mind in its students which applied those principles logically to new situations.[39] The presidencies of William L. Rodgers and Austin M. Knight at the Naval War College marked a new aspect in the college's history. During their terms, coinciding with the tenure of Josephus Daniels as Secretary of the Navy, both Rodgers and Knight found the Navy Department appreciating the War College's role in educating officers and promoting professionalism within the service. Together, Rodgers, Knight, and Daniels succeeded in putting the college on a stronger basis and enabling it to reach a wide spectrum of officers, for the first time, through Navy-wide General Orders and the Secretary's personal and direct support of the college.[40] As Austin Knight described it in 1916, the Naval War College had finally become "an institute of definite aims, pursued by definite and above all organized methods."[41]

It is clear in retrospect that when the college used the applicatory method for problem solving, it found a logical and practical approach which revolutionized its outlook. "Of all the changes the last years have wrought," Austin Knight told the students, "the greatest is this— that the college has been vitalized by a new comprehension of its mission and a new consciousness of its power."[42] The staff was well aware that it could not hope in a year's time to make its students finished tacticians or finished strategists, but it hoped to ground them in the elementary principles of warfare, acquainting them with the methods by which the principles might be studied and applied. It was hoped the students would also be inspired with ambition to continue their self-education with widened reading, continuing with the foundation they had received in Newport.[43] If the college did no more than bring naval officers together for discussion, it would provide a valuable service, but it did more by promoting the German approach in the applicatory system. The college "not only makes us understand each other's ways of thinking," Knight reminded the students, "but it makes us think alike, this of course, through the guiding influence of the college superimposed upon the mere association of mind with mind."[44]

Significantly, the introduction of the applicatory method brought about an unintended development: it coincided with the demise of theoretical work at the college. The central focus changed to an emphasis on tactics rather than strategy. Although the case study method had originally been intended to form the basis for an inductive approach that would develop naval theory and help to formulate broad principles, the use of case studies with the applicatory system, in fact, moved the students' interest away from a synoptic view of naval science. No historian had been a resident member of the staff since Mahan's departure in 1893, and no similar general studies on the nature of naval warfare were undertaken by anyone in the years to come. The result was that instead of dealing with fundamental questions of naval warfare, War College students after 1912 were encouraged to concentrate on smaller areas with emphasis on the procedures of higher tactical command.[45]

On 16 February 1917, Captain William S. Sims succeeded Rear Admiral Knight as president of the Naval War College. Sims was certainly the leading officer in the Navy who could carry on with the new program at Newport. Sims had not been happy when he had been ordered to the War College as a student in 1911, but by the time he completed the first long course, he had completely changed his view. "Any man who compares certain opinions he brought to the Naval War College at the beginning of the long course with those he took away at the end," Sims said in 1914, "must realize the unrivaled advantages of full and free discussion; and now recognize the extreme improbability that his own undiscussed opinions are always infallible."[46]

A year after leaving the War College, Sims had been assigned command of the Atlantic Fleet Destroyer Flotilla in July 1913. With about 30 destroyers in his flotilla, Sims was allowed to develop his own organization and to choose his own staff. This was an entirely new development, since his predecessor had no staff at all. Sims chose officers whom he had met at the War College, including Commander W. V. Pratt from the War College staff, who would command his flagship and serve as his chief of staff, and Dudley W. Knox, a graduate of the second long course. Sims went to his new command with the idea that "the torpedo fleet could be made an enormous game board . . . for trying out all kinds of maneuvers at small expense. There is a lot to be learned . . . . But one thing is sure, and that is that it can only be learned by study combined with actual maneuvers with the fleet."[47]

Sims' idea was clearly to apply War College methods to fleet problems. He did so first by using the conference approach which came from the applicatory system. Unlike the "old man idea," which was entirely dependent on a single leader's understanding, Sims believed that the "organized team idea produced the maximum result of which the organization is capable."[48] Sims stressed that it was impossible for a commander in chief to provide detailed orders with every new and changing situation. A captain must know what to do without any particular orders from his superior beyond an initial one. With no established doctrine, Sims created what he called a War College afloat. "I am not a practical man in these affairs," Sims told his officers. "I am not capable of knowing from one station to the other in the night what to do, but you people ought to know that . . . . Here is the cabin floor, and there are a dozen or so model ships, and we will work out a scheme."[49]

Plans were made, tried out in varying conditions, revised and redevised until a doctrine of attack was worked out and reduced to 31 coded words for radio use. Using ideas drawn from the applicatory system learned at the Naval War College, Sims and his staff created an effective naval doctrine for destroyers, the first naval doctrine developed and used in the U.S. Navy.[50]

In 1916, just before returning to the Naval War College, Sims published an article in the Naval Institute *Proceedings* entitled, "Cheer Up!! There is No Naval War College."[51] In suggesting the demise of the college, Sims wanted to stress to naval officers the changes that had taken place in recent years. The Naval War College, he said, was "no highbrow institution that imposes theoretical ideas on the fleet in words that had to be looked up in a dictionary." It was now conducted and controlled as part of the fleet; "let the fleet officers therefore cheer up," he wrote,

> and instead of criticizing their own fleet War College across the wardroom tables, get busy, read the books, take the correspondence courses, get up chart maneuvers, and learn the great game the successful playing of which in war is their only reason for existence.[52]

By the time Sims relieved Knight as president of the War College, it was clear that America would soon enter the war. Sims was called to Washington for conferences with the General Board and National Advisory Committee in February and March. During those periods, Captain Benton C. Decker directed the activities of the college. On 19 March, Sims was promoted to rear admiral, and on the same date, the first of a long series of students and staff were detached for duty elsewhere, interrupting the course. In the last week of March, Sims received a telephone call ordering him to proceed secretly to Washington. Returning briefly to Newport, Sims sailed under an assumed name from New York for Liverpool on 31 March. It was several weeks before it was public knowledge that Sims had gone to begin discussions to prepare for cooperation with the Royal Navy.

By the time Congress declared war on 6 April 1917, regular War College instruction had already been suspended. From that time until January 1919, the War College building was devoted to training naval reservists in the Second Naval District. Only a nucleus War College staff was retained under the direction of retired officers who had been recalled to active duty for the purpose. Since Sims had only been relieved as president of the college temporarily, in the following year and a half his place was filled by a series of acting presidents: Commander Charles P. Eaton, Commodore J. P. Parker, and Captain R. R. Belknap, who would become head of the strategy department in 1919. The Chief Clerk's Office, the Secretary's Office, and the Library were maintained. The Secretary's Office received copies of naval attaché and intelligence reports, filing them in the vault and indexing them. Correspondence courses were continued and various War College publications continued to be distributed to the fleet. One of the most important of these was Commander W. S. Pye's, mathematical tables developed from war games that were designed to assist in fleet maneuvers. The library's collections were maintained and expanded, and the library was used extensively by officers assigned to the training station, particularly by reserve officers.[53]

Although the War College course of instruction had been suspended, the spirit of the college survived with Sims in Europe. Once again, he employed War College methods as his work in London expanded from that of a diplomat and advisor to commander over 370 ships of all classes, 5,000 officers, and 70,000 men distributed over 45 bases. The Planning Staff at Sims' London headquarters consisted entirely of Naval War College graduates who applied and developed further what they had learned in Newport. Among the men assigned to the Planning Staff were H. E. Yarnell, F. H. Schofield, Dudley W. Knox, R. H. Dunlap, Luke McNamee, and Louis McCarty Little. The performance of that pioneer group in actual wartime planning seems to have been the force that inspired the establishment of its regular counterpart in the office of the Chief of Naval Operations at the end of the war. War planning finally had become a separate duty. As H. E. Yarnell put it, there was "a considerable number of capable youngsters with War College training and full of vim and vigor"[54] to get on with naval planning.

On 27 July 1917, Stephen B. Luce died at the age of 90. In the two years prior to his death, he had given up most of his active association with the college. His death marked the end of the first generation of War College men. Of the leading lights in that generation, Henry Taylor had died an early death in 1904; Mahan died suddenly in December 1914;

and William McCarty Little in March 1915. Chadwick lived until January 1919, and only Stockton and Goodrich survived until 1924-1925. The deaths of these men and the suspension of classes in 1917 marked the end of an era in War College history. They were the men whose prolonged and dedicated efforts had firmly established the Naval War College. Its future course would be determined by other hands from another generation.

Yet the seeds of the college's influence in later years had already been planted. Among the students and staff at the War College in the years 1910-1917, W. B. Caperton, W. S. Sims, Josiah McKean, Royal Ingersoll, Yates Stirling, W. V. Pratt, Halsey Powell, Reginald Belknap, W. D. Puleston, D. W. Knox, H. E. Yarnell, Nathan Twining, Mark Bristol, and V. O. Chase were names that would come to be remembered in the U.S. Navy. It was while many of them were students that the Naval War College first came to develop the method of creating an effective naval doctrine for fleet operations.

Notes

1. Damon E. Cummings, *Admiral Richard Wainwright and the United States Fleet* (Washington: Govt. Print. Off., 1961), p. 243.

2. George S. Pappas, *Prudens Futuri: The U.S. Army War College 1901-1967* (Carlisle Barracks: Alumni Assoc. Army War College, 1967), pp. 33, 37, 49, 51, 78.

3. NWC Archives, RG. 2, Box 37, File A-12: W. L Rodgers to Secretary of the Navy, 14 Feb 1921 enclosing "Memorandum Regarding the History of the Naval War College," p. 6.

4. Ibid.

5. Ibid.

6. J. H. Russell, "A Fragment of Naval War College History," U.S. Naval Institute *Proceedings*, vol. 58, (August 1932), pp. 1164-65.

7. Hattendorf, "Technology and Strategy" in B. M. Simpson, III, ed., *War, Strategy and Maritime Power* (New Brunswick, NJ: Rutgers Univ. Press, 1977) Quote from W. P. Cronan, "The Greatest Need of the United States Navy: Proper Organization for the Successful Conduct of War, An Estimate of the Situation," U.S. Naval Institute *Proceedings*, Vol. 42 No. 4, (July-August 1916), p. 1153.

8. NWC Archives, RG 14: lecture by F. N. Schofield, "Estimate of the Situation and Formulation of Orders," Summer Conference, 1912.

9. W. L. Rodgers "Memorandum..." op. cit., p. 7.

10. Luce "On the Relations Between the U.S. Naval War College and the Line Officers of the U.S. Navy," U.S. Naval Institute *Proceedings*, Vol. XXXVII, No. 3., (1911), pp. 787-99. Quoted in Hayes and Hattendorf, *Writings of Stephen B. Luce*, (Newport: Naval War College Press, 1975), p. 233.

11. Ibid.

12. Naval Historical Collection: Staff-Student File: Ellis; J. J. Reber "Pete Ellis: Amphibious Warfare Prophet," U.S. Naval Institute *Proceedings*, Vol. 103, No. 11, (November1977) pp. 53-64.

13. E. E. Morison, *Admiral Sims and the Modern American Navy*, (Boston: Houghton, Mifflin, 1942), Chapter 2.

14. Ibid., pp. 278-79.

15. Ibid., p. 287.

16. Ibid., p. 289.

17. Gerald Wheeler, *A Sailor's Life—Admiral William Veazie Pratt* (Washington: Govt. Print. Off., 1974), p. 70.

18. NWC Archives RG 15, W. V. Pratt, Lecture, "Aspects of Higher Command," 30 Aug 1929.

19. NWC Archives RG 12: Report of 1912 Summer Conference, p. 3.

20. Ibid., pp. 3-4.

21. NWC Archives, RG 12: Report of 1911 Conference, Vol. I, p. 20. For Mahan's criticism of the 1911 Orange War Plan, see Mahan to Rodgers, 22 Feb, 4 March, 1911, in Seager and Maguire eds., *Letters and Papers of Alfred T. Mahan*, (Annapolis: Naval Institute Press, 1975), Vol III, pp. 380-388, and 389-94.

22. Quoted from Black Plan in J. H. Maurer, "American Naval Concentration and the German Battle Fleet, 1900-1918," *The Journal of Strategic Studies* vol. 6, no. 2, (June 1983), p. 164.

23. Ibid.

24. NWC Archives, RG 2, op. cit., W. L. Rodgers, "Memorandum," pp. 7-8.

25. Ibid., and Knight and Puleston, Unpublished Typescript "History of the Naval War College 1913," p. 3.

26. Typescript "History of the Naval War College to 1937," pp. 66-67.

27. Ibid., p. 68.

28. NWC Archives, RG 2, op. cit., W. L. Rodgers "Memorandum," p. 8.

29. Ibid.

30. Knight and Puleston, op. cit., 1914, pp. 4-9.

31. Bradley A. Fiske, *From Midshipman to Rear Admiral* (New York: Century Co., 1919), pp. 544-549.

32. P. E. Coletta, *Admiral Bradley A. Fiske and the American Navy*, (Lawrence: Regents Press of Kansas, 1979), pp. 151-52.

33. Fiske, *Midshipman to Rear Admiral*, p. 585. But see David F. Trask, "William Shepherd Benson" in R. W. Love, *The Chiefs of Naval Operations* (Annapolis: Naval Institute, 1980), pp. 3-20.

34. Ibid., p. 592.

35. NWC Archives, RG 8, Series II: Attache Reports: November 1916: U11:1, pp. 30-34, 43; Navy Department, Office of Naval Records and Library, *German Submarine Activities on the Atlantic Coast of the United States and Canada* (Washington: Govt. Print. Off., 1920), pp. 18-23.

36. NWC Archives, loc. cit., p. 30.

37. Ibid., p. 33.

38. NWC Archives, RG 14, Faculty and Staff Presentation, 1915-17; RG 15 Guest Lectures, 1915-17; RG 8, Series I: UNOpM 1915-17; XTAP: Rough NWC staff notes on C-in-C, Atlantic Fleet's "Tentative General Plan for Operations of the Fleet in an Engagement with the Enemy," April 1916; UNS: Submarines 1915-17.

39. NWC Archives RG 16, Opening Addresses: A. M. Knight, 5 July 1916, pp. 15-16.

40. Spector, *Professors of War* (Newport: Naval War College Press, 1977), p. 125.

41. Knight and Puleston, op. cit., 1916, p. 2.

42. NWC Archives, RG 16: Opening Addresses: Knight, 2 Jan 1917.

43. Loc. cit., Opening Address: Knight, 5 July 1916.

44. Loc. cit., Graduation Address: Knight, 22 Dec. 1916.

45. Spector, op. cit., pp. 128-129.

46. W. S. Sims, "Naval War College Principles and Methods Applied Afloat," U.S. Naval Institute *Proceedings*, Vol. 41, No. 2, (March-April 1915), p. 385. Published version of 1914 War College lecture.

47. E. E. Morison, *Admiral Sims*, p. 292.

48. W.S. Sims, op. cit., p. 307.

49. Morison, op. cit., p. 297.

50. Ibid., p. 296.

51. U.S. Naval Institute *Proceedings*, Vol. 42, No. 3 (May-June 1916), pp. 857-860.

52. Ibid., p. 860.

53. "Brief History of the Naval War College from 16 Feb. 1917 to 31 Dec. 1919," (NWC 1921), in typescript "History of the Naval War College to 1937."

54. Morison, op. cit., p. 369; R. G. Albion, *Makers of Naval Policy 1798-1947*, (Annapolis: Naval Institute Press, 1980), pp. 89-90. Yarnell quote in Albion, p. 90. W. S. Sims, *Victory at Sea* (New York: Doubleday, 1920), pp. 253-54.

GENERAL ORDER, No. 325.

October 6, 1884.

A college is hereby established for an advanced course of professional study for naval officers, to be known as the Naval War College. It will be under the general supervision of the Bureau of Navigation. The principal building on Coasters' Harbor Island, Newport, R. I., will be assigned to its use, and is hereby transferred, with the surrounding structures and the grounds immediately adjacent, to the custody and control of the Bureau of Navigation for that purpose.

The college will be under the immediate charge of an officer of the Navy, not below the grade of commander, to be known as the President of the Naval War College. He will be assisted in the performance of his duties by a faculty.

A course of instruction, embracing the higher branches of professional study, will be arranged by a board, consisting of all the members of the faculty and including the president, who will be the presiding officer of the board. The board will have regular meetings at least once a month, and at such other times as the president may direct, for the transaction of business. The proceedings of the board will be recorded in a journal.

The course of instruction will be open to all officers above the grade of naval cadet.

Commodore S. B. Luce has been assigned to duty as president of the college.

WM. E. CHANDLER,
Secretary of the Navy.

1. Navy Department General Order No. 325 of October 6, 1884 establishing the Naval War College on Coasters Harbor Island, Newport, R.I. and designating Stephen B. Luce president.

ADMIRAL LUCE.

2. Stephen B. Luce at about the time the Naval War College was established. *Harpers Weekly* illustration.

3. The Naval War College, former Newport Poorhouse (built 1819). *Harper's Weekly* illustration, 1885.

U. S. Naval War College.
September 2nd, 1885:

Order;

     Lectures will begin on Sept. 7.
The working days will be Monday, Tuesday,
Wednesday, Thursday & Friday.

     The lectures on International Law
will be delivered daily at 10. A M.

     The Lectures in Military
Science will be delivered daily
at 11.30 A. M.

     Additional Lectures on Naval &
Military Science will be delivered
at 1 P.M. on Monday, Tuesday,
Thursday, & Fridays.

S. B. Luce
Commodore U. S. Navy.
President Naval War College.

4. First Naval War College Order, September 2, 1885, signed by Commodore Stephen B. Luce, War College president.

THE INFLUENCE

OF

SEA POWER UPON HISTORY

1660–1783

BY

CAPTAIN A. T. MAHAN
UNITED STATES NAVY

BOSTON
LITTLE, BROWN, AND COMPANY
1890

5. Title page of Stephen B. Luce's copy of Mahan's first book on seapower.

6. Captain Alfred Thayer Mahan, lecturer on naval history and strategy and War College president, 1886-1888, 1892-1893.

7. Army-Navy Joint Exercise, Newport, R.I., November, 1887. The North Atlantic Squadron under Rear Admiral Luce passes Fort Adams at the entrance of Narragansett Bay. *Harper's Weekly* illustration.

8. Naval Torpedo Station, Goat Island, ca.1880. The College was transferred to Goat Is.

9. Naval Training Station, Coasters Harbor Island, Newport, R.I., 1889. View showing *USS New Hampshire*, headquarters and recruit quarters ship, tied up at South Point.

LIEUTENANT T. A. BLISS, U.S.A.

PROFESSOR SOLEY.

10. Lt. Tasker A. Bliss, USA, lecturer on military strategy and tactics, 1885-1887. Later, Army Chief of Staff, 1917; Member, Supreme War Council in France, 1917-1918, and Commission to Negotiate Peace, 1918-1919. *Harper's Weekly* illustration.

11. Professor James Soley, lecturer on international law, 1885-1888. Director, Office of Naval Records and Library, 1882-1890. Later appointed the first Assistant Secretary of the Navy, 1890-1893. *Harper's Weekly* illustration.

12. Classroom lecture, 1888. *Frank Leslie's Illustrated Newspaper* illustration.

13. Naval War Gaming, 1894. Illustration by the noted naval illustrator Rufus F. Zogbaum, Sr. Representatives of a delegation from China, which was visiting the War College, are in the background.

14. First foreign students: Commanders Carl-Gustaf Flach (right) and Gösta af Ugglas (left), Royal Swedish Navy. From a student and staff photograph of 1894.

15. Lieutenant William McCarty Little, about the time he joined the Naval War College Staff, 1885.

16. Captain Henry Taylor, War College president, 1893-1896.

17. Luce Hall, built in 1892 and named in honor of the founder of the War College in 1934. View of about 1910 showing Naval Training Station recruits on Dewey Field.

18. President Theodore Roosevelt arrives at Coasters Harbor Island for the Battleship Conference at the Naval War College, 1908.

19. George Grafton Wilson, Harvard Professor of Law and Naval War College Lecturer on international law, 1901-1937. Courtesy of the Harvard University Law School.

20. Staff and students, 1897, with visiting Assistant Secretary of Navy Theodore Roosevelt.

U. S. Naval War College

Administ

United States Nava

21. View of the Naval War College and the Naval Training Station, ca.1903-1907. The tw

22. Interior of the Library, 1923. A Library-Archives annex was built directly behind Luce Hall in 1904. The building was named in honor of Rear Admiral Alfred Thayer Mahan in 1936.

al Training Station vessels in the foreground are the USS *Hist* and the USS *Constellation*.

23. A Naval War Game on the third floor of Luce Hall, ca.1910.

24. Lt. Colonel Earl Hancock Ellis, USMC, one of four students of the first Long Course, 1911-1912. Ellis was the principal proponent of the advanced bases concept for a possible Central Pacific offensive strategy. Courtesy of the Marine Corps Historical Center.

25. Secretary of the Navy Josephus Daniels with Rear Admiral Austin Knight, War College president, staff and students, 1914. Captain William S. Sims, wearing armband, is seated on right.

26. The President's house (Quarters AA). View of ca.1914, when Rear Admiral Austin Knight and his family were in residence.

27.   View of Coasters Harbor Island, 1915, showing the Naval War College, a naval recruit parade, and ships of the Atlantic Fleet in the bay.

28.   German Submarine *U-53*, anchored south of Coasters Harbor Island, October 7, 1916 USS *Birmingham* is in background. Courtesy of the Naval Historical Center, Washington D.C.

29. Visiting Japanese delegation, February 13, 1924. Included are Vice Admiral K. Ide and aide Captain I. Yamamoto.

30. Rear Admiral William S. Sims, Naval War College president, and staff and students, 1922. Commander Chester W. Nimitz, future World War II Admiral, is in the last row directly behind Sims.

31. Pringle Hall, to the left of Luce Hall, in this view of 1963 was built in 1934. It was named in honor of Rear Admiral Joel Roberts Poinsett Pringle, president, 1927-1930.

32. War Gaming Room, Pringle Hall. A game in progress, ca.1950.

33.   World War II Admirals Nimitz, King and Spruance, graduates of the Naval War College during the interwar period. Taken on board the USS *Indianapolis* in the Pacific, 1944.

33.a.   NWC Class pictures: Nimitz '23, King '33, Spruance '27.

CHAPTER 5

SIMS CHARTS THE NEW
COURSE, 1919-1927

By the time the Armistice was signed in November 1918, Admiral William S. Sims had become an American naval hero. When he became president of the Naval War College in 1917, he had had a full and distinguished career which few other officers could equal, earning him both national and international prominence. He had been promoted to the temporary grade of vice admiral in May 1917, only nine months after he had been selected for rear admiral, the junior officer on a list of 30 rear admirals in the U.S. Navy. In December 1918, he was promoted to admiral. Praise, gifts, and honors showered on him and it seemed that any high office of his choice might have been open to him. Commander in Chief of the U.S. Fleet, Chief of Naval Operations, or Chairman of the General Board were all conceivable options had he wanted to choose them. Instead, Sims requested Secretary of the Navy Daniels to reappoint him president of the Naval War College, then a rear admiral's position.

When his request was granted in December 1918, Sims wrote on the bottom of Daniels' telegram, as it was received in his London Headquarters, "Note how pleased all hands are to give me the college. It relieves them from the embarrassment of not knowing what to do with me."[1]

For Sims, the office of Chief of Naval Operations was too limited in authority to make it as effective as it should be. A return to the fleet would seem to be an anti-climax after the war to end all wars. In Sims' mind, the Naval War College offered the greatest possibility for making a contribution to the Navy. Sims was highly critical of the manner in which the Wilson Administration conducted the war and, undoubtedly, he was happy to avoid a role that would require him to act on similar postwar policies. The presidency of the Naval War College attracted him not because it was a post in which he could play elder statesman but because the Naval War College carried the seeds of the Navy's future.[2]

From his London office, overlooking Grosvenor Gardens adjacent to Victoria Railway Station, Sims composed a long letter to the Secretary of the Navy which summarized his general recommendations concerning the War College in January 1919. "It is my conviction," he wrote, "that the Naval War College should be made one of the principal assets of the Naval Service." Brains, information, and professional training for officers were the essential elements that made the fleet useful for national defense, Sims declared. "Ships and equipment taken alone mean nothing other than the quantity of material they represent." "Therefore," he argued, "the art of command and coordinated effort, should be given precedence over all other considerations."[3]

Attacking directly the long-standing reluctance of the Navy Department to assign appropriate numbers of officers to the college, Sims urged that its personnel needs be given precedence over all others. "In fact, I would go as far as to say," Sims wrote, "that the college should be maintained with a capable and adequate staff and student body even if such a course can be carried out only by actual reduction of the size of the fleet." In other words, it might "be necessary to place a ship out of commission in order to avoid decreasing the efficiency of the education of our officers."

While the detailed plans for the War College would necessarily wait until the college's staff could be reassembled in Newport, Sims had several important ideas that would guide those plans when they were made.

First, he believed that the college must be closely defined as an educational institution. Too many people misunderstood its mission and attempted to show or to deny concrete results accomplished by the college. "The aim of the college is to cause officers to educate themselves in many lines, which the unavoidable limitations of the course at the Academy and the routine duties at sea prevent. It should be well understood by the service that the college is in no sense a planmaking body, nor has it any administrative or executive functions." The college's accomplishments, he remarked "are not subject to specific compilation or statement."

Second, Sims recommended that the principal members of the staff, or at least the two principal chairs of strategy and tactics, should be held by flag officers. Because Sims viewed their functions primarily as supervising war games and tactical problems, he believed that the conclusions drawn needed to be impressed upon the students with the full weight of authority. In this respect, the head of each department was put in the role of a teacher and an authority. Rejecting as "wholly illogical" Luce's belief that the students were mature professionals who were capable of deriving their own lessons from the course, Sims maintained that it was impossible from a psychological point of view to disassociate the staff from the role of teacher. For that reason, he recommended that the two principal staff members be senior to the students.

Third, officers for the college teaching staff should be conversant and sympathetic with its work and be men "who are generally popular, and of all-round, so-called good 'practical' service reputation." In recommending that the college avoid staff members who had great ability, but who might suffer, even unjustly, from unpopularity, Sims was concerned that the college would give a bad impression to the service in general. Careful selection of staff was important to give "the college a fair start."

Fourth, Sims saw that the War College had suffered in the past from a lack of continuity in its policy and in its methods. The dedicated and voluntary efforts of Stephen B. Luce and William McCarty Little had provided only an informal continuity which counteracted the constant change of naval personnel. To remedy this, Sims recommended that the War College employ at least four civilians who were experienced men from university life. At a minimum, these should include a civilian in both the strategy and tactics departments, an experienced librarian, and an archivist. These four appointments would ensure that historical and actual experience was obtained and employed along proper lines while also affording permanent contact with the university world and maintaining continuity in shaping the courses. "There are many important branches of education which are, of necessity, neglected in a naval officer's education," Sims reflected. Civilian academics could be extremely valuable "for example, in the field of economics as it affects international law, trade relations and government interests, and in the broad field of political science and many other subjects." To obtain the right type of men, Sims believed that the college should establish attractive pay levels corresponding with university appointments and academic standard titles beginning with assistant professor.

Finally, Sims recommended that funds be increased in order to provide for leading authorities on "international law, history, political science and government, economics, trade relations, policy, logic, psychology, scientific management, and many other subjects which should have an influence on our profession." In addition, he recommended that the two resident courses begin in November and May rather than January and July as they had previously done. In this way, college students avoided competition for housing with summer residents and tourists. He also pointed out the need to refurbish the college building and provide new equipment.

Sims requested that as college president he be given complete discretion to spend college appropriations and to select the staff to be assigned to the college for its first six to twelve months "regardless of any other considerations which may be advanced." He stressed the importance of the college presidency; Sims pointed out that it should be the sole duty of the officer assigned. No other administrative or military duties, such as naval district commandant or base commander, should be added.

Sims forwarded his ideas to the Secretary of the Navy through the Chief of Naval Operations. In reviewing Sims' recommendations, W. S. Benson approved nearly all of them, but did not agree to give Sims free rein in obtaining all the officers he wanted or to allow him to spend college funds without first reviewing an estimate of funds necessary for each fiscal year. Having no direct experience of the War College, Benson sought the advice of Rear Admiral H. S. Knapp, who had studied at the War College in 1897 and been a staff member in 1903-1904 and 1906. Following Sims' departure from London, Knapp succeeded him as both naval attaché and Commander of U.S. Naval Forces in Europe. Although Knapp and Benson agreed that the War College had outgrown "the town meeting idea" and that "the staff should be looked upon as teachers," they saw no need to assign flag officers to head the strategy and tactics departments. While it might be desirable, the men selected for those jobs "must of necessity be specialists in their line, and no right-minded man can object to learning from specialists whether they be senior or junior, and whether they be older or younger."[4]In disagreeing with Sims' views on assignments to the War College, Knapp noted that the value in attending the college had "been so demonstrated by this war that any doubts about it should forever be dissipated. Yet it is a very large demand that the college be given precedence over every other personnel need. . . . " Furthermore, as the Navy returned to peacetime duties, it was important to consider the personal interests of officers. Certain officers whom Sims had in mind had served long periods on staff duty ashore and were overdue for assignment to sea. "Before being ordered to the War College," Benson concluded his endorsement, "they should be given a chance to express their wishes as to whether or not they are willing to take the chances which are perfectly apparent from a casual reading of the statutes governing promotions at the present time."

Despite Sims' notion that the college was a practical extension of the fleet, his view of it as the Navy's most important resource conflicted with the promotion regulations based on the view that practical sea experience was more important than intellectual preparation.

The implementation of Sims' ideas had to await his return to Newport from London. In the meantime, work had begun to prepare the buildings in Newport to be used once again by Naval War College students. Plans for extensive renovation were halted, however, by

Benson's personal opinion that the college was best located in or near Washington.[5] Despite this, improvements were made to the existing building which would allow the college to handle more students. The four sets of quarters at the east and west ends of the building were converted into offices, but the mantelpieces and oak trim were left in several rooms, giving them a gracious and formal ambience. The interior staircases were relocated to provide better access between the old apartments and the main section of the building. The heating system was revamped and exterior repairs made. The third floor received additional rooms, and space was provided in the basement for library storage, the chart collection, and the college printing shop.

Sims' Return to Newport

After a series of farewell celebrations in March, Admiral Sims left London and sailed for America. Arriving in New York on board the liner *Mauretania,* he was greeted by flags flying, whistles blowing, and people shouting. Traveling by train, he was received in Washington by Secretary Daniels and other senior naval officers at the train station.[6] After a brief stay in the capital, Sims traveled home to Rhode Island for a reunion with his wife and children.[7]

Arriving by train in Providence, Sims made the remainder of the journey down Narragansett Bay in the destroyer *Sampson* (DD-63), escorted by both a torpedo boat and a low-flying seaplane. Appropriately, *Sampson* had seen extensive wartime duty in European waters and was named for the admiral who had so effectively supported the college in its early years.

Sims' arrival in Newport on 11 April 1919 was a gala occasion for the city. Business had been formally suspended for half a day, but many enthusiastic shopkeepers closed their doors early to join the growing crowds that lined the streets and crowded the wharves to catch a glimpse of the returning hero. The city's fire whistle sounded a prearranged signal as *Sampson* hove into sight. After the destroyer anchored in Newport's inner harbor, Sims boarded a steam launch for the trip to Government Landing in downtown Newport, near Bowen's Wharf. It was a short and rough journey, but Sims was seen at the hatchway waving a greeting to his wife and children on the wharf.

Government Landing was jammed with official, civilian, and military greeters. Mayor Mahoney of Newport solemnly declared, "Newport and its people rise as one man today to bid you a sincere, cordial, and hearty welcome home." Sims inspected the military honor guard and then he and the other dignitaries boarded their carriages for a triumphal parade through the streets of Newport.

Sixteen carriages led the parade, made up of veterans, civic, and local groups, such as the Italian Progresso Society, the Congregation of Jeshuat Israel, and school children, accompanied by several bands. Several thousand Newporters turned out to give the returning hero a tumultuous reception. While all the ships in the harbor sounded their whistles, the bells of nearby Trinity Church chimed joyously and the crowds shouted their welcome.

The parade followed a circuitous route through the city to the Sims house on Kay Street at Mann Avenue. First it went south on Thames Street, then onto Young Street, and back north on Spring Street. Up the hill at Pelham Street, down Bellevue Avenue to Touro Street and Washington Square, out Broadway to Powel Avenue, and finally onto Kay Street they went. A reviewing stand had been erected in front of the Sims house, and it was here that the admiral finally joined his family.[8] Sims stood before the cheering crowd to review the parade that followed him, wearing his old uniform blouse with two stars on each side of the high collar. Thus, he signified that he had reverted to his permanent grade as a rear admiral to take up the presidency of the Naval War College.

Sims and his wife had already decided against moving into their old home. Instead, they rented it and moved into the War College President's House. But it was government quarters, and Mrs. Sims quietly attended to the many chores necessary to turn it into a home for the Sims family.

Sims spent much of the following month away from Newport on an extensive speaking tour of the midwest on a "Victory Bond" drive.[9] When he settled in to his work at the college, Sims found most of the staff there, already hard at work making the multitudinous preparations for the incoming class of 31 officers who would arrive at the end of June and for another class of 30 officers who were due in December. Within two years Sims convinced the Bureau of Navigation to send only one class of 60 or more officers instead of two classes of 30 or so each year.

Sims was not able to realize all his plans. He had been able to obtain two rear admirals for the staff, but one of them, C. S. Williams, took up the duties of chief of staff, while the other, A. H. Robertson, served only a short time as head of the tactics department before he had to succeed Williams who had been ordered back to the fleet. Several civilians were also obtained. Dr. Edwin Wiley was appointed librarian, and Tracy B. Kitteridge, a reserve lieutenant formerly with the Hoover Relief Commission, was appointed archivist. Professor George Grafton Wilson of Harvard continued to be the college's professor of international law and J. M. Scammell became the technical assistant in the tactics department. The civilian position envisaged for the strategy department, however, was not filled.

The College Reopens

Opening day arrived on 1 July 1919. Many officers from the Training Station, from Fort Adams, and from the Atlantic Fleet vessels present in the harbor joined the staff and students of the Naval War College in the gymnasium of Training Station Barracks B. Among the 31 student officers were two army officers, two marines, a Navy doctor, and a naval constructor. Captain Joel R. P. Pringle, a future president of the college, and Captain Joseph K. Taussig, a future chief of staff of the college, were among their numbers, as well as Sims' close friends and former London colleagues, Commander J. V. Babcock and Captain Hutch I. Cone. The opening ceremony was simple, consisting of an address by Sims in which he explained his views of the college's purpose, its relation to the Navy Department and to the fleet. "You will thus recognize," Sims told his audience,

> . . . this is not really a college. Perhaps it would have been better if it had never been so designated, for in reality this assemblage is nothing but a board of practical fleet officers brought here to discuss and decide the extremely important question of how we would best conduct naval war under the various conditions that may arise.

Taking his point further, Sims stressed that "our work is wholly practical, because we base our conclusions upon our own experience and upon that of those who have gone before us; and that therefore there can be nothing theoretical about the principles of fighting that we decide to be the correct ones . . . . "[10]

The employment of the applicatory system by W. L. Rodgers and "The introduction of the long course marked the most radical and progressive step in the development of the college that has ever taken place . . . with a continuing student body in which individual work and development was a prominent object," Sims believed.[11]

In his view the college existed solely to develop and to teach certain general principles. He did not propose to establish a code or rules by which naval warfare could be conducted. Rather, he believed, through training, students could acquire a habit of mind which applied the basic principles "logically, correctly, and rapidly to each situation that may arise." The principles that Sims had in mind were the three cardinal points of the applicatory system:

1. A clear conception of the *mission* to be attained.

2. An accurate and logical *estimate of the situation,* which involved a mustering of all information available, and a discussion of its bearing upon the situation under consideration.

3. A *decision* that was the logical result of the *mission* and the *estimate.*

It was a strict and practical method of problem solving, which correlated ends with means and objectives and directed attention to operational and tactical issues. It did not attempt an analysis of the assumptions behind the objectives.

At the same time, Sims denied that the Naval War College "is, or should be, the planmaking branch of the Navy." Undoubtedly its staff and students were capable of doing this if there had been more of them and if they were supplied with the data not readily available outside of Washington. In light of those limitations, Sims argued that such a planning section should not be located at the War College. Moreover, planning would detract significantly from the ability of the staff to carry out its teaching functions. "While we cannot supply strategic plans required by the Navy Department," Sims pointed out, "we hope to supply officers who can formulate such plans." Similarly, while the College was unable to provide tactical plans for the wide variety of circumstances the fleet would meet, "if the college course proves successful it will supply commanders-in-chief and fleet staff officers competent to prepare and carry out such plans." Planning work, Sims emphasized, would force the college to cease teaching to supply plans instead of supplying trained officers.

Correspondingly, Sims believed that as the college stressed principles and made no claim to show what should be done in any particular situation, it should never pass judgment upon actual operational decisions made by the U.S. Navy in tactics or in strategy. To do this would put the College in a controversial position, creating antagonism between it and the rest of the Navy. "If the college is to succeed in teaching the art of war to willing pupils," Sims concluded, "it must at all times work in complete harmony with the service."[12] To do this, Sims organized the college to concentrate on promoting a common methodology in the officer corps for dealing with the practical aspects of naval planning.

The Reorganized College

Under Sims' tutelage the college was organized into four major departments: command, strategy, tactics, and the correspondence department. In addition, there was a fifth department for administration.

The command department had cognizance of such matters as plan making, estimate of the situation, and formulation of orders; that is, the various elements of the applicatory system as developed in the years immediately before World War I. It also included doctrine, dissemination of information, art of command, discipline, organization, administration, and leadership. Nominally headed by the War

College chief of staff, the command department was effectively directed by Captain Dudley W. Knox.

The strategy department was concerned with policy, strategy, logistics, chart maneuvers, and international law. The major focus of the work was on war gaming where the problems under consideration were tailored to consider actual geographic areas with opposing forces from fleets of existing nations which could conceivably be a possible enemy of the United States. This focus required rules and problems that stressed current conditions and the practical experiences of the 1914-18 war rather than abstract ideas. The requirement for students to write theses, which had been introduced for the long course in 1912, was maintained and expanded by adding a topic on command. But instead of making them abstract considerations, Sims directed that they be devoted to specific, concrete subjects. A thesis on policy was required in the strategy department; so as to make it conform to the new emphasis, the students were told to examine U.S. policy in the Far East, a subject which continued to be a major interest for many years.

In dealing with strategic war games, free discussion of every problem was an essential characteristic, but a staff solution was also presented along with a critique by staff members of the student solutions. Through this approach, staff members were able to perform more effectively as teachers while also encouraging free and general discussion. In addition, discussion was aided by showing game moves on slides immediately after the game was completed. This was a vast improvement over the old, slow method of preparing blueprints for each move. Finally, the strategic war game was improved by significantly increasing the numbers of ships involved in the games. Submarines and aircraft were added, using more careful definitions in defining the missions of various types of ships.[13]

The tactics department was modified to respond to the same changes. The development of aircraft and submarines as well as a clearer definition of types and classes of ships required a change in the way tactics was taught at the college. New tactical war games were developed to include submarines and aircraft which had to be formed and maneuvered in accordance with fleet standing orders. A tactics department staff member, Captain Luke McNamee, was responsible for rewriting all the instruction pamphlets used in tactics. In undertaking this task, McNamee attempted to reflect the latest fleet practice as well as the experience of the war. Under his direction, Commander J. T. G. Stapler provided the college's first text on "Submarines and Submarine Operations" and Admiral Sims' aide, Lieutenant Commander W. A. Edwards, prepared a similar compilation for aviation. One important wartime idea that was developed further in war gaming at Newport was the idea of the aircraft carrier. In December 1920, Sims told the General Board during its consideration of converting scout cruisers, aircraft carriers were in use on the gameboard at the War College, and problems in which they were used showed their efficiency in scouting to be such as to refute the statement that "experimental work is in reality the main argument for the conversion of the scout cruisers," as assumed by the General Board.

> The more urgent argument is that the fleet needs aircraft carriers, and that these converted cruisers will supply them in much less time than we can hope to get the larger vessels. But the principal argument in favor of the proposition is that converting two of the ten scouts to aircraft carriers will very materially increase (1) the areas the ten vessels can cover in scouting; (2) the efficiency of the group as a scouting line—as an information getter; and (3) the efficiency of the group as a fighting force, particularly if opposed by vessels of greater individual gunpower than the unconverted scouts.[14]

In the tactical war games the staff did not submit a solution as it did in strategy, but the head of the tactics department critiqued the maneuvers, called attention to various issues, and encouraged discussion. The general thrust of the game, however, was to coordinate the students' ideas and to indoctrinate them in methods which could be applied to fleet practice.[15]

Sims sought to strengthen the library by increasing its collection and improving its staff. Writing to the Assistant Secretary of the Navy, he declared that the college librarian should be

> a man who combines the expert knowledge of library science, a special knowledge of the literature, history and techniques of naval and military science, of international law, and, in addition, must be capable of translating material on these subjects from French, German, Spanish, Italian and other modern languages.[16]

To meet these increased demands, the library staff was increased and small collections of books in great demand were placed in convenient locations throughout the college. In 1920 alone, the collection grew by 7,000 to a total of almost 45,000 items. During that same period, 5,000 items were borrowed, averaging 83 volumes per student per year. Not surprisingly, naval science, history, political science, and international law were most popular, but a significant amount of fiction was also borrowed.[17]

The correspondence course was also emphasized by Sims as the best means to get the college's work to the fleet. In the first five years of its existence, 828 officers enrolled and a small number continued to submit work during the war. By 1919, however, only 30 officers had completed the entire course by correspondence. Sims introduced a stronger system to follow up students' work and to monitor their progress.

By 1920, the rejuvenated Naval War College had reached a level such that Secretary Daniels could write in his annual report, "I hope to see the time when every officer will be able to take advantage of the courses offered by the War College, and it will be as much a part of preparation for high command as is the course at the Naval Academy for commissioned rank."[18]

While the Secretary lauded the College, his 1920 report also raised an old issue recommending that the college was better situated in Washington than in Newport. This time the rationale was slightly different. Daniels stressed that the 1914-1918 war had taught the great need for close cooperation between the Army and Navy. Now that the Army War College was established in Washington, "the best" reason to move the Naval War College to Washington was to develop close cooperation between the two colleges as well as to bring the Naval War College in closer touch with the Navy Department and the Naval Academy. In mid-December 1920, a small notice buried in the middle of the *New York Times* reported that Daniels was drafting a bill for Congress to transfer the Naval War College to the District of Columbia where it would be established in a special building as a naval war memorial.[19]

Sims protested against the renewed effort to move the college, and after the inauguration of Warren G. Harding in March 1921, the issue died, not to be raised again. In some respects, Daniels threat to move the college was only an incident in the wider dispute that arose between Sims and Daniels in 1919 and 1920.

The Sims-Daniels Controversy

Sims' controversy with Daniels, which quickly turned bitter, arose from questions involving decorations awarded for wartime service. Prior to World War I no decoration other than the Congressional Medal of Honor and campaign ribbons were authorized. In early 1919, Congress made provision for awarding the Distinguished Service Medal and the Navy Cross. Commanding officers were authorized to recommend awards, and Daniels established a board to review these recommendations. Its chairman was Rear Admiral Austin M. Knight, Sims' predecessor as president of the Naval War College. However, Daniels abolished the board before it had completed its work.

In December 1919, Daniels published his annual report as Secretary and appended his own list of "Medals of Honor, Distinguished Service Medals, and Navy Crosses Awarded." The list reflected significant changes in the recommendations of both the respective commanders and those that the Knight Board had made. Daniels' list was based solely upon his judgment and he awarded higher decorations to some men and lower ones to others.

Sims took great exception to Daniels' handling of this matter for a number of reasons. First, he believed a commanding officer was in the best position to judge the merits of each case. Second, he disagreed with Daniels' view that sea duty was more important than staff duty ashore. Third, the DSM had been awarded to many commanding officers who had lost their ships. Fourth, and perhaps most important of all, Daniels had failed to provide any guidance or clear Navy Department policy upon which recommendations could be made.[20]

The immediate upshot was that Sims refused to accept the DSM awarded to him, and he hoped that other officers would spontaneously refuse their decorations in protest over what he saw as a grave injustice, destructive of good morale. As a result, the Senate Naval Affairs Committee commenced an investigation into the controversy and Sims became a star witness.

At one session in January 1920, Sims was told that if he had any further correspondence with Daniels about the "question of awards and their effect on the morale of the service," the committee would receive it. Sims then produced and read a lengthy letter he had written to Daniels about "Certain Naval Lessons of the Great War." The substance of this letter had already been leaked to the press. The *Washington Post* a few days before described it as "a frank and fearless exposé of the hopeless story of maladministration, mistakes, and blunders into which the American Navy has fallen as a result of Mr. Daniels' policies."[21]

This letter was a bombshell. It had the effect Sims intended: a widening of the committee's inquiry into the preparations of the Navy for war and its conduct of the war. Sims returned to Newport where he prepared for the forthcoming March hearings. Returning to Washington, he took with him his closest associates, Captain Hutch I. Cone, Commander J. V. Babcock, and Captain Dudley W. Knox, as well as Captain Joseph K. Taussig, and the college archivist, Tracy B. Kittredge.

Sims was aware that his letter would produce an uproar. Nevertheless, he persisted in his testimony because he was convinced that until the Navy could be properly organized and run it would not operate effectively under all conditions. A better reorganization of the Navy, not a personal vendetta against Daniels, was Sims' motive. Moreover, he was being entirely consistent with what he had done before in a career marked by his insistence that the Navy organize itself and operate as a modern professional fighting force.

In order to justify a reorganization of the Navy, Sims had to prove that in 1917 it was unprepared for war and that it was slow to act in the first five or six months of hostilities. He marshaled and presented convincing evidence that in April 1917 the material condition of the Navy was not in shape for war; that personnel readiness in terms of numbers and training was unsatisfactory; that war plans and overall strategic planning were inadequate; and that the Navy Department failed to grasp the nature of the sea war within the first few months of American participation.[22]

Part of the problem, especially in discretionary areas, could not be attributed to Daniels alone. It lay with the policies of the Wilson Administration, which precluded prudent moves such as systematically placing existing ships on some kind of wartime footing and organizing flotillas of destroyers and other potential antisubmarine ships and craft because such preparations were warlike and might be considered overt acts by the Germans.[23]

To make his case effective and to convince not only the Senate Committee but ultimately influential segments of public opinion, Sims had to overcome several obstacles. The chief one was partisan politics. It was an election year. Wilson and his supporters, of whom Daniels was one of the staunchest, had recently suffered a humiliating defeat in the Senate over the peace.

Also, Sims was faced with demonstrating that a navy which had been on the victor's side had failed to do what it should have done. It was an insurmountable task to prove to the public that it had been successful despite the Navy Department's failure to prepare properly for war or to conduct it more efficiently.

The hearings degenerated into a game of partisan politics, thick with slander. Sims' opponents painted him as a commander with a grievance and an Anglophile who loved Britain more than America. The serious professional issue which Sims had in mind was ignored as Daniels won support for the traditional, populist view that capable forces could always be effectively mobilized whenever war came.[24]

With the controversy past after a new administration came to power on 4 March 1921, the Naval War College continued its development unscathed. The college, however, remained clearly identified with Sims' viewpoint. On the eve of Sims' retirement in 1922, the admiral was feted by War College students at a dinner in Newport's Clambake Club. Spirits ran high that evening as the well-wishers sang irreverent parodies of popular songs. The chorus of one in particular, rang through the rafters rhyming Daniels' first name with Sims' wartime telegraphic address:

Away, away with Josephus
He's the one that made the muss,
His brand of bull don't go with us,
For we are strong for Simsadus.[25]

On 14 October 1922, Sims retired from active duty in the U.S. Navy after 42 years of service. He read his orders and saluted, transferring command to his chief of staff who would administer the college until the arrival of Rear Admiral C. S. Williams. Sims shook hands with each of the officers on the college staff, and walked down the hill, across Dewey Field, between two rows of recruits from the Training Station. When he reached the waterfront landing, he boarded his barge for the trip to Government Landing in Newport. As he was piped aboard, a 13 gun salute rang out. Moments later, his two-star flag was struck from the mizzen of the old frigate *Constellation*, moored alongside the quay at Coasters Harbor Island. The Sims years were over, but the spirit lived on for many more years in the course of study he had devised for the Naval War College.

The Course, 1919-1927

The college curriculum and organization changed little in the following years. Each department scheduled lectures on the matters under its cognizance and provided a required reading list for the students. In addition, a recommended reading list was an expansion of the required list. The books on these extensive lists were well chosen and included not only the standard works in the area but also classics of military history and analysis. One student, Commander Harold R. Stark, compiled for his colleagues a 179-page digest of the 113 books on the policy, command, strategy, and tactics reading lists. It was printed and distributed to students as an intelligent and useful encapsulation of the principal works that an educated naval officer at that time should read.[26]

The lectures covered a wide variety of topics, some of which were chosen on the basis of general interest and others because they provided necessary professional information. New developments in warfare were not neglected.

In addition to the instruction provided by lectures and the self-instruction derived from reading widely and in depth, the students were required to write a thesis for each department. The purpose of this exercise was to force each student to come to grips with the relevant materials and to set them forth in a logical and coherent manner. Most papers were approximately 50 typewritten pages in length, but frequently they extended to almost 100 pages. Commander Chester W. Nimitz expressed the typical concerns of the time in his paper on policy. Nimitz noted the climatic and geographical factors and their influence on policy. Like many, he worried about the effect of racial heterogeneity in the United States and its inhibiting effect on the formulation of a coherent national policy that would enjoy wide, popular support. Nimitz thought immigration ought to be suspended and an intensive campaign of education for newer citizens be undertaken. Immigration policy was hardly a professional problem for a naval officer and Nimitz's policy essay was an ordinary piece of work, but his thesis on naval tactics properly reflected his professional brilliance. The duty of a naval tactician is "to plan the employment of available forces in battle against any opponent, and to ensure that the utmost strength is developed at the crucial time and at the decisive point," Nimitz wrote.

> To accomplish this task the tactician has available not only such experience as he can bring to bear on the problem but, in addition, he can draw on the lessons to be learned from the innumerable examples of failure and the comparatively few instances of decisive victory recorded in history. A study of the mistakes of the past will usually yield a better harvest than a study of the successes. In most instances, it has been the errors of the vanquished rather than the brilliant tactics of the victor that brought success to the latter.[27]

Another student, Captain Thomas C. Hart, wrote that militaristic ideas and institutions were losing ground in Japan and that "probably many Japanese were forsaking their teaching that war pays."

Hart's thesis on tactics was a model statement of the subject, reflecting mature consideration and a wide practical experience at sea. Several men had deduced the principles of war from a study of history, and along broad lines they were in agreement, Hart wrote,

> Knowing those principles and enunciating them is an easy task for many men. It is in the *application* of principles that the difficulties lie—and wherein the dozen or so of really great leaders have excelled all others. They have frequently succeeded by entirely *new* applications—have thus surprised. Able to estimate the attendant conditions better than others, they have often subordinated theory and rules to the needs of the moment and have even discarded them. In so doing, those leaders have seemed to disregard principles. But in all cases having that appearance it has rarely, if at all, been violation of fundamental principle but rather new *application* which surprised by diverging from the stereotyped methods that inferior men had come to regard as thoroughly established *principles*. In that same way will the "great" leader of the future surprise his enemy.[28]

In 1923 fellow students and future admirals such as Hart, Nimitz, and Stark all considered the same problem. They each wrote a three-part tactics paper which examined a naval war against Britain, a war against Japan, and an examination of the Battle of Jutland. As the college viewed the situation, future wars in the Atlantic and the Pacific would be different. In the Atlantic "the War College conception of the naval battle of the future . . . follows closely the general plan employed by both fleets in the Battle of Jutland."[29] Future war in the Pacific, however, would be a slow battle of attrition and logistics. Nimitz's reflection on his War College year, written in response to a request from college president Charles Melson in 1963, has been often quoted:

> The enemy of our games was always Japan, and the courses were so thorough that, after the start of World War II, nothing that happened in the Pacific was strange or unexpected. Each student was required to plan logistic support for an advance across the Pacific, and we were well prepared for the logistic efforts required to support the operations of the war.[30]

It was a kind and generous statement by an old graduate, but what he actually wrote in 1923, trying to analyze a future war, is more interesting:

> To bring such a war to a successful conclusion Blue must either destroy Orange military and naval forces or effect a complete isolation of Orange country by cutting all communication with the outside world. It is quite possible that Orange resistance will cease when isolation is complete and before steps to reduce military strength on Orange soil are necessary. In either case the operations imposed upon Blue will require the Blue Fleet to advance westward with an enormous train, in order to be prepared to seize and establish bases en route . . . The possession by Orange of numerous bases in the western Pacific will give to her fleet a maximum of mobility while the lack of such bases imposes upon Blue the necessity of refuelling en route at sea, or of seizing a base from Orange for this purpose, in order to maintain even a limited degree of mobility.[31]

From 1921, most games involved Blue versus Orange forces in the Pacific, although often other forces were considered, namely those of Britain and Germany.[32] The purpose behind the Blue-Orange conflict was for Blue to impose its will on Orange, disrupting its economic life and for the Navy "to gain and to exercise command of the sea, and to operate offensively against Orange.[33] These studies were important reflections on American thinking about a future war with Japan at a time when the U.S. Navy still had little experience in the Pacific. In the summer of 1925, the Battle Fleet, augmented by a division of new cruisers from the Scouting Fleet, made a six-week cruise to Australia and New Zealand; it was the first such deployment to the Antipodes since the Great White Fleet of 1908.

One historian has described these war games against Orange as "So intense . . . so hypnotic was the ritual rehearsal, repeated in unnumbered war games at Newport, that historical reality flowed, naturally, effortlessly, necessarily."[34] In more stereotyped style, Secretary of the Navy Curtis Wilbur wrote in 1925, "The Naval War College tests *strategic policies* of the department by making them the basis for problems which are worked out and played on the gameboard."[35] In the next 15 years naval weapons changed rapidly and so did tactics; but the focus on Orange did not change.

While naval men were generally enthusiastic about the approach, some Marine officers were not. Holland M. Smith was a member of the first class to convene after the war. He found that Sims was too narrowly naval in his outlook and Smith thought it

> bogged down in obsolescence. The lessons learned from World War I appeared to point backward instead of forward and the mass of pertinent timely information furnished by the war just concluded had been ignored in favor of long established principles which a novice could see would never apply to future problems.[36]

While Smith saw Sims as brilliant within his own particular field he considered Sims hidebound in his opposition to the changes needed in the Navy to develop amphibious warfare.

By a curious coincidence, as this intense interest in a possible war with Japan was being created in the 1920s, the College received a visit from some distinguished Japanese naval officers. On 13 February 1924, the Japanese naval attaché and his assistant arrived with the director of training for the Japanese Navy, Vice Admiral K. Ide, and his aide, Captain Isoruku Yamamoto, the man who would insist on the Pearl Harbor attack nearly 18 years later.

The Junior Course Established

In 1923, one of the innovations that Sims had hoped to establish finally became reality. As far back as 1919, Secretary Daniels had questioned both the Naval Postgraduate School and the Naval War College on their proposed budgets. In response to these questions, the Chief of the Bureau of Navigation decided that more systematic guidance was needed in planning for officer education in the future. He therefore ordered Captain Ernest J. King, Head of the Postgraduate School, Commander Dudley W. Knox of the Naval War College, and Commander William S. Pye, Executive Officer of USS *Pennsylvania*, to study the subject and to recommend a policy for advanced naval education. In the next nine months these three men met periodically and, in the summer of 1920, they submitted a 28 page report, charting the education of officers through their service careers. As with many reports submitted to the Department, this one was approved but not fully implemented. In all probability it would have been completely forgotten except that King submitted it to the Naval Institute and it was published in the *Proceedings* for August 1920.

The three members of the board believed strongly that a naval officer needed to have a working knowledge of a wide range of arts, sciences, and technical developments, which were each continuously developing. It was impossible, they believed, to equip an officer at the outset of his career with all the knowledge he would need as he advanced through his service. The board concluded that naval officers should be given periods of education at recurring periods in their career, each period building on the previous one and appropriate to the duties an officer would expect to meet at the next phase in his career. Knox, Pye, and King identified four phases in a naval officer's career, each of which should be preceded by a course that they outlined. As they outlined the plan, the Naval Academy prepared an officer for the first phase as a division officer, but a general line course was needed to prepare for the second phase as a department head. Similarly, a junior War College course was needed to prepare for command of a single ship, and a senior War College course was appropriate to prepare for flag rank.[37] The Knox-Pye-King Board, as it was known, not only incorporated Sims' ideas on progressive education represented by Knox, but suggested paralleling the Army course at Fort Leavenworth, Kansas. Graduation from this Army Command and General Staff course had by this time become a prerequisite for further advancement in the peacetime army. The footnote to the Board's published report echoed a typical reaction to suggestions for improving officer education:

> This report is published by permission of the Navy Department for the information of the service. The report of the Board has been approved, but the shortage of officers will not permit the recommendations to be carried into effect at present.[38]

Two years later, however, in December 1922, Assistant Secretary of the Navy Theodore Roosevelt, Jr. convened a conference to consider the entire War College effort. Besides Rear Admiral C. S. Williams as college president, the conferees included the Chief of Naval Operations, the Fleet Commander-in-Chief, the Superintendent of the Naval Academy, the Chief of the Bureau of Navigation, and the Commandant of the Marine Corps. On his return to Newport after the meeting, Williams believed that the battle for a junior course had been won, and directed the staff to prepare its implementation.

On 6 March 1923, Secretary of the Navy Edwin Denby issued General Order 98, which in essence provided what the college needed to go ahead. Included was the requirement that students assigned must have "special aptitude." The initial junior class opened in the summer of 1923 under the direction of Captain William McDowell. There were 22 officers, who had been commissioned between 1907 and 1915. The Department announced a goal of 60 officers per class, but it was never attained. In 1929 there were 52 officers, the largest group until the 1950s when the title changed from Junior Course to the Command and Staff Course. Physical facilities of the college were severely strained, but by the time funds for new facilities were approved in the 1930s, the junior class had grown smaller because of the requirements of the expanding fleet for more officers. The Bureau never agreed to the concept of progressive education, and the curriculum of the new course gradually paralleled the existing senior course, with both classes participating in some of the same operations problems and gameboard work. Both groups attended the lectures. By the beginning of World War II, only a few officers had attended both junior and senior courses.

Pratt Reorganizes College Administration

In September 1925, Rear Admiral William Veazie Pratt relieved C. S. Williams as college president. A highly regarded officer, Pratt felt the need to revitalize the college and to assure that it remained responsive to change within the Navy. A few months after his arrival in Newport, Pratt saw that the college was not achieving the goals he felt it should achieve. The statement of the college mission in Secretary Wilbur's report for 1925 said, "The mission of the Naval War College is to furnish a medium whereby naval officers in peacetime may study the conduct of naval warfare and the art of command in relation thereto." Pratt objected, "That most important work, the conduct of joint operations in a grand campaign of war" was not even mentioned. Furthermore, he said, "The mission of the Navy is not only how to conduct efficient war in time of war, but in time of peace the Navy must know how to keep the peace."[39] To implement his ideas, during his second year in Newport, Pratt restructured the War College staff to parallel more closely the organization of the General Staff of the Army and the Office of Naval Operations.

Pratt believed that a new arrangement would repair the unnatural emphasis that he believed had been created by dividing strategy and tactics into two separate departments. In his view, strategy and tactics were inseparable. Moreover, Pratt was convinced that future naval operations would fail unless naval leaders viewed the totality of modern warfare. Strategy and tactics should "merge together under the head of operations," Pratt said, because

> operations, even purely naval, cannot hope to succeed unless careful attention is paid to materiel, personnel, and the thousand detailed difficulties attendant upon war.[40]

Pratt concluded that there were six principal elements in warfare: (1) personnel, materiel and supply; (2) information; (3) operations; (4) policy; (5) inspection; and (6) finance.

Heretofore, the college had stressed the operations segment and paid little attention to the other equally important areas. In order to rectify this and to make the college curriculum a more appropriate preparation for practical staff duty in Washington, Pratt reorganized academic instruction into four departments and designated by letters:

(A) Logistics.
(B) Information.
(C) Operations.
(D) Policy and Command.

Under this scheme, the logistics department would deal with issues of material, personnel, supply, transport, and relative priorities. The information department would deal with the library, intelligence and archives. Operations would teach war planning, estimate of the situation, order forms, military and naval operations, and the policy and command department would deal with the correspondence course, the lecture courses, policy, international law, and foreign relations.[41]

With the changes, Pratt believed he had brought the college into closer resonance with both the development of the office of the Chief of Naval Operations and the way in which the U.S. Army was thinking. Joint Army-Navy operations would be extremely important in the future, and Pratt believed it was important to further the similarity of professional thinking. "After all, there is no difference in principle," he wrote, "between naval and military strategy and tactics, though there are essential differences in movement and time."[42] While Pratt stressed the similarity in principles he also saw that one area which required greater emphasis for naval education was the study of international relations. Pratt believed that the Army only became involved in foreign affairs after a war was declared. The Navy, however, was constantly involved in international relations in both peace and war. "The Navy is the external buffer between our federal state and other sovereign states," he declared.[43] With this in mind, Pratt substantially increased the number of lectures that students heard on topics relating to current affairs.

Joint Exercise, 1927

Complementing Pratt's efforts in the Naval War College's classrooms, the U.S. Navy participated in the largest joint Army-Navy exercise which had been staged up to that time. In May 1927, just as Pratt's war college presidency was coming to an end, the joint exercise took place off the coast of southern New England. The Battle Fleet had come east to the Caribbean and joined the Scouting Fleet for their annual Fleet Problem. In the spring of 1927, Fleet Problem VII had a number of phases. In its first stage, Blue forces were sent to establish a base of operations against Black in the West Indies and to exercise in the wartime operation that would be required to support a large, expeditionary force at Panama. In the second stage, a Blue fleet attempted to rendezvous from dispersed bases in the West Indies and to concentrate its forces while threatened by a Red fleet with heavier guns, but fewer ships. Third, enroute from the Caribbean to New York, the fleet exercised its torpedo tactics. In early May, after the entire fleet had enjoyed leave and liberty in New York City, the final phase of Fleet Problem VII was the week-long, joint Army-Navy exercise between Blue and Black, conducted this time near the entrance to Narragansett Bay. Blue forces included army units in the New England area, units of the Scouting Fleet, and some Marine aircraft flown up from Quantico and based at Newport Airport, then located in the Wanumetonomy area of Middletown, as defending fighters. Black forces consisted of the Battle Fleet, including the carrier *Langley* ("the Covered Wagon") and its two squadrons of planes. Black attempted to land an expeditionary force somewhere between Cape Cod and Long Island. Newport was the headquarters for the defending forces as well as for the umpires of the war games.

There was considerable press interest, and a war correspondents' center was set up at Fort Adams with regular briefings on the progress of "the war." There were air and surface contacts at sea, a simulated bombardment of Newport by the Black battleline of nine ships, and a simulated landing near Watch Hill, R.I., which the umpires ruled a failure. While these exercises were being carried out by the fleet, War College students played a parallel game on the college's gameboard and then joined the fleet officers for the discussion. On May 21, the same day that Charles Lindbergh flew solo across the Atlantic, the entire fleet entered Newport for a week's visit during which time the Commander in Chief, Admiral Charles F. Hughes, presided over the critique of the exercise at the Naval War College. For the first time since 1901, the main body of the fleet and the Naval War College were directly involved in working together on an exercise. The class of 1927 heard the exercise discussed by umpires and opposing commanders. They could see that the views of Rear Admiral Joseph M. Reeves, recently head of the tactics department at the college, were correct when he told Pratt a few months before the exercise,

> I have long felt that one of our weakest spots was in the Plans Division of Naval Operations because of its wholly inadequate personnel. I felt this so keenly while I was at the War College as to be apprehensive that in a large overseas operation of the amphibious nature, we would find the Army plans forced upon us because of lack of any adequate plans of our own.[44]

From this point onward, amphibious warfare assumed an increasingly important role in college studies at the same time that the Fleet Marine Force was gradually evolving during the 1930s.[45] At the same time, Pratt's emphasis on joint operations in the college curriculum developed further the connection with the Army War College, emphasizing further the development of the joint war games between the two colleges.

Emphasis on Logistics

While joint operations had an important place in Pratt's thinking, it was no accident that in the college's reorganization, a department was devoted to logistics. The subject was not new to the college; visiting lecturers had dealt with the subject since the 1890s and Mahan had written that "logistics is as vital to military success as daily food is to daily work."[46]

In 1911, Commander C. T. Vogelgesang told college students, "Logistics comprehends all the operations outside the field of battle and which lead up to it—it regulates the execution of those movements which in combination become the function of strategy."[47] Pratt had been on the staff with Vogelgesang at that time and he undoubtedly heard his lecture. A few years later, World War I mobilization showed the importance and complexity of logistics to the nation. The Army had recognized this by establishing the Army Industrial College in 1923, but within military education, the Industrial College was viewed as something on a lower plane than a War College course. In the Navy as well, there was a widespread view that logistics was a problem for staff corps specialists, not an issue of great concern to line officers. Pratt argued against this line of thinking and stressed the importance of logistics in studying the whole subject of warfare. By creating a separate department for logistics, Pratt raised that area of concern to equal status with operations, plans, and intelligence.

The new logistics department had four officers, but not a single naval line officer among them. It was headed by Captain R. E. Bakenhus, CEC, assisted by Colonel Frank E. Evans, USMC; Captain A. H. Van Keuren, CEC, and Lieutenant Colonel Walter A. Reed, U.S. Army.

In its first studies, the logistics department worked on developing plans for a joint overseas expedition, which was later carried out by a Navy and Marine Corps landing force on the north side of Hawaii. As a result of this work and in preparations for the Joint Army-Navy exercise on the southern New England coast in 1927, the logistics department developed a rational system of designating transport capacities and troop loads. Since much of the college's work was devoted to the problem of a fighting fleet opposing an enemy's fighting fleet, the logistics department devoted its primary attention to the control of trade routes over the ocean, the object for which the fleets were fighting.[48]

The academic year 1926-1927 saw the formal implementation of Pratt's concepts into the college curriculum. These changes emphasized and expanded upon the vision which Sims had charted in 1919. More than ever, the college was an institution for the practical training of officers in fleet and staff positions. While Sims had emphasized the fleet aspect, Pratt had recognized the rapid growth of staff and planning positions, both ashore and afloat, and he attempted to meet the need for proper training in these new areas. By the end of Pratt's term as president of the Naval War College, he had established firmly the two courses, senior and junior, envisaged by Sims and recommended by the Knox-Pye-King Board. The two courses were closely related, and during the latter part of the academic year, the junior course students assisted the senior students in both operations problems and committee work. Similarly, the correspondence course was related to the work of the resident students as preparation for the junior course.[49] These courses related to the three phases that Pratt saw in a naval officer's career: preparatory, executive, and command. Each was paralleled by a course at the Naval War College. In the highest phase, Pratt told the graduating class in 1927, "Through careful reading, training, experience, and thought, you should have arrived at a position where your services become invaluable to the government on account of the good and sound advice which you are able to give." In the exercise of supreme command, "character and knowledge display themselves in breadth of vision, determination, undeviating purpose when once a decision has been thoughtfully arrived at, unselfishness, simplicity, knowledge of men and of fundamental principles, based upon a background of sound practical experience."[50] In this, the Naval War College played an important role as a place to learn and reflect on the established, fundamental principles of warfare.

Notes

1. E. E. Morison, *Admiral Sims and the Modern American Navy* (Boston: Houghton Mifflin, 1942), pp. 333-34, 466-469. Quote from p. 467. The Title Commander in Chief U.S. Fleet, was in use during the first half of 1919. It was then dropped and not revived until 1921.

2. Ibid., pp. 467-68.

3. This and the following paragraphs with their quotations are taken from W. S. Sims to Secretary of the Navy, 15 January 1919, with endorsement of W. S. Benson, 23 January 1919. NWC Library, typescript, "History of the Naval War College to 1937," pp. 88-99.

4. Ibid., p. 97.

5. Ibid., p. 98.

6. "Welcomed in Washington; Navy Department Heads at Station to Greet Sims." *The New York Times*, 9 April 1919, p. 10:7.

7. Morison, *Sims*, p. 432.

8. *Newport Daily News*, 12 April 1919.

9. Gerald J. Kennedy, "United States Naval War College 1919-1941: An Institutional Response to Naval Preparedness," unpublished typescript, 1974, Naval War College Advanced Research Project.

10. NWC Archives, RG16: Opening Address. W. S. Sims, 1 July 1919.

11. NWC Archives, RG2, Box 37, File A-12: Sims to SECNAV, 5 Jan 1921.

12. Sims "Opening Address," op. cit.

13. "History of the Naval War College to 1937," pp. 105-06.

14. Norman Friedman, *U.S. Aircraft Carriers* (Annapolis, Naval Institute Press, 1981), p. 38. See also pp. 7, 33, 40, 57, 81, 84.

15. "History of the Naval War College to 1937," p. 107.

16. Sims to T. Roosevelt, Jr., 27 August 1921. Quoted in G. J. Kennedy, op. cit., pp. 33-34, fn 25.

17. "History of the Naval War College to 1937," p. 115.

18. Ibid., p. 115.

19. Daniels to Draft Naval College Bill," *New York Times*, 15 December 1920, p. 14:7.

20. E. E. Morison, *Admiral Sims*, p. 436.

21. Joseph Morrison, *Josephus Daniels, The Small d Democrat* Chapel Hill: University of North Carolina Press, 1966), p. 124.

22. Tracy B. Kittridge, *Naval Lessons of the Great War* (Garden City, N.Y.: Doubleday, 1921), p. 76.

23. Harold Sprout and Margaret Sprout, *The Rise of American Naval Power* (Princeton: Princeton University Press, 1967), p. 357.

24. E. E. Morison, *Admiral Sims*, pp. 455, 458.

25. NWC Archives, RG27: Presidents File: Sims. The chorus is to the tune of "Away, Away with Sword and Drum," widely known from Naval Academy days.

26. NWC Archives, RG17: Staff Studies 1923, H.R. Stark, "Extracts from Books Read in Connection with War College Reading Courses: Policy, Command, Strategy, and Tactics," arranged alphabetically by author, two volumes.

27. C. W. Nimitz, "Naval Tactics," *Naval War College Review*, November-December 1983, p. 9. Excerpt from 1923 thesis in NWC Archives, RG12.

28. NWC Archives, RG12: student theses, T. C. Hart, 1923.

29. NWC Archives, RG15 Staff Presentation, 1922: Harris Laning, "The Tactics Department of the War College and the Relations between it and the Fleet."

30. E. B. Potter, *Nimitz*, (Annapolis: Naval Institute Press, 1976), p. 136.

31. Nimitz, op. cit., pp. 12-13.

32. For a detailed list of games, see M. Vlahos, *The Blue Sword* (Newport: Naval War College Press, 1920), pp. 166-178.

33. Ibid., p. 121 quoting War Plan Orange: WPL-8-16.

34. Ibid.

35. Navy Department, *Annual Report . . . 1925*, p. 20.

36. H. M. Smith and Percy Finch, *Coral and Brass* (New York: Scribners, 1949), pp. 47-54.

37. "Instruction and Training of Line Officers," U.S. Naval Institute *Proceedings*, Vol. 36 (1920), p. 1265-1292.

38. Ibid.

39. *NWC Archives* RG28: Pratt, President's File: "The Mission and Work of the Naval War College," April 1926.

40. Ibid., p. 13.

41. Ibid., p. 16.

42. Ibid., p. 17.

43. Ibid., p. 18.

44. NWC Archives, RG2: J.M. Reeves to Pratt, 24 March 1927; quoted in Kennedy, op. cit., pp. 136-37 footnote 9.

45. George S. Pappas, *Prudens Futuri* (Carlisle Barracks: Army War College Alumni Assoc., 1967), p. 118; NWC Archives, RG8 Series I, UNOpP.

46. A. T. Mahan, *Armaments and Arbitration* (Boston: Little Brown, 1912), p. 196.

47. NWC Archives, RG14, C. T. Vogelgesang lecture, 1911: "Logistics: Its Bearing on the Art of War."

48. "Outline History to 1937," p. 181.

49. Ibid., p. 208, president, NWC to CNO, Annual Report, 14 June 1927.

50. NWC Archives, RG16: Graduation Address, W. V. Pratt, "The Three Phases of a Naval Career, Some Reflections of an Older Officer," 27 May 1927, pp. 10, 12.

CHAPTER 6

EDUCATING LEADERS FOR WORLD WAR, 1927-1939

The concept of the Naval War College, which Sims had established in 1919 and Pratt had refined in 1926, formed the basis for War College work in the years leading up to World War II. There were administrative readjustments, course modifications, and gradual expansion during these years, but the philosophy of education and methodology of the War College remained the same. The college limited itself to training officers for practical work in their future assignments; during these years it did not attempt to encourage original research as Luce and Mahan tried to do, or to emulate the practice of a university graduate-level course. The Naval War College stayed within the limits of a professional training institution.

Through William Veazie Pratt, the college achieved the widespread recognition that Sims and others had fought to achieve. Recognized early as a man with a future, Pratt was the only president in the college's first century to become Chief of Naval Operations. The role the college presidency played in Pratt's career and the stress Pratt placed on the Naval War College as he continued to rise to prominence promoted the college's image.

The importance of a War College diploma was symbolized by an incident that occurred during the 1927 graduation ceremony. Secretary of the Navy Curtis Wilbur delivered the address on that May day and personally handed diplomas to each of the 70 graduates. To everyone's surprise, he produced one more diploma which he presented to Pratt. From 1928, Pratt's name in the *Navy Register* was followed by the code number indicating that he was a graduate of the 1927 senior course at the Naval War College. Navy watchers of the day considered Wilbur's surprise diploma an indication of both the importance of the War College course to an officer's career and Pratt's imminent advancement.[1] Two months later, Pratt was promoted to vice admiral and ordered to command Battleship Divisions, Battle Fleet. He was relieved by Rear Admiral J. R. P. Pringle.

Newport—Hometown for the College

Newport, Rhode Island, a city of about 30,000 in the 1920s, was both a summer colony and a navy town—a base for the fleet in the summer and home of the Training Station, War College, and Torpedo Station year round. The summer residents who occupied the magnificent "cottages" along Bellevue Avenue and the Ocean Drive included many of New York's fabled 400. Property taxes from these estates helped the city. Its other sources of income were the Navy and naval families who moved through the community. Up to the early 1930s, the summer visits of the Scouting Fleet brought swarms of bluejackets ashore on liberty, but their pay was small and only a few waterfront areas benefited. During the remainder of the 1930s up to World War II, most of the Navy's ships were in the Pacific, although the fleet came east in 1934 and again in 1939.

The civilian work force at the Torpedo Station, Newport's largest industry, had become long-term residents. The War College classes, of up to 100 officers in the 1930s, provided a lush market for local real estate, particularly for the rental of homes that would otherwise remain vacant during the long New England winter. No systematic housing arrangement for the students existed. In the several Newport naval shore activities, only a few officers or senior enlisted personnel were assigned government quarters.

Early in his tour as president, Admiral Sims had tried to change the situation. He urged the Navy to acquire quarters for student officers, stating that "real estate agents here are fully informed as to every officer's circumstances and his urgency in obtaining a house, and they do not fail to take advantage of such urgency."[2] Sims' efforts failed at this time; bachelor officers and, on occasion, married officers with their families continued to find lodging in the many boarding houses in the Kay Street and Touro Park areas of Newport, where weekly rates for the winter continued at high summer levels.

The War College presidents continued to occupy the commodious President's House on Coasters Harbor Island. As senior officer present for most of the year, the president led naval social life and was also included in many of the summer colony's activities, with honorary memberships at the Newport Reading Room and Spouting Rock Beach.

Few other War College officers were offered or could afford memberships in such exclusive clubs.

The students often appreciated a year of family life devoid of naval responsibilities and sea duty. Noticeably warmer in winter and cooler in summer than nearby Boston, Newport had a pleasant atmosphere that gave students a chance to unwind and enjoy their families.

William F. Halsey, a student in the class of 1933, recalled,

> Few years in a naval officer's life are more pleasant than this one. It is restful because you have no official responsibilities, and it is stimulating because of the instruction, the exchange of ideas, the chance to test your pet theories on the game board, and the opportunity to read up on professional publications.[3]

Another student, Ernest J. King, remembered his War College year as "refreshing and valuable." During that time he had

> in addition to the prescribed course of study, time to browse in the excellent library, to reflect upon ... past and future service, and to consider the world situation, particularly in those aspects that appeared to be leading toward war.[4]

For the wives and families living in rented accommodations in Newport, life was relatively pleasant. The naval medical officer would make house calls, groceries ordered from the commissary would be delivered to the door, and the Navy Exchange laundry made home pickups and deliveries.[5] But there were problems to face. Remembering her Newport year in 1922-1923, Mrs. Catherine Nimitz wrote,

> My memories of the War College are vivid! Three children who took that time to have all the contagious diseases in succession. A coal shortage, a hard winter, a house really meant only for summer, etc. We had to burn soft coal and could only buy one half ton at a time. The house had five bedrooms and was very large. We arrived late in a Transport from Honolulu and had to take what we could get. The situation was laughable *afterwards*, but not at the time. On the day of graduation I awoke to find Chester lying beside me and reading 'The Last Engagement of the Battle of Jutland.' I laughed and congratulated him on getting that battle over. He remarked he knew that battle *by heart*. What memories I have.[6]

Working hours during the six-day work week at the War College were appealing, 0900 to 1530, with afternoons free on Wednesday and Saturday. Although the college courses were demanding and most evenings had to be devoted to writing papers and reading, there was plenty of social activity, particularly on the weekends. In the era of national prohibition, which began in 1919 and did not end until December 1933, and before World War II brought officers' clubs, entertaining was largely confined to individual homes, where small dinner parties were commonly followed by a table or so of bridge.

Domestic help was within reach of commanders and captains in Newport, adding another facet to a pleasant year for the wives. By 1927 duty on the War College staff enhanced a naval career. Students selected for continuation on the staff were generally pleased to stay on in Newport, and a few were lucky enough to move into quarters on the Naval Training Station.

There was little in the way of sports facilities. In 1919, Sims had complained, officers

> are left to their own devices as regards the matter of their physical fitness. Newport, for example, offers little or no encouragement for exercise outside of the few tennis courts .... It is true, of course, quite true that walking facilities exist in the vicinity of Newport, but this is not, to my mind, a successful solution to the problem.[7]

In 1926, several Army officers organized a league for "kitten ball, indoor baseball played out of doors." Played every Wednesday afternoon and Friday after a lecture, weather permitting, the War College teams were pitted against officers from the Training Station and the Torpedo School. As one Army student wrote, the games "were always well played and closely contested but not withstanding the 'youth' of the junior class, 'the old men' of the senior class won the majority of the games." The half-hour games "helped them physically more than any of them really know ... so that when they came back to work at 1:30, they were wide-awake and ready for 'an estimate of the situation' or a lecture."[8]

For the college, the Newport scene of the 1920s and early 1930s would not have been complete without the presence of William Sowden Sims, who, like Stephen Luce 35 years earlier, had settled in Newport until retirement. After moving to Boston for the winter, he continued to spend the pleasant part of the year in Newport. Sims knew his successors well. Williams, Pratt, Pringle, and Laning had all served under him or with him in Europe and at the college. In these years Sims was a familiar figure in the city and at the college, as a parade marshal on Memorial Day, in cap and gown at graduation at St. George's School where he was a trustee, or riding straight and tall on his bicycle, escorting his youngest son Ethan to Miss Weaver's Day School where the Newport Creamery now stands on East Main Road. Sims in this period was truly an elder statesman at the college and on Aquidneck Island.

Curriculum Modifications

In 1927 the United States made another effort to limit the world's navies by convening a conference of major naval powers at Geneva to discuss limiting the construction of ship types not included in the 1922

Washington Treaty. France and Italy refused to participate, and the other three Washington signatories, Great Britain, Japan, and the United States held divergent views on the proper size and gun power for new cruisers. By the time Admiral Pringle relieved Pratt in Newport, the conference had become a stalemate with each country wanting parity of naval force solely in terms of its own strategic requirements.

In Washington, plans were made to push ahead with modernizing battleships and building carriers, cruisers, and destroyers as well as resuming battleship construction in 1931, when the Washington Treaty expired. It was an ambitious program, but an exciting one for the future naval leaders in classes at Newport. Against this background, Pringle's first classes followed a curriculum largely planned by the previous college president, but the next year saw changes. The new classes of 1929 found some of Admiral Pratt's innovations modified. The separate logistics division was now combined with strategy and tactics into an operations department, beginning with the academic year 1928-1929. Pringle, drawing on his previous staff background at the college, believed that tactics flowed from strategy (national, military, and naval) and that operations were based on both strategical and tactical decisions. Although logistics disappeared from the organizational chart, it remained a vital element in each operations study and a part of game board play.

War College student problems continued to focus on the Pacific area with the Blue-Orange games reworked and updated to reflect the modernization of the fleet. Using updated rules and scoring techniques, the senior classes concentrated on the strategic, logistical, and tactical elements for a Blue advance westward across the Pacific, which required taking advance bases to support the fleet. Concurrently, the class also developed Orange plans for thwarting a Blue advance. Throughout the entire academic program, increasing emphasis was placed on Japan as a likely enemy.[9]

The operation department's plan for the senior course attempted to broaden the students' perceptions by concentrating on four areas:

1. Joint Army-Navy attack on and defense of islands.
2. Defense of and attack on lines of communication.
3. Naval defense of a specified area.
4. Fleet use in a naval campaign.

The department envisaged that this concentration would facilitate student effort in thinking about a future war in the Pacific. At the same time, the plan for the junior course was similar but focused at a slightly lower administrative level of fleet organization. Both classes, however, worked together in their studies of World War I battles and campaigns at Jutland, Coronel, Gallipoli, Dogger Bank, and the Falkland Islands.

The experience of World War I continued to play an enormous role in the way officers envisaged the future.

In tactical theses, the battle of Jutland continued to receive the greatest attention. The names of the opposing admirals in that engagement became a litany of basic responses for the students. Examining the battle from the standpoint of tactics, performance of ship types, and leadership, it was only in the area of individual leadership that the student officers revealed any variety in their perception.[10] The student theses on policy stressed the historical development behind policy decisions, but the authors often failed to pursue their analyses thoroughly. In 1926, Commander H. E. Kimmel's thesis on policy followed the usual form, with fundamental definitions of types of policy, factors influencing the formulation of policy, and the relationship of war to policy. In his conclusions, however, Kimmel argued against the general feeling that Japan would be a major opponent for the United States. American policy in the Orient, he believed, was "consistent and sound." The most probable conflict in that region would be between Japan and Russia over Japanese policy in China. Only intensification of Japanese imperialism could bring European nations and the United States into that war.[11] In 1927, Commander Royall E. Ingersoll thought that American foreign policy in the twentieth century had changed from one "purely political in character" to one more shaped by economics. His classmate, Raymond Spruance, concluded that America had become unpopular because of her overemphasis on the collection of war debts and failure to participate in the settlement of postwar political problems. "Time will serve to soften this," Spruance wrote, "and then it is hoped that the real United States will be seen."[12]

In 1929, Commander J. B. Oldendorf was exceptional in his class for focusing on Europe rather than the Far East. He maintained that the reparations question was a substantial problem in achieving European peace. Commander Alan G. Kirk thought that although American isolationism was admirable in the past, America must now step forward. Taking another view, Commander John S. McCain approved of American policy which avoided "entangling alliances."[13]

Looking back over the immediate past, War College President Harris Laning told the class of 1933 that too many students came to the college with the assumption that all matters pertaining to war had already been thought over and should be presented to the students on a silver platter. Students often became discouraged and critical of the college, he warned, when they found that most of their theses were considered only a "rehash" of the obvious and that the college expected hard, perceptive, and innovative thinking. However, he admitted, "very few of the two preceding classes did any such reasoning."[14] His exhortation for change brought little result.

Renewed Emphasis on Tactics

Captain Reginald Belknap had written to Admiral Sims in July 1923, "In any war within fifteen years our naval leadership would be in the hands of those who served under you at the War College." Belknap was right, considering the size of the Navy in 1923. The influence of Sims can be directly traced to the 1930s through Harris Laning, who had been one of Sims' "band of brothers" in the Torpedo Flotilla of 1913-1914. After World War I, Laning's year as a student and a subsequent year as head of tactics at the college explain the emphasis he gave to tactics in the curriculum during his three years as president. At the end of his term, in 1933, he spelled out this emphasis:

> Those to whom the handling of forces in war is entrusted are in duty bound to so handle them that those forces will exert their maximum power in the battle that is the campaign's crucial and decisive point.[15]

Although strategy was not forgotten, the tactics of the fleet action received greater attention than before. After guiding and observing the 1930-1931 academic year that was based on a curriculum planned by Pringle, the new president significantly altered the staff when he created a research department for statistical studies. As head of the tactics department, he had emphasized the value of statistics in planning for battle; now a new department housed a separate group that included statisticians. The work of the new research department, headed by Captain Wilbur R. Van Auken, was

> 1. To keep full records of the details of all games played and from study and analysis of these records to ascertain the salient points and features relating to gunfire, torpedo fire, bombing, smoke screens, damage received and inflicted by the different types, use of aircraft, etc., together with statistical data as to material features and
> 2. To make a complete study of all questions presented to the War College for consideration from time to time.[16]

In addition, special consideration was given to the operation of *types* of ships, their speed, armament, ammunition, supply, and their use. An intensive historical study was begun in 1931 on battleships, cruisers, aircraft and carriers, destroyers, and submarines.[17] This work was later expanded after 1933 to include the accuracy and damage effect of aerial bombing, a study of grand strategy in World War I,[18] and a number of historical studies on ship types, as well as collating and editing translations by naval reservists of the German official history of the World War and parts of Raoul Castex' multi-volume work, *Théories Strategiques.*

The work of the research department stressed the increased emphasis placed on the fleet battle tactics, which by 1931 formed most of the operations study program. Engagements on the maneuver board between opposing battle lines eventually reverted to the lessons learned in the one great modern battleship engagement, the Battle of Jutland. That battle was studied and analyzed throughout most of the 1930s. Laning, in a letter to Commander John Shafroth, a recent War College graduate, spoke in glowing terms of the improvements made in student execution of tactical problems:

> We start them out with a verbal picture of The Naval Battle, then give them some papers Captain Coffey (tactics instructor) has prepared on the tactical handling of the battle line, and the tactical handling of light forces. Other papers on the tactical operations of air forces and submarines are now about ready . . . . With revised procedures, the students are getting a lot of splendid groundwork in fundamentals that heretofore were only brought home by the trial-and-error method, which method wastes a lot of time and doesn't always take anyhow.[19]

The emphasis on tactical handling of the fleet was sensible not only in Laning s view but also in the view of many others. They felt then, as many were to feel half a century later, that a war would be fought with what was available. Depression, tight budgets, a national administration committed to disarming for economy as well as for its own sake, and few new developments produced an outlook that emphasized the tactical handling of existing forces. The prevailing view was clearly stated by Pratt when, commenting on Fleet Problem XII, the annual fleet exercise for 1931, he emphasized

> the inexorable advance of the heavy battleship, even though encumbered by a large convoy. There are many who believe the day of the battleship is over. It is my opinion those who hold this view don't know what they are talking about, and that most of them belong to a pure pacifist class who would like to see the Navy done away with altogether, or else they belong to that class of people who when ill go to the quack, instead of the specialist.[20]

Naval War College Operations Problem IV, the last of the annual war games in Laning's term, formed the basis for college recommendations to the General Board and was studied and analyzed more thoroughly by the college than any such operation problem up to that time. In this particular problem, the Blue Fleet commander was Captain Ernest J. King, the senior student officer, and a man who a month before had been selected a year early for promotion to rear admiral. In the problem scenario, Orange had already seized the Philippines and King's objective was to work out their recapture by Blue forces. There were several possible routes for Blue forces based in Hawaii. King favored a movement north of the Marshall and Caroline Islands, then through the Marianas to retake the Philippines, but Admiral Laning insisted that King use the route south of the Marshalls and Carolines. King objected that Blue forces would be subject to flank attacks by Orange along the entire route and then be caught in a bottleneck between New Guinea, Morotai, and Mindanao.

The head of the operations department, Captain Stephen C. Rowan, told King that he could continue to play only if he would agree to play the "school solution." King replied that he would carry out "the solution of a berth-deck cook" rather than miss the chance to manage a fleet, even on the maneuver board.

King kept his war game command, but still attempted to persuade Laning to use the northern route. Laning, however, was not convinced. Laning believed that by changing Blue Fleet's speed from 12 to 14 knots, the southern route would be easy.

If only for the sake of peace in the game room, it was probably fortunate that King was unexpectedly detached in the middle of the game to become chief of the Bureau of Aeronautics. This sudden assignment for King was necessitated by the death of Rear Admiral William A. Moffett in the crash at sea of the dirigible *Akron* on 4 April 1933. King was not disappointed when he suddenly gave up command of the Blue Fleet, knowing the outcome would frustrate him.[21]

A long critique of Operations Problem IV followed. It emphasized the effects of the lack of logistical support for the Blue Fleet west of Hawaii, particularly the absence of repair facilities for battleships in the Philippines. Furthermore, the Japanese, with fewer capital ships than the Americans, were not likely, at first, to seek out a battle line engagement, preferring to attack with light forces and wear down the U.S. Fleet as it steamed further and further from its own bases. The student Orange Fleet commander, Captain C. R. Train, spoke for many students who doubted the viability of the Blue plan when he asked, "Is it a good thing for us to give so much attention to this [trans-Pacific] crossing, when it is pretty well established that it could not be done?"[22] Captain Adolphus Andrews, chief of staff at the War College, replied by saying that because of the treaty ratios as applied to battle fleets, even with casualties, the United States could expect to reach the Philippines with a battle fleet equal to Japan's. Many students were unconvinced and they urged that other methods of a campaign against Japan be explored, even "strategic" bombing. King, who finished his final thesis in pencil before hastening to Washington, foresaw actual events eight years later when he wrote:

> Japan will assume the offensive initially to acquire an advantage where she can assume the defensive and defy us to alter the situation, not that her defensive attitude will be in any degree passive—it will not.[23]

The difference of opinion in this war game was typical of the whole range of games that were played throughout the inter-war year. By 1940 two separate schools of thought had developed in Newport over the best way to deal with a war against Japan. One argued for a quick dash across the Pacific to relieve Manila and to establish a base there, bypassing Japanese forces in the Marshalls, Marianas, and Carolines. This plan held that battleships were essential to controlling the sea and also involved a decisive naval battle between the two fleets as the U.S. Fleet approached the Philippines. The opposing school of thought advocated a step-by-step method, in which the fleet, with its Marine force, advanced first to the Marshall Islands, then moved westward, establishing bases across the Pacific to the Philippines. Less hazardous than the quick dash plan, the step-by-step plan always kept the fleet within range of an advanced base and avoided risking everything in one large battle.[24]

These war games typified the Naval War College's approach to educating officers in the 1920s and 1930s. After completing the 1933 course at the Naval War College, William F. Halsey went on for an additional year of study as an exchange student at the Army War College in Washington. Looking back, he compared the two:

> At Newport we had studied the strategy and tactics of naval campaigns with emphasis on logistics. At Washington, we studied on a large scale—wars, not campaigns—and from the viewpoint of the top echelon . . . .[25]

Halsey had correctly described the situation when he was a student. College presidents and staff had long sought a higher-level course for a selected group of students at the Naval War College.

The Advanced Course

A week after the 1933 graduation, Rear Admiral Luke McNamee relieved Laning as college president. Coming ashore from a four-star assignment in command of the Battle Force, McNamee, like Sims before him, now reverted to the rank of rear admiral. At the age of 62 he anticipated a two-year tour in Newport before mandatory retirement. McNamee, a former student staff officer, may have realized that it would be difficult with retirement so near to make a real contribution or to effect specific changes in so short a time at the college. In any event, a year after his arrival he requested early retirement to become president of the Mackay Radio and Telegraphy and Federal Telegraph companies; but in that short year, he accomplished something his predecessors had been unable to do. He obtained approval for the establishment of the advanced course.

McNamee had also been on Sims' staff in London and carried with him the ideas of his wartime leader. Sims tried unsuccessfully as college president to establish such a course, which would provide one additional year of study for selected graduates of the senior course. In Sims' mind, however, the establishment of a junior course took priority. He believed that the work he had undertaken at the college was beneficial, first as a student in the traditional short summer course of 1911 and then the advanced work in the first long course in 1911-1912. Presidents following Sims had continued to recommend an advanced course, but a reluctant Navy Department, more specifically the Bureau of Navigation, had pigeonholed these recommendations. In 1927, Secretary of the Navy Curtis Wilbur had issued a General Order which specified that an advanced course, when established at the War College, would include "the drafting of war plans and advanced phases of naval campaigns,"[26] but the course was not implemented. Various boards on education and training had continued to support the need for an advanced course, including the most recent one headed by Captain Joseph K. Taussig in 1929.

In 1933, even before arriving in Newport, McNamee took up the campaign for an advanced course. Looking at the *Navy Register*'s pages of flag officers and senior captains, McNamee noted to the Chief of Naval Operations that there were few who had not completed the senior course. With planned reductions in the Navy's shore establishments, senior officers should be available for additional study at the college. At the same time, completion of the new wing under construction would provide badly needed facilities. He recommended that an advanced course commence in the summer of 1934 with ten senior officers, five from the present senior course and five from the fleet. Also, the course should include an Army and a Marine officer, who were graduates of either the Army or Naval War Colleges or the Army Industrial College. In August 1934, Admiral W. H. Standley, the Chief of Naval Operations, approved McNamee's recommendation, but observed,

> The drafting of war plans referred to in the request is only for the purpose of training and would have no connection with war plans which are now prepared in the Office of Chief of Naval Operations.[27]

McNamee and his staff laid out an initial curriculum with the expectation that succeeding courses would evolve from it. He was particularly concerned with selecting the highest-quality officers who would be ordered to the first advanced class and with the identity of its senior student who would work directly with the president of the college in developing the course. Finally and with agonizing slowness, the Bureau of Navigation issued orders, but ignored the college's recommendation that selected students of proven capacity from the present senior class be continued for a second year. Similarly, the Bureau ignored McNamee's request that the students be ordered for a two-year period to the advanced course. Several early nominees, such as Rear Admiral E. C. Kalbfus and Captain W. F. Halsey, Jr., were unavailable. By July 1934, however, a class of 11 officers assembled in Newport as the first advanced class. The senior student was Rear Admiral W. S. Pye, who had long been interested in naval education. Other students included Robert A. Theobald, Walter N. Vernou, Byron McCandless, Ellis B. Miller of the Marine Corps, and Edward M. Offley of the Army. The advanced class took over the old General Board room in the lower floor of the library for classes and committee work, and each officer was assigned a separate office in the first floor of the east wing of the main building.

The advanced class was not in the same category as other classes at the college. There was no connection between the college staff and the class, although students attended the lectures given by prominent educators. Instead, the immediate supervision of the class was given to the senior member of the class who consulted almost daily with the college president and carried out the policy laid down by the president.

The advanced class was concerned with international relations, major strategy, and the broader aspects of warfare, with particular attention to German and Japanese aspirations. There was no set curriculum, but the class investigated subjects of immediate concern to policymakers in Washington. The first class analyzed the policies of the United States and Japan, the conflicts between those policies, and the probable political objectives that would develop in event a war should occur between the two countries. In addition, a plan for American grand strategy was formulated along with an outline for joint Army-Navy action in a war against Japan.[28]

The results produced by the first class were not encouraging. By and large, the college staff placed the blame on the failure of the Navy Department to order the best-qualified students to the advanced course. What was needed were the officers of greatest analytical ability in the service, but the college was unable to convince the Navy Department that this criterion should override a qualified officer's assignment to other duty. Up to 1940, subsequent advanced course students continued with the same studies in preparation for a future war with Japan, yet their work, too, was plagued by late arrival of several students and early detachment of others.[29]

College Expansion

Since the reopening of the college in 1919, college presidents had repeatedly requested funds for physical improvements. By 1928, student numbers had already reached nearly 80 a year, and the staff steadily expanded from 14 in 1919 to 35 in 1934. Students crowded into offices with four and five to a study room, and the library had outgrown the quarters built 30 years before. With the exception of the library, the college was confined to the 1892 building that had been constructed to house four officers and teach only 18. During the 1920s, no funds had been available for construction. Finally in 1933 the urgent pleas of the college were heeded. Under the Emergency Relief and Construction Act of 1932, $360,000 was allocated to construction of a new wing to house an auditorium, a large gaming room, and additional office space for staff and students. Approval for this expansion came at the same time that Admiral McNamee was able to obtain approval for the advanced course.

Looking forward to the completion of the wing, McNamee thought it appropriate to name the two buildings in honor of Luce and Mahan. McNamee recommended that the older building with the 1904 library annex be named for Luce and the new building named for Mahan. Chief of Naval Operations W. H. Standley approved the selection of Luce's name, but directed that the new wing be named after Admiral Pringle, noting it was when he was Chief of Staff [1924] that the first steps were taken in regard to the new War College wing and during his incumbency as president [1930-33] that the plans of the building were completed and approved. In addition, Pringle had distinguished himself in a number of ways but had not been widely recognized. During World War I, he had commanded USS *Melville*, Sims' flagship at Queenstown, Ireland, and served also as Chief of Staff, Destroyer Flotillas, European Waters. Mahan, the CNO noted, was honored in so many ways throughout the Navy that there was no impelling reason to name for him a building "with which he had no connection whatever."[30]

Since 1932 a move had been afoot in Washington to transfer the college from the direct responsibility of the Chief of Naval Operations back once again to the Bureau of Navigation. The Chief of the Bureau, Rear Admiral F. B. Upham, argued that the college was "primarily a technical school for the training and education of line officers"[31] and that it was best administered through the Bureau of Navigation in the same way as the Postgraduate School and the Naval Academy. In October 1934, the Naval War College was placed under the administrative jurisdiction of the Bureau, but policy decisions regarding the War College remained subject to the approval of the Chief of Naval Operations. At the same time, the president of the Naval War College was removed from the now perfunctory ex-officio membership on the General Board.

The change in administrative responsibility raised a hope that further construction funds could be obtained to expand the college library. In 1934, the college president complained that

> the library was completely inadequate, the small adjoining room, which is used as a reading room for newspapers and periodicals, contains but two small tables, both completely covered with current publications. There can be no provision at present for retention of important magazines.[32]

With little space for the main collection, the library continued to divert some of its holdings into the small reference collection that had first been dispersed to convenient locations around the college in 1920-1921. By 1940, these small collections had grown from the original 10 to 54, averaging 60 to 100 volumes apiece.

In 1935, the Bureau of Navigation agreed to name the 1904 library annex in honor of A. T. Mahan. This time, the building was one in which Mahan had actually worked, albeit briefly during his few visits between 1908 and 1912. Finally in 1937, construction was begun on an addition to the 1904 building. A large, paneled reading room with a stack area to the north was added and completed in the spring of 1938.

Mahan Hall and the library it housed made an impressive memorial as well as being an integral feature of the life of the college. Only a portrait of Captain Mahan was lacking. In 1939 Rear Admiral C. P. Snyder started a campaign for subscriptions to provide the necessary funds to commission such a portrait. His successor, Rear Admiral Kalbfus, continued the effort by a direct appeal to the nearly 1,400 living graduates of the college for contributions of only one dollar from each man. This appeal was made following the observation of the centennial of Mahan's birth in September 1940. It was successful, and Alexander James, son of the Harvard philosopher and psychologist William James, was commissioned to paint the portrait using photographs and a specially made rear admiral's uniform from the 1906 period. James received $1,650 for the portrait, which was unveiled at the brief ceremony in August 1945, commemorating Mahan's arrival at the college in August 1886. It was designed to hang above the fireplace in the rotunda of Mahan Hall.[33]

In the college's physical expansion, the immediate need was to accommodate the increased numbers of staff and students as well as to provide larger space for long-established activities such as the library and war gaming. The construction of the large auditorium in Pringle Hall reflected the change in instruction methods that had followed the reopening of the college in 1919. Lectures had always played a role at the college, but from 1919 the number of lectures reached 50 a year from noted civilian and service experts, in addition to presentations by staff members. In tone and purpose, the lectures supported the general proposition that the college was involved in training, not advanced education. There were lectures to inform students about current issues, part of the college's mission "to develop and coordinate systematic courses of *instruction* and *training* for officers."[34]

In 1932, Harris Laning explained the rationale for lectures, as he saw it:

> We use all the lecture time to cover certain things not coverable by reading ... lectures on policies, especially the present-day policies of our own and other countries and the conflict between them. Then we have lectures on the happenings in our own and other countries to show the conditions, the state of mind, etc. in these countries .... Our next series of lectures have to do with economics, international trade, commerce, etc., arranged in such a way to bring home to the student some idea of how to use economic strangulation in the strategy of war .... Although economic pressure through control of the sea has always been a particular role of the Navy in war, very little has been done in our Navy in the past to perfect ourselves for carrying out that role.[35]

There were also lectures on international law and recent historical subjects such as the Gallipoli campaign, which provided the substance of a lecture nearly every year. The new auditorium was used for the first time to house these lectures on 20 April 1934 with a lecture by Professor W. S. Myers on "Comparative Organization of Government for War."

The year 1934 marked the War College's semicentennial. To begin its second 50 years, the college received a new president, Rear Admiral Edward C. Kalbfus. Relieving McNamee in mid-June, Kalbfus had already been a flag officer for four years, two in the Navy Department as Director of War Plans, and two in the fleet as Commander, Destroyers, Battle Force. A 1927 War College graduate, he stayed on the staff for two years, first as head of the logistics department, then as head of the intelligence department. In succeeding years, he kept in close touch with War College presidents and senior staff officers. When he returned he needed little briefing to take up his new duties.

Kalbfus arrived soon after the Navy and the War College had taken a new and more confident look into the future. The day after ground had been broken for the new wing to be named Pringle Hall, a new American president had been inaugurated. He had the personal interest, reliance on, and knowledge of the Navy that his distant cousin, Theodore Roosevelt, had shown 30 years earlier. Both had been Assistant Secretaries of the Navy and both were well known within the naval service. During their terms of office, both followed the operations of the fleet closely. Both enjoyed being with the fleet, and both sponsored major fleet expansions. From 1933 on, classes at Newport were looking at an expanding and more modern Navy in their problem solving, and the college physical plant would also benefit from having a sailor in the White House.

Narragansett Bay was a busy place in the summer of 1934. President Franklin D. Roosevelt visited Newport in Vincent Astor's yacht *Nourmahal*, and there was another British challenge for the America's Cup. The white American J-boats were already competing in the waters west of Coasters Harbor Island for the honor of meeting the blue-hulled British challenger *Endeavor*, soon to arrive. For the past two summers, only ships of the U.S. Navy's Training Squadron had visited Newport. But in early June 1934, the United States Fleet, after being reviewed by President Roosevelt off New York on 31 May, arrived in Narragansett Bay. It was the fleet's first visit to the East Coast since 1927, and it received an enthusiastic reception Newporters were jubilant; the *Daily News* editorialized, "Newport loves the Navy, and at last it has come back."[36]

On 11 July, the new auditorium in Pringle Hall was the scene of a gathering of some 200 fleet officers of all ranks. The principal speaker was the new Commander-in-Chief, U.S. Fleet, Admiral Joseph Mason Reeves, the first fleet commander-in-chief to be qualified in aviation, and a former head of the college's tactics department. Tall and picturesque with an impressive white goatee that reputedly concealed an anchor tatooed on his chin, Reeves was a gifted extemporaneous speaker. Only a month after he took up his command, the charismatic admiral delivered an extemporaneous address to the fleet that marked the beginning of the transition from a peacetime fleet to one in which men were mentally and emotionally prepared for a future war. Appropriately, he chose the Naval War College as the place to launch fleet reform. Addressing fleet officers in Pringle Hall, he said,

> In everything we do, we must ask ourselves: does this directly advance preparation for war?
>
> Our Fleet today is over-organized, over-educated, over-theorized, over-instructed, over-administrated, over-complicated, and overwhelmed with red tape, correspondence, paperwork and books!
>
> I believe the Fleet can be handled far more effectively and practically than is the case today if the number of tactical books used by the Department is limited to four. Any commander may indoctrinate his command in any way he chooses, except by complicated books and pamphlets on tactical procedures.
>
> If war comes, this Fleet must fight 'as is.' You must fight at sea and not on paper. Victories are won by practical results. Practical results are obtained by application at sea of our studies, theories, and analyses on shore.
>
> You will get licked with your nose in the wrong book and your pocket full of red tape and fine forms unless you lock your library in

the safe, stand up, and face a practical sea situation in a practical seamanlike way, using your own brains and making your own decisions.[37]

Reeves was making a point long supported by the Naval War College that theories and analyses belonged properly within its walls, but the application of the ideas it developed should be embodied in doctrine, standardized procedures, and order forms which avoided overwhelming paperwork. It was the basic assumption of the college's "estimate of the situation" teaching.

The Concept of the College in the 1930s

By the late 1930s the concept behind the War College had developed into a clear educational philosophy, the result of the cumulative efforts of several presidents and many staff officers spanning two decades. Since William S. Sims resumed the college presidency in 1919, the college had consistently perceived a clear role for senior naval officers in the defense of the country. They were being groomed in the practical, mental discipline necessary to command naval forces at sea rather than to manage a bureaucracy or to make policy. Their education, training, sea duty, and practical experience were directed toward making the existing naval forces work at all levels. The college took for its area of work the education of senior officers in problems of command.

In this the college staff believed that its principal role was to teach naval officers how to make sound decisions when in command positions. A commander's subordinates, whether on a staff or in a ship, tended to the multitude of administrative and operational details associated with his decisions. Thus, as the college saw it, the chief quality a naval commander must have is good judgment. That judgment must be perceptive and must produce the best possible decisions under existing conditions. Good judgment might be the result of rare, inherent genius. It could also be developed through study, reflection, and mental exercise. In the 1920s and 1930s, the college saw its purpose as the development of judgment by these means.[38]

In practice this meant that students were first required to master "accepted principles of reasoning" through study of the methodology first introduced in 1908 as the applicatory system and further developed in the ensuing quarter of a century. Then, they applied it to the solution of assumed strategic and tactical problems, which they expressed in terms of military decisions. Finally, they drew up plans and formulated orders to translate their military decisions into effective action.

When all this had been accomplished, the students played their solutions first as chart maneuvers, with every member of the class participating in a command or staff capacity, and then later on the tactical game board. In 1934, this war gaming activity was shifted to the commodious second floor of recently completed Pringle Hall, where the tile floor resembled a large checkerboard, its squares providing scales for distance and range. A gallery extending along the four sides of this large room permitted close observation without encumbering the players.

The prime motive for playing war games was to provide mental exercise so as to develop sound judgment. Student preparation began with an estimate of an assumed situation for which they formulated plans and orders. This estimate of the situation had to be rigorous and demanding, and it provided the basis for the plan. It embraced a systematic procedure for the selection of appropriate objectives to be achieved by naval forces. Thus it was necessary for the commander in each hypothetical problem to understand the underlying strategic purpose of the campaign, so the achievement of the immediate naval objective could further that purpose, and to weigh the relative fighting strengths of his own and enemy forces, as influenced by the various characteristics of the theater of operations.

In addition, these problems provided a means of familiarization with the composition and capabilities of foreign fleets and with important strategic areas such as the Caribbean and North America's Atlantic Coast. Primarily, however, games were set in the central and western Pacific. The college intended the increased mental facility the students gained from meeting assumed situations to be practical grounding in the fundamentals of strategy and tactics. This was a clear echo of Sims' insistence that the college course be predominantly practical rather than theoretical. The games were a means to that end; they provided a means to link theory with practical application.

By this time the college had also come to follow a clear philosophy of the role of armed forces in the affairs of the state. It was reflected in a lecture by Captain C. W. Magruder in 1938, when he told students that national policy will initiate war and will prescribe the political objective. Echoing Clausewitz, he said, "Policy throughout the war will continually exercise a guiding hand over its conduct and finally the policymakers—not the military leaders—will have the last word in deciding when hostilities shall cease." Continuing to expand on his exposition of the classic Clausewitzian concept of war as an instrument of national policy, he told his audience, "War for us should not mean that diplomacy has failed—that the armed forces are called in to bail out the State Department—but rather it should signify the decision by the administration to employ violent means to accomplish national ends that cannot be attained by peaceful purposes."[39] Obviously, a competent government will have a clear conception of its political objectives, and it must decide their relative importance by identifying which are vital and which are subordinate; and competent statesmen will know where the objectives their country seeks conflict with the rights and desires of other powers. These objectives, Magruder concluded, grow and develop from basic causes. They are frequently of long standing "while statesmen are often mere political accidents of temporary tenure."[40]

The "Green Hornet"—Sound Military Decision

The crowning expression of the college's philosophy during this period came with the publication of *Sound Military Decision*. During his first term as president from 1934 to the end of 1936, Kalbfus commenced a revision of the college's pamphlet, *Estimate of the Situation*, which had been used since 1910 to teach the applicatory system to the students. The *Estimate* was small, only 42 pages, and was already in its eighth version since it first appeared during the presidency of Rear Admiral R. P. Rodgers. The revised editions had been written under the direction of W. L. Rodgers in 1911-1912, Austin Knight in 1915, W. S. Sims in 1921, C. S. Williams in 1924, W. V. Pratt in 1926, J. R. P. Pringle in 1929, and Harris Laning in 1932. Most of the revisions were minor, but in 1915 Austin Knight stressed the importance of logical progression. "The estimate is not for the purpose of justifying a decision previously arrived at," Knight wrote "It is a reasoned solution of a problem where each step in the process approaches a decision, [which] without those steps could be arrived at by accident only."[41]

The 1924 and 1926 editions obscured some of the simple logic behind the process by adding a detailed series of questions that needed to be answered in order to identify a commander's mission. The manner in which these questions were framed led to confusion in differentiating between "missions" and "tasks." This confusion caused the estimate to become only a recurring process for a commander as he went from one crisis to another, always in hope he was accomplishing "the ultimate mission of the superior" in the process.[42] A further difficulty was presented by the 1926 edition which combined *The Estimate* pamphlet, for the first time, with another War College pamphlet, *The Formulation of Orders, Doctrine, and Dissemination of Information*. Although the two pamphlets appeared between the same covers, they were not yet effectively united as a single conceptual work.

The 1929 edition made conceptual progress by defining a commander's mission as an assigned task coupled with an explanation of the purpose of the task. Then after considering the situation as a whole, a commander should analyze all the obstacles opposing accomplishment of the task, including the strength and capabilities of both the enemy's and one's own forces. With this done, a commander could proceed to analyze the courses of action open to him and to select the one best suited to accomplish the task of the mission. This in turn provided the basis for making auxiliary decisions and formulating tasks to be carried out by subordinates.[43]

Further minor amendments were made in the 1932 edition under Laning. Both Laning and his predecessor, Pringle, had felt that previous editions of the pamphlet had become too long. Pringle's staff tried to "cut it down and simplify it."[44] Laning declared that his version "contains solid meat and that not one idea can be overlooked even though expressed in only one sentence." But, he added pensively, "Perhaps we were too optimistic as to what one sentence can do."[45]

In 1933, Captain Forde A. Todd, the head of strategy studies for the senior class in the department of operations, prepared a booklet entitled, *A Study and Discussion of the Estimate of the Situation*, as an adjunct to the *Estimate of the Situation*, to provide students with a keener appreciation and clearer understanding of the basic elements. Todd dealt with many of the common difficulties that student officers experienced with the *Estimate*, using a dialogue format between a typical student and staff officer. At the end of the booklet, the hypothetical student asked what benefit derives from this study. The staff officer replied

> A. As I conceive it, the principal benefit of this course is acquiring mental and moral experience.
> Proficiency in any art can only be had by practice. This practice is to increase our experience so that we unconsciously, as it were, do the right thing.
> In peacetime we can only have complete practice in war by such sub-caliber war as we conduct here. But in all our games and maneuvers here, the elements of chance, courage, and material efficiency are, necessarily, incapable of being injected into the solutions. They remain units for each side.
> Consequently, striking out the elements of units on both sides, as in mathematics, we have left only the intellectual qualities of knowledge and experience and the moral quality of character to develop.

After listening to some further advice, the student exclaimed,

> Q. Well, with all these, I'm sure that I can tackle the next problem with more intelligence.
> A. No, experience. You can't add a iot to your intelligence. Well, so long.
> Student officer (to himself): He seems to expect me to be a Jove, Neptune, and Mars combined in one.
> Staff officer (to himself): That chap had me crowding on all sail. He knows much more than he thinks he does.[46]

To add credence to the effort, the college staff looked for some estimates that were actually made in wartime and rewrote the original documents in the format the college used. As an appendix to Todd's book, Captain R. B. Coffey translated into War College form General Grant's order to Major General G. G. Meade of 9 April 1864 for the Potomac campaign. To supplement this, a version of a battle order was prepared by a member of the junior class, using Nelson's Trafalgar Memorandum as a basis.[47] Undoubtedly good fun, it was also the first published attempt by the college to explain *The Estimate* more fully.[48]

When Kalbfus took up the college presidency in 1934, he believed that a new revision was essential. "At the time that this change was in process of contemplation," Kalbfus recalled,

> it was not generally accepted by the Navy that their business was to fight although, of course, if confronted with this question, they would have agreed that that is what they were hired for. But, within the range of my own observation, both ashore and afloat, I saw that the keeping of office hours and the performance of sundry routine tasks were more in order than an intensive study of the Navy's real business.[49]

Todd's work had already suggested that the *Estimate* pamphlet had become too short, and Kalbfus believed it was vague, misleading, and confusing. Kalbfus sought more than a revision, he wanted a complete recasting of the pamphlet, turning its terse outline form into a book on the art of logical thinking, which would be appropriate to every military situation.

To Kalbfus, the key to improving the work was developing it along more logical lines. To do this, he sought outside assistance. Since 1920, W. E. Hocking, professor of philosophy at Harvard University, had been a regular lecturer at the college, speaking on a variety of subjects such as "Morale," "Psychology," and "Leadership." In 1934, Kalbfus asked Hocking to change his usual topic to a new one that would directly help the college revise *The Estimate*. Using this lecture, "Logic and its Process," as a basis, Kalbfus ordered the staff to begin rewriting the pamphlet. A year later, however, little had been accomplished. In the summer of 1935, an army infantry major, Edward S. Johnston, reported as a student in the senior course. A University of Indiana graduate and writer on the art of war, he had made a name for himself by publishing a critique that condemned the *Army Field Service Regulations* for their failure to deal with fundamental values, rather than changing factors in warfare. In the year before coming to Newport, Johnston had served on an Army War College committee devoted to discovering the basic factors in planning and executing joint operations. Its purpose touched on the same ideas which Kalbfus sought, and it may be that Kalbfus arranged for Johnston to be assigned to the Naval War College with that thought in mind. At any rate, Johnston soon became a collaborator in Kalbfus' work, serving also as a sounding board for his ideas and stimulating his thought.

In addition, Johnston was directly responsible for the idea which Kalbfus called "the fundamental principle for the attainment of an end." This was a three part text for suitability, feasibility, and acceptability which asked

1. Will the course of action accomplish the mission?
2. Will the available resources allow the mission to be carried out?
3. Is the cost worth the price?

The first draft of Kalbfus' work was completed in May 1936 and distributed to staff and students for comment and criticism. Committees were established to review the comments during the summer. Three of them were headed by distinguished staff members: Captain Robert A. Theobald, head of strategy in the senior class; Captain Raymond A. Spruance, head of tactics in the senior course, and Captain Richmond Kelly Turner, assistant for air operations in the department of operations and one of the college's most effective lecturers on naval strategy.[50]

The draft was controversial. Many thought the book had become too long, others said it was too complex. Some staff members disapproved of Kalbfus' innovative work, but hesitated to earn the admiral's wrath. Others, such as Raymond Spruance, objected to Kalbfus' ponderous style and his rejection of the so-called "principles of war." In 1934, the list contained nine principles: objective, offensive, superiority, cooperation, simplicity, economy, surprise, movement, and security, and had been part of the basic doctrine in the Army since 1921,[51] but they had never been fully accepted by the Navy. In 1933, Captain Todd's explication of The Estimate declared that if war could be conducted by formula, one "could not have distinguished Nelson, John Paul Jones, Decatur, or Farragut from their fellow officers." It is a simple matter to collect maxims, but "the difficulty always lies in applying rightly those deductions. Sound decisions depend, fundamentally, on character, knowledge, and experience."[52] These ideas were long engrained at the Naval War College and Kalbfus was their latest exponent. The use of the principles of war as a means of exercising effective command was, in Kalbfus' opinion,

> a very dangerous condition, for it led the unwary to believe that if he remembered the names of these nine so-called principles, which were, however, merely nine nouns and not statements of cause and effect, he could feel that he did really understand the fundamentals of warfare, particularly if this practice were approved and in effect at the only institution we had which covered the study of naval warfare.[53]

Spruance disagreed with Kalbfus on this and argued with his boss, Captain J. W. Wilcox, head of the operations department. Wilcox thought Kalbfus' work was magnificent and forbade Spruance to criticize it. In Spruance's view, Wilcox lacked courage to tell the truth. The two argued; Spruance disobeyed Wilcox and went directly to Kalbfus with his criticisms. Outraged, Wilcox threatened to destroy Spruance's career for his insubordination. When the incident finally came to the admiral's attention, Kalbfus vindicated Spruance, over-ruling Wilcox's demand that Spruance be punished.[54]

With all the criticisms collated, Kalbfus proceeded to put his book in print, but in the process he came to the conclusion that his work should supersede the old *Estimate* pamphlets and not be merely another edition. In order to differentiate it, his new 91-page booklet was titled *Sound Military Decision*.

Kalbfus was just leaving the college to take up his new position as vice admiral commanding Battleships, Battle Force, when the book came off the press. His successor as president of the Naval War College, Rear Admiral C. P. Snyder, evaluated the book for a year and then issued his own version in May 1938. Snyder recast part of three chapters and attempted to make a more precise treatment of the order form while clarifying portions of Kalbfus' text.[55]

Kalbfus was outraged that Snyder had tampered with his text. Promoted to full admiral in command of the entire Battle Force in 1938, Kalbfus was persuaded by his chief of staff, Captain C. J. Moore, to avoid a public confrontation with Snyder over the issue. In June 1939, when it became apparent that he would not be given a Washington appoint-ment, Kalbfus requested a return to the Naval War College to finish his work on *Sound Military Decision*. Resuming his two-star rank, Kalbfus brought back with him Edward S. Johnston, now a lieutenant colonel. As a result of Kalbfus' intervening experience as Commander, Battle Force, he was able to make an important addition to the book. Up to that time, the work only examined the process up to the point where a decision had been made. Now Kalbfus could see clearly that it had been a serious omission not to include a chapter on "The Supervision of the Planned Action." He immediately added it and in 1940, several drafts of the new and expanded version were circulated, with another draft appearing in 1941. From 1940, the book was given a green paper cover and soon became known among the students as the "Green book" or the "Green Hornet." In March 1942, a full edition appeared and was reprinted several times during the year. It was distributed widely throughout the Navy as the only published guide for naval planning that was available to officers involved in writing the multitude of plans and orders used during the war.

At the Naval War College, the staff under Kalbfus' successor, Rear

Admiral W. S. Pye, revised the book three times between 1943 and 1945 for purposes of instruction within the college and distributed new versions in mimeographed copies. One version came into use in October 1943 and was superseded by another revised version in January 1944. In June 1944, Pye issued a new mimeographed book entitled *The Operational Function of Command, Including Sound Military Decision,* which he claimed superseded Kalbfus' work. An abridged version of this was used in the college from April 1945. In 1944, Admiral Ernest J. King issued a portion of *Sound Military Decision* as COMINCH P-1: *Naval Directives and the Order Form.* In issuing it, King wrote "the matter contained in this publication is prescribed as standard in the United States Fleet for use in the formulation of Naval Directives."

The most widely known and used edition of *Sound Military Decision* was Kalbfus' own 1942 version. Like the *Estimate* pamphlet which it superseded, *Sound Military Decision* was prey to revisionists who would follow. The significance of the 1942 version, however, is that it presented a fairly comprehensive theory of war. A work of this kind is an enormous undertaking; that it was undertaken by a man whose training and background were more naval and military than scholarly and philosophical makes it even more remarkable. Kalbfus' purpose was to elaborate upon the methodology of the applicatory system, encourage deep thinking on the nature of professional judgment, and to relate the role of armed forces to the implementation of national policy.

Kalbfus' view of war as the *ultima ratio regum* was a statement of the classic concept espoused by Clausewitz, Mahan, Corbett, and other leading philosophers and commentators whose works formed the bulk of the required and suggested reading lists at the college. Kalbfus went further. He related this concept to the military commander whose task it is to lead and to direct armed forces in combat. As a professional naval officer, he recognized that the commander must keep uppermost in his mind the strategic effect that would be achieved by the successful accomplishment of the military task at hand. He emphasized that the chief task of the commander was to make sound military decisions through the exercise of good judgment, obviously based upon known and knowable facts.

The methodology of the applicatory system as it was used at the college was the tool by which a commander and his subordinates could order data, relate them to ultimate purpose, and ascertain the best or most likely means of producing the desired effect. In this sense it was essentially a descriptive theory, meeting the requirements that Clausewitz elaborated. Even so, it was not abstract. It was eminently practical. Many believe it was and still is the most valuable contribution to military thought made at the Naval War College in the past century.

Despite its high purpose and the weighty and useful ideas and techniques it contained, *Sound Military Decision* was flawed. Its chief flaw was that it did not illustrate its excellent ideas by practical, concrete historical examples that would impress practical-minded readers. Moreover, its prose was ponderous. The final product was more of a treatise, albeit an excellent one, than a useful publication for other naval officers.

In any event, as the protracted struggles of Luce and others at the college had clearly shown, the U.S. Navy as an institution has always had difficulty reflecting on the art and science of war. *Sound Military Decision* enjoyed only a short period in vogue before it was shelved by more literal-minded officers after World War II.

By the time Japanese forces attacked Pearl Harbor in December 1941, the Naval War College had already made its most significant contribution to the war effort by its earlier training of officers in a methodology for problem solving. Kalbfus' *Sound Military Decision* was the most important expression of the college's philosophy, embodying both the focus and understanding expressed in college classrooms throughout the inter-war period. When the United States entered World War II, every flag officer qualified to command at sea, but one, was a graduate of the Naval War College,[56] and had become accustomed to think in terms it had established.

Notes

1. "The Naval War College," *New York Times*, 19 Sept. 1927, p. 24:3, and *Army-Navy Journal*, 4 June 1928.

2. NWC Archives, RG 2: W. S. Sims to Chief Bureau of Navigation, 20 September 1920.

3. Fleet Admiral William F. Halsey, Jr., USN, and Lieutenant Commander J. Byran III, USNR, *Admiral Halsey's Story* (New York: McGraw, Hill, 1947), p. 54.

4. Fleet Admiral Ernest J. King and Walter Muir Whitehill, *Fleet Admiral King* (New York: Norton, 1952), p. 242.

5. Thomas B. Buell, "Admiral Raymond A. Spruance and the Naval War College—Part I," *Naval War College Review* (March 1971), p. 36. Based on Naval War College, *Information for Student Officers* (Newport, 1927), pp. 3-10.

6. NWC Archives, Staff-Student File: Nimitz: Mrs. Catherine Nimitz to Vice Admiral Stansfield Turner, 2 April 1973.

7. Sims to Secretary of the Navy, 16 June 1919, quoted in G. J. Kennedy, "Naval War College," p. 179, fn. 44.

8. "Outline History," p. 189.

9. G. J. Kennedy, "Naval War College," p. 160.

10. Ibid., pp. 172-73.

11. Ibid., pp. 166-67.

12. Ibid., p. 168.

13. Ibid., p. 170.

14. NWC Archives, RG 16: Harris Laning, Opening Address, 1 July 1932, p. 3.

15. NWC Archives, RG 4: Harris Laning, "The Naval Battle," May 1933.

16. "Outline History," pp. 369-371: Research Department Memo of 18 May 1932.

17. Ibid.

18. Ibid., pp. 388; Research Department Memo of 17 July 1933; p. 398, "Research Department, 1933-34;" and p. 411, "Research. 1934-35."

19. NWC Archives, RG 2, Box 34, P11-3 Lectures 1930-32: Laning to Shafroth, 28 Nov. 1932.

20. *Army and Navy Register*, 14 March 1931, interview with W. V. Pratt.

21. King and Whitehill, *Fleet Admiral King*, p. 239.

22. NWC Archives, RG 8: Operations Problem IV: Captain C. R. Train critique notes.

23. King and Whitehill, *Fleet Admiral King*, p. 237.

24. Frederick C. Sherman, *Combat Command* (New York: Dutton, 1950), pp. 43-44.

25. Halsey and Byron, *Admiral Halsey's Story*, p. 54.

26. General Order 168, 21 Sept. 1927.

27. NWC Archives, RG 2, File A 3-1: CNO to Chief, BuNav, 16 Aug. 1933.

28. "Outline History," p. 409. These plans have not been located. See Kennedy, p. 279, footnote 22. See also, Staff Study, *U.S. Naval War College*, 1954. Annex N: E. C. Kalbfus "Memorandum Notes on NWC History."

29. "Outline History," pp. 434-35; Kennedy, pp. 280-281.

30. Kennedy, pp. 215-216, 233-35, 272. Quote on Pringle, pp. 234-35.

31. Ibid., p. 210. Quoting Chief, BuNav letter to CNO, 6 August 1932.

32. Ibid., pp. 273-74.

33. NWC Archives, RG 2, Box 28. File PG-5. For appeal, see "Secretary's Notes," USNI *Proceedings*, Vol. 65, No. 5 (May 1939), p. 779.

34. Navy Department, Annual Report of the Secretary . . . 1933, p. 34.

35. NWC Archives, RG 2, Box 34, File P11-3: Laning to Shafroth, 28 Nov. 1932.

36. *Newport Daily News*, 22 June 1934.

37. Quoted in John D. Hayes, "Admiral Joseph Mason Reeves, USN (1872-1948): Part II - 1931 to 1948: Commanding the U.S. Fleet and in World War II," *Naval War College Review*, (January 1972), Vol. XXIV, No. 5, p. 59.

38. NWC Archives, RG 19: "Prospectus of the Naval War College Courses, 1938-40."

39. NWC Archives, RG 14: Staff lectures: C. W. Magruder, "Policy and Warfare," 8 Dec. 1938.

40. Loc. cit., C. W. Magruder, "The Potential Economic Strength and Weakness of Japan," 24 April 1939.

41. C. W. Cullen, "From the Kriegsacademie to the Naval War College: The Military Planning Process," *Naval War College Review* (January 1970), Vol. 22, No. 5, p. 15.

42. Ibid., p. 16.

43. Ibid.

44. T. B. Buell, "Admiral Edward C. Kalbfus and the Naval Planner's Holy Scripture: Sound Military Decision," *Naval War College Review*, Vo.. 25, No. 5 (May-June 1973), p. 32. Quoting J. K. Taussig letter to J. T. G. Stapler, 18 January 1929.

45. Ibid., quoting Laning to M. H. Simons, 10 October 1932.

46. F. A. Todd, *A Study and Discussion of the Estimate of the Situation* (Newport, 1933), pp. 36-37.

47. Ibid., pp. 38-46.

48. Cullen, op. cit., p. 16.

49. Staff Study, 1954, op. cit., Kalbfus "Memorandum," p. N-5.

50. Buell, op. cit., pp. 33-35.

51. Russell F. Weigley, *The American Way of War* (Bloomington: Indiana University Press, 1977), pp. 212-14, 512, footnote 42.

52. Todd, op. cit., pp. 22-23.

53. Staff Study, 1954, op. cit., p. N-6. See also *Sound Military Decision* (1942), pp. 25-28.

54. Buell, *The Quiet Warrior* (Boston: Little, Brown, 1974), p. 73.

55. *Sound Military Decision* (Newport, 1938), p. 1.

56. The exception was Rear Admiral, later Vice Admiral, Randall Jacobs, Chief of the Bureau of Personnel, 1941-1945.

CHAPTER 7

INTERLUDE: THE WAR
COLLEGE DURING
WORLD WAR II, 1939-1946

In 1938 and 1939, the Naval War College reflected the slow adjustment of Americans to the possibility of a second world war. German, Italian, and Japanese ambitions posed threats to the long-term national interests of the United States; yet, like most Americans in those years, the lecturers, students, and staff at the Naval War College did not anticipate the international arrangements that would be required to forestall those threats.

Even in 1938, the theoretical possibility of a war between the United States and Great Britain was still entertained at the college. Admittedly, it was unlikely to occur, but the staff thought it was of interest as an academic discussion as well as a means to measure the capability of the U.S. Navy. In Tactical Operations Problem VI, conducted in February 1938, the students grappled with a Blue-Red War in the Atlantic, with Crimson (Canada) coming in as an ally of the British. Blue planned to capture Halifax, and to engage the Red Fleet off Sable Island. Repeatedly played in 1932, 1933, and 1934, the final "Battle of Sable Island," demonstrated American naval capability by conceiving of British forces turning away with a dozen disabled battleships.[1] While measuring American capabilities against traditional British naval prowess, the college did not go further to examine the now likely need to cooperate with the Royal Navy in combat against a common enemy. Moreover, the exercise was fought against a similar fleet, not the dissimilar navy the United States eventually faced in battle.

In discussing current issues, opinion varied widely and, with hindsight, some of it appears quite inaccurate. A few weeks after

Germany's attack on Poland, a visiting lecturer, Bruce C. Hopper, expected "the boot [will] tighten on Germany," and he thought at that time Hitler would offer to abdicate. Clearly, the Führer would be forced to leave Germany. Hopper sarcastically told the student body, "No nation is equipped to give refuge to a man-made god, unless it be the United States; there is always Hollywood."

In a more serious vein, he expected a changed world to emerge from the war, explaining, "A civilization that spends up to 50 percent of its income for war is doomed to disaster." Despite the portents of doom that were so clear late in 1939, Hopper was optimistic. Taking a long view, he stated, "This war is only one violent aspect of that change which is nothing less than the rebirth of all human society, comparable in historical significance and greatly exceeding in magnitude the previous rebirth of Western society beginning 400 years ago—the Renaissance."[2]

In the tactical area, the role of aviation in modern warfare continued to excite interest at the college. Captain A. H. Douglas of the staff pointed out in December 1939 that "aviation can be counted upon for the execution of important tasks in the three fields of information, of security, and of attack." It is "no mystery, nor is it the property of any small group of military specialists," he declared; naval aviation is "here to stay."[3] Following the German conquest of Western Europe and the start of the Battle of Britain in 1940, Commander Henry S. Kendall surveyed the employment of aviation in naval warfare for the staff. He clearly and accurately saw that one operational effect of aviation would be an enlargement of the "area of tactical contact and action [by] merging along the coastline of the spheres of influence of the military and naval forces." Moreover, carrier-based aircraft heralded "the availability of a new weapon, effective . . . in the tactical offensive against all classes of vessels." One result of this development, in Kendall's opinion, would be the "relative reduction in the importance of destroyers and submarines as a means for inflicting attrition." Therefore, he concluded, it would be necessary to expend considerable strength and effort toward "the early destruction of enemy air power and the continuous protection of our own."[4]

The enfolding developments of the war in Europe showed that new techniques had to be mastered and that new lessons had to be learned. Nevertheless, according to Captain John L. Hall, head of the strategy department, the fundamental concept for the strategic employment of the fleet remained unchanged. Echoing old concepts, he declared, "The only reason for the formation of a fleet is to provide battle power. Therefore, the chief strategic function of the battle fleet is the creation of situations that will bring about decisive battle under conditions that will ensure the defeat of the enemy."[5] It would not be long before a wider concept of naval warfare became current at the college.

By early 1940, however, the War College had begun to come to grips with the implication of American participation in the war. In April, the advanced class, under the direction of Captain Hall, presented the results of its study of possible American involvement in a two-ocean war. Although at the time it seemed unlikely that the President would take the recommended action, the class believed that the United States should increase its military power and assist other democratic states. Should America become involved in the war, the group held that the prime responsibility for the United States was the defense of the western hemisphere. In naval terms, this meant concentrating the fleet in the Caribbean with patrols in the Atlantic, leaving only a secondary force on the West Coast. The students' most significant conclusion was that in the event of war with both Germany and Japan, American forces should first be concentrated against Germany, remaining on the defensive against Japan. Then as forces became available, the United States should begin a limited offensive against Japanese sea lines of communication.

This study was an early step toward official acceptance of the "Germany first" strategy. Admiral Harold Stark's "Memorandum on National Security Policy" in November 1940—"Plan Dog," as he called it—was likely to give the United States the most advantage by stressing "Germany first." It became official policy through the ABC-1 staff agreement with Britain in March 1941, and the United States Joint Army and Navy Basic War Plan, "Rainbow 5," developed in May and June 1941.[6]

Kalbfus's Valedictory

As the war progressed in Europe and tensions increased in Asia, American naval leaders realized that it would probably not be long before the United States was directly involved. At any rate, the world crisis and the rapid American naval buildup under President Roosevelt's direction required increasingly more naval officers at sea and in major billets ashore. This, of course, made it hard to find suitable students for the War College. The experiences of the Spanish-American War and World War I suggested that, as in earlier conflicts, the college might be closed shortly. Immediately after war broke out in September 1939, the Bureau of Navigation advised the college to be prepared to have all or part of its staff and students detached. Making a hasty trip to Washington, Kalbfus first persuaded the Chief of the Bureau of Navigation, Rear Admiral Chester W. Nimitz, that depletion of the college staff beyond a certain point, would make it impossible to do any worthwhile teaching. Nimitz agreed to a compromise which required only 27 students to be detached, but a further problem arose when the

Army ordered all its students at the Naval War College withdrawn. In Kalbfus's view, "These Army students, who had already benefited by the superior educational system of the Army, made a real contribution to the college and to the advancement of the military because of their mature views and opinions."[7] Returning to Washington, Kalbfus was successful in having the Army not only restore its students but double their number.

At the same time, Kalbfus discovered that the existing war plans required, in the event of national mobilization, that the War College would be automatically closed and turned over to the First Naval District for use as quarters and offices. Kalbfus pointed out to Nimitz that such a decision, without knowledge of the circumstances that might exist at the time of mobilization, violated the first precepts of planning, as taught by the college. Although unable to refute entirely the idea that the college might be closed, Kalbfus was able to have the plans amended to include the phrase, "if and when ordered."

Kalbfus saw clearly that it was unlikely for officers to be sent to the War College for a full 11-month course during wartime. During several visits to Washington, Kalbfus and Nimitz worked out a plan to keep the college open, but with abbreviated courses. Although the plan was formulated in February 1940,[8] it was not until March 1941 that Nimitz issued the order that prevented the exigencies of war from closing the college. When the three regular college courses, the advanced, senior and junior, were completed on 15 May 1941, Nimitz directed that "these courses in their current form will be suspended for the duration of the present emergency."[9] The advanced course was terminated, but the college's correspondence courses were to continue without modification. In place of the two resident courses, two new ones were established: the command course and the preparatory staff course. Both were designed to provide, through a series of lectures, a background for the study of world politics, economics, and strategic geography. Satisfactory completion of either course was regarded as qualification in tactics and strategy for promotion examinations.

In particular, the command course was designed to cover in five months the area previously dealt with in twice that time by the senior course. It was open to both line and staff officers with more than six years' commissioned service. The Navy also encouraged the State Department, Army, Marine Corps, and Coast Guard to send students.[10]

The preparatory staff course was intended primarily for junior Naval Reserve officers who had already seen some service. The instructors in this course sought to promote familiarity with staff procedures, with the elements of tactics and strategy, and with the application of international law to likely situations at sea.[11] At the outset, the preparatory course was composed of carefully selected officers, most of whom were graduates of the Naval Academy. Later, the course included officers who had demonstrated high ability in civilian life.

Interestingly, the courses were designed to run for five months and one day, instead of five months. The additional day was added when the college discovered that five months' duty or less constituted temporary duty and did not allow for transportation of dependents and household effects.[12]

Despite the shortened time available for study under the new system and the need to take as students some officers merely because they happened to be available, Admiral Kalbfus believed it essential that the college be kept open so that after the war it could resume its long-range function. In particular, he feared that the value of the college could be destroyed if "the equipment peculiar to the exercise of its functions" were not maintained. Continuity, he believed, was the key to preserving the essential and irreplaceable elements such as the library, the archives, and the uniquely qualified civilian staff. The brief courses, with their obvious educational shortcomings, were only one means to achieve this goal. Kalbfus moved simultaneously in another direction to achieve the same thing.

As the U.S. Navy began to react to the increasing possibility of entering the war in 1940, it began to examine its own command structure, including the shore establishment and naval districts. In 1919, Admiral Sims had convinced Secretary Daniels that the War College president should be separated from these administrative duties that fell on naval district commanders.[13] This position was reaffirmed by the Chief of Naval Operations, William D. Leahy, in 1937.[14] Kalbfus suspected that in wartime a flag officer would be appointed to the college presidency only if he were saddled with additional military and administrative duties. He believed a flag officer was essential in the billet to preserve the prestige of the college and to prevent it from being dispersed while the Navy, at large, was concerned with the war. "Even though his duties as Commandant of the Naval Base may occupy most, if not all, of his time during war," Kalbfus told the CNO, "his office as President, Naval War College, will remain alive and the college will continue as an entity."[16]

With these thoughts in mind, Kalbfus recommended that the various naval activities in the Narragansett Bay area be administered through a single base commander. As the senior officer in the area, the president of the Naval War College would naturally be appointed the commandant.[15] Kalbfus' recommendation was approved and the Secretary of the Navy created the Naval Operating Base, Newport, on 31 March 1941. Kalbfus took charge as commandant of the base on 2 April. In addition to the presidency of the Naval War College, he took administrative charge over the commanders of the Naval Training Center, Naval Net

Depot, Naval Air Station, Quonset Point, Naval Torpedo Station, Naval Fuel Depot, Melville, and the Naval Hospital. When Kalbfus's two-star flag was broken at the flagstaff atop Luce Hall as Commander, Naval Operating Base on 2 April 1941, it was the first time that an admiral's flag had been flown over the college since Sims' request to be relieved of military duties had been approved.[17] The base commander was given a separate staff to administer the base, and no officer other than the president was given additional duties, thereby preventing administrative functions from interfering directly with the work of the college. This arrangement remained in effect until 23 June 1944 when the college was removed from the administrative control of the Commander, Naval Operating Base, Newport, and reestablished as a separate activity under the Chief, Bureau of Naval Personnel, Vice Admiral Randall Jacobs. With this move, the college returned to the same bureau, which before 1942 had been known as the Bureau of Navigation and had so often administered the college in previous years.

By the time Kalbfus completed his second tour of duty as president of the Naval War College on 2 November 1942, he had already drafted his views and recommendations for future War College education in a paper entitled, "The Study of the Science and Art of War in Relation to the Safeguarding of the Nation's Future."[18] His recommendations became, as he intended, the guidelines which two of his successors, Raymond Spruance and R. L. Conolly, used in reviewing the college's courses in the late 1940s and early 1950s.

Kalbfus believed that to exercise command efficiently an officer must understand the fundamentals of war. "There are fundamentals common to all, irrespective of whether the sphere of action has been land, sea, or air."[19] The best means to understand these fundamentals is through concentrated study of military and political history. "Technological evolution has always exerted great influence on methods of operation, but the extent of this influence cannot fully be understood and measured unless there be ability to sift technical details from fundamental truths,"[20] Kalbfus wrote. Peacetime is the proper time to prepare officers in this way, but in peacetime it is particularly difficult to detect the early need for subtle changes in method required by technological advances. At the same time, these changes cannot be skillfully applied to particular situations unless "with the science of war as a basis, war against a particular (potential) enemy or enemies be continuously made the subject of study by resourceful, competent, and suitably trained officers."[21]

The Naval War College was the only naval institution where, without the distraction of administrative or technical matters, officers could study the fundamentals, debate views, and discuss military topics. But the Navy's educational policy up to that time showed a disturbing trend. Those in high command in 1942 had attended the college, but in the previous decade attendance by the junior officers who would eventually succeed those presently in command had fallen off. The 1942 *Register of Naval Officers* listed 2,510 line commanders and lieutenant commanders. Only 241, or about 10 percent, had been given the opportunity to study at Newport. Kalbfus pointed out to the Secretary of the Navy that these figures "indicate a forced trend away from the guided and undisturbed study of war by those upon whom the burden of conducting war necessarily falls."[22] Since the rapid buildup of American naval forces, which began about 1933, operational, technical, and administrative demands had progressively forced the study of war into the background. By 1943, only a handful of junior naval officers had been properly educated. Kalbfus urged that the United States maintain a strong armed force in the peace that would follow World War II, so he was particularly concerned that there be proper provision for the continuing study of war. The nation expected officers to be proficient in the art of war, but "mere mastery of a particular technique, without the fundamental knowledge from which it emanates, does not meet this requirement."[23] Without a grounding in the fundamentals, the experience and associations of individual officers provided them with only a narrow viewpoint and basis of judgment with which to conduct warfare.

Kalbfus believed that it was vital for officers to learn the fundamentals early in their careers. To delay such education until an officer reached the rank of commander or captain yielded results "far from what they should be." Such delay meant that the senior course had to be devoted to the fundamentals rather than to advanced work. In consequence, it paralleled closely the content of the junior course. "To have it otherwise," Kalbfus wrote, "would have been to lay undue stress on the greater practical experience of the officers of the senior class and to have assumed, without justification, that all who have attained command rank are grounded in fundamentals."[24] To rectify this unsatisfactory situation, Kalbfus recommended that

1. All line officers receive compulsory grounding in the fundamentals of warfare in a Naval War College staff course between the time they reach the middle of the lieutenant's list up to the time they reach the middle of the lieutenant commander's list. This course would be a prerequisite to promotion to commander.

2. The senior or command course be composed of officers "selected for this assignment because of demonstrated capacity and probable future usefulness."[25]

One of the great advantages of study at the Naval War College, Kalbfus declared, was "a rubbing of elbows as between officers of the college staff and the students, and among the students themselves."[26] With that in mind, Kalbfus strongly believed that both courses should be taught by the same faculty members at the Naval War College in order to achieve uniformity of thought and method as well as the utmost opportunity for staff and students to exchange views. Above all, Kalbfus concluded, a coordinated postwar educational system among all government departments was necessary. Within that system an obligatory study in the art and science of war should be an integral part of the Navy's educational program. With those sentiments, Kalbfus left a fund of views based on his nine years' association with the Naval War College. Although not especially original, they revitalized old ideas and provided a basis for others to plan postwar educational policy at the Naval War College.

Newport in Wartime

If there was a "front line" in the continental United States in World War II, Newport was on it. Army units garrisoned forts and batteries from Sakonnet to Point Judith. The Torpedo Station at Goat Island went to three-shift production. The new Naval Air Station at Quonset Point grew as air groups formed, an overhaul and repair facility was organized, and specialty schools opened. At Davisville, battalion after battalion of Seabees were trained and sent overseas. At the Melville fuel depot, a motor torpedo boat base was established in 1941, and PT boat crews formed, trained, and shipped out to man new boats.

Of particular significance to the fleet and the Navy's wartime training system was the Precommissioning Training Center, formed from the old Naval Training Station. That station, which had reopened in 1937, was gradually transformed into a center for training crews of the many large combat, amphibious, and auxiliary ships being constructed in East Coast shipyards. For three years practically every such crew was collected and trained on Coddington Point. Under the command of Commodore Cary W. Magruder, a rare three-time graduate of the War College (junior, senior, and advanced courses), several hundred thousand officers and men went through periods of up to three months of rigorous training. It was the Navy's largest receiving station in history. Liberty for the embryo crews was closely controlled and the term *concentration camp* was used on more than one occasion as a fast-moving, production-line type of training evolved. When possible, a ship enroute to war would be delayed to permit some on-board training for the organizing crews, but usually training was shorebound.

With the new crews were a proportionate number of ships' officers, some of whom brought their families to Newport, compounding an already serious housing shortage. War College students, about 100 at any time, had to compete for housing with the large numbers of officers attached to other commands. Bachelor officers could find rooms in hastily constructed barracks, which provided the basic necessities but few comforts. Many of these temporary buildings continued in use for more than 30 years.

The college received numerous inquiries from incoming students as to the availability of quarters. One Army colonel who was ordered to the Joint Army-Navy Staff College for one month wanted to bring his family. He had been abroad for 18 months and expected another long separation. He told the college that he required two bedrooms, a bathroom, kitchen, living room, and garage. A house meeting his needs was available, but two other students living in an attached apartment would have joint use of the kitchen with his family. The college chief of staff, Captain H. H. Crosby, "strongly advised" him to accept this house.[27]

Many townspeople made houses, apartments, and even spare rooms available to military tenants. The owner of one mansion on Ocean Drive offered several apartments in his summer "cottage" to War College students. However, rents were high. Two rooms, the occupants of which shared a bath, at 91 Rhode Island Avenue rented at $10 weekly. An unfurnished six-room apartment on Red Cross Avenue was offered at $70 per month. House rentals were even more expensive. Most exceeded $100 per month.

One of the most practicable arrangements was offered by St. George's School in Middletown. Rooms were made available for $15 per week, which included not only the room and a linen change but also three meals daily. Even though the rooms were in the dormitory of a boys' preparatory school, they stood in sharp contrast to many of the inflated local rents.

In order to prevent rent gouging by unscrupulous landlords, the Office of Price Administration established wartime regulations governing rent. Landlords were required to produce a registration statement showing the approved rent on their property. Repeated student complaints about the failure of some landlords to produce the statement and about the excessive rents they were charged prompted the War College president to write to the Area Rent Director. He cited specific examples. Commander C. M. Block was charged $43 per week for a furnished room and bath at 19 Greenough Place. This complaint was typical of many the college received, but given the large number of military tenants the relative percentage of complaints was actually very small.[28]

By 1944 Newport's recreational facilities for officers were excellent. The Navy rented the second floor of the Newport Casino on Bellevue Avenue for an officers' club. Ping-pong tables, a juke box, and a reading room were available. A good meal could be purchased in the dining room for a mere $1.25. Four of the exceptionally fine grass tennis courts at the casino were permanently available for club members and their guests. Fees were 25 cents per day, or $2.50 monthly.

The officers' club planned the usual activities. There was a tennis tournament in the summer of 1944 for officers in the Narragansett Bay area. Matches were scheduled "so as not to interfere with official duties." Entrants competed for the Mrs. M. Barger-Wallach Challenge Cup. There was also a fashion show for the benefit of the Navy Relief Society, which featured fall and winter clothes by Peck and Peck. Married students were asked to take the notice announcing this event home to their wives. There was also a get-acquainted tea dance in December 1943, presumably for single officers and local young ladies.[29]

At the conclusion of the war, it was apparent that an officers' club at the Newport Casino would no longer be practical. The advisory committee met at the end of November 1945 and discussed the future use of Building 95 on Coasters Harbor Island. Soon thereafter this building, which was no longer needed as a machine shop, was converted into what is now the NETC Commissioned Officers Mess (Open), "The O Club." Situated at the foot of the hill below the War College, the club boasts a magnificent view of Narragansett Bay. It is convenient to the War College as well as to the other commands in the Newport area. One additional benefit of moving the officers' club back onto the base was that it was possible to remove the package store from the basement of Mahan Hall where it had been located for most of the war.[30]

ANSCOL: The Army-Navy Staff College

Admiral Kalbfus was succeeded by Vice Admiral W. S. Pye in November 1942. A graduate of the college, a former staff member, and a participant on the well-known Knox-Pye-King Board, he had long been keenly interested in the War College and in the development of naval education. Although Pye was undeniably well qualified by his experience, his appointment to the presidency of the Naval War College followed an unfortunate set of circumstances. At the time of the attack on Pearl Harbor, Pye had been Commander, Battle Force, and Task Force One of the U.S. Pacific Fleet. When Admiral Kimmel was relieved following the attack, Pye succeeded him as acting Commander in Chief, Pacific Fleet, until Admiral Nimitz could arrive in Hawaii. During that brief period, Pye appeared to be reluctant to engage the Japanese, and he was blamed for allowing the enemy to occupy Wake Island without dispute from the Pacific Fleet.[31] Unfortunately, the stigma of these controversial events followed Pye and reflected on the prestige of the college as an institution devoted to promoting excellence of command in wartime.

Under Pye the college continued to carry on the wartime courses which Kalbfus had instituted. Early in 1943, however, General H. H. Arnold, Commanding General of the Army Air Forces, recommended to the Joint Chiefs of Staff that a course be set up to prepare officers for duty on joint staffs. The early experience of World War II stressed the need for mutual understanding of the roles and functions of the various armed services so that staff officers could "have at least a rudimentary knowledge of the technique of operations of all types of armed forces, ground, sea, and air, and of the methods of coordination of such forces in joint operations."[32] When Admiral Pye reviewed the proposal, he said "the number of officers who possess such knowledge is negligible. The need for officers who possess such knowledge is urgent."[33] He saw that Newport was the best place to give the proper education on the naval aspects of the problem. Unlike the Army War College in Washington, whose buildings had largely been taken over by Headquarters, Army Ground Forces,[34] at Newport the facilities were readily available in Luce Hall.

In response to the obvious need, the Joint Chiefs established the Army-Navy Staff College to coordinate a four to five-month course for senior officers. Established in Washington, D.C., in buildings at 21st and Virginia Avenue NW, 12 classes attended the new Staff College in 1943-1945. The classes first went to the Army Air Force School of Applied Tactics at Orlando, Florida, for a four-week course. For the second four weeks, Army and Marine officers were sent to the Naval War College to learn about the Navy, while the naval officers in the course went to the Army Staff College at Fort Leavenworth to learn about the Army. The group reunited again in Washington for the final eight weeks of the course. After the fourth class, the course was lengthened by four weeks so that all officers could have the same background and attend classes at both the Naval War College and Fort Leavenworth. Between June 1943 and September 1945, 337 students were trained at the Naval War College. Of this total, 213 were Army officers, 77 Naval officers, and 19 Marine Corps officers.

The classes also included the first Foreign Service officers to attend the college and the first foreigners (Britain, Canadian, and Australian) to attend a Naval War College course since 1895. This mixture of foreign officers, civilian government officials, and officers from all the armed forces studying joint operations together provided a successful model.

At Newport, the school was allotted the entire third floor of Luce Hall. There the Naval War College contribution was conducted by Captain F. S. Steinwachs, assisted by Commander Thomas A. Brown, SC, USN, and Miss Willie Mae Owenby.

One student described the naval phase of the ANSCOL course in irreverant verse:

We were sent up to Newport, R.I.
To that barracks of wood known as "ply"
Op Problem X was a terrible bore
Logistics of clambakes a more pleasant chore
We can handle a cruiser with skill
Our objective the top of a hill
In the heat of a battle
This knowledge will rattle
Around in our heads like a pill.

So we're saying goodbye to Pye Tech
To the Washington windstorm we'll trek
Bless the PT boats
We cruised in the Sound
Bless those dammed busses
That bounced us around
We are calloused in points to the rear
The state of our eardrums we fear
Destroyers and tankers
Torpedo net anchors
Do you wonder we left with a cheer.[35]

Newport was the last stop before the students went on to the final portion of the course in Washington. The first class did not reach there until August 1943, but when the class finally convened in the capital, it was met with an enthusiastic official welcome. Commodore Foy, the senior naval staff member in Washington, described it for Admiral Pye:

> We got off to a pretentious start last Thursday. Admiral King, Generals Marshall and Arnold spoke. All the rank in town were here, including the General Board (in a body), the representative of the British Chiefs of Staff, the Marine Band, etc., etc.[36]

The Pye Board

In March 1944, Secretary of the Navy Frank Knox appointed Vice Admiral Pye to the presidency of a board of officers to study the methods of educating naval officers. This group of five naval officers, a Marine Corps officer, and a civilian educator, Dr. F. B. Snyder, president of Northwestern University, were directed to study the entire field of officer education, except that for chaplains, medical and dental officers. Heading the first study since the Knox-King-Pye Board of 1920 to view the entire picture, Pye sought once again to stress the need for a complete system of education, taking into account the deficiencies that the war had revealed. According to the board, the present war had demonstrated that:

1. All naval officers must have a more thorough knowledge of the capabilities, limitations, and general principles of employment of forces and their logistic support.

2. A larger percentage of officers must be educated and trained for operational staff duties.

3. A larger percentage of officers should be specially qualified in applied communications.

4. Officers should be given special education and training for command at an earlier age. For officers of the command branch, education and training in material is important but distinctly secondary to education and training for command.

5. Education must be progressive and must be provided at appropriate periods in an officer career . . .

6. Periods of education should precede periods of increased responsibility . . .

7. While no one man can be master of all aspects of the naval profession, the Navy as a whole must include and means must be provided for the education of some officers specially qualified in each of the various arts, industries, and sciences, which can, in any way, contribute to the advancement of the conduct of naval warfare.[37]

In examining an officer's education after he had received his commission, the board decided that the conclusions of the 1920 Knox-King-Pye Board were still sound. In the postwar period, the 1944 Board envisaged that at all times approximately 15 percent of naval line officers would be engaged in educational pursuits. For officers being trained for command, the board believed that a typical career fell into five phases. For the first stage, as a division officer, the Navy provided adequate education before commissioning. After five years of service, however, an officer had reached the department head level. Before entering this phase, he needed a general line course. Then, in preparation for the third phase, in command of a large ship, an officer required a command and staff course. The fourth stage was that of division commander. Before entering into those duties, an officer required a Naval War College course and, in addition, some officers should go on to take either the Army-Navy Staff College course or the Army War College course. The fifth and highest phase of an officer's career was as a flag officer commanding forces or fleets or filling high administrative posts ashore. To be prepared for these duties, the board recommended that a flag officer attend an advanced War College course.[38]

Pye envisaged three tiers at the Naval War College, the command and staff course, the War College course, and the advanced course. With a large postwar Navy, this would involve expansion of War College facilities to deal with 1,000 students, nearly ten times the capacity of the buildings available. Consequently, the board recommended that the Naval Training Station on Coasters Harbor Island be closed and its facilities turned over to the War College. "The need for these expanded courses will be urgent. Each year's delay after the armistice means the loss of vital periods of postgraduate education."[39]

Just as its predecessor, the Pye Board's recommendations were not implemented fully, but its views would be repeated over and over again in future years. The Naval War College continued its series of abbreviated wartime courses up until the summer of 1946. Pye received orders that he would be relieved by Admiral Raymond A. Spruance as college president, but Spruance would not arrive in Newport until the middle of the tenth shortened course in March 1946. As soon as the war had ended, Pye had begun to make preparations to reopen the college on its normal schedule, teaching two full-year courses. By the time Spruance arrived in Newport, Pye and his staff had been working for more than six months on the new curriculum and he was able to present Spruance with a well-grounded plan for the new president to implement. It could not be merely a return to old ways at Newport; the experience of World War II had clearly changed the Navy. It was now a much larger Navy with wider responsibilities, but naval officers had also come to view their needs for professional education in a different light.

Notes

1. NWC Archives, RG 4: "Operations Problem VI, 3 Jan. 1938; Michael Vlahos, *The Blue Sword* (Newport: Naval War College Press, 1980), p.109.

2. NWC Archives, RG 15: Lectures, Bruce C. Hopper, "The Role of Soviet Russia in the European War," 1939.

3. NWC Archives, RG 14: Staff Presentation, Captain Archie Douglas, "The Employment of Aviation in Naval Warfare," 14 Dec. 1939.

4. NWC Archives, RG 14: Staff Presentation, Commander Henry Kendall, "The Employment of Aviation in Naval Warfare," 14 Sept. 1940.

5. NWC Archives, RG 14: Commander John Hall, "The Strategic Employment of the Fleet," 2 Nov. 1939.

6. R. G. Albion, *Makers of Naval Policy 1798-1947* (Annapolis: Naval Institute Press, 1980), pp. 550-53.

7. NWC Archives, RG 17: Staff Study, The United States Naval War College (Newport: Naval War College, 1954), Annex N: "Memorandum Notes on Naval War College History—RADM E. C. Kalbfus," p. N-9.

8. NWC Archives, RG 2: File: A 2-12(b 1940), Kalbfus to Nimitz, 5 Feb. 1940.

9. NWC Archives, RG 2:, Box 37, A3-1 (1937-1943), Chief of the Bureau of Navigation to All Ships and Stations, "Modification of Naval War College Courses During Current Emergency," 25 March 1941.

10. Loc.cit., Chief of the Bureau of Navigation to Commandant, U.S. Coast Guard, 27 March 1941; Secretary of the Navy to Secretary of State, 26 May 1941.

11. Loc.cit., BuNav to All Ships and Stations, 25 March 1941.

12. NWC Archives, RG 17: Staff Study, 1954, pp. N-10, 11.

13. NWC Archives, RG 2, Box 37, file A-12: Sims to Daniels, 15 May 1919. See Chapter 5.

14. NWC Archives, Loc.cit., Commandant, First Naval District to All District Units, 26 April 1937. Quoting OPNAV letter to COMONE, No.Op 13C-jc A2-9 (370330) of 15 April 1937.

15. NWC Archives, Loc.cit., CNO to Commandant First Naval District and President, Naval War College, Op 13A-1-jc (No. 259513) of 27 Dec. 1940 with COMONE to CNO, NONB/NC3, of 31 Dec. 1940; National Archives, Washington, D.C. RG 24: Records of the Bureau of Navigation. General Correspondence 1925-1940 Box 573, NC3: Kalbfus to Stark, 31 Dec 1940.

16. Ibid. Kalbfus to Stark, 31 Dec 1940.

17. NWC Archives, RG 17: Staff Study, 1954, p. N-12.

18. NWC Archives, RG 28 President's File: Kalbfus. R. L. Conolly memo of 26 March 1951 transcribing Kalbfus to Secretary of the Navy, 15 January 1943.

19. Ibid., p. 5.

20. Ibid., p. 6.

21. Ibid.

22. Ibid., pp. 7-8.

23. Ibid., p. 8

24. Ibid., p. 10.

25. Ibid., p. 12.

26. Ibid., p. 14.

27. NWC Archives, RG 2, Box 26, Files N4-1, N4-5.

28. Ibid.

29. Ibid.

30. Ibid.

31. For a study of this action, see S. E. Morison, *History of Naval Operations in World War II*, vol. 3: *Rising Sun in the Pacific, 1939-April 1942* (Boston: Little, Brown 1948), pp. 250-54.

32. NWC Archives, RG 27, Subject Files: Army-Navy Staff College: CDR Thomas A. Brown, SC, USN, "ANSCOL at the Naval War College." Appendix A, "Study of the Desirability and Practicability of Establishing a United States Staff College," by W. S. Pye.

33. Ibid.

34. George S. Pappas, *Prudens Futuri, The US Army War College 1901-1967* (Carlisle Barracks: Alumni Association of The U.S. Army War College, 1967) p. 139.

35. CDR Thomas A. Brown, op.cit., p. 15.

36. NWC Archives, RG 2, Box 4, File A2-12 (1943) "Army-Navy Staff College, Foy to Pye," 10 August 1943.

37. NWC Library, W. S. Pye, "Report of Board to Study the Methods of Educating Naval Officers, 1944." Photocopy of typescript. Shelf number: V411.U56., pp. 6-7. See also NWC Archives, RG 3 Box 2: File 5216: Pye Board Correspondence.

38. Ibid., pp. 20-21.

39. Ibid., p. 91.

CHAPTER 8

THE NAVAL WAR COLLEGE IN QUANDARY, 1946-1953

For two decades following the end of World War II, the Naval War College was in a quandary. The college was widely acclaimed within the Navy as the apex of professional education; yet it encountered insurmountable obstacles in carrying out the actions that would logically flow from that position. First, as Vice Admiral Robert B. Carney told War College students in 1947, "World War II upset our neat little Navy world and necessitated the inclusion of many specialized skills, which could not be mastered by what we used to call the 'well-rounded officer.' "[1] Second, naval officers, in general, had no clear concept of sea power or of maritime strategy. In the aftermath of the war, it became apparent that strategic thinking involved a broad range of knowledge that spanned several academic disciplines and, at the same time, lacked a coherent theoretical basis upon which an effective study could be constructed.

These problems gave rise to doubts about the curriculum and course content, and other problems brought into question the very purpose and function of the college. In order to carry out its stated mission, War College staff members saw the need to expand the size of the classes to accommodate the increased size of the naval officer corps. These plans were consistently approved by the Navy Department, but funds, staff, and student officers to carry them out were not forthcoming. The situation exacerbated the trend begun in 1933 with an increasingly smaller percentage of officers attending the college. At the same time, the increased demand for officers at sea made it impossible for the Bureau of Personnel to select only the best officers as staff and students.

Often officers were assigned because they happened to be available when vacancies at the college occurred, not because they were particularly qualified or talented for War College work. A result was that a decreasing number of War College graduates were selected for promotion to flag rank.

In contrast to the prewar view, the Naval War College no longer appeared to be an essential step in the promotion process or in preparation for higher command. Two factors made it extremely difficult to reverse this process easily. The pattern of a naval officer's career and cycle of promotions had been dramatically shortened in comparison to the prewar period. Total length of service was generally shorter and subsequently time in each grade was shorter. Therefore, there was much less time available for each officer to have the necessary sea and shore responsibilities that would prepare him for high command. Finally, the Naval War College found that the establishment of the joint service colleges had inadvertently created a threat to its function by drawing away from it some of the most highly capable students. These successful naval officers went on to high command with a joint service college education, but without the experience of their own service college. The success of many of these officers began to create a pattern that supported joint service education rather than single service war college education. Because the Naval War College continued to be devoted to professional naval matters, it was not successfully competing with the joint service colleges which focused on higher levels of national policy.

The Naval War College experienced many of the same problems that other service colleges also faced in the period from 1946 to 1966. During these years, however, the college was more or less left to adapt to circumstances as best it could. The college was in the position of trying to carry out an educational concept that required both expansion and development of its own program as well as coordination with other service colleges. At the same time, though, it lacked the necessary power and influence at high levels within the Defense and Navy Departments that would enable it to carry out the program.[2]

Plans for Postwar Naval Education

In 1944, the Joint Chiefs of Staff (JCS) directed Admiral J. O. Richardson to head a board to consider the unification of the armed services in peacetime. Following one of the recommendations of this group, the Joint Chiefs also appointed Lieutenant General J. L. DeWitt, commandant of the Army-Navy Staff College in Washington, to prepare a "General Plan for Postwar Education of the Armed Forces." Approved by the Joint Chiefs in June 1945,[3] the plan carried forward one of the recommendations made by the Navy's Pye Board a year earlier, proposing a college of national defense with students from all the armed services as well as the State Department. All the services agreed on the need for such a college,[4] and the success of ANSCOL during the war seemed to support continuation and expansion of its approach on a permanent basis as the National War College. The JCS Plan made three basic recommendations.

First, a small number of officers would be sent early in their careers to schools of other services in order to broaden their outlook and prepare them for joint service. This relatively small group would provide a core of officers that could adequately meet expected joint service requirements. Second, there would be a new level of military education above that provided by the Naval War College and its sister colleges in other services. Only selected students would be sent on to this new level of education but then only after they had completed their respective service's war college course. Students at this new higher level would be educated in "military strategy and war planning" by a broad appreciation of the interrelationship between national and international policy and the military force by which such policies are sustained and enforced. "The factors that enter these relationships are many and complex, and include social, political, and economic considerations as well as those of a military nature."[5]

In this general scheme of education, the Naval War College would continue to carry out its prewar function as the highest institution devoted to in-depth study of naval affairs, but would not focus primarily on the broadest questions of warfare. The JCS, however, went further, and recommended that the War College also provide a joint service function by having 30 percent of its student body come from other services.[6] As envisaged by the JCS plan, a naval officer would proceed from fleet schools to the Postgraduate General Line School at Monterey, California, in about the sixth year of service, complete the junior or naval command and staff course at the Naval War College in about the fourteenth year, then proceed to the senior or Naval War College course, reaching the joint college level in about the twenty-fifth year of service.[7]

In September 1945, the Secretary of the Navy convened a board to study the proper form, system, and method of postwar naval education. The board was headed by Rear Admiral James L. Holloway, Jr., who had served as aide to Admiral Laning at the Naval War College in 1931-1932. It included among its ten members James P. Baxter, president of Williams College; Henry T. Heald, president of the Illinois Institute of Technology; and Captain Stuart H. Ingersoll, a future War College president. In Part III of the report devoted to all aspects of naval education, the Holloway Board considered graduate education, taking into account the recommendations of both the 1944 Pye Board and the JCS General Plan.[8]

Following these earlier studies, the Holloway Board concluded that the General Line School was the cornerstone of education for all officers, regardless of their source in receiving a commission. Beyond that step at the eighth to twelfth year of commissioned service, the Holloway Board wanted the two Naval War College courses to be equivalent to the courses offered by the joint service colleges, and for the Naval War College to have an advanced course for flag officers above both the senior War College course and the National War College course. Approving the earlier recommendation for the exchange of students among the various services, the board concluded that

> this policy of mutual understanding should include a lively awareness of the strategic tactical implications of scientific development at all levels of graduate education. The subject of logistics has assumed such dominant importance in modern war, and is of such complexity, that the Board likewise believes positive provision must be made for its inclusion in all line courses subsequent to the General Line School.

The board went on to suggest that line courses, such as those offered by the Naval War College "should fill the gaps in . . . experience left by limitations in variety of duty at sea."[9] At the same time, the board agreed it was fundamental that all courses relating to naval staff work should be located at the Naval War College, even though this required an expansion of facilities in order to produce "a cohesive effect." The board also took into account the recommendations made by the board headed by Captain H. A. Spanagel on the new postgraduate school to be established at Monterey, stressing its role as a general line school, but cautioning "that maximum use should be made of the facilities of civilian colleges for graduate education of specialist officers."[10]

Admiral Holloway later summarized his view of the plan by noting the changed functions of naval officers:

> From the springboard of professional knowledge and ability, our officers, particularly upon and after attaining command rank, must operate effectively in manifold areas in addition to the technical, tactical, or operational. To mention a few, there are personnel research, public relations, foreign commissions, legislative and congressional liaison, organization and direction of research, instruction and education, all types of administration, duty with Reserve components, fiscal control, and planning at high levels involving historical, political, sociological, and economic perceptiveness of the highest order. All these are things to which a diverse intellectual input into the Line of the Navy should contribute, through creation of a synthesis of thinking, expression, and

experience which will serve to improve the capacity of the corps of officers in a while.[11]

The success of this plan, however, depended on several uncertain factors: the expansion of educational facilities to meet increased student numbers, the rapid rotating of officers to and from specific sea billets with appropriately placed periods of education, and a sufficient excess in the number of officers in the service to allow for manning responsible positions as well as assignments to student and instructor billets.[12]

Return of Spruance

Admiral Raymond Spruance relieved Pye as president on 1 March 1946. Spruance was well acquainted with the college having graduated in the class of 1927, served as head of the correspondence course in 1932-1933, as head of the tactics section in 1936-1937, and as head of the operations department in 1938. Some four months before returning to Newport, Spruance had relieved Fleet Admiral Nimitz as Commander in Chief, Pacific Fleet and Pacific Ocean Area when Nimitz moved on to become Chief of Naval Operations. Always a strong supporter of the college, Nimitz had a more important task for Spruance than command of a shrinking fleet with diminishing responsibilities. He wanted to revitalize the Naval War College and to restore its prestige. With a thin postwar budget and a plan for naval education based on some uncertain factors, Spruance faced a difficult task.[13]

He entered his task with the conviction that the Naval War College was best suited to seek out and to develop thinkers. It was not the appropriate place, he believed, to instill a fighting spirit. Knowing his fellow officers, Spruance put them into three categories: (1) "tactical types" who were good on the bridge of a ship, but were deficient in abstract imagination and reasoning; (2) the energetic and industrious who were not themselves creative, but who could grasp the ideas created by those who were; and (3) "the strategical type" with inventive intellect. The second and third types were those best qualified to attend the Naval War College, Spruance believed. "If imagination, tempered and guided by common sense and reason is the scarce and valuable quality which I believe it to be, it behooves us to recognize the individuals who possess this disciplined imagination, to encourage and make full use of them."[14] This was Spruance's goal as he set about revitalizing the college. If he could stimulate at least one creative mind in each class, each year, Spruance believed that the college would be successful.[15]

The curriculum, the staff, and the student body were the three crucial elements in revitalizing the college. First, Spruance sought to build understanding and cooperation between the various specialties within the Navy by bringing officers of all branches to the college. He particularly tried to avoid the prewar situation in which he believed the college had been dominated by battleship-oriented officers and shunned by naval aviators.[16] Moreover, he knew that interservice rivalry had on occasion hampered the American war effort, and he emphasized the example of ANSCOL in bringing officers from all services together with Foreign Service officers at the Naval War College. Above all, he wanted academic freedom, so students and staff might express their views uninhibited by official policy. "The Naval War College advocates no dogma, nor doctrine, nor any set of rules by which campaigns can be conducted or battles won," Spruance said.

> There are no such rules. But it can and does endeavor to show that there are certain fundamentals, the understanding of which assists a commander in orderly thinking and planning necessary to solve a military problem.[17]

With that thought, Spruance clearly echoed the basic theme that War College leaders had stressed since the founding of the college. But Spruance was not merely content with prewar ideas. He was clearly concerned with new problems in warfare, while stressing the need to attend to fundamentals in approaching them. "We study military history for the lessons it has to teach us," Spruance warned, "but we must not expect necessarily to obtain from history the correct answers to future problems."[18]

Immediately upon his arrival at the War College in March 1946, Spruance directed that a new curriculum be readied for the year-long courses, which would start again in July of that year. In constructing a revived War College, Spruance moved in several directions simultaneously, but each of them complemented his conception that in planning for the future one must deal with fundamentals and take into account the lessons of experience. He appointed Commodore Penn L. Carroll to develop strategic problems and war games which stressed the tactics and weapons of the future: nuclear weapons, air warfare, missiles, mines, electronic sensors.[19] At the same time, he began an entirely separate course in logistics, under Captain H. E. Eccles, built on the experience of World War II but directed toward future operations. Then, he arranged for Commodore Richard W. Bates to head a battle evaluation group that would analyze the combat experience of World War II. Finally, Spruance sought to publish a permanent, uncontroversial naval planning manual. He hoped it would provide the basis for college teaching and establish standard procedures throughout the service. While reviving the basic structure of the college along the lines which Kalbfus had recommended after his retirement in 1942,

Spruance's main contribution to the college involved these three topics: the logistics course, the battle evaluation program, and the planning manual.

World War II: A Logistician's War

While the principal thrust of the wartime ANSCOL course was on building an understanding between the services that would promote more efficient joint operations, the continuing thread that ran through the course was an emphasis on logistics. The experience of World War II continually stressed supply and transport of necessary goods as well as production of war materiel and the use of a wide variety of industrial, technical, and professional expertise that had previously been thought of as remote, civilian occupations. During World War II, officers began to realize that the armed forces had become intricately complex communities in which the traditional distinction between combatant and noncombatant skills had become blurred.

Despite Admiral Pratt's early initiative in creating a logistics department in 1927, the emphasis on the subject gradually had dwindled and been incorporated into the many subjects dealt with under the rubric "naval operations." At the beginning of World War II, the American naval officers had some general knowledge of the principles involved in logistics but knew nothing of its theory and little about either the interdependence of logistic matters, general logistic planning, or its organization.[20]

It had been battle problems that had excited great interest among professional naval officers. At the Naval War College the Battle of Jutland continued to be studied, analyzed, and commented upon from 1919 until World War II as a segment of every year's curriculum. This interest channeled much thinking in the Navy at large along the tactical lines of a major battlefleet action, and tactical proficiency naturally continued to be a requisite for promotion. There was a corresponding tendency to brush aside as too academic the study of the business of supply and resupply of overseas forces, although there were a few notable exceptions.[21]

The global aspects of World War II changed these concepts. As allied forces gathered momentum to mount the final offensive, naval officers found themselves busily engaged with planning for and carrying out jungle-based air operations, surface and submarine operations, and amphibious operations. To do this, naval officers discovered they must also support a large floating air force of their own, operate freight lines, engage in base construction, stockpile materials, and do dozens of other jobs that were foreign to their prior training. The Navy became acutely aware of such things as tons-of-supplies-per-man and usage rates of all manner of ammunition and equipment—in short, with the down-to-earth spadework of what it takes to wage war. World War II proved that "strategy and tactics provided the scheme for the conduct of military operations and . . . logistics provided the means therefor."[22]

In light of these facts a board, convened to study postwar naval logistics training, recommended that study of the subject begin at the Naval Academy or college NROTC and continue at the Naval War College. It also recommended establishment of a separate naval logistics institute. After being approved by the Secretary of the Navy, this latter recommendation was modified by another committee, which recommended that instead of an institute, the Naval War College be expanded to include a logistics course. This new course would be co-equal with the senior course at the college. Both courses should be headed by an officer of flag rank, directly under the president of the college.[23]

Henry Eccles and the Logistics Course

Henry E. Eccles and the study of logistics at the Naval War College are synonymous. Drawing on his extensive first-hand experience in the Pacific during the war, Eccles returned to the college in the late spring of 1946 to lecture on advanced base development. A few months later he received orders to command the battleship *Washington*. Shortly after he assumed command, the Navy Department decided to decommission the ship within a few months and she proceeded to the New York Naval Shipyard in Brooklyn to make the necessary preparations. Eccles, then a senior captain, started looking for his next billet. He soon found it.[24]

On a trip to Washington a friend showed him the directive signed by the Chief of Naval Operations, Fleet Admiral Nimitz, which established the logistics course at the Naval War College and called for a flag officer to head the course. Eccles was asked if he could suggest anyone for the job. When he mentioned two or three names, he was told those officers were either not available or not interested. Finally, he was asked if he might be interested. He was. He said he would take either the number one or the number two position. Admiral Spruance knew Eccles and, believing that commitment and knowledge were more important than rank, eagerly approved assigning him to lead the course even though he was not a flag officer.

There was important high-level interest in establishing the course. The Deputy Chief of Naval Operations for Logistics, Vice Admiral Robert B. Carney, who supported the idea, made $90,000 available to convert the then unused Training Station Barracks "C" (later named Sims Hall) into suitable spaces. For more than two months Eccles alternated his weekends, commuting from his ship in Brooklyn to either the college in Newport or to Washington in his efforts to recruit qualified officers for his staff and to oversee the renovation of the barracks.

Gathering a staff was a difficult matter. Eccles was told that his number two man should be an aviator. He requested the assignment of either of two captains, who were also aviators: George W. Anderson and James H. Russell. The detail officer for captains laughed at such presumption, reflecting the widespread attitude within the Navy that duty in connection with logistics was the kiss of death for a line officer in the furtherance of his career. Nonetheless, Eccles was able to gather a competent staff and have them on board in sufficient time to prepare for the opening of the course in July 1947. He received unqualified assistance and support from the Bureau of Supplies and Accounts, which assigned several outstanding Supply Corps officers.

Soon after Eccles reported to the college, an attractive young blonde was assigned from the demobilizing Naval Station to be his secretary. Miss Mary V. Murphy was extraordinarily competent. Her quick wit, calm disposition, and ability to cope effortlessly with the hurly-burly connected with establishing a new course qualified her to work directly with the dynamic Eccles. Upon Eccles' reassignment in 1951, the president, Vice Admiral Richard L. Conolly, appointed Miss Murphy as the president's secretary, and she remained in that assignment until her own retirement in 1979.

By early July 1947, 46 officer students, representing all the U.S. armed forces and also Britain's Royal Navy, reported for the logistics course. This new course was co-equal with the regular course in strategy and tactics. Both courses were integrated for the first two months, which were devoted to common background work in general principles and in the capabilities of ships, planes, and weapons, and other combat forces. There was also study of weather, communications, and intelligence.

Then the logistics students broke off and concentrated for eight months on their subject. A considerable amount of time was devoted to joint amphibious operations. Moreover, the logistics students solved naval problems, working them out on the game board. These ranged from a quick tactical problem to a major one involving a global war. In addition, each student was required to write papers on two subjects, "A Comparison of the War Potential of the United States and the U.S.S.R." and "The Effect of New Weapons on Naval Logistics." Besides the obvious educational benefits of research, arriving at conclusions, and reducing thoughts to writing, the thesis topics had the additional virtues of requiring every student to look forward in regard to the most likely enemy and of requiring each one to focus on problems that logisticians might have to face in the future.

Among other things, the logistics war games examined the concept of a "one-stop" replenishment ship. As early as 1948, Eccles proved the effectiveness and efficiency of a concept that did not become an operational part of the fleet until 1964 when USS *Sacramento* (AOE-1) was commissioned. In addition, Eccles wrote the Navy's first logistics manual, *Operational Naval Logistics*, which was published in 1950. It was a philosophical approach to the study of logistics as a command responsibility "devoted to the thesis that while we can expect to make new mistakes in the logistics of a future war, we should not repeat the old ones."[25]

In the succeeding three years refinements were made to the logistics course, but the basic concept remained the same: to teach logistics from the point of view of command. In 1950 the name of the course was changed to strategy and logistics in recognition of their close relationship. Considerable difficulty attended the search for a qualified relief for Eccles in 1951. Although logistics was a responsibility of the line, officers of the line failed to support the course. Thus, shortly after Eccles' reassignment, the logistics course was fully integrated into the regular college curriculum and the subject was once again relegated to a position of secondary importance.

The Logistics Library

Emphasis on logistics study at the college brought about a local problem in logistics. The Navy's wartime efforts produced an enormous body of logistical experience, which was recorded in a great variety of ways in literally millions of pieces of correspondence, reports, directives, manuals, instructional texts, standard operating manuals, plans and orders, reference data, and the like. These records were stored in desks, file cabinets, and offices throughout the Navy.[26]

The problem was how to collect, organize, catalogue, and make available a representative cross section of this recorded experience, organize it, catalogue it, and make it available to those who would come to depend on it in the future. Probably the first logistics library was established in 1944 at the Advanced Supply Base Training Center, Williamsburg, Virginia. When that command was decommissioned the following year, the library was absorbed by the Logistics Research Library at Bayonne, New Jersey. By January 1947, this library comprised approximately 20,000 accessions. When the logistics course was established at the War College later in 1947, it seemed only natural to transfer the library from Bayonne to Newport.

Commander C. C. Mathas of Eccles' staff at the War College concluded that only about 3,000 items of the entire collection at Bayonne were of any value to the Naval War College. Transferred to

Newport in June 1947, the 3,000 items, combined with material from other sources, formed the nucleus of the logistics library. As originally conceived, the library would not only serve the college but would be directly useful to the entire Navy.

Unfortunately, only Eccles, his staff, and a handful of others in the Navy had a grasp of the field of logistics broad enough to know what was involved, what were its limitations, and how best to organize it for future reference. The life of the logistics library was short. The high classification of its documents required security, but there was no appropriate place for it to be separately housed. It was moved from place to place and eventually was dispersed.

World War II Battle Evaluation Group

During the course of World War II, the Combat Intelligence Branch of the Office of Naval Intelligence prepared a confidential series of combat narratives to give naval officers "a clear view of what has occurred, and form a basis for a broader understanding that will result in ever more successful operations."[27] These studies gave the most reliable current information, but they were no substitute for a detailed analysis of all accounts of battle experience.

In September 1944, Admiral E. J. King directed that the Naval War College answer all requests made for analysis of battle action reports. In May 1946, Admiral Nimitz ordered the college to study and to evaluate those World War II battles in which the U.S. Navy participated, using all sources available.[28]

To undertake this task, Spruance selected Commodore Richard W. Bates. "This is a new and important responsibility for the War College," Spruance told Bates, ". . . success will depend upon obtaining especially selected officers, and particularly upon the officer who heads up the group."[29] Bates had both War College training and battle experience. A graduate of the Naval War College senior class in 1941, he had stayed on to be an instructor in strategy, 1941-1943. In 1943-1944 Bates commanded the heavy cruiser *Minneapolis* and then became chief of staff to Admiral J. B. Oldendorf. He was with Oldendorf in the battle of Surigao Strait, at Lingayen Gulf, Luzon, and Okinawa. In May 1945, he assumed command of the Motor Torpedo Boat Squadrons, Pacific Fleet.

Bates headed the project of analyzing battle reports until it was disbanded in 1958. The group began as the department of analysis, was then renamed special projects department, and in 1952 became the World War II battle evaluation group.

The group's purpose was to derive lessons from war experience for the benefit of officers seeking to improve their professional judgment. By attempting to portray the mental processes, decisions, and actions of combat commanders, Bates emphasized the study of command and decision.[30]

By 1950, Bates' group had published confidential, single-volume studies on the battles of Midway, Coral Sea, and Savo Island. In 1950, the group embarked on an eight-volume study of the Battle of Leyte Gulf, of which only volumes 1-3 and 5 were completed. Portions of volumes 4, 6, and 7 were drafted, but only a few notes were gathered for the projected volume 8, which would have distilled the lessons to be learned from the experience at Leyte. In 1958, the Chief of Naval Operations, Admiral Arleigh Burke, ordered the project discontinued for lack of funds. Despite attempts by Admiral Claude Ricketts and others to reestablish the project, using private funds, it was not continued.

In lengthy and detailed technical analyses of each battle action, Bates and his team were often critical of individuals, but throughout they attempted to maintain the analysis on professional terms of judgment, which reflected the long-established principles that the college had taught in its work, culminating with Admiral Kalbfus' *Sound Military Decision*. Bates elucidated some of these abstract principles in the context of recent battle experience. Interpreting the Coral Sea operation as a raid, for example, Bates wrote:

> This whole operation stresses the strategic principle that a raid may have strategic consequences far above those originally contemplated. This raid was too small to do substantial physical damage, yet its political effect, caused by fear of additional raids, was great and, in this case, appears to have caused Japan to alter military timetables for other theaters.[31]

Examining the Battle of Midway, Bates noted that both the Japanese and Americans relied on surprise in their basic planning, but neither was as successful as had been hoped. "Surprise must not be counted on too strongly in planning," Bates concluded, "although it should be considered as the soul of every operation. There must be sufficient means available to ensure success even though surprise be not obtained."[32]

Looking carefully at American defeat in the Battle of Savo Island, Bates said that the Navy can best prepare its prospective commanders for command in four ways:

> 1. By instilling in them as early as possible the fundamentals of warfare, which in turn requires a knowledge of history by land, sea, and air.
> 2. By providing them with the maximum mental training in the art and science of war.
> 3. By giving them the opportunity for study and reflection, and for exchange of views within and among the several echelons of command.

4. And finally by providing them with the maximum practical training in the fleet and task group maneuvers as well as in maneuvers of lesser scope.[33]

After this, "there should be ... a ruthless and impartial elimination of those whom such maneuvers and mental training show to be lacking in initiative or to be lacking in the ability to make prompt and sound decisions under the pressure of fast moving events."[34] In writing his studies, Bates followed his own precept in judging commanders in action. The results, as one might expect, caused a great deal of controversy among senior naval officers. Many opposed the project and tried to stop it.[35]

Despite this, Bates' work earned praise from Samuel Eliot Morison. In his inaugural address as president of the American Historical Association for 1951, Morison spoke to the gathered historians about the importance of intellectual honesty in their work. He used as an example the two years of work that Bates and his assistants had devoted to the 42 minutes of the Battle of Savo Island. "They have tried to find out exactly what happened and why, sparing nobody, praising few, although shocked to the core at the faulty tactics that their search revealed," Morison said. Of Bates he said,

> Like the best professional historian, he took no shortcuts, tested all *a priori* generalizations by ascertainable facts, and hesitated not to scrap his charts and shape a new course whenever new soundings revealed uncharted reefs. His *Savo Island* monograph is a fine example of intellectual honesty, because it was motivated by an earnest desire to explain the event exactly as it happened.[36]

Morison was fully aware of Bates' methodology and procedures in his research work. In early 1942, Morison, who held the Jonathan Trumbull chair of American History at Harvard, volunteered his services to the Navy to write a *History of U.S. Naval Operations* in the war. Approved personally by President Roosevelt, Morison was commissioned a lieutenant commander in the naval reserve and given authority to read official reports, visit ships, and interview senior officers. "The Navy Department did everything possible to enable Morison to make his research exhaustive and to afford him first impressions,"[37] Secretary of the Navy James Forrestal wrote. The result was the work of an independent scholar, published privately. It was not an official history reflecting official conclusions. During the war, Morison had been assigned an office in the Naval History Division of the Office of the Chief of Naval Operations,[38] and that office continued to assist him in later years. In the summer of 1946, however, Morison with two officers, a yeoman and a cartographer, brought his project to Newport. Morison lived aboard his 36-foot yawl, which he requested be berthed "close aboard USS *Constellation*,"[39] in Coasters Harbor. Morison wrote to

Spruance, "It will be a great help in writing the history to work in such pleasant surroundings and to be able to ask your advice on many subjects."[40] Morison had met Bates in the Pacific, and in 1946, he and his research assistants were already housed at the Naval War College when Bates arrived to take up his official work on the classified analyses of battle.

The two projects were entirely separate.[41] Morison's official assignment to the Naval War College was limited to the brief period from June 1946 until his return to regular teaching at Harvard in the autumn of that year. Although the official connection was brief, Morison continued to make good use of advice he obtained at the college throughout the period he was writing the history. From time to time, he worked on it in the college library and archives,[42] giving credit for the assistance he received from Bates and other staff members, as well as from librarians and cartographers.

Naval Planning Manual

The third area that Spruance directed the college to develop was the publication of a standard manual to guide officers in planning. These, of course, were waters in which the college had fished for half a century, but Spruance wanted to avoid the constant revision to which the old "estimate of the situation" pamphlet had been subjected. Remembering clearly his dislike of Kalbfus' *Sound Military Decision*, Spruance wanted a reduced and simplified standard publication "which is not to be changed by a shift in command at the War College or by new ideas of individuals every one or two years."[43] Spruance was not opposed to the purpose for which the earlier publication had been written. However, he thought that the constant revisions were not only unnecessary but prevented the work's full acceptance and use throughout the Navy. By simplifying and standardizing the text, Spruance believed, "a fixed meaning will grow up from midshipman to flag officer as to certain features of the estimate of the situation."[44]

Spruance was not alone in his views on the subject. As early as November 1945, Captain Bern Anderson of the college's strategy department had submitted to Admiral Pye a proposed draft of a naval planning manual. Based on his own experience as planning officer with the Seventh Fleet and teaching at the college, Anderson, like Spruance, wanted it "to be purely a practical guide," omitting "insofar as practicable theoretical and philosophical discussions."[45]

Spruance recommended to the Chief of Naval Operations in March 1946 that a manual be published with a standardized "check off sheet" for the estimate of the situation and standard format for orders. The latter agreed.[46]

By March 1947, the college had published for its own teaching purposes the *Naval Manual of Operational Planning*, and forwarded it to the Chief of Naval Operations for approval and servicewide distribution. In the foreword, Spruance wrote that the new manual "attempted to combine, in the clearest and simplest terms, the various existing instructions in effect for planning naval operations."[47] In 1948, the book became the U.S. Navy's basic planning manual. In 1953, after several, perhaps unavoidable, revisions, the college issued the manual under a new title, *Naval Operational Planning (NWP-11)*. With minor revisions, it has continued in use since that time.[48]

There were no formal retirement ceremonies on 30 June 1948 when Spruance hauled down his flag. No senior Navy Department official was on hand, and no relief had been designated. Rear Admiral Allen E. Smith, chief of staff, assumed the presidency temporarily. By special act of Congress, Spruance would receive the pay and allowances of a full admiral for his lifetime, the best the Navy Department could do to give this World War II leader and hero equal status with the dashing Fleet Admiral William F. Halsey, Spruance's opposite number in the Pacific campaigns and admired friend. On the morning of 1 July, Admiral Smith's two-star flag had already replaced Spruance's four stars at the War College flagstaff on Luce Hall as Admiral and Mrs. Spruance got into their fully laden car at the President's House and drove to Gate 1, expecting to slip quietly by the sentry. There in the early morning sunlight were the Naval Base Band, a full guard from the Marine Barracks, War College staff officers, and many others from the Fleet and the Base. Watching from the sidelines were many families. The band sounded off with four ruffles and flourishes and the admiral's march while all hands saluted. Spruance got out of his car and greeted those who had come to say "farewell," then drove on. World War II's "Quiet Warrior" retired quietly from the Navy in which he had served for 45 years.[49]

Spruance succeeded in reasserting the college's position as the Navy's senior educational institution, lending it both dignity and prestige. Yet, essential questions relating to course curricula, student selection, educational philosophy, and institutional purpose remained to be answered as the Navy grappled with understanding its own role and function in a new era of warfare.

By 1948, the recommendations of the Pye, JCS, and Holloway boards had still not been fully implemented in respect to middle-and senior-level officer education. In March 1948, the Chief of Naval Personnel, Vice Admiral T. L. Sprague therefore convened another board under Rear Admiral C. C. Hartman to recommend a program of education and training of line officers to provide the best feasible means to prepare them for high command.

In preparing its recommendation, the Hartman Board emphasized that "high command requires an education ensuring knowledge of the capabilities and limitations of all the tools with which modern naval warfare is waged." This education must be progressive and, as an officer advances in rank, concentrate less on specialized duties and more on broad areas of high command. "In other words," the board noted, "his identification with any particular specialty or branch becomes less marked as he moves on in his career."[50]

The board perceived the basic problem to be that "new weapons produce dominant groups of officers."

> The importance of each new weapon, if only because it is new, gives prestige to the officers skilled in its use. That acts as an incentive for that group to seek special privilege, authority, and autonomy. This is natural and normal. Therefore, it becomes incumbent that the Navy establish a training and educational system which constantly emphasizes the importance of high command relative to any specialty.[51]

In its final recommendation, the Hartman Board revived the Pye Board's proposal for a command and staff course to replace the Naval War College junior course. After completion of this course a specified number of officers should then be sent on to one of the command and staff or war college courses provided by the Army, Air Force, or Marine Corps. Above this level, the board recommended two further educational assignments in an officer's career, one in the grade of commander and another at the captain or flag officer level. These levels of education would be controlled by a career planning board under the Chief of Naval Personnel, which would balance an officer's qualifications and experience with the future needs of the service and "ensure that . . . no group of officers subconsciously imposes their ideas on the naval service."[52]

Both these Navy boards agreed on the basic principles of an educational structure for the Navy, but, at the same time, none of their recommendations were able to remedy the existing situation of the Naval War College which needed high-quality officers to be diverted from operational, administrative, and staff positions, and Navy funds to be diverted for service education.

Postwar Newport, a Year-Round Fleet Base

Vice Admiral Donald B. Beary hoisted his flag as president of the Naval War College on November 1, 1948 as Spruance's successor and became Senior Officer Present, Narragansett Bay. The postwar Newport Naval Base was in full operation, commanded by Rear Admiral T. Ross Cooley. The primary mission of the base was to support units of the Atlantic Fleet with home ports in the Bay.

The Naval War College continued to be a tenant activity located at Naval Station, Newport. Other activities included the Quonset Point Naval Air Station, the Naval Hospital, Naval Supply Depot, and the Naval Station. In the years ahead there would be various base reorganizations as new commands, such as the Naval Communications Station and the Naval Schools Command, were formed. The important postwar change for the city of Newport was that it became the home port of more than one quarter of the Atlantic Fleet. With the exception of station ships and experimental craft at the Torpedo Station, no units had called Narragansett Bay home port before 1946.

In 1949 Newport's portion of the Atlantic Fleet included a carrier division, berthed at the large pier at Quonset, and Commander Destroyer Force, Atlantic on board a tender at Melville, with berthing there for a squadron of destroyers. There were also a cruiser division and several more destroyer squadrons with tenders and Service Force ships mooring to buoys in the East Passage of the bay. For the crews of these ships it was a perilous existence in wintertime, and the arrival of additional ships during the Korean war compounded the problem. Boating between ships and shore was frequently suspended, and Newport as a home port for ships had few votes of approval from the sailors. Reenlistment figures of the period in Newport emphasize this point, as do police statistics for the Thames Street and West Broadway areas. In March 1953, the sinking of a loaded liberty launch from U.S.S. *Yellowstone*, in which some 20 lives were lost, finally brought Navy Department approval of money for piers at Coddington Cove. In another four years there was pier space for most of the destroyers. The cruisers were then based in Boston, and only a lonely oiler could be seen swinging to a buoy off the War College.

The fleet making its home port in Newport brought economic benefits to the area and, although the Navy constructed several housing projects, private construction boomed, particularly in Middletown and Portsmouth, which grew rapidly. In 1951, the Army vacated Fort Adams and the Navy took over the property, using its old and spacious officers' quarters for the War College staff. A low-cost housing project, known as Brenton Village, was constructed on the former parade ground. Here both War College students and fleet officers vied for housing to be allocated by the Naval Base Commander. Traditionally, the designation and allocation of quarters ashore have been a delicate administrative problem, often settled only at the top level of command. Newport, with its large Navy population from many divergent commands, was no exception. Stacks of correspondence on the relative merits of sea or shore duty in the assignment of quarters attest to a never-ending problem for Newport's base commanders.

With the fleet based in the Bay area, one important goal of Luce, Sims, and later War College presidents seemed to have been realized as fleet officers often attended lectures at the War College and analyzed and evaluated fleet exercises in Pringle Hall. The War College and the fleet were drawing closer together once again.

Command and Staff Course

When regular War College classes resumed in the fall of 1946, the junior course, originally established in 1923, consisted of 35 officers in the rank of commander and lieutenant commander, including officers of equivalent rank from the other services. The course curriculum paralleled the senior course, with most of the lectures attended by both classes. Game board problems found the junior class taking subordinate positions on each side. When the logistics class was formed in 1947, the junior class continued in concert with the senior strategy curriculum, attending certain logistics lectures with them.

By 1947, the college was making plans to reorient the junior class curriculum toward more detailed staff work, following the recommendations of the Pye Board. The Army since 1900 had operated its Command and General Staff College at Fort Leavenworth, graduation from which was almost mandatory for promotion and further education. An Army Air Corps Command and Staff School had opened in 1946 at Maxwell Field, Alabama, and in the next year the Armed Forces Staff College opened in Norfolk. The Navy needed a similar course with a larger output of graduates to educate its intermediate-level officers. For naval officers there was no adequate stepping-stone from initial postgraduate-level, technical education at the General Line School to the senior-level war colleges. Spearheaded by Captain Claude Ricketts of the college's strategy department, Admiral Beary's staff reorganized the junior class curriculum with emphasis on understanding the fundamentals of warfare. The new course, which would begin in 1950, stressed operational planning, staff organization, staff functions, and headquarters procedures afloat and ashore.

Round Table Talks—Broadening the Curricula

During Admiral Beary's presidency, the college made a significant attempt to broaden the students' view by bringing knowledgeable civilians to Newport for a conference. The seeds for these discussions were sown with the arrival at the college of Rear Admiral C. R. Brown in 1948. At first, Brown was special assistant to Admiral Spruance, and with the departure of Rear Admiral Smith that fall, he became the college's chief of staff. Brown had been the Navy's representative at the

Air War College after the war and as such had first-hand knowledge of the Air Force's view of service unification and of Air Staff philosophy. He had been impressed by the contact which the Air Force fostered at every opportunity with the world of business and industry. In his first few months as chief of staff, Brown organized a week of round table talks to take place shortly before graduation of the three college classes in May 1949. In these talks prominent civilians and a few senior officers from the three services joined the staff and students for a five-day period of study and discussion on "the future strategy of the United States." Visitors were carefully integrated in student sections to participate in this final exercise of the academic year and to expose them to the ideas and thinking of the prospective graduates. In turn, the graduates about to return to the fleet would hear the views of leading civilians as well as officials from Washington on many current issues with military implications.

Initially, most of the invited participants came from the business community to support the economic and logistic portion of the year's study. In view of the important work of the World War I War Industries Board, the Army Industrial College had already established close relations with industry. Bernard Baruch, head of that board, lectured in the Naval War College's logistics course in 1947-1948, and he may well have encouraged the War College to follow a similar pattern in its round table discussions. After three years, the round table talks were renamed Global Strategy Discussions, and gradually included a broader segment of civilians. Each day's session included one lecture from an important civilian or military visitor for the entire group.

These sessions were and still are an important part of the school year. Invitations are eagerly sought after, and the sessions are as much a benefit for visitors as for their hosts. By 1954, Global Strategy Week had become an institution, requiring detailed planning, funding, and assistance from Newport's fleet units to provide accommodations and transportation for the visitors. Students were enthusiastic but also quite exhausted by the end of the busy week of lectures, seminars, and reports plus a busy social schedule in the evenings. More than one weary student's wife exclaimed, "What a wonderful week, but why do we have to pack up and move three days later?"

The Naval War College Review

In a separate attempt to widen the contacts of the war colleges, the Chief of Naval Personnel, Vice Admiral T. L. Sprague, suggested in early 1948 to the commandants of all the joint service colleges and the president of the Naval War College that they begin to publish a lecture reprint series, in order to make them "available to the majority of officers, who for various reasons are not able to attend the college."[53] Responding to this suggestion, Admiral Spruance told Sprague that the college was prepared to institute an "Information Service to Officers" upon receipt of definite authority. The contents of the publication, he advised, would be at the discretion of the president, Naval War College. It would be highly selective, not normally classified higher than "Restricted" and available only to individuals, not activities. Published by the correspondence course department, it appeared in October 1948 with Vice Admiral Robert B. Carney's lecture, "Logistical Planning for War" as its lead piece. Initially planned for distribution to officers in the grade of commander and above, the college was authorized in June 1949 to expand its distribution to lieutenant commanders and Marine Corps majors. Beginning with 3,000 copies in its initial issue, it was expanded to 6,000 copies per month by 1952 and distributed to major commands. In its fifth year, the college altered its name to *The Naval War College Review*. It continued to publish predominantly college lectures and to retain its "Restricted" classification until December 1953 when it was downgraded to "For Official Use Only." The classification of the *Review* sharply circumscribed its reading audience, a fact which Chief of Naval Operations Admiral Arleigh Burke noted in a memorandum in 1958:

> Both the Air Force and the Army have non-classified publications, published primarily by their war colleges, which are distributed to civilian subscribers and which probably have great influence on civilians who are interested in military affairs. Our Naval War College publications are For Official Use Only and, consequently, have practically no influence on civilian thought.[54]

The situation, however, was not altered until the September 1964 issue when all classification was removed. The change to include articles written by academics did not occur until the editorship of Commander R. M. Laske, 1968-1975, when the lack of articles forced Laske to search for contributors at American Political Science Association conventions and the Inter-University Seminar on the Armed Forces and Society.

The Search for Civilian Faculty

As Spruance was preparing to leave the college in May of 1948, he approved a plan to employ a professor of history and education because he and other officers on the staff felt the need for continuity and professional advice in the field of education. At the same time, Spruance saw the importance of having a lecturer who could broaden the outlook of the staff and students by giving lectures on social, political, and naval history.[55] As the concept for the position evolved, the acting president of the college, Rear Admiral A. E. Smith, wrote to the Secretary of the Navy, "At the present time, there is widespread confusion of thought in the evaluation of the effect of science, industry, and new weapons on national strategy and the conduct of war." As a result of this, the American public seemed to have lost sight of sea power in the country's national development, and the Navy had also lost prestige because it had failed to explain the case for sea power. All the new developments had both increased efficiency and complicated modern living, but as Smith wrote, "they have not changed the basic facts of life, either in peace or in war." The case for sea power was as strong as ever, he believed. "It only needs to be spelled out, as Mahan was able to do once before when sea power was under challenge." While the short-range effort in convincing Congress and the people lay with leaders in Washington, "The Naval War College is ideally suited to exert long-range leadership in our efforts to bring land, sea, and air power back into true perspective." The presence of a military and naval historian at the college would provide both continuity and a rallying point "for those within the Navy who possess the energy and the perspective to reinterpret sea power in the light of modern war."[56]

As C. R. Brown, the chief of staff, told Admiral Beary,

> We seek more than anything else a student of military history. We seek a thinker who, with the aid of practical students of sea power, can apply his background of military history and his ability to think to the problem of sea power. A professor of military history will be one of the means by which we clarify our thinking on the significance of sea power and maritime transportation in modern civilization. He will be one means by which the Naval War College will regain, maintain, and exercise world leadership in naval thought.
>
> As I see it, it is the task of a lifetime's work. If properly chosen, he will not get into a rut but will constantly develop and grow richer in experience and knowledge.[57]

This proposal was approved by the Secretary of the Navy on 29 December 1948, but "for lack of funds" the chair was not filled until three years later.[58]

Vice Admiral Richard Conolly

A second series of round table talks in early June 1950 preceded graduation, at which Admiral Forrest P. Sherman, the Chief of Naval Operations, spoke. Vice Admiral Beary, undergoing medical treatment in late June, was detached, and the college presidency was once again temporarily delegated, this time to Rear Admiral Cooley, Naval Base Commander. Cooley allowed the college's capable chief of staff, Captain Harry Felt, to deal with almost all issues relating to the college.

Students arriving in the summer of 1950 found that the Navy was at war. On 25 June, a well-organized North Korean army invaded South Korea. It was an act which seemed, at the time, strangely reminiscent of Hitler's moves in 1939.

On 11 August 1950, the college's first command and staff course convened with only 31 officers. The Korean war can be blamed in part for the smaller number of students than the last of the junior courses that had preceded it. But there were clear suggestions that the War College continued to have low priority in the eyes of detail officers at the Bureau of Naval Personnel.

Some students and staff were ordered to sea because of the Korean war, but Naval War College classes convened on schedule and were welcomed by Rear Admiral Cooley. Cooley was detached two months later, turning the college over to Captain Felt. By this time the orders for a new president had been published. He was Admiral Richard L. Conolly, then serving as Commander-in-Chief, U.S. Naval Forces, Europe and the Mediterranean (CINCNELM). On 2 December 1950, he hoisted his flag as a vice admiral over Luce Hall.

Conolly came ashore after almost continuous command and staff assignments in the fleet since May 1939. A destroyer man and amphibious leader, he brought a wealth of war and postwar experience to Newport. In his four years as CINCNELM with headquarters in London he reorganized the Navy's forces in the European area, changing the structure from one primarily in support of U. S. occupation forces to a tactical fleet, the backbone of NATO's naval power in the Mediterranean Sea. Like Luce, Sims, Pratt, and Spruance, he came to the Naval War College with a clear and up-to-date knowledge of the Navy's operational problems and commitments.

New Courses

Conolly marked his presidency by attempting to broaden the curriculum. Shortly after he arrived at the Naval War College, he quickly realized the dilemma the institution faced. The Bureau of Naval Personnel continued to pursue its general policy, which allowed a proportion of officers the opportunity to attend only one War College level course in their careers. Following the reopening of the Army's War College, first at Fort Leavenworth in 1950 and then moving to Carlisle Barracks in 1951, the Army revised its policy of officer assignment to the junior colleges. The Navy followed suit, and both services thereafter sent officers in the rank of lieutenant commander and major to the Armed Forces Staff College. The Navy viewed the three remaining colleges, National War College, Industrial College of the Armed Forces, and Naval War College, as the highest level of education for naval officers.

The Bureau of Naval Personnel declined to follow the Army's example in issuing a policy statement identifying its own War College as the apex of the Navy's educational system. Instead, the Navy merely established a policy by which only 47 percent of each promotion group of naval officers would be assigned to a senior war college course. Of the total number, 29 percent would be sent to the Naval War College, 9 percent to the National War College, and another 9 percent to the Industrial College of the Armed Forces. Despite this policy, staff members in Newport believed that the Army and Air Force continued to evaluate the Naval War College senior course as one of relatively lower standard than senior courses at other war colleges because the Navy had failed to implement the recommended policies requiring prior attendance at the General Line School and War College junior-level courses.[59]

Conolly had his own clear views of strategy, based partly on his own studies as a student and then as a staff member at the Naval War College in 1929-1931 and partly on his experience as a destroyer squadron and amphibious commander in the Atlantic and Pacific during the war plus his postwar experience as a Deputy Chief of Naval Operations and as CINCNELM.[60] In approaching the presidency, Conolly sought to revitalize the institution through new courses. His first move was to establish a course in advanced study in strategy and sea power and to create a research and analysis department.

Approved by the Chief of Naval Operations, Forrest Sherman, in July 1951, the new course in advanced study in strategy and sea power was headed by Captain J. C. Wylie. Officers ordered to the new course were expected to stay up to three years and to be limited to flag officers, selectees for flag rank, and captains who had completed the resident course.[61]

The motivation behind the course was the college's dissatisfaction with the state of thinking on sea power. "The poverty of contemporary naval strategic thought is, I think, self-evident," Captain Wylie wrote. He added,

> Naval participants in the unification hearings displayed a considerable degree of confusion, internal contradiction, and lack of originality whenever they spoke about strategic meanings of sea power. Navy professional journals show a striking reluctance to discuss controversial strategic problems. The Navy, it would seem, has been unable to successfully educate the American people in the imperatives of modern naval strategy and largely because the Navy has no clear concept of just what its strategic necessities are.[62]

Wylie attributed this situation to the lack of any person in the Navy who was assigned the primary job of speculating, evolving, and forming strategic naval thought. To change this, students would first have to be given a sound working relationship with the relevant social sciences. "The Navy has, to a reasonable degree," Wylie wrote, "isolated itself from the general cultural developments which bear directly upon modern strategy."[63] Students needed contact with social psychologists, anthropologists, economists, political scientists, and other groups which were unknown to the classical thinkers such as Clausewitz, Jomini, and Mahan.

This process would take at least a year. It would be paralleled by participation in the senior course at the War College plus an intensive course in naval history to give depth to the students' only superficial understanding of their own profession. In the second year, the students would undertake a piece of research which in a third year could be worked up to a book or article. After that, each student would be ready to undertake a piece of original writing on strategy. "If the project were wildly successful," Wylie suggested, "we might discover two or three men every five or six years who have a real feel for strategy, a creative impulse in expressing themselves, and with the broad conceptual type of intelligence that would allow them to become strategic thinkers of the first quality."[64]

There were seven members of the first group to undertake the course: Rear-Admiral Ralph Earle, Jr.; Captains George R. Phelan, James H. Hogg, Robert A. Theobald, Jr., Charles J. Odend'hal, Jr., and Marine Colonel George A. Roll, with Captain J. C. Wylie as the staff member. Of the seven, five continued to the second-year stage, but only two, Phelan and Theobald, completed the three-year course of study. During that period a number of individual studies were undertaken, including an examination of "Strategies Open to Russia", "Malta and Restricted Waters," and other aspects of maritime strategy.[26] Rather than seek wide publication of their work, the group decided among themselves that the best means of disseminating their ideas was to volunteer their services as speech writers to senior flag officers and civilian officials. At the same time, they offered their services to planning officers on fleet staffs who were writing or revising fleet operation plans. Through these methods, they focused attention on the purposes for which sea power was used. In particular, they stressed the idea that the end purpose of sea power was not command of the sea, but to project American power on distant shores, in a variety of ways.

In order to support the high-level course, Admiral Conolly moved to revive the 1948 approval of civilian professors at the Naval War College. "The naval officer, in general, is a man trained and experienced in dealing with concrete facts," Wylie explained. "The problem in this course is the different one of dealing with ideas in their abstract form."[27] The question was one of intellectual reorientation for the student, so the question as to what kind of professor filled the chair of history was extremely important. Wylie suggested that there were three types of knowledge to be had from historians: knowledge of what happened, knowledge of how to fight better based on an analysis of mistakes, and the study of historical interpretation as a tool to improve analysis. "It is the third area of knowledge—that of how to think better—that we are interested in here at the War College."[67]

But this was easier said than done. The interpretative historian interested in the matters that related to naval strategy and who could stimulate current thinking by careful thought about the past was "a very rare bird indeed." The college needed a thinker who had devoted his lifetime to an academic exploration of strategy, military philosophy, and naval history; yet there were few such people available. With a few notable exceptions, American historians seemed to be recorders and narrative historians rather than interpreters of the type the War College had in mind. This posed a problem. The college was looking for someone in Mahan's mold who could provide a knowledge of what had happened in the past and at the same time pursue an analytical thread that crossed academic boundaries in the study of international relations, historical synthesis, political science, economics, military science, philosophy, and other disciplines. Eventually, the college staff realized that it was unlikely to find all these attributes in a single man and moved, instead, to obtain the advice of several scholars whose work would complement each other in producing the wider outlook that the college sought.

In searching for an appropriate scholar, Conolly obtained the advice of Rear Admiral Charles J. Moore, Dr. James Phinney Baxter III, and Professor Harold Sprout. But even together, they found serious additional problems in finding scholars who were willing to alter their focus and move entirely out of the university environment to devote a career to the area the college wished to explore. Captain Wylie and his assistant, Lieutenant Commander Eugene Burdick, consulted a number of other academics in the search. Among them, Professor John von Neumann at The Institute for Advanced Study in Princeton and Professor Harold Lasswell, a sociologist at Yale, impressed upon Wylie the need for a theory of sea power and a vocabulary to talk about the theory.[68]

Although the college was unsuccessful in finding an academic to come to Newport for a long-term appointment, Professor Thomas C. Mendenhall of Yale University agreed to accept the professorship on a part-time basis from September 1951 to March 1952. He offered a series of ten seminar discussions on maritime history from the Age of Discovery to 1900, concluding with a two-day session devoted to defining the role of sea power in the contemporary world in the light of the historical overview. Finishing the course, Mendenhall told Admiral

Conolly, "I have nothing but praise to say of my students. They had been admittedly a little rusty in the kind of intellectual activity we were proposing, but their innate ability, industry, and willingness to lose themselves in the subject of a piece of research soon became apparent." The course, he said, was "a long-term investment in education, the fruits of which will become apparent only as these men return to their professional duties."[69]

The first year of the course was a further step in the college's postwar attempt to establish the study of "war and strategy, and particularly maritime strategy, as manageable units of study in theory and in generality."[70] Secretary of the Navy Robert B. Anderson clearly supported the idea behind it when he told the 1953 graduating class,

> It is true that genius such as Mahan's shows itself rarely. Whether or not another man of his calibre comes along within fifty years or five hundred is something over which you have no control. What you can control, and which is of the utmost importance, is the intellectual climate of the Navy's highest educational institution. Upon that factor, more than any other, depends the success or failure of your mission. It is an essential ingredient to the success or failure of the Navy itself. Axiomatically, the intellectual failures of today are the strategic failures of tomorrow.[71]

Stressing the need to go beyond the traditional goal of furthering an understanding of the fundamentals of warfare, Anderson said, "This War College has the duty of providing intellectual leadership in sea power and maritime strategy, not only for the Armed Forces, but for the United States as a whole."[73]

In the second year of the advanced study course, with assistance from outside scholars, the college strived to maintain the intellectual climate. After 1953, when Wylie was detached as staff member for advanced study, the course turned increasingly away from its initial emphasis on theory and became more of a problem-solving effort. But the need for both historical background and training in interpretive analysis led the college to seek the establishment of more civilian professorships and to establish three visiting professorships, each to be filled for a full academic year. In July 1951, the Chief of Naval Personnel authorized a full-time professorship of international law in addition to the professorship of military history. Since the 1890s, the college's professor of international law had continued his full-time teaching duties elsewhere with occasional visits to the War College to lecture and to edit the *International Law* "blue book." Since 1946, the international law position had been held by Manley O. Hudson of Harvard. Ill health prevented Hudson from accepting the new full-time position, although he was retiring from Harvard. Through his assistance, the college was able to appoint Professor Hans Kelsen as the first full-time resident professor of international law. In November 1951 a chair of social sciences was also authorized, and in 1953 the Secretary of the Navy approved naming two of the chairs, the Ernest J. King Chair of Maritime History and the Chester W. Nimitz Chair of Social and Political Philosophy.

The first full-time resident holder of the history chair was Professor J. H. Kemble, followed by Professor Charles H. Haring, who occupied the chair at the time it was named in honor of Fleet Admiral King. The social sciences chair was first held by Professor W. M. McGovern, followed by Professor W. T. Jones.

In the following year, 1954, the college saw the need to expand further the civilian faculty and requested the establishment of three additional civilian academic positions, one each in political, economic, and social elements of national power at the assistant and associate professor level, to teach for six months. Titled as academic consultants, the first to hold these positions were Dr. Alfred D. Chandler, Dr. William Reitzel, and Dr. Robert E. Osgood, in 1955. The civilian staff was further expanded by the establishment of a chair of physical science, first held by Professor W. E. Albertson.[73]

All these civilian appointments were short-term ones, changed usually once a year. Through this method, the college was able to expand its contacts in the university world and broaden both its outlook and perspective by using civilian academics in all areas of the curriculum. At the same time, however, the constant rotation of both military and civilian staff prevented continuity in curriculum development.

Research and Analysis Department

Concurrently with the establishment of the advanced study in strategy and sea power, Admiral Conolly created a new department devoted to research and analysis. Begun with Captain W. W. Strohbehn as its first head, the research and analysis department was separated from the advanced study of strategy and sea power course. The latter aimed toward the higher education of officer students and the enlargement of knowledge on the nature of strategy and sea power. Conolly designed the department of research and analysis to provide a service to the other departments of the War College and to the Navy, as a whole, by furnishing tools for more effective solution to operational problems, and to deal with specific research projects and problems.

The department worked on the naval planning manual, began to collect data on the Korean war, and undertook extensive work on naval logistics. To support the work on logistics, the George Washington University Logistics Research Project supplied the department with a secretary, and retired Rear Admiral Henry E. Eccles was engaged by George Washington to work part-time in the research and analysis department. From the series of research papers which Eccles wrote at this time, he produced his book, *Logistics in the National Defense*,[74] a study which President Henry Wriston of Brown University commended to a wide audience.

Naval Warfare Course

To complement the advanced work done by the research and analysis department and the advanced study of strategy and sea power, Conolly wanted to upgrade the regular courses. When Conolly took command at the Naval War College, the command and staff course was already in its first year of operation. At the senior level, the curricula of the strategy and logistics courses were separate, but had grown closer. Following the Pye report, which called for increased strategic-level education, including "joint military thought such as combined staff procedures and combined exercises,"[75] more speakers brought a greater variety of topics to the Pringle Hall podium. Conolly continued this trend but soon realized that there was a limit to what could be effectively assimilated during a ten-month academic year.

To solve the problem, a lengthened senior course seemed a good option. With support from the new Chief of Naval Operations, Admiral Robert B. Carney, who had urged the 1947 establishment of the logistics course, and his new Chief of Personnel, Vice Admiral James L. Holloway, the War College staff planned a revised senior education program, combining the separate strategy and logistics courses into a single two-year course, titled naval warfare. Conolly directed three members of the staff, Captain S. M. Barnes, and Commanders W. M. Kaufman and H. T. Gannon, to prepare a staff study exploring the rationale for a new course, but before their work was completed, Conolly went ahead and proposed a new two step course. Starting from the basic premises that had been approved by Admiral Carney, the new course, naval warfare 1, would lead directly into the second year, naval warfare 2 (which could be taken in whole or in part).

The first year would be suitable for commanders and junior captains, and the second year was a high-level course suitable for senior captains in preparation for flag rank. This change to the curriculum was designed to make the college courses available to the maximum possible number of officers and at the same time make allowance for a full and useful education for high command, taking into account "the complexities and advances in modern and future warfare."

This approach was based on the premise that the Naval War College must carry through to the highest level and not be relegated to an intermediate role. If naval officers were to make proper military decisions that related to political reality, they had to be educated in international political factors, military decisions, the theory of strategy, social and political science, natural economics, mobilization, international law, and the principles of logistics. As the staff committee declared, "Lack of more thorough and widespread education in higher military matters has hampered the Navy . . . in the past and will continue to operate against the best interest of the Navy, the national defense, and the nation unless and until remedied."[76]

The staff committee's work was deep and broad, ranging from consideration of the basic purpose of the college to its relation to the exercise of high command. The committee asserted, "higher education in the Navy must so prepare senior naval officers [that]—in future positions of great responsibility, harassed by the daily pressures created by the conduct of important affairs—called upon suddenly for thought, they need not rely entirely on memory of past experiences to guide their decisions."[77]

As explained by the staff study, the first year naval warfare course was devoted to the fundamentals of warfare. It emphasized the integrated employment of all the elements of naval power, seeking at the same time to develop the students' powers of logical thought in military affairs. In the second year, the course was to further an understanding of fundamentals by emphasizing strategic employment of the Navy in relation to national objectives, and developing breadth of vision and highly developed reasoning power. Conolly hoped that the two-year course sequence would be temporary; it really represented "catch-up" ball. He planned that much of the naval warfare 1 curriculum would soon be included in the command and staff course. Then, as attendance at the latter course increased, officers returning for the senior-level courses could go directly to naval warfare 2.

The separate strategy and logistics courses ended in Conolly's last year, and in August 1954 naval warfare 1 and 2 classes convened for the first time. The two-year curriculum lasted for five years before further changes were made. Actually, few students stayed for two full years. The Bureau of Naval Personnel filled the classes to about 60 each, but the War College segregated them on the basis of their qualifications. From those who stayed for the entire two years, there was a mixed reaction. Most lectures were attended by those in both courses, and in more than 150 talks each year duplication was inevitable. The distinction between the courses was lost in a few years' time. At the War College "cabaret" in 1955, a group of second-year naval warfare students serenaded the president and an amused audience with the "Song of the Bilgers," using the old Naval Academy term suggesting that they had been failed and held over for a second year of Newport study.

Conolly's reforms to the War College were substantial and important ones, which reflected many of the insights gained in World War II; however, the college still lacked a clear Navy or Defense Department policy that firmly defined the college's role and purpose. Moreover, the constant flux in faculty and staff appointments prevented the long-term continuity Conolly's new plans required. Conolly's retirement from the Navy in 1953 to become president of Long Island University left the reforms without their prime mover.

Notes

1. "Lecture Remarks by Admiral Carney at the Naval War College, 1947," Part VI of Annex G, p. G-35 of S. M. Barnes, W. M. Kaufman, and H. T. Gannon, Staff Study, "The United States Naval War College," 1954. NWC Library, shelf number U420 U5 1954. [Hereinafter, staff study 1954.]

2. Nepier V. Smith, "Historical Analysis of the Organizational Success of the Naval War College During the Twenty-five Years Following the Second World War," NWC Advanced Research Project, 1974, pp. 145-149.

3. JCS 962/2 of 22 June 1945.

4. John Masland and Lawrence Radway, *Soldiers and Scholars* (Princeton, Princeton University Press, 1957), pp. 130-34.

5. NWC Archives, RG3, Box 2. File A2-12(B) ANSCOL: JCS 962/2, 22 June 1945. Annex D to Appendix A, p.30.

6. Masland and Radway, op. cit..

7. NWC Archives, R6 3, Box 2. File A 2-12(B): JCS 962/4 of 17 Aug 1945.

8. Loc. cit. Report of Holloway Board. 29 Sept 1945.

9. Ibid., p. 2.

10. Ibid., p. 3.

11. J. L. Holloway, Jr. "The Holloway Plan—A Summary View and Commentary," U.S. Naval Institute *Proceedings*, Vol. 73, No. 11 (Nov. 1947), p. 1303.

12. NWC Archives RG 3, 1945-68, Series Box 2, File 5213. "Education of Naval Officers of the Post War Navy," Briefing presented to Secretaries Sullivan, Kenny, and Brown, 3 Nov. 1947 by Captain J. M. Will, USN.

13. Thomas Buell, *The Quiet Warrior*, (Boston: Little, Brown, 1974), pp. 383-4.

14. Quoted in ibid., p. 385.

15. Recollection of RADM H. E. Eccles. Conversation with J. B. Hattendorf, 20 Dec. 1983.

16. Buell, *Quiet Warrior*, p. 387.

17. Quoted in ibid., pp. 387-88.

18. Quoted in ibid., p. 388. Commencement Address, University, 1948.

19. Ibid., p. 390.

20. Robert M. Leighton and Robert W. Coakley, *Global Logistics and Strategy, 1940-43* (Washington: Office of Chief of Military History, 1955), pp. 62-68.

21. Henry E. Eccles, *Operational Naval Logistics* (Washington, 1950), p. 2.

22. NWC Archives, RG 27, Subject File: Logistics Course: Lecture by Ralph E. Smith, "A History of Logistics at the Naval War College."

23. Ibid., p. 4. Quoting address of VADM Robert B. Carney at Naval War College, 12 July 1947.

24. Interview with RADM Eccles, 27 June 1980.

25. NHC, MSS Collection 52: H. E. Eccles Papers: Eccles to F. H. Whitaker, 2 Dec. 1947. These paragraphs are based on conversations with and comments by

RADM Eccles. The quotation is from H. E. Eccles, *Operational Naval Logistics* (Washington: Bureau of Naval Personnel, April 1950) NAVPERS 10869, p. iii.

26. NWC Archives, RG 27: Logistics Course Subject File: Lecture by Ralph E. Williams, "A History of Logistics at the Naval War College," pp. 25-32.

27. E. J. King, "Foreword" dated 8 January 1943, printed in each volume of the series "Combat Narrative" by Publication Section, Combat Intelligence Branch, Office of Naval Intelligence, United States Navy, 1943-45.

28. NWC Archives, RG 23: Battle Evaluation Group Records, Box 3, File H: Official Correspondence 1946-56. CNO to President, Naval War College ser. 0331P34 of 24 May 1946 and COMINCH Conf. memo 03072 of 4 Sept. 1944.

29. NHC Bates Papers, Ms. Coll. 28, Box 5, Folder 17: Spruance to Bates, 19 June 1946.

30. NWC Archives, RG 23, Box 3, File 5: "Relief Folder," p. 1.

31. NWC Archives, RG 23, Box 1: *The Battle of the Coral Sea: Strategical and Tactical Analysis* (1947), pp. 114-15.

32. Loc. cit., *The Battle of Midway: Strategical and Tactical Analysis* (1948), pp. 213-14.

33. Loc. cit., *Battle of Savo Island: Strategical and Tactical Analysis* (1950), p. 359.

34. Ibid., p. 360.

35. H. E. Eccles, "Rear Admiral Richard W. Bates, 1892-1973," NWC Review (May-June 1974), p. 7.

36. S. E. Morison, "Faith in An Historian," *American Historical Review* LVI (Jan. 1951), pp. 261-75. Reprinted in *By Land and By Sea: Essay and Address by Samuel Eliot Morison* (New York: Knopf, 1953). Quote from pp. 349-50.

37. James Forrestal, "Preface" to S. E. Morison, *History of U.S. Naval Operations in World War II* (Boston: Little Brown 1947), Vol. I.

38. NWC Archives, RG 3, Box 12, File A-12: Naval History Memo-2-49 of 25 May 1949.

39. NWC Archives, RG 3, Box 2, File A12-2.

40. Loc. cit., Morison to Spruance, 13 May 1946.

41. HC Ms. Coll. 28: Bates Papers, Box 5, Folder 17: RADM A. E. Smith to R. W. Bates, 26 July 1946.

42. Loc. cit., Box 33, File A-12 (1981), Morison to R. L. Conolly, 16 May 1951.

43. NHC, Ms. Col. 37: T. B. Buell (Collector) Research Materials Relating to Raymond Spruance. Box 2: Chief of Staff Memo for the Staff, 12 March 1946.

44. Ibid.

45. NWC Archives, RG 3, Box 1. File A16-1. Captain Bern Anderson to President, NWC. 5 Nov. 1945.

46. NWC Archives, RG 27: Subject File, Military Planning Process: CNO to President, NWC, serial 321P30 of 3 Oct. 1946.

47. Loc. cit., Subject File 1947.

48. C. W. Cullen, "From the Kriegsacademie to the Naval War College: The Military Planning Process," *NWC Review* (January 1970), p. 17.

49. Buell, *The Quiet Warrior*, p. 398.

50. Loc. cit., Hartman Board report, p. 2.

51. Ibid. chart #5.

52. Ibid. chart #7.

53. NWC Archives, R63: 1948 Box 11 File P11-3: CNP to War College Commandants, 26 April 1948.

54. NWC Archives, RG33: CNO Memo for OP-90 of 22 Jan 1958, copy to NWC. Quoted in NWC Review Editor Memo to President, 6 March 1970.

55. NWC Central Files: 12040, chairs, establishment of: President, NWC, to SECNAV, 28 July 1948.

56. Loc. cit., President, NWC to SECNAV, 20 Oct 1948.

57. NWC Archives, RG3. 12040: (P-11) Chair of Military History, Folder 1: C. R. Brown Memo to Admiral Beary, 18 Nov 1948.

58. NWC Central Files: 12040: Chairs. Chief of Naval Personnel to President, NWC, 28 Jan 1949.

59. Staff Study, 1954, pp. 27-28.

60. See Donald G. White, "Admiral Richard G. Conolly: A Perspective on his Notions of Strategy," *NWC Review* (Nov. 1971), pp. 73-79.

61. NWC Archives, Advanced Study in Strategy and Sea Power Records: CNO to President, NWC, Ser 130PO3 of 3 July 1951.

62. Loc. cit. J. C. Wylie to Adm C. J. Moore, 13 July 1951.

63. Ibid.

64. Ibid.

65. Captain J. C. Wylie's study, "On Maritime Strategy," appeared in the USN *Proceedings*, Vol. 79, No. 5 (May 1953), pp. 467-477.

66. NWC Archives: Advanced Studies in Strategy and Sea Power Records. J. C. Wylie Memo to President, NWC, 9 June 1953, para. a.

67. Loc. cit., J. C. Wylie Memorandum on Military History, 2 April 1951.

68. Conversation: Hattendorf-Wylie, 18 January 1984. Wylie letter to B. M. Simpson, 23 March 1982.

69. Loc. cit., T. C. Mendendall to R. L. Conolly, 19 March 1952.

70. Loc. cit., J. C. Wylie memo to President, NWC, 9 June 1953.

71. NWC Archives, RG16: Graduation Address: Robert B. Anderson, 10 June 1953.

72. Ibid.

73. NWC Central Files: 12040: Case file: Chairs, establishment of

74. H. E. Eccles, *Logistics in the National Defense* (Harrisburg: Stackpole Co., 1959). See also NWC Archives, RG 27: Subject File: Research and Analysis Department.

75. Staff Study, 1954, pp. 1-3.

76. Ibid., p. 117.

77. Ibid., pp. 89-90.

34. Admiral Edward C. Kalbfus, Naval War College president, 1934-1936, 1939-1942.

COMDR. BS ARRIVES NAVAL W.C. JULY, 1937 PREPARED FOR A SERENELY MEDITATIVE YEAR, WITH STIMULATING EXERCISE AND SOME LIGHT PROFESSIONAL READING. THROUGH RENEWING OLD ASSOCIATIONS AND IMPROVING HIS GOLF, HE HOPES TO RECOVER FROM HIS STRENUOUS SEA CRUISE.

TIME MARCHES ON! COMDR. BS IN MAY, '38.

35. Student cartoon on Naval War College education, 1938.

36.   Admiral Raymond Ames Spruance, cla of 1927, staff member 1932-1933, 1936-19 and War College president, 1946-1948.

37.   Command Class, 1943. Commander Henry E. Eccles is in second row (extreme left)

38. Entrance to Sims Hall, former Naval Training Station Barracks C, acquired by the Naval War College in 1946 to house the Logistics Department.

39. A Logistics war game, Sims Hall, ca.1950.

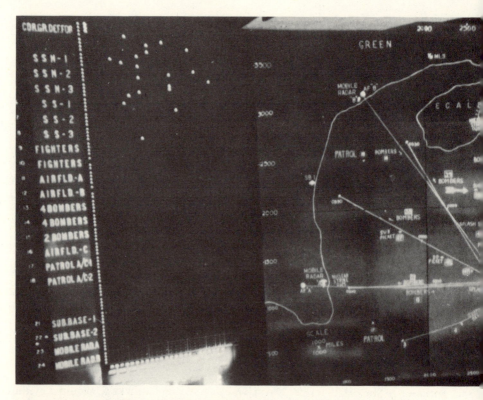

40. Umpire Area, Naval Electronic Warfare Simulator, Sims Hall, 1960.

41. Rear Admiral Henry E. Eccles, Head the Logistics Department, 1947-1951, a authority on military philosophy, strate and logistics in association with the Na War College for over thirty years.

214

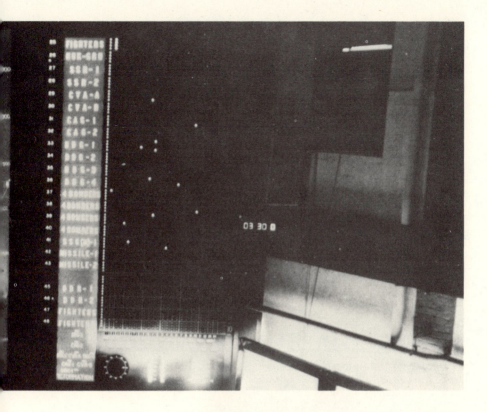

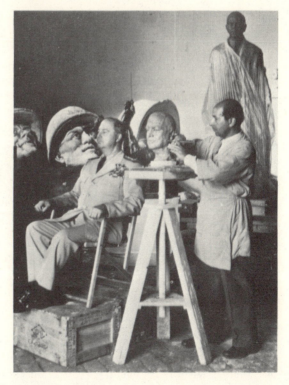

2. Admiral Richard L. Conolly, College president, poses for a bust by noted sculptor and friend of the College, Felix deWeldon, 1953.

43.   Students and staff of the first Naval Command Course, September 1956, during a visit to the Capitol, Washington, DC. Captain Richard Colbert, director of the course, is in the back row (second from right).

44.   Summer visitors President Dwight D. Eisenhower and Fleet Admiral Chester W. Nimitz, USN (Ret.) confer with Naval War College president Vice Admiral Bernard Austin, 1960.

45. President John F. Kennedy, 28 September, 1961. With the President are Allen W. Dulles, retiring Director of the Central Intelligence Agency and John A. McCone, his replacement. President Kennedy announced the change in a news briefing at the War College.

46. Naval War College campus, 1968.

47. Vice Admiral John T. Hayward, War College president, 1966-1968.

48. Vice Admiral Richard G. Colbert, War College president, 1968-1971.

49. Vice Admiral B.J. Semmes, War College president, 1971-1972, comments after the unveiling his official college portrait by college artist To Sarro at a Hail and Farewell party, June 1972.

50. Naval War College Foundation Board of Trustees, November, 1981. (left to right) Messrs. Freund, Anderson, Mrs. Crown, Mr. deWeldon, Rear Admiral Wadleigh, Ambassador Estes, Commander Albrecht, Ambassador Middendorf Board President, Rear Admiral Welch, NWC president, Mr. MacDonald, Mrs. Sturtevant, Messrs. Ruger, Caragianis, Mays, and Fairchild.

51. Civilian faculty line up for academic procession, convocation, June 1970. (left to right) Clyde Sargent, Oliver Lissitzyn, Neil Huntley, John M. Roberts, T.H. Williams, Stephen E. Ambrose, Phillip L. Gamble, J.C. Aller, Frederick H. Hartmann, August Miller, and Earl Schwass.

52. Vice Admiral Stansfield Turner, College president, presides at convocation, 1973. Seated to the right of Vice Admiral Turner is Secretary of the Navy William J. Middendorf.

53. First Naval Staff Course, 1972. College deputy president Rear Admiral W. Harris and course director Captain J. Quinn are in the front row.

54. Vice Admiral Julian LeBourgeois, College president, participates in a Rhode Island Independence Day celebration in downtown Newport, May 4, 1975. With Admiral LeBourgeois are members of the Newport Artillery Company.

55. Rear Admiral Huntington Hardisty, College president, with the Naval War College Board of Advisors, May 1977: seated, Professor Lyman B. Kirkpatrick, Jr.; Hardisty. Standing left to right, Admiral Horacio Rivero; Dr. David M. Abshire, Lieutenant General W.K. Jones, USMC; Vice Admiral James F. Calvert; Mr. Malcolm Forbes; Dr. Robert E. Ward; Mr. Richard Beverly Corbin, Jr.; Admiral Charles K. Duncan.

56.   Lecture in Spruance Hall auditorium. Spruance Hall, the first of three new buildings constructed during the 1970s, was completed in 1972.

57.   View of the Naval War College campus, 1978.

58. Interior of the Naval War College Museum, Founders Hall, 1981.

59. Change of command, August 1979. Rear Admiral Edward F. Welch, Jr. relieves Vice Admiral James B. Stockdale as president during college convocation ceremonies. In background (left to right) are Naval War College Foundation representative J. William Middendorf, II and Under Secretary of the Navy R. James Woolsey.

60. Center for Naval Warfare Studies, 1981. Strategic Studies Group I with visiting CNO Admiral Thomas Hayward, college president Rear Admiral Edward Welch, Jr., and center director Robert J. Murray.

61.   Umpire Area, Center for Naval War Gaming, Sims Hall, 1981.

62.   Convocation on Colbert Plaza, August 1983.

63.   Close-up of faculty group, Convocation, August 1983.

64.   A group of key civilian employees and staff, 1984.

65.   Rear Admiral James E. Service, College president, and foreign officer delegates with Secretary of the Navy John Lehman, International Seapower Symposium, 1983

66.   Naval War College Executive-Policy Group, May 1984, plus CNO.

Front row: Rear Admiral James E. Service, President, Naval War College
                 Admiral James D. Watkins, USN, Chief of Naval Operations
Second row: Professor Frederick H. Hartmann, Special Academic Advisor
                 Professor Robert S. Wood, Dean/Director of Naval Warfare Studies
                 Captain James M. Conway, USN, Dean of Academics
                 Captain Robert B. Watts, USN, Deputy
                 Captain Richard D. Coogan, USN, Dean of Administration
                 Captain William K. Sullivan, USN, Dean of Students
Third row: Mr. Edward L. Killham, Department of State Advisor
                 Professor Earl R. Schwass, Director of Library Department
                 Captain Robert A. Hall, USN, Director of Continuing Education
                 Captain Wright H. Ellis, USN, Director of Naval Command College
                 Captain Joseph P. Marnane, USN, Director of Naval Staff College
                 Captain Marshall B. Brisbois, USN, Director of Center for War Gaming
Fourth row: Colonel Laurence R. Gaboury, USMC, Advisor, U.S. Marine Corps
                 Colonel Richard E. Bauchspies, USA, Advisor, U.S. Army
                 Captain Nelson H. Keeler, USCG, Advisor, U.S. Coast Guard
                 Captain David A. Albrecht, USN, Staff Judge Advocate
                 Professor Alvin H. Bernstein, Chairman, Department of Strategy
                 Captain Jerome F. Watson, USN, Chairman, Department of Naval
                    Operations

CHAPTER 9

THE CONTINUING
QUANDARY, 1954-1966

The problems of the immediate postwar decade continued unsolved. Following Admiral Conolly's retirement from the Navy, the Bureau of Personnel delayed naming a new president of the Naval War College. The chief of staff, Rear Admiral Thomas H. Robbins, Jr., was named acting president in November 1953. A thorough military scholar, Robbins took a deep personal interest in naval strategy and in international relations.

The delay in assigning a new president came at an inopportune time for the college. Not only did it create uncertainty at a time when the college was trying to implement a new curriculum, but the delay gave the impression that the college was being given low priority. This impression only added to the doubts which the college already faced in terms of its role and position in service education. The delay in making the appointment also gave rise to speculation as to what type of officer was most suitable for the position and what impression his assignment makes to the naval officer corps. For some officers in the Navy, it seemed most appropriate that the college president be a man who was seen to be rising in the Navy and who had potential for the highest positions, instead of a final comfortable post for a man who was about to retire and to leave the service. For others, the college seemed to be the best place for a man of great experience, a kind of elder statesman among naval officers, who could help to educate younger officers in the light of his long career.

After a six-month delay, the Navy Department appointed Vice Admiral Lynde McCormick as president, allowing Robbins to resume his position as chief of staff in May 1954. McCormick was a distinguished officer who had already served 39 years in the Navy when he arrived at the college. Qualified in submarines, he had been a Naval War College student in 1937-1938 and commanded battleships in World War II. Appointed Vice Chief of Naval Operations in 1949, he served as Acting Chief of Naval Operations in 1951 following the sudden death of Admiral Forrest Sherman. He returned to the Naval War College after serving as Commander-in-Chief, Atlantic Fleet and Atlantic Command. In that position, McCormick had been the first to be Supreme Allied Commander, Atlantic.

Clearly McCormick was an elder statesman and he set about carrying out, in a quiet yet forceful manner, the plans which Conolly had laid. The basic college courses were stabilized, but in 1956 McCormick dealt with two important changes. First, the course in advanced study in strategy and sea power was discontinued and a new course for senior officers from other navies was established.

On 16 August 1956, before these changes could be fully developed and the day before a new class was to convene, the flags of more than 40 warships in Narragansett Bay and all local shore installations were lowered to half staff. An "All Ships and Activities" radio message from Commander Naval Base announced the sudden death of Lynde McCormick, president of the War College and Senior Officer Present, only a few days after he had celebrated his sixty-first birthday.

On 17 August, Rear Admiral Robbins, the chief of staff, and once again acting War College president, greeted the 1957 classes in Pringle Hall. The 287 officers in four incoming classes constituted the largest group that had convened up to that time. Noting that Admiral McCormick would have wanted no delays or changes in the routine of the college, Robbins stated, "The Admiral's love and devotion to this college could not be excelled. He spent his last days here devoting himself selflessly of his energies, broad experience, and wisdom to keep this college in the forefront of the military education field and in preparing officers to better serve our country in these perilous times."[1]

Establishing the Naval Command Course

Two weeks after the 1956-1957 academic year started, Robbins received orders to become president of the college in his own right for his fifth and last year on Coasters Harbor Island. The most significant event that year was the inauguration of the naval command course (NCC). Thus, at McCormick's death, the Naval War College entered a new phase in its history, for among the officers greeted by Admiral Robbins as the year began were senior naval officers representing 23 free world navies. They were the members of the naval command course. From then on, the Naval War College was more than a national school. By embarking on an international course, it became a school to influence both the strategy and thinking of allies and friends of the United States worldwide.

The establishment of the NCC put on a permanent and regular basis the participation of foreign officers in college courses, which had first occurred in 1894-1895. After that, foreign officers had not been seen in the classroom again until the ANSCOL course in 1943-1945, and the assignment of 15 officers from the Royal Navy as students in Naval War College courses between 1947 and 1951.

The move toward putting allied service education on a more systematic basis got a start in 1951 with the establishment of the NATO Defense College in Paris. When Admiral McCormick reported to Newport after two years as NATO's Supreme Allied Commander, Atlantic, graduates of the NATO College were appearing in both European and Atlantic allied staffs. McCormick had commanded several Atlantic NATO operations, including the largest allied peacetime sea operation up to that time, Mainbrace, in the North Atlantic. He was well aware of the need for better understanding among the allied navies and for better knowledge of each other's intentions and methods of operating. Admiral Arleigh Burke, too, realized this need, and in 1955, his first year as Chief of Naval Operations, he started working toward a solution.

Ten years earlier Burke had been chief of staff to Vice Admiral Marc Mitscher, Commander, Task Force 58, the Pacific Fleet's fast carriers. Off Okinawa, TF 58 was joined by the new British Pacific Fleet, built around four carriers. Rather than attempt to integrate the two groups, Mitscher assigned the British separate target areas, thus avoiding the complications of different operating procedures.

Soon after the end of the war, Burke was again Mitscher's chief of staff in the new Eighth Fleet, preparing for possible Mediterranean duty. Early in 1946 Burke accompanied his superior on a trip to Europe to talk with naval officers in Great Britain, France, and Italy concerning a possible war with Soviet Russia. Referring to Allied cooperation at that time, Burke reminisced, "We didn't have time to do much, but even that would have been a godsend if we had had trouble with the USSR."[2]

Six years later in 1952, Burke was director of OpNav's Planning Division (Op30). Here he found that NATO planning was difficult because American officers did not know their opposite numbers in London, Paris, and other NATO capitals. In the winter of 1955, as Commander, Destroyer Force, Atlantic Fleet, Burke had a chance to see how NATO plans were working out in operation. In the weekly coffee hours that Burke hosted for his captains based in Newport, the subject of NATO exercises came up frequently. Reports from the destroyer captains reinforced Burke's conviction that a most important factor in war was to know your friends. It followed naturally that soon after becoming CNO, Admiral Burke began laying the groundwork for bringing the U.S. and other NATO navies closer together. From a global viewpoint he also realized the need for closer coordination with friendly navies in the Pacific and the Americas.

In the next few months Burke made contact with leaders of several navies concerning ways of improving Allied naval operations. One option was to offer a year's course of study for senior officers at the Naval War College, a course modeled generally along the lines of the curriculum for the naval warfare 1 course. NATO naval officers seemed generally enthusiastic Burke said:

> As I remember, about the only objection they voiced was sending the wives over with their husbands. This was not a requirement, but it took a couple of years before foreign Navy Departments decided it was worth the extra cost to let the wives come too.[3]

By the spring of 1956, 23 navies had accepted Burke's invitation and had assigned officers for the first class, to convene that summer.

In Newport, Vice Admiral McCormick, at that time still in command, was convinced of the value of such a course to future naval planning and operations around the world, and he cooperated fully with Burke's plans. If enthusiasm at lower levels in Newport was initially restrained, it was because of worry that such a course might impinge on regular courses at the college. Burke later commented:

> He [Admiral McCormick] was absolutely correct that this new course should not reduce the caliber of the other work the War College was doing. The president and his staff made many helpful suggestions right from the start and after it was going awhile, their enthusiasm grew, perhaps due to the quality of foreign officers assigned.[4]

Burke continued to be involved in getting the new course off to a successful start:

> I had already learned that the CNO could not just give an order and expect to have it carried out. He had to get somebody who was in agreement with the project, who was just as enthusiastic about it, who was capable of running it without supervision, who could get things done, and who could use the authority delegated to him wisely to take charge of the project. That man was Dick Colbert.[5]

In January 1956, Captain Richard G. Colbert was a student in naval warfare 1 at the college. Recently promoted to captain, he had already been selected to remain for the next academic year as a student in naval warfare 2. Colbert was well known to Admiral Burke, having been one of his action officers when Burke was director of the Plans Division in OpNav. At that time Colbert was serving in the International Affairs Division with an office directly across the hall from Burke in the

Pentagon's "E" ring. Colbert had worked closely with Burke on many position papers and plans. Friendship and a mutual respect developed. Burke realized that few of the many staff action officers with whom he worked had Colbert's competence and background in the field of international relations. Colbert had not only been aide to Admiral Conolly, Commander in Chief, U.S. Naval Forces, Europe, for two years but he had served temporarily as aide to Admiral Forrest Sherman during his trip to Europe in the summer of 1951.

Putting his studies behind him, Colbert undertook to organize, guide, and instruct a most diverse group of senior seagoing officers. Four years earlier, while in Washington, he had written a brief staff study recommending such a course, and much of what he had learned then helped him to get started. As a relatively junior officer and with a myriad of personnel and logistic matters to be tackled, Colbert had to proceed with tact to find adequate resources. The east wing of Sims Hall had to be renovated to provide a separate area of offices, lecture rooms, and a small library for the foreign students on the social, political, and cultural background of the United States. One civilian professor was added to the college staff to work primarily with the new course. He was August C. Miller from Wheaton College. Miller was assigned as professor of international relations, a position which in 1961 was named the Milton E. Miles Chair of International Relations. Miller held the chair until his retirement in 1974. There was little holiday leave for Captain Colbert in the summer of 1956 following his graduation from naval warfare 1 and serving as a student moderator for a global strategy seminar group. Less than eight weeks later, the students for the new course had arrived.

The naval command course generally followed the curriculum of naval warfare 1. Students were included in as many of the regular War College lectures as consistent with security. When the other War College classes concentrated on highly classified matters, such as nuclear operations, the foreign officers took field trips. Using his extensive personal contacts, Colbert arranged for visits not only to U.S. military and naval activities but also to industrial plants in Buffalo, the International Telephone and Telegraph laboratories near New York, and the New York Stock Exchange.

On 25 August, the members of the new naval command course joined 1,000 U.S. officers from the fleet and shore establishment to hear and to question Admiral Burke in the base theater. Socially in Newport and professionally at the college, the class soon proved that Admiral Burke's request for topnotch officers had been understood well and acted upon in the capitals of the Allied nations.

The naval command course has continued much along the lines pursued by that first 1956-1957 group. The problems that faced Captain

Colbert, Professor Miller, and six other staff officers have changed little. Predictably and foremost, there is a language barrier to be overcome in varying degrees by both students and instructors, but the security problem has diminished with time. As a 1959 student wrote:

> It is surprising how much classified information is released to this course. It certainly looks to me as if an effort has been made by the U.S. Navy Department to go as far as it possibly can. In addition, officers of flag and general rank have made short and exceedingly frank 'off the cuff' remarks at our lectures. In general I am surprised anyway at the amount of information concerning the U.S. armed forces that is continually being released to the general public.[6]

At the beginning of the course, staff and students resembled a mutual admiration society. That gradually gave way to greater frankness in criticizing problem solving, presentations, and lectures. The same 1959 student pointed out that with more than 20 nationalities present there would always be reluctance knowingly to hurt another's feelings.

Changes in Courses and at the Helm

As Robbins approached the end of his term as president, the college faced a difficult problem in managing the curriculum that Admiral Conolly had established. Conolly had envisaged that in 10 years it would be possible to revert to a one-year naval warfare course. The two-year course was needed only to prepare for the senior course those students who had been unable to attend a command and staff course. Conolly had hoped that by the 1960s the Bureau of Personnel would be able to send enough officers to command and staff level courses that there would be a sufficient number of appropriately educated captains and commanders who could attend the naval warfare course without having to provide a preparatory course.

In less than three years from its establishment, Robbins faced the fact that the Bureau of Naval Personnel had not been able to carry out the commitment to the two-year program. The demand for officers at sea and in staff positions was so great that the Bureau was not able to allow students completing naval warfare 1 to proceed on to the second year of the course; with the exception of officers on the college staff who had received certificates of completion, only 13 student officers had completed the full two-year course.

In March 1957, Robbins recommended to the Chief of Naval Operations that in view of this situation, the naval warfare courses should be combined as soon as practicable and be pitched at the naval warfare 2 level. Approved to take effect in 1958, this alteration would put the college's courses more in line with those offered by the other war colleges. At the same time, it simplified the task of the Bureau of

Naval Personnel and those assigned to schedule and administer courses at the college.[7] However, it marked the end of Conolly's idea to expand and deepen the education of senior naval officers. The shortening of the course meant, also, the end of logistics as a distinct part in the study of strategy and high command in the college's curriculum. In the years immediately following World War II, prominent naval officers such as Spruance and Carney had believed that logistics had been ignored in naval education before World War II. Only a dozen years after the end of the war, this initial "lesson" of that war's experience was put aside.

The inability of the Bureau of Personnel to find enough senior officers to fill billets afloat and ashore has always been the main rationale for the Bureau's reluctance to assign students to the Naval War College. In 1956, Vice Admiral James L. Holloway, Jr., used the same reasoning when he advised the War College that no further officers were available for the course of advanced study in strategy and sea power. "The reason is a simple one;" Holloway wrote, "our commitments are already beyond our resources."

> The bare fact is that we are operating our naval establishment with a practical deficit of some 250 line captains . . . .
>
> No one could be more appreciative than I of the benefits likely to be gained from a full staffing of the Advanced Study group. We are in an era of transition of the very nature of sea power, faced with the absolute and over-riding requirement to maintain our present forces at maximum effectiveness while striving to ready our personnel for the technological advances they must cope with in the future forces. In this transition, our operating forces must rely heavily on the experience existing in our captains. One hundred fifty-one of such captains are now assigned as students or staff to the Senior Service Schools. To immobilize any additional captains in a purely academic area is not justifiable.[8]

Although the problems that the Bureau of Personnel faced were undoubtedly difficult, Holloway's statement played down what others would argue was the even greater importance of theoretical study in a time of transition. At the same time, however, it was a recognition that good theoretical work requires long years of intellectual development and exploration. If Naval War College staff members clearly saw the need to continue in this area, Washington policymakers had little interest in it. For them, studies that helped to justify the Navy's policy positions were more appropriate and useful.[9]

In June 1957, Robbins officiated at the largest graduation up to that time, including the awarding of diplomas to students of the first class of the newly established naval command course. Among the graduates were 24 members of the college staff who, although they had not taken the course, were given diplomas in recognition of their teaching it.

Shortly after the ceremony, Robbins received orders to the Office of the Secretary of the Navy, and later went on to be Commandant of the Potomac River Naval Command. He was the first college president since World War II who did not immediately leave active service.

The incoming president, Vice Admiral Stuart H. Ingersoll, was also an aviator. When he came to Newport he had already served for 12 years as a flag officer, and he brought not only aviation expertise but a broad background of planning and command assignments in post-World War II unified commands, including the directorship of strategic planning in OPNAV. He had no Navy or joint postgraduate education and he was the first president in many years not to be a Naval War College graduate. He was forceful, direct, and blessed with a dry wit. Ingersoll summarized bluntly his aims while commanding at the War College:

> The United States today is engaged in a protracted conflict and needs more people who are conflict-minded and who can develop into conflict managers.[10]

Long-Range Studies Project

In 1958, in an attempt to deal with rapid technological development within the Navy and its relationship to naval strategy, doctrine, and operations, the Chief of Naval Operations, Admiral Arleigh Burke, directed the formation of the naval long-range studies project at the Naval War College, following a recommendation from the Naval Research Advisory Committee.

The purpose of this project was to assist the CNO in forecasting long-range requirements of the operating forces of the Navy for equipment, personnel, and supporting services. The Naval War College had been selected as headquarters because of its naval-oriented, academic atmosphere, library, educational responsibilities, and location away from Washington, yet near to centers of learning and industry.[11] Six officers under the leadership of a newly selected Rear Admiral, Edwin B. Hooper, reported to Newport in the fall of 1959 and were given office space and support by the college. Admiral Ingersoll's War College directive supplementing Burke's instructions pointed out that "although the project headquarters is located at the War College, it is not an integral part of the Naval War College."[12] It would come under the college president's direction only for the portions of the work carried out by the college's students or staff.

Some early cooperation took place between the college's research and analysis department and the long range studies project, but by and large their functions were entirely separated, with the project director reporting directly to OPNAV as one of its component offices. The original designation OP-93X, was changed in May 1960 to OP-09E to indicate more accurately the OPNAV office through which the director reported. At the suggestion of the Vice Chief of Naval Operations, the name of the project was changed in February 1961 to the Institute of Naval Studies. In 1960 that same name had been given to a civilian contractor representing the Institute for Defense Analysis, an association of universities engaged in research at Cambridge, Massachusetts. The naval portion of that group, also located in Cambridge, was a component of the War College group.

In 1961, the War College staff joined with the Institute in its Limited Warfare Symposium, and the same year staff and students joined in an Institute panel discussion of "Future Naval Tasks." Following the Navy Department's long-standing desire to consolidate its study effort through one contractor, the Institute was removed from the Naval War College in 1963 to form the Center for Naval Analyses, coordinating with other contract groups.[13]

In 1965, the college made a short-lived attempt to establish a Maritime Strategy Group under Captain Thomas H. Stetson. Its purpose, however, was to promote study and research rather than to undertake it.[14]

Electronic War Gaming

During the Ingersoll presidency a major change in war gaming took place. The old game board in Pringle Hall was replaced with the commissioning of the Navy Electronic Warfare Simulator (NEWS) on 7 November 1958 in the central wing of Sims Hall. Since 1945 this complex giant had been under design and construction by the Navy Electronics Laboratory of San Diego and various subcontractors including the Navy Training Devices Center. It was the post-World War II successor to game board and chart maneuvers introduced by William McCarty Little in the 1880s.

NEWS continued the traditional war game, blending it with modern techniques. The unveiling of the NEWS in 1958 completed 13 years of design and construction at a cost of $7.25 million. The machine was described enthusiastically as

> the most flexible and intricate training device ever built, here a war game can be laid out simulating any section of the globe, varying from 40 to 4,000 miles on a side. The flag plot, individual command centers, umpire plots, twenty individual command centers, communication centers, and allied equipment to accommodate a wide range of variables in weapon, ship, missile, and aircraft performance occupy 35,000 square feet of floor space.[15]

Fleet commanders, seeing its value to train fleet units, heartily supported funding for the NEWS. Since 1947, Newport-based destroyer squadrons had exercised their tactical teams on the BZ trainer of the General Line School. At a higher level, the Naval War College's NEWS offered simulated operations for task group, force, and fleet commanders. Proper scheduling ensured no interference with the college classes. In May 1958 the NEWS was included as a major element in the new Navy war games program under the direction of the Chief of Naval Operations. The NEWS staff became the war gaming department in 1959, and operations in support of fleet forces were integrated with the war games of the naval warfare, command and staff, and naval command courses.

In 1965 the NEWS devoted 36 days to war games for the college, 15 days for various Atlantic Fleet staff exercises, and 12 days for the Destroyer School classes from Newport. By the mid-1960s the NEWS was able to provide

> the basic elements of mobility, firepower, vulnerability, and intelligence so that opposing commanders might exercise their professional judgment in the employment of assigned forces during a war game.[16]

Summer White House, 1957-1962

In September 1957, President Dwight D. Eisenhower moved to the Naval Base for a month's vacation. It was the first of three summers during which Newport was host to the President of the United States, his staff, and a large press contingent. The Executive Offices were established in the original building of the War College. Although the President had little direct contact with the college, he made a point of meeting with the foreign officers in the second naval command class. In September he informally received them in front of Founder's Hall for a few minutes while photographers crowded around for picture taking.

During their first visit, the Eisenhowers occupied the quarters then assigned to the base commander, directly across the street from the War College president's house. In the following summer and again in 1960, President Eisenhower and his family occupied the old post commander's home at Fort Adams, designated at that time as quarters for the War College chief of staff. In these two years, the chief of staff was tactfully on leave or traveling during the presidential visit. In 1958 the chief of staff, Rear Admiral Charles H. Lyman, made a South American trip, visiting the war colleges of that area.

Eisenhower's successor as President, John F. Kennedy, also came to Newport on several occasions during his term, visiting at Hammersmith Farm, the estate of his mother-in-law, Mrs. Hugh Auchincloss. In September 1962, President Kennedy saw the America's Cup Races on board the destroyer *Joseph P. Kennedy, Jr.,* named for his older brother. Other destroyers were sent out to serve as escorts and assist the Coast Guard in patrolling the race course. The rush for passes to ride aboard these ships was phenomenal, and last-minute directives from White House and naval authorities were often conflicting. The Destroyer Force chief of staff, who was responsible for operations of the participating Navy units, commented

> There were two crises in this Force in 1962, the America's Cup Races at Newport in September, and the Cuban Missile Crisis in October. Of the two the former was by far the most traumatic.[17]

The Military Media Conference

The increasing presence of the civilian press corps in Newport was reflected also in the establishment of the Naval War College's first Military-Media conference in 1960. For the two-day affair, modeled in part on the successful global strategy discussions, the press announcement of the first session stated:

> Over fifty experts in the Public Relations and Press, Radio, and Television industries will gather with the War College classes to study Public Relations as it affects the U.S. Navy as a part of the nation's defense establishment.[18]

The chief of Navy public information, Rear Admiral C. C. Kirkpatrick, was a featured speaker. He was followed by several newsmen, a panel discussion with questions from the floor, and an afternoon of seminars in 24 groups.

Since the 1960 conference, military-media sessions have continued almost annually. The format has generally remained the same, and each year has brought interesting speakers from press and television, representatives from some of the nation's leading periodicals, and senior public information officers from the Department of Defense. At times, debate and questions have been acrimonious, and although it is doubtful that either government officials or members of the press changed long-held convictions, they each may have come to a better understanding of one another's views.

As the *Naval War College Review* reported about a later conference,

> Government-press relationships have been described as a game of cops and robbers. The object of the cops is to conceal information, while the robbers seek to disclose it. The cops seldom ask themselves why they want to conceal particular bits of information, and the robbers often fail to analyze why they choose to disclose the information they do.[19]

During the Vietnam war, relations with the press may have reached a low point, but in 1972 the War College president closed the conference with words that echoed the original purpose of the gathering:

> I think nothing could endanger our nation and its freedom more than to generate a military-media complex. I feel the adversary relationship is a healthy one and in the interest of a free and effective media.[20]

Four-Year Term for College President

On 30 June 1960, Vice Admiral Bernard L. Austin relieved Admiral Ingersoll as president. Austin, the college's twenty-seventh president, remained for four years in that position, the longest presidency in the college's history. A veteran of submarines and destroyers, he had a service record unexcelled in breadth and diversity in this era of the U.S. Navy. A wartime destroyer captain and squadron commodore, Austin was a veteran of several actions in the Solomon Islands, sailing with Arleigh Burke's "Little Beaver" squadron. Later as a spot-promoted commodore on Admiral Nimitz' Pacific Fleet staff, Austin became the Navy's youngest flag officer. He had had NATO duty in Europe and had been Director of the Joint Staff in the Pentagon. He reported to Newport after a year as Deputy Chief of Naval Operations for Plans. At the age of 58, Austin was truly an "elder statesman" in the service. His nickname "Count" had been acquired as a plebe in the Naval Academy, and befitted this dignified, courtly, and articulate college president. One Austin innovation, the president's hour—periodic sessions where students could address any question to the admiral—led to a later comment by Austin that these sessions too often produced questions from the same students, those who in any lecture "must" be heard.

The change of administration in Washington in 1961 brought a new civilian team to the Pentagon under Secretary of Defense Robert McNamara. They recommended that the naval command course include more pro-American propaganda for the visiting foreign students. With up to 25 different nations represented, NCC staff officers had studiously avoided any glossing of subject matter or any attempt to guide students' attitudes. Austin talked with emissaries from Washington interested in guiding the curriculum. His statement that "the very best propaganda in the world is no propaganda" carried the day. It remains the basis of instruction at the naval command course.

The terms of both Ingersoll and Austin were interrupted, often on short notice, by special assignments. Ingersoll participated in planning for future disarmament talks between the United States and the Soviet Union, the forerunner of the SALT talks of later years. Austin was ordered to head investigations on three separate occasions. The most important was the Court of Inquiry into the loss of the nuclear submarine *Thresher* east of Cape Cod on April 10, 1963. Although a military organization is geared to accept successive commanders, such absences did not contribute to continuity in policy. Senior education at Newport still needed a higher priority within the Navy.

The George Washington University Program

A growing area of concern for naval officers from the 1950s onwards was their perception that an advanced academic degree enhanced an officer's chances for promotion, and hence, a more successful career. In 1956, an after-hours voluntary cooperative program was begun with the Graduate School of Boston University. This program offered interested staff members and students an opportunity to earn a Master of Arts degree in political science (international relations). At the end of the first year, Boston University found that the Naval War College's students had not performed successfully enough for them to continue, but the university allowed staff members to continue up to 1963. Similar attempts were made to further the education of staff members with other institutions. In 1955, for example, two officers on the staff attended the summer course in Arctic geography offered by McGill University in Canada. From 1956 to 1960, a number of staff members also participated in Harvard University's defense policy seminar, under the direction of Barton Leach, Edward L. Katzenbach, Jr., and later, Henry A. Kissinger.

In 1960, the commandant of the Army War College established a cooperative master's degree program in international affairs with George Washington University in Washington, D.C. The purpose of the program was to complement the Army War College's curriculum in the international affairs field, to further the mid-career development of officers, and to provide recognition to successful students in the form of an academic degree.[21]

The plans for this trial course were discussed at the first annual meeting of heads of senior, joint, and service colleges in the autumn of 1960. This conference, later known as the Military Education Coordinating Conference (MECC), had been created that year as an alternative to unified control of the war colleges by the Joint Chiefs of Staff. It provided a means for the war colleges to discuss common problems in dealing with similar basic curricula for students from all services.

The Bureau of Naval Personnel was strongly in favor of implementing the program at the Naval War College, and Admiral Austin approved a trial course for Newport for the academic year 1961-1962, to be put into full operation the following year. The course found support in

Washington, particularly in the Bureau of Naval Personnel.[22] As established at the Naval War College, staff and student officers were given the opportunity to undertake, on a voluntary basis, four nine-week terms ending in May each year. Each class met twice weekly for two hours and carried three hours of academic credit. Three more hours of academic credit, for a total of 15, were earned in an outside reading course. The degree program also included writing a thesis. The course was taught by a team of professors from George Washington University. The first resident head of this team was Dr. Hiram M. Stout, followed in later years by J. K. McDonald, Clyde Sargent, and Peter A. Poole.

In announcing the inauguration of the George Washington University program, Austin recognized the need for a high level of education in the officer corps and for a clear understanding of foreign affairs officers exercising high command. But, he warned,

> Participation in The George Washington University Cooperative Program is an after hours activity. Work in connection with the program must not infringe upon nor interfere with the performance of regularly assigned duties or the resident courses at the Naval War College. . . . Only those students who have the capacity for a very heavy academic work load should participate.[23]

Traditionally, senior naval officers had always been involved in international affairs during peacetime, but most officers on duty in Washington or on large staffs had generally received only on-the-spot training in the subject. During three Washington tours as a flag officer, Austin had seen Army and Air Force officers outshine and sometimes outmaneuver their Navy cohorts on the multitude of international problems tackled in the Pentagon. Both the Army and Air Force had made great efforts to provide academic education in international relations to middle-grade officers. By the early 1960s, the Navy was far behind the other services in the number of officers who had graduated from university postgraduate courses at such institutions as Oxford, Tufts University's Fletcher School of Law and Diplomacy, Harvard, and Stanford. Officers who had earned degrees from these institutions were often designated subspecialists in international relations, but the Navy had few of them.

The planners in the Bureau of Naval Personnel saw that the new course at Newport would quickly increase the number of officers with the qualification of an academic degree who could be designated international affairs subspecialists without taking them away from active service for additional courses in civilian universities. Officers who volunteered for the additional course found the Navy ready to pay the tuition, and often, the Bureau of Naval Personnel allowed time after War College graduation for thesis work.

Although many naval officers thought that the course was a successful one, there were some reservations on the part of the War College faculty. There was a growing feeling that the requirements of the degree course, which represented an additional 20 percent work load on a student, detracted from the regular curriculum. Similar worries surfaced in the other service colleges and were brought out in the 1963 Military Education Coordinating Conference, at which the college commandants concluded:

> Realizing that the military have now become involved in many non-military matters, we nevertheless agree that the Service War Colleges should consider whether the trend toward non-military subjects has gone too far.[24]

Moreover, as the program spread to all the war colleges, critics thought that its quality declined. At the same time, some officers who wanted to go on with advanced academic work found that course credits from the George Washington War College program were not recognized.

After Vice Admiral Charles Melson relieved Austin as college president in July 1964, he expressed doubts about the true value of the course:

> Personally I did not place a great deal of credit in these degrees. It seemed to me there was something lacking, and to give a man a degree while working on an outside course like that just seemed to me he was missing something. He either wasn't doing his work at the War College and that was my big objection, or he wasn't doing the proper amount of work on his course to get a degree. In short, I felt the degrees were not demanding enough of the individual and that their standing would not be very high in the educational world.[25]

In May 1965 Admiral Melson and his staff hosted the Military Education Coordination Conference at Newport. As chairman of this gathering of commandants and members of the staffs of the senior, joint, and service war colleges, Melson prepared a report to the Chairman of the Joint Chiefs of Staff. It stated:

> The George Washington University master's degree program detracts from college mission accomplishment to a prohibitive degree. The student conflict in meeting both sets of requirements is too often solved in favor of the George Washington University.[26]

Despite this comment, the JCS made no move to stop similar programs in the joint service colleges under their jurisdiction. The Navy Department stood by its position on subspecialization. Although the other service colleges found great difficulty in their relationship with the George Washington University, the program at the Naval War College ran smoothly and successfully. Vice Admiral Benedict J.

Semmes, Chief of Naval Personnel, stated, "The Navy Department considers the George Washington University cooperative program an asset in the subspecialty program of officer education."[27] Despite some reservations in Newport, the program continued. In 1964, the Graduate Record Examination was introduced to raise standards, screening out those with low aptitude for the master's program. As a result, the 1965 enrollment at the Naval War College was reduced by more than 100 students to 115.[28]

Melson's Presidency, 1964-1966

Looking back on his term as War College president, Melson recalled, "I really had no tangible objective in mind, but I had always enjoyed the War College—I'd been a student there—and I just thought it was a fine way to end my career at the War College."[29] During a part of his year and a half in command, Melson was assigned additional duties as Commander, Newport Naval Base. Taciturn and direct, "Charlie" Melson supported greater emphasis on basic naval subjects, questioned the value of the George Washington University program, and expanded the use of the NEWS for war gaming by both courses. If at times he wondered about the support given his college from the Navy Department, he could reflect on a letter Fleet Admiral Nimitz sent him shortly before Nimitz's death:

> I credit the Naval War College with giving me the wisdom and foresight to see the need for many important changes in our personnel war planning. I regard your job as President as being second only to that of the Chief of Naval Operations in importance.[30]

Early in Melson's term, Congress appropriated $335,000 for a much needed addition to the Mahan Library. It was the first significant addition to the college's physical plant since Sims Hall was acquired from the Naval Station at the end of World War II. The new addition permitted space for another 110,000 volumes. But classroom and student office space was crowded for the student population of about 350. Melson considered the possibility of using land at Fort Adams, but favored expansion on Coasters Harbor Island, with Luce Hall as the center. As U.S. participation in the war in Vietnam expanded during Melson's War College tour, there was little enthusiasm in the Navy Department to support additional buildings. Melson's later view of the financial support the college received during his presidency is a classic understatement: "Speaking as an ex-War College president, I would say the Department was not very liberal."[31]

In September 1965, Melson saw that the quandary in naval education had not been solved, and he urgently recommended that the Navy "develop and issue a policy providing for the orderly growth and progression in formal professional education of naval officers through the grade structure." Melson's proposal was approved and Vice Admiral B. J. Semmes, the Chief of Naval Personnel, initiated a study.[32]

On the basis of Melson's recommendations, Admiral David L. McDonald, the Chief of Naval Operations, slightly revised the formal definition of the college's mission:

> To provide naval officers advanced education in the science of naval warfare and related subjects in order to improve their professional competence for higher responsibilities.[33]

But in a private letter to Melson, McDonald revealed more explicitly his view of the college's function:

> At the career point at which naval officers attend the Naval War College, they have been working hard at sea and ashore. Our career progression is such that the pace is intense. A year at the Naval War College offers an opportunity for a needed change of pace, a change in perspective and in pressure. In addition to formal matters of substance and procedure, the Naval War College opportunity to think in relative tranquility, to research against the largest backdrop, to exchange searching broad ideas and ideals, to weigh comparatively the ideas of distinguished speakers and stimulating classmates, and to argue alternatives through to meaningful conclusions are indeed energizing processes of the first order. How to think clearly, then, is as important as what to think.[34]

About the same time, the college's three academic departments were redesignated as the school of naval warfare, school of naval command and staff, and school of correspondence, but the curricula and administration were only slightly affected. The distinction between the naval warfare and the command and staff curricula continued along the lines Admiral Austin had established in 1960 when he told incoming students that in the naval warfare course the emphasis was on education and in the command and staff course emphasis was on training.[35] In both schools after 1965, lectures and emphasis were given more than before to the subject of counterinsurgency, and a correspondence course in this subject was initiated.

As Admiral Melson's term drew to an end, he and his staff received a visit by a Department of Defense group of 12 civilian and military officials, formed by Secretary of Defense McNamara to report on the service and joint colleges providing education for senior and middle grade officers. It was one sign of the increasing and direct interest in the Naval War College and service college affairs that was now evident at high levels in the Department of Defense. By coincidence the visit of this group under Thomas Morris, Assistant Secretary of Defense for Manpower, took place on 1 December 1965, the day the Navy

Department announced that Melson would retire on 31 January 1966 and be relieved by Vice Admiral John T. Hayward.

Five years earlier, McNamara had arrived in the Pentagon, bringing his team of young thinkers and planners from industry and academia. The Navy adjusted slowly to the innovations brought by this new administration, and it was a while before the Naval War College became directly involved. Staff and students had been caught up in the many problems of the Cuban missile crisis of 1962 as they translated them into lectures, operational scenarios, and war games. They noted the efforts of Secretary McNamara to carry out civilian command as distinguished from civilian control of the armed forces. It was public knowledge that Admiral George W. Anderson, Chief of Naval Operations from 1961 to 1963, had served only a two year term because he had disagreed with the McNamara philosophy. The current Chief of Naval Operations, Admiral David McDonald, found himself wrestling with the same problem, as U.S. participation in the Vietnam war slowly grew. Already he had addressed the War College classes three times, and these concerns were reflected in his comments. In Washington, the McNamara team, with support from President Lyndon Johnson, was taking an ever more detailed role in combat operations in Southeast Asia. The President was not averse to giving direct orders to units in the combat area. By the time Admiral Melson's retirement was announced, McNamara's young "Whiz Kids" seemed to be in "complete domination of the Department of Defense."[36]

In March 1965, Dr. Edward L. Katzenbach, Jr., who, before becoming a director of the American Council on Education, had served under McNamara as deputy assistant secretary of defense for education, sounded a clarion call in an article in the U.S. Naval Institute *Proceedings*, entitled "The Demotion of Professionalism at the War College."[37]

"At the War Colleges . . .," Katzenbach wrote, "the sense of military professionalism has been on the wane. The mystique—that sense of mission and that excitement of being part of a tightly knit professional body—is barely felt. Service may be becoming a job."[38] Katzenbach charged that the War Colleges had civilianized their curricula to a degree that they were no longer service-oriented; at the same time they did not reach the high quality of civilian universities. Among the service colleges, only the Naval War College retained a major concentration upon its warfare specialty, but its curriculum, too, was "something between great issues courses and extended Administration policy briefings."[39] Katzenbach pointed out that there were four characteristics of war college courses:

1. The faculty did not teach in the classical sense of imparting knowledge from a storehouse of knowledge.

2. The students claimed to learn more from their fellow students than through instruction.

3. The student had the opportunity to earn a master's degree at another institution while studying full time at the war college.

4. The breadth of view presented by the curriculum was so extreme that it precluded depth of view in any subject.

There was a baffling sameness in the programs of all the war colleges, and none dealt effectively with systems analysis, the major intellectual tool used by the McNamara team in the Defense Department. In Katzenbach's view, the solution was a simple one. The curriculum should be reoriented.

> To date the trend in the war colleges has been to discuss national problems, hopefully tying these in some way to military problems. This should be reversed. Military problems should be central to the discussion and due reference made to the pressures, political, economic, and technical which prescribe the peripheries within which solutions must, or can, or cannot be found.[40]

Case studies of military problems should be developed, war college staffs should include research analysts to develop suitable teaching materials where none existed, and more use should be made of political-military war games. Finally, he argued, high standards should be used to select faculty, staff, and students, and officers should be sent to the War College before, not after, a staff assignment. In short, the college should be the locus of the teaching, development, and analysis of strategic concepts, tactics, weapons, and criteria, "that gamut of matters which encompasses military professionalism."[41]

Katzenbach's views reflected some of the traditional ideals which the Naval War College had espoused in years past. But few agreed with them when stated by a civilian in a professional military journal. Katzenbach was accused of "shooting from the hip," for confusing the missions of the senior war colleges and the command and staff level schools. Naval leaders accused Katzenbach of forgetting "that in the world of 1965, a senior officer must be knowledgeable of a variety of national and international problems."[42] He was also criticized for advocating essentially "a Prussian approach" to senior officer education in "the teaching of established doctrine."[43] A future four-star admiral, then a newly promoted captain, noted that Katzenbach's recommendations would make the war colleges into advanced schools "producing graduates who had clocked a certain number of hours in a certain number of subjects. The present system turned out more professional officers than Katzenbach offered."[44]

Not everyone defended the status quo. One Naval War College graduate and former staff member indicted the Navy's policy on senior officer education:

With our philosophy of the supreme importance of command, it is understandable that the Navy has the least effective educational plan for training top-notch staff officers. We send our best officers to junior and senior war colleges, but rarely to both. This is equivalent to sending our youngsters to high school or college, but not to both. We do not ordinarily seek out at junior officer level those outstanding officers who are most 'educable' and progressively educate them for top staff assignments.[45]

The Naval War College had faced an ever increasing problem in obtaining appropriate students since the 1930s, partly because of shortages in officer strength, more because of the lack of a systematic, progressive system of professional education for middle grade and senior naval officers. The problem had only grown in proportion as the Navy expanded over the years and took on more operational assignments. The newer problem, however, was how to incorporate into the War College course the new perceptions of professional needs gained during and since World War II. In the 20 years since the war had ended, the Naval War College had succeeded in broadening the outlook and perspective of its students. But it had not yet succeeded in achieving consistently high academic standards, or linking broad perspectives with a professional understanding of naval power.

Notes

1. NWC Archives, RG 16: Address by T. H. Robbins, 17 August 1956.
2. Letter, Arleigh Burke to J. R. Wadleigh, 12 December 1980.
3. Ibid.
4. Ibid.
5. Ibid.
6. E. H. Van Kee, "Reflections of a foreign student," U.S. Naval Institute *Proceedings* (February 1959), p. 39.
7. NWC Archives, RG 3: President, NWC, letter, serial 485-57 of 15 March 1957; CNO letter, serial 140P60 of 17 April 1957.
8. NWC Archives, RG 3 File A3-1 (5400) Course of Advanced Study in Strategy and Sea Power. J. L. Holloway, Jr. to L. D. McCormick, 5 April 1956.
9. Nepier Smith, "Historical Analysis of the Organizational Success of the Naval War College during the Twenty-five years following the Second World War," NWC Advanced Research Project, 1974, pp. 119-20.
10. NWC Archives, RG 16: S. H. Ingersoll Convocation Address, 23 August 1959.
11. OPNAVINST 5010.16 of 31 March 1959.
12. Naval War College Instruction 5400.24 of 20 May 1959.
13. NWC Archives, RG3 File 5400/Naval Long-Range Studies Project, 1959-1965. See also, D. A. Rosenberg, *Historical Perspectives in Longrange-Planning in the Navy* (Naval Research Advisory Committee Report, 1980), pp. 39-59.
14. Loc. cit., File 5420: Maritime Strategy Study Group, 1965.
15. NWC Archives, RG 32: *Command History*, 1958, p. 44.
16. *Command History*, 1965, p. 28; See also F. McHugh, "Games at the War College," USNI *Proceedings* (Sept. 1959), p. 53.

17. Conversation during turnover of duties, Captain D. Willman, USN, to Captain J. R. Wadleigh, 14 March 1963.

18. NWC Archives, RG 7: NWC press release, 14 April 1960.

19. "Military Media Symposium at the Naval War College," *Naval War College Review* (Jan-Feb 1973), p. 49.

20. Vice Admiral Stansfield Turner, Ibid., p. 50.

21. Robert Carter Burns, *George Washington University Program inInternational Affairs at the War Colleges* (Washington: George Washington University School of Public and International Affairs, 1982), p.7.

22. Ibid., pp. 37-39; Nepier Smith, op. cit., pp. 108-09.

23. NAVWARCOL NOTICE 1550, July 1962. Quoted in Burns, *George Washington University Programs*, p. 40.

24. Nepier V. Smith, op. cit., p. 109.

25. NHC Oral History Collection: Charles Melson, p. 392.

26. NWC Archives, RG3: Report of Third Annual MECC. President, NWC to Chairman, JCS. 30 June 1965.

27. Loc. cit., Chief of Naval Personnel Endorsement on Combs Board Report, 1965.

28. NWC Archives, RG32: *Command History*, 1965, p. 38.

29. NHC Oral History Collection: Charles Melson, p. 384.

30. NWC Archives, RG28: President's file, Melson: Nimitz to Melson, 24 September 1965.

31. NHC Oral History Collection: Charles Melson, p. 384.

32. NWC Archives, RG3, Box 123: File 5400; Mission and Tasks: Melson to CNO, 17 September 1965, serial 2355; B. J. Semmes to Melson, 11 October 1965, Op10 serial 12425.

33. OPNAV Instruction 1520.12B of 3 April 1965.

34. NWC Archives, RG3, Box 123, File 5400: Missions; McDonald to Melson, 25 Nov. 1965.

35. NWC Archives, RG16: Convocation Address, B. L. Austin, 19 August 1960.

36. R. J. Stillman "The Pentagon Whiz Kids," USNI *Proceedings* (April 1966), pp. 53-60.

37. Edward Katzenbach, Jr., "The Demotion of Professionalism at War Colleges," USNI *Proceedings* (April 1965), pp. 34-41.

38. Ibid., p. 34.

39. Ibid.

40. Ibid., pp. 40-41.

41. Ibid., pp. 38 and 41.

42. Anthony Harrigan, "Comment" in USNI *Proceedings* (September 1965), p. 112.

43. E. R. Schwass, "Comment" in USNI *Proceedings* (June 1965), p. 110.

44. H. E. Shear, "Comment" in USNI *Proceedings* (September 1965), p. 112.

45. Paul R. Schratz, "The Ivy-Clad Man on Horseback," USNI *Proceedings* (April 1965), pp. 47-48.

CHAPTER 10

WATERSHED FOR
CHANGE, 1966-1972

The year 1966 marked the beginning of the first of two major periods of change and reform that took place at the Naval War College between 1966 and 1974. The origins of these changes can be found in the growing criticism directed toward service colleges since the mid-1960s. The critics gained the attention of high level officials in the government, and a search for solutions to the problem was stimulated by pressure from both President Lyndon Johnson's staff in the White House and Secretary of Defense Robert S. McNamara's in the Pentagon. The first series of resulting changes stemmed from the appointment to the college presidency of Vice Admiral John T. Hayward, 1966-1969, and from the personal interest taken by Admiral Thomas B. Moorer, first as Chief of Naval Operations, 1968-1970, and later as Chairman of the Joint Chiefs of Staff.

Essentially, the college faced three major issues: the longstanding need to improve and expand its facilities, the need to provide an appropriate and demanding curriculum, and the need to educate students in a progressive manner.

In late 1965 and early 1966, both the Department of Defense and the Navy Department were beginning to examine seriously the educational problems faced by service colleges at the same time that a new president was needed to succeed retiring Vice Admiral Charles Melson. Secretary of the Navy Paul Nitze had strong views as to the type of man who should be chosen. He believed that the Navy should

> seek out a 3-star admiral who had distinguished himself intellectually, as well as professionally. On top of that, [the Navy] needed someone with dash, creativity and push. It is a truism to say that the sum of a man's knowledge is an inadequate measure of his

intellectual capacity. The extraordinarily capable man is one who uses this knowledge in a creative way—an innovator. Such a man is particularly needed to head an educational institution to resist the natural trend to conservatism which blocks attempts at curricular reform.[1]

The man chosen to fill these requirements in 1966 was the Navy's senior vice admiral, John T. Hayward. A naval aviator with a probing mind and seemingly unlimited energy, he had an established reputation as a dynamic officer. Soon after World War II, as a commander, Hayward had flown a large, land-based Navy bomber from the deck of an aircraft carrier to demonstrate that the Navy could deliver nuclear weapons. His passengers on this experimental flight included the Secretary of the Navy and the Chief of Naval Operations. The flight justified the construction of aircraft carriers to help deliver these weapons. This in turn ended the monopoly of them by the new U.S. Air Force and its Strategic Air Command.

Hayward's Innovations

A high school dropout and a bat boy for the New York Yankees, Hayward began his long naval career in Newport. In May 1925, he enlisted in New York and was sent on a Fall River Line steamship to the Newport Naval Training Station for recruit training. At that time Barracks C (now Sims Hall) was used to house the newest recruits, or "boots," and Hayward underwent his first naval training there. He disliked it intensely.

The Catholic chaplain, Commander John J. Brady, took an interest in him and successfully tutored him for the Naval Academy entrance examination. Following graduation from the Naval Academy in 1930, Hayward's career was marked by a driving desire for professional excellence through education. Scientific study at a variety of universities complemented his wartime service in the Pacific and his subsequent assignments in the development of rockets and of atomic weapons. As Deputy Chief of Naval Operations for Development, he was closely involved in the construction of the world's first nuclear powered aircraft carrier, the USS *Enterprise,* and later flew his flag in her as the first commander of a nuclear powered task force.[2]

When Hayward took command at the Naval War College, he was determined to bring new academic and intellectual vigor to the curriculum. He had no preconceived notions and was willing to search and to experiment. The concurrent examination of education policy within both the Navy and the Defense departments, however, gave him the material with which to work.

Shortly after taking up the War College presidency, Hayward wrote to Under Secretary of the Navy R. H. B. Baldwin:

My overall appraisal at this time is that the course has not been
demanding enough of the better students, and that changes are in
order for both them and us to derive maximum benefit from their
attendance.[3]

Hayward saw the process of education as a complex one which must
be tailored to promote individual growth as well as to impart a basic
professional knowledge. "As a philosophy at Newport, I attempted to
make it an intellectual experience for each individual,"[4] Hayward
wrote. In restructuring the college curriculum, he sought the advice of
specialists such as Dean Fuller of the Harvard Business School and
Alain Enthoven on McNamara's staff in Washington, and also
attempted to develop closer ties with neighboring universities. "Our
reorganization program, to be effective without being disruptive, must
be evolutionary," Hayward decided. "I believe that one of our troubles
here has been the fact that the evolution in curriculum development
has not kept pace with either the other educational institutions or the
surrounding world environment."[5]

The lack of continuity in the college's curriculum had been evident
for many years. The constant rotation of naval officers was matched by
the even faster rotation of civilian academics who came to the college
for six-month or one-year appointments. However, even before
Hayward's arrival at the college, the appointment of one civilian
professor on an extended-term contract had been approved in principle
by the Vice Chief of Naval Operations.[6] The holder of this position as
special academic advisor was to provide continuity in curriculum
development, to offer academic expertise, and to serve as a link to
civilian universities. On 1 July 1966, Professor Frederick H. Hartmann
took up this position, first holding the Nimitz chair, then assuming the
newly created Alfred Thayer Mahan chair of maritime strategy.

Core Curriculum and Civilian Faculty

Utilizing Hartmann's advice, Hayward started with the premise that
he could not deal with students as a homogenous group. He knew that
their professional and educational backgrounds were extremely diverse
and he sought to revise the curriculum to take this diversity into
consideration. First, incoming students were required to take the
graduate record examination. The results would be used to determine
their overall academic capabilities. Then, following a pattern common
to many leading universities to deal effectively with diverse backgrounds, he established a basic curriculum to give the students a
common professional beginning point. The instruction of both the
school of naval warfare and the school of command and staff were
consolidated during the initial period of the academic year in order to

provide the academic and military fundamentals common to both.[7] The title of the course, "Fundamentals of Strategy," was a misnomer. It implied an elementary level of inquiry; however, its scope and pace were hardly elementary. It was a wide-ranging review designed to bring the students rapidly up to a graduate-level course in international affairs and strategic issues. Students had to come to grips with the essentials of international relations (including conflict resolution), economics, the functioning of the U.S. economy and its relationship to military expenditures, international law, the history of strategic thought and theories of war, the organization of the federal government, and the roles and missions of the armed services.

Without great financial resources, the college could not hire a large faculty to teach each of these areas in depth to small classes. In order to meet the needs of the course on a limited budget, Hayward chose to expand the system of visiting professors by widening the range of academic disciplines they covered. In addition to the chairs already existing, Hayward took the initiative in establishing the Theodore Roosevelt chair in economics, first held by Professor Franklin Root of the Wharton School of Finance; the James V. Forrestal chair of military management, first held by Professor Z. S. Zannetos of the Sloan School of Management at the Massachusetts Institute of Technology; the Stephen B. Luce chair of naval science, first held by retired Captain Edward L. Beach; and the chair of comparative cultures, first held by Professor J. M. Roberts.

The greatest drawback to this system of professorial chairs was their small number. The college lacked enough qualified academicians in any one discipline to lead the dozen or so small student seminars on that subject. The faculty instead delivered lectures in their discipline to the assembled student body. In addition, the professors gave introductory lectures on the research approaches in their respective disciplines and went on to supervise student research efforts, thus enriching the overall program. It was less than an ideal teaching arrangement, but considering that the college faculty was predominantly military, the result produced a broadening of perspective in a curriculum heavy in military value and outlook. With this in mind, Hayward specifically fought against the notion that there was a military mentality. "It is ridiculous ... how people try to isolate today something called the 'military mind,'" he wrote. "There is no such thing. The armed forces have been intimately involved in all the progress of this Nation . . . ."[8] It was clear that

> if the military were to take their rightful place in the scheme of things, they had not only to be better educated themselves in all areas but also better educate others with whom they deal on just how broad and deep their knowledge has become.[9]

The civilian chair holders played an essential role in this, both to broaden the students' perspective and to carry a knowledge of this breadth back to their civilian colleagues in other institutions. Each of the civilian chair holders, after his portion of the fundamentals course, in the later portion of the academic year pursued his subject with the two separate courses and in giving electives.

Once the students had finished the fundamental portion of the course and had received a common background, the seniors began a study of how policy was made, then applied it to major geographical areas. In addition, they became acquainted with questions raised by the New Left and New Right, the news media, and their effects on public opinion and public diplomacy. Additional topical and contemporary problems followed, such as national strategy, foreign policies, the economic, political, military, and the socio-psychological sources of national power.

As the academic year progressed, the course turned to naval matters. The naval warfare course examined the historical implications of sea power and the maritime capabilities of the United States, the Soviet Union, and their respective allies. The final two months of the core curriculum were devoted to enhancing the knowledge of the students in the art and science of naval warfare generally. Specifically, they examined naval capabilities of the United States to engage in world-wide operations in support of national policies. They conducted war games to confirm or to disprove their assessments. While the senior level course studied such issues, the command and staff course concentrated on operational matters and especially on the complexities of planning for military operations. Gaming played a large role.

Throughout the year the core curriculum was pitched to the "average" student. An electives program was designed to enrich the curriculum and to provide either further background courses or to challenge the most advanced students. The students chose from an extensive list of diverse elective courses, such as maritime history, economics of war, foundations of modern China, Cold War operations, and the legal aspects of modern warfare, among others. The educational background of the students was extremely varied. Some had advanced academic degrees and others lacked undergraduate education. Arrangements were made with neighboring universities to assist the college. The University of Rhode Island allowed some War College students to earn credits for their bachelor's degree. In addition, qualified students could gain entrance to work for advanced degrees in oceanography and ocean studies with War College courses counted for academic credit and a common thesis for both institutional programs. Nearby Brown University in Providence admitted a few selected students to pursue advanced seminars in political science.

By far the most elaborate and extensive degree program at this time was the already established George Washington University curriculum to provide a master's degree in international affairs for resident War College students. Hayward strongly supported it, regarding the George Washington professors as, in effect, an augmentation of college resources. Their classes were treated by the War College as an additional set of electives, but were held after regular college hours. Credits earned from these courses, plus satisfactory completion of the War College course, entitled students to a master's degree in international affairs.

Consequently, the George Washington curriculum was not simply laid on in addition to the regular War College courses. It was carefully coordinated with the resident course of study to the extent that credit earned in an appropriate college elective had sufficient academic worth to be applied toward the George Washington degree. Similarly, work done in the George Washington course was acceptable to satisfy War College requirements.

Military Management Studies

The basic program that Hayward established contained some new subjects for the college. One of these new areas of study involved the related subjects of military management, economics, and systems analysis. For the six years since Secretary of Defense McNamara had come into office, many officers in the Navy had scoffed at the approach to management that McNamara had introduced. Part of this reaction may have been caused by McNamara's failure to develop a cohesive team feeling between the men in uniform and the civilians who accompanied him. "These bright, developing military leaders were astonished at first. That quickly changed to resentment and was probably one of the biggest incentives our young people had," Hayward wrote. "They became determined to know more than the so-called 'whiz kids.' Today they are spread all over the land, attending universities ... in many areas once thought foreign subjects for military training."[10]

Hayward saw military management as part of the broad spectrum of knowledge that is required for a professional officer. Emphasizing this point, he wrote:

> We should not let strong differences be drawn between these components of national strategy. These are all areas in which we must be knowledgeable and be able to contribute. We must avoid becoming mere technicians. Economics must concern us as well as other facets of our profession. Military deployments contribute to our balance of payments problems, so if we are to be able to evaluate them one must of course be familiar with the economics of the situation.[11]

In modifying the War College curriculum to include "systems analysis," the current approach to evaluating weapons systems in the light of their cost effectiveness, Hayward established a three-part program. He included a segment on the principles of management and the Department of Defense's program planning system in the introductory fundamentals course, established an elective for more in-depth study in operations research and defense programming, and increased emphasis on current issues in this area.[12] In addition, a three-week management course for newly selected flag and general officers was offered during the summer recess and taught by faculty from the Sloan School of Management at MIT. Hayward sought to make the study of management as relevant to actual problems as possible by using drafts of recent memoranda in this area from the Joint Chiefs of Staff and the White House. Commenting favorably on the innovative use of these documents, the Vice Chief of Naval Operations, Admiral Horacio Rivero, wrote, "Not only will they create an awareness of the many new concepts being generated, but they will also show how essential the quantitative analytical approach is to the justification of force levels."[13]

Hayward believed that field study was an important ingredient in the curriculum and he took steps to increase it. "The perspective which can be gained by actually witnessing events which are carefully curriculum-integrated can not be duplicated in textbooks or on lecture platforms," Hayward declared.[14] Among other visits, he arranged for the school of naval warfare to visit the United Nations and for command and staff students to visit the headquarters of Strike Command, thus emphasizing the two different levels at which these courses were pitched. In addition, he was able to obtain additional funds to support extensive travel and conference meetings for students involved in research work.

In general, Hayward sought to widen the outlook of future naval leaders and to stimulate them. Neil Ulman, staff reporter for *The Wall Street Journal*, described his impression of Hayward's curriculum changes after a visit to the college in 1968:

> Its 10-month course has traditionally concentrated on battle planning, fleet maneuver and control, logistics and weapon systems.
> But now a guest lecturer blasts the U.S. presence in Vietnam. A professor tells his class that the State Department's rationale for the Cuban quarantine is all wet. A picture of Ho Chi Minh hangs prominently in an administrative office. And a favored new text is Che Guevara on Guerilla Warfare.[15]

In Hayward's view, open discussion and complete academic freedom went far in stimulating intellectual growth. "When I got here," Hayward said, "there was an obsession with the procedures of military planning. That's strictly mechanical—not an intellectual exercise."[16] The curriculum that Hayward designed to produce this effect was a basic one which assumed little prior knowledge by the students but at the same time gave them as broad a view as possible and increased the level of study in increments, reaching the graduate level in January.

The College and Its Place in an Officer's Career

Revising the curriculum was only one aspect of the problem Hayward faced. The quality of the student body and the role of the college in an officer's professional career was an important issue and one which lay in the wider realm of educational policy within the Navy and the Department of Defense. Along with all War College presidents, Hayward believed that the quality of the student body was central to the future of the college. He saw that far too many students were not destined for important and sensitive positions in whatever time remained in their careers. Although he believed that the college should do more than educate future admirals, he was committed to the idea that the student body should consist of officers with excellent service records. Obviously, if the student body did consist of such men, a fairly high proportion of them would be elevated to flag rank some time in the future.

A review of the 1966 *Navy Register* indicates that of 229 line flag officers on active duty, only 64 were graduates of a course at the Naval War College. Eighty-seven were graduates of the National War College, where the 20 classes since World War II had contained far fewer Navy students than the comparable classes at Newport had held. The status of the senior joint service college and the convenience of a one-year Washington tour close to the center of power were obviously attractive. At the same time, the relative importance of the Naval War College to the professional development of ambitious naval officers had declined. Such men tended to think they could no longer spare a year away from cockpits, reactors, ship's bridges, and staff duty in Washington. By the 1960s, officers expected much shorter service careers than they had in previous generations. In order to be promoted up through the grades, officers needed to have specific types of experience at different promotion levels. To do this within the constraint of a relatively short service career created pressures to exclude any duty assignment that did not obviously meet the accepted criteria for promotion. The competition among officers to obtain such "career enhancing billets," as they were called, was swayed toward technologically oriented positions. The armed forces needed a large number of officers who could swiftly assimilate technical data and master rapidly changing technology. This need put a premium on technological education over the analytical and broadening approach which the Naval War College represented. In short, the college was unattractive in an era of relatively short service careers and emphasis on technology. If officers with promising futures were to be attracted once again to Newport, either the college had to offer them and the Navy something more than it was doing, or career pressures and patterns had to be altered. The college faced a dilemma in that its longstanding belief in progressive education required that students proceed from one level to another in a structured manner. Every trained educator who looked at the issue supported this notion; yet it was an idea that appeared to be impractical. The Deputy Chief of Naval Operations for Manpower, Vice Admiral B. J. Semmes, put the issue clearly when he told the college:

> The philosophy of providing for the professional development of officers through a formal education process must be carefully weighed against other 'high priority' programs of the Navy.[17]

The demands of the nuclear power program, Vietnam, anti-submarine warfare, research and development, and increasing requirements from outside the Navy meant that in 1967, for example, there was a shortage of 1,154 lieutenant commanders in the Navy, with only 86.5 percent of the lieutenant commander billets being filled. "To enforce a hard and fast rule," Semmes continued, "that an officer must attend a junior service college prior to attendance at a senior college could discriminate against many outstanding officers who could not be spared from operation type billets."

The attempt that Admiral Conolly had made to institute progressive education in 1953 had lasted only three years. "In analyzing the reluctance of the Navy to establish an effective progressive professional military education program," Hayward protested in December 1966,

> it is very evident that greater emphasis has been placed on the importance and prestige of formal, specific, specialized postgraduate education than on the less tangible, but equally important War College type [of] progressive officer education. It is insupportable for the records to show through the years that the Navy cannot produce the funds and facilities, as well as program personnel, to provide the long agreed required number of senior officers with progressive education in the broad fundamentals of their profession . . . . The continuing lowering since World War II of the percentage of professionally educated senior officers in the Navy is a phenomenon that can only invite criticism.[18]

Unable to move the Navy Department in its view toward progressive education, the War College turned to other issues relating to the role of the college in an officer's career. In early 1966, Assistant Secretary of Defense for Manpower Thomas D. Morris had observed a wide divergence in the ways that senior service colleges evaluated their students' academic achievement. The Naval War College had no grading system, but the Industrial College of the Armed Forces and the Army's Command and General Staff College used grades and established a student's class standing. At the same time, the National War College faculty evaluated students and prepared lists of class standing, but this information was not made known to the students. With Morris's criticisms in mind, the Navy Department directed the Naval War College to institute some kind of a system, which, at least, would select the top 10 percent of the students for outstanding academic achievement. Replying to this directive in 1966, Hayward cautioned:

> Considering the maturity of the officer students and the important objective of encouraging them to develop their reasoning power and decision-making ability, overemphasis upon academic competition in an evaluation system would be self-defeating. However, even an unobtrusive evaluation process will provide a subtle extra stimulus.[19]

Hayward went on to suggest that a specifically designed officer fitness report be used for naval officers under instruction. This suggestion, however, was not taken up by the Bureau of Naval Personnel.[20] At the same time, Hayward experimented with a grading system at the college. After about a month, he found that it could not be effectively employed without a larger academic staff, which would have more time to spend with individual students.

The basic difficulties the college faced were still unresolved, and the college continued to decline in importance for the general pattern of officer careers. In 1967, for the first time in the naval warfare course, students from other services actually outnumbered Navy students: 57 from other services to 38 naval officers. Moreover, the proportion of naval officers sent to the college failed to increase commensurately with the growth of the total number of officers in the Navy. If this trend were not reversed, the Naval War College would end up educating primarily officers from the other services, if it remained open at all. In terms of the Navy's educational policy, the outlook was no better. In 1968 the Navy's quota of seats at all senior service schools was 196, of which 129 were filled. Given the demand for officers in operational assignments, filling two thirds of senior service school quotas might appear credible. However, all the empty seats but one were at the Naval War College. Further, only 59 percent of Navy captains had some service college education, compared to 73 percent of the Air Force colonels, 79 percent of the Marine Corps colonels, and 96 percent of the Army colonels. At the same time, 1,442 naval officers of all ranks were enrolled full time in a variety of postgraduate and other educational programs. The Navy had not turned its back on advanced education. Only professional military education had been eclipsed.

Support from Admiral Moorer, CNO

Hayward and his staff and faculty received valuable support from the new Chief of Naval Operations, Admiral Thomas H. Moorer, a 1953 naval warfare course graduate. About the time that he became CNO, Moorer recalled in a U.S. Naval Institute lecture that World War II had made him aware of the interdependence of all the armed services and the Korean war impressed upon him the close relationship between military strategy and national policy. It was in the midst of the Korean war (during Admiral Conolly's presidency) that Moorer came to the Naval War College to study and had his first opportunity to develop his ideas about large military issues, particularly about American foreign policy and joint strategic planning.[21] This was an important personal experience which Moorer believed should be encouraged in younger officers.

Soon after his appointment as CNO, Moorer asked Hayward to focus his efforts in making a "hard-hitting presentation" to convince high-level officials in the Navy and the Defense departments of the necessity for the advanced professional education of middle-grade and senior officers.[22] To prepare for this effort, Hayward ordered a thoroughgoing review of the necessity for professional education, an examination of the state of Navy professional and postgraduate education, and an ambitious concept for expansion of the physical plant of the college. This review for the CNO was written by Hayward with the assistance of Captains Aloysius J. Pickert, Jr., and Daniel J. Morgiewicz.

The review argued that it was time to redefine both the requirements for being a naval officer and the concepts with which naval officers viewed their own profession. The purposes, they said, for which military and naval forces existed had expanded far beyond the relatively narrow and familiar uses of World War II. Because policy goals and military means were inextricably related, they believed it was necessary for officers to understand the realities of practical international politics. They recognized the post-World War II development within the armed forces that encouraged reliance on new insights from the social sciences to questions of national security.

Hayward's presentation to the CNO emphasized that the formation of policy, the preparation of plans, and the execution of programs had both a military and a political character. The critics of the war colleges had insisted that professional military officers needed to understand the political consequences of their actions, whatever they might be or however they might be made. This could be accomplished best when officers were freed from immediate administrative and policy concerns but still had access to upper levels of the military policymakers. This,

Hayward argued, was a need that the Naval War College could clearly meet.

In order to carry out the plans that Hayward and his staff formulated for the college, two groups were established. At the local War College level, the Secretary of the Navy established on 2 March 1967 a 12-member board of advisors to recommend improvements in the curriculum, augmentation to the faculty, plans for the library, and a 10-year construction program for new college facilities. The board, designed to provide general policy guidance to the president, was composed of leaders in a variety of fields. As a group, their ideas and recommendations could provide effective weight when necessary to counter opinions expressed by senior civilians in the Department of Defense. The board met three times a year; its first members were Vice Admiral Bernard L. Austin, USN (Ret.), Chairman, Inter-American Defense Board; Mr. Emilio Gabriel Collado, Executive Vice President and Director, Standard Oil Company of New Jersey; Mr. John S. Dickey, President, Dartmouth College; Mr. William W. Foshay, Senior Partner, Sullivan and Cromwell, New York City; Vice Admiral Stuart H. Ingersoll, USN (Ret.), Beachmound, Newport, R.I.; Professor George F. Kennan, Institute for Advanced Studies, Princeton, N.J.

Also, Mr. S. M. McAshan, Jr., Chairman of the Board, Anderson, Clayton and Company, Houston, Tex.; Mr. Stanley Powell, Jr., President, Alexander and Baldwin, Inc., San Anselmo, Calif.; Mr. Henry S. Rowen, President, Rand Corporation, Santa Monica, Calif. Dr. Maurice F. Tauber, Melvil Dewey Professor of Library Science, Columbia University; Dr. Edward Teller, Associate Director, Lawrence Radiation Laboratories, University of California; and Mr. Thomas J. Watson, Jr., Chairman of the Board, International Business Machines.

A year later, Admiral Moorer as CNO established a steering group under the direction of the Vice Chief of Naval Operations to develop a schedule and feasible plan to carry out Hayward's objectives for the Naval War College. The group consisted of the VCNO as chairman; the Director, Navy Program Planning; Chief of Naval Personnel; Deputy Chief of Naval Operation (Plans and Policy); Deputy Chief of Naval Operations (Logistics); and Assistant Vice Chief of Naval Operations/Director of Naval Development. Simultaneously, Admiral Moorer ordered that the Naval War College have a clearly delineated sponsor within the OPNAV staff.[23] In November 1968, this was done by appointing the Deputy CNO for Manpower (OP-01) as the college's sponsor, with command and support of the college delegated to the Chief of Naval Personnel.[24]

Admiral Moorer's personal interest in the College was undoubtedly a key factor in carrying out the administrative reorganization necessary to success. The very words used within the Navy to describe functions were constantly being changed in this period, adding to the difficulty involved in normal development. Commenting on the creation of a new administrative relationship for the college, the Commandant of the First Naval District referred to the Navy's overall administrative problem when he wrote, "We have been reorganizing continuously for five years and are getting more muddled all the time . . . . In our constant change syndrome, we simply can not permit a system to work long enough to make the adjustment in the mind of the participants."[25]

But that was not the only difficulty. After the CNO's steering committee had established the Naval War College development plan in 1968, the Department of Defense delayed approving the necessary "program change requests" which would put the plan in effect. Finally, Admiral Moorer personally obtained the coordination of various offices within the Department of Defense, without using the normal administrative methods, so that the plan could be implemented.

Construction Program

The expansion plan announced by the Chief of Naval Operations was an ambitious one. If it could actually be carried out, it would ensure that a significantly greater proportion of unrestricted line officers would be educated at the college. It would also make the existing facilities hopelessly inadequate. Hayward and his staff faced the enormous task of identifying specific needs, arranging for preliminary studies, garnering congressional support for funds, and finally, starting the work.

The plan to increase enrollment to 700 students at the college by 1980 spurred the most comprehensive review and plan for the expansion of the physical plant in the college's 80-year history. From 1891 to 1968 the total cost of construction at the college had been only $1.636 million. The proposal in 1968 for three additional buildings carried an estimated price tag of $7.625 million.

The first and most important item in the 1968 proposal was a Professional Education Center containing a divisible auditorium with 1,200 seats plus academic study office area for 50 students. The second was a combined academic, command, and administration building. It would accommodate 100 students in addition to the academic, planning, and administrative functions then currently performed in Luce Hall, including a fully equipped print shop. The Secretary of the Navy approved naming these two buildings, respectively, for Admiral Raymond A. Spruance and Vice Admiral Richard L. Conolly, both former presidents of the college.

The next priority was another academic building, originally referred to as "Conolly second increment." It was to replace Sims Hall to house the command and staff course and the correspondence course.

The 1968 expansion plan had at first included both a separate, new library building, and a new structure for war gaming. But as student increases lagged, plans for these buildings were cancelled.

Although there was little real opposition within the Navy Department to a major physical expansion of the college, there was little real interest in it. Using his considerable powers of persuasion, Hayward did not hesitate to approach members of Congress whom he had known in earlier tours of Washington duty and to use key members of his board of advisors to help carry the message. Two influential members of the Armed Services Committees, Senator Henry Jackson of Washington State and Congressman Robert Sikes of Florida, agreed with him on the necessity for expansion. With these two powerful allies, the initial appropriations for military construction were obtained from Congress, and the ground for Spruance Hall, first of the new buildings, was broken in 1971. As Hayward recalled some years later, "People knowing the infighting in the Navy itself for military construction funds know the problems we faced. These strong allies [in Congress] won the day for me and deserve the credit . . . . if we had not fought, it would never have happened; as in Luce's day, Congress was the key to success."[26] Retiring in 1968, Hayward left the college demonstrably better than he had found it with an expanded curriculum and a sound, detailed program for expansion and construction.

Colbert's Return to Newport

Hayward's successor was Richard G. Colbert, then serving in Norfolk as Deputy Chief of Staff to Admiral Ephriam Holmes, Supreme Allied Commander, Atlantic. Colbert had been aide to Admiral Conolly in 1948 and had absorbed some of his views toward professional education. As a student in the War College in 1956, Colbert had been chosen by the then CNO, Admiral Burke, to head the first international course at Newport. In 1968, Hayward thought that Colbert, although a relatively junior rear admiral, was the ideal man to succeed him, and he said so in Washington. In July, Secretary of the Navy Paul R. Ignatius announced that Colbert would succeed Hayward upon the latter's retirement from active duty. This selection represented a break in Department policy prevalent since World War II. College presidents since Edward Kalbfus had all been in their final tour of active duty, and in every case could be termed "elder statesmen" in the Navy hierarchy. Colbert at the age of 53 was serving in his second flag assignment, and after a normal tour at Newport could expect further duty afloat and ashore. Colbert, known as a "comer" among his contemporaries, was also familiar with the Naval War College and its progress in the years since he had been a student.

The Colbert presidency remained deliberately low-key with respect to the evolution of the academic program, which he believed was then in excellent shape. After the ferment of the Hayward years, the college needed a period of relative calm and stability. Colbert's mission was not to revolutionize the college; Hayward had already done that. The new president consolidated and strengthened the academic program initiated by his predecessor. He added a new civilian chair of war gaming, however, to increase the rigor and scope of the expanding games being played on the NEWS. Assuming the presidency in July 1968, Colbert quietly declared his belief in the role of the Naval War College. "In the face of the challenge that confronts us, I would hope that 'on my watch' we will be able to generate new and meaningful thinking," Colbert declared. "If the kind of research and creative thinking necessary to sound military knowledge is not done at the Naval War College, there is danger that it will not be done at all."[27]

Colbert's primary attention was given to enriching the existing overall program through better student housing, creating a War College Foundation, and establishing Newport as a center for international naval discussions through symposia, conferences, and courses. He wanted to expand the influence of the college by providing the means by which the U.S. Navy and other navies could seek out common ground and start working toward common solutions to common problems. At a time when the United States government officially recognized in the Nixon Doctrine that this country alone could not bear the burden of the defense of the free world, Colbert's contribution in furthering this policy in the maritime community of the free world navies was significant and remains largely unsung.

Expanding the International Role of the College

Colbert was a happy choice to continue the reforms started by Hayward and to add to them in a broader field, the arena of international naval discussions. When Colbert reported to Newport for the second time, he had added significantly to the experience gained in his years with the naval command course from 1956 through 1958. He had had service in the planning directorate (J-5) of the Joint Chiefs of Staff and later on, the policy planning group of the Department of State. Afloat, he had spent a year commanding an auxiliary ship with the U.S. Sixth Fleet whose home port was Barcelona, Spain. This tour had been followed by command of the guided missile cruiser *Boston*, serving on occasion as flagship for the Commander, Sixth Fleet. In both these assignments he visited many Mediterranean ports and observed as well as partook in the power projection role of the Navy. His most recent position at the Norfolk headquarters of the Supreme Allied Command,

Atlantic, provided a fertile field for expanding his knowledge of dealing with U.S. allies and meeting their senior naval officers. After Hayward, an intellectual and a scientist, who improved dramatically the academic credibility of the college, Colbert was well suited to carry on and to develop the plans further. Fully accepting the Hayward curriculum, Colbert turned his considerable skills to the delicate but important task of quiet naval diplomacy.

Since the U.S. Navy was broadly connected with other countries through their navies, it was possible through Colbert's informal contacts and more formal symposia to discuss a wide range of ideas and concepts. From the first, these conferences were largely out of the public eye. What made them feasible was the deliberate decision to cast them as an exchange of views between professionals on common problems under a mantle of academic freedom rather than as an official negotiation among governments. In this way, it was possible to test and to discuss new ideas without appearing to challenge official government positions and policies. Under Colbert's immediate guidance and with the express blessing of CNO, Admiral Thomas Moorer, the Naval War College in 1969 hosted the First Seapower Symposium attended by the chiefs of naval staff and senior officers from 37 navies. In addition, Colbert hosted a meeting of the presidents of the war colleges of the Americas in 1970. The next year, the new CNO, Admiral Elmo R. Zumwalt, sponsored the Sixth Inter-American Naval Conference, which was also held at the college under Colbert's aegis. All of these international events were administered by Captain Clarence O. Fiske, who had also been elected the coordinating secretary of the Conference of the Naval War Colleges of the Americas.

The sea power symposium was a meeting of heads of the free world navies to discuss matters of mutual interest. Going to sea, operating ships, and running navies have many similar characteristics the world over, regardless of the size of the navies or the number of ships. There is a bond among men who have gone to sea and have experienced both the thrill and the challenge of experience at sea. There is also an unspoken feeling that sailors have problems and concerns that landlubbers cannot fully comprehend. Whatever the reason, naval officers the world over, regardless of the size or mission of their navy, have much in common. In making his closing remarks at the first international sea power symposium, Colbert stressed his view of personal, international naval diplomacy,

> Over the years each of us has had the opportunity to observe developments on the world maritime scene . . . . [Our] points of view—the basic beliefs which have arisen from them—and the pure professional naval competence which each of us can bring into the consideration of these matters—all could provide

threads of a cloth which might be woven into a durable and serviceable fabric.[28]

Colbert capitalized on the common experience and outlook of the naval profession. Working closely with the Chief of Naval Operations as the official host, Colbert arranged for the sea power symposium to meet in Mahan Hall for wide-ranging official discussions. There was also plenty of opportunity for the various foreign naval leaders to meet with one another and with their American hosts. The sea power symposium quickly achieved popularity around the world, and others have followed. In 1983, the seventh symposium took place at Newport and was attended by representatives of 49 navies, including 22 chiefs of naval staff, many of whom were graduates of the naval command course.

Similarly, the Conference of Presidents of the Naval War Colleges of the Americas brought together the senior officers of the various hemispheric war colleges for discussions of mutual problems. These meetings had begun in 1962 and have continued every two or three years at Newport or in Latin America. The point, which Colbert emphasized, was that the war colleges had much in common and that each college had something to offer the others. The list of countries participating was impressive: Argentina, Bolivia, Brazil, Canada, Chile, Colombia, Dominican Republic, Ecuador, Mexico, Paraguay, Peru, Uruguay, and Venezuela. It is difficult to measure the effect of these navy-to-navy contacts, but their intent is to bring about, at the very minimum, a mutual awareness of common problems and to construct a community of common maritime interests.

Carrying Modernization Programs Forward

These major international conferences were only a part of Colbert's extensive efforts to bring the college to the attention of the broader community, not by press releases alone, but by substantial performance; and to bring the broader community to the college. The global strategy discussions were an excellent vehicle to attain this goal on a broad national scale. Started 20 years earlier as round table discussions, the global strategy discussions by 1968 had evolved into major five-day meetings of prominent civilians, numerous flag and general officers, and the entire staff, faculty, and student body of the college. Colbert put to good use his extraordinary web of contacts and succeeded in attracting unusually distinguished and influential men and women to the college.

Within the college he kept going the momentum that had already been started. He refused to make changes for their own sake, building instead upon the foundations of his predecessor. The focus of the curriculum was on foreign affairs and on the military concerns at higher levels as well as at operational and planning levels. As Hayward had found before him, Colbert was unable to obtain a sufficiently large civilian teaching faculty to permit a radical departure from the traditional lecture format of the college curriculum, but he did make a determined effort to upgrade his military faculty, creating a system of 10 military chairs in 1969. Each such chair had a sponsor within the planning and operational divisions of the Office of Naval Operations in Washington. The idea behind the military chair system was clearly stated by Colbert when he wrote to the Chief of Naval Personnel:

> In the military area, however, the developments in all naval warfare areas of new weapons systems, tactics and doctrine brought on by the tremendous rate of technological change, and the need for the Naval War College students to receive a thorough background in these areas have created a challenge in the study of military subjects. Changes in the world balance of sea power, coupled with these technological changes, pose major problems in naval strategy. In the past, there has been no institutional provision for military specialists as effective as the civilian scholars have been in their area. A program of military chairs, therefore, is being established to improve the balance of military and academic curriculum programs.
>
> To ensure that the individuals who occupy the Military Chairs are of the highest caliber and represent the best and most current thought in their specialty areas, nominations will be solicited from the Bureau of Naval Personnel, requesting that the Division of OPNAV bearing principal responsibility in each warfare area be called upon for advice.[29]

The first chairs to be established were those of air strike warfare and naval strategy. While the addition of these chairs brought more academic and professional talent to the college, there were still too few professors available to change the chief mode of instruction from the lecture system, but students exchanged ideas raised in the lectures in discussion groups under the guidance of a uniformed faculty member. The extensive offerings of the electives program coupled with the requirement to do independent research on a given subject individualized the academic program to suit the needs and desires of the students. George Washington University continued to offer courses leading to a master in science degree in international relations. The cooperative degree program with the University of Rhode Island, now including a maritime affairs option, continued.

Colbert was able to maintain the momentum for the building program. He used his skill and influence to bolster congressional support for necessary funding when required. During his administration he oversaw the refinement and the final design of the three major additions to the college complex—Spruance, Conolly, and Hewitt Halls. Working with the noted sculptor Felix de Weldon and with Carter Brown, head of the National Gallery of Art in Washington (both were Newport residents), Colbert arranged to use granite facings for these new buildings which would weather to the color of the granite used in Luce Hall in 1891 and subsequently in the other buildings, Pringle and Mahan Halls. This meant reopening the original quarry and transporting a significant amount of granite several hundred miles.

Student housing at Fort Adams was deteriorating at an alarming rate. Colbert conceived the idea of new student housing on vacant land near the old fortifications. His concept was an extensive housing development in a style compatible with colonial Newport. With the support of Rhode Island Senator John O. Pastore, he was able to obtain funds and congressional authorization for it and other projects. By 1975 it was largely completed. The design of the project met Colbert's high standards of impeccable taste, and many of the units have an unexcelled view of the narrow entrance to the east passage into Narragansett Bay.

The Naval War College Foundation

One of Colbert's lasting and most significant achievements was the creation of the Naval War College Foundation. His experience while head of the naval command course and in global strategy discussions through the years convinced him that there was a wealth of civilian interest in improving the college to mutual advantage. The board of advisors whose task was to furnish guidance and recommendations to the president was already in existence, but some of the board's proposals were impractical because of budgetary limitations. An alumni organization or other group of supporters was needed to help the college. Most educational institutions depended on help from foundations in various ways.

The Naval Academy had an active alumni association as well as the Naval Academy Foundation, both nonprofit organizations contributing significantly to the projects that the superintendent believes necessary. Rear Admiral Richard W. Bates, who had stayed in Newport and who had been closely associated with the Naval War College since 1946, along with several important civilian attendees at global strategy sessions were enthusiastic about such an idea. In 1969, the Secretary of the Navy approved organizing a Naval War College Foundation, and it was chartered as a nonprofit organization under the laws of the state of Rhode Island and Providence Plantations. John Nicholas Brown, former Assistant Secretary of the Navy for Air and a prominent Rhode Island philanthropist, became the first Foundation president, with Rear Admiral Bates as executive director. With more than 100 founding members, including corporation heads and many Rhode Island citizens, the Foundation was off to a good start. By its charter, support could be provided for activities and projects which the War College president wished to carry out that would benefit the institution but could not be funded officially.

The Era of "Z-Grams"

Two years after Colbert's arrival in Newport, Secretary of the Navy John H. Chafee selected Vice Admiral Elmo Zumwalt, Commander, Naval Forces, Vietnam, as Chief of Naval Operations, succeeding Admiral Moorer, who had been picked to be the new chairman of the Joint Chiefs of Staff. Zumwalt, 14 years junior to Moorer, became the youngest CNO to date. He had graduated from the command and staff course at Newport in 1953, the same year his predecessor had graduated from the senior strategy and tactics course.

The new Chief of Naval Operations assumed his post on 1 July 1970 and lost no time in instigating a number of radical changes in traditional personnel policies, based on his experiences as naval commander in Vietnam. He wanted to ensure that modern youth would be attracted to serve in the Navy and was willing to change time-honored rules and traditions to do so. Within a few weeks, the Navy was receiving serially numbered "Navops," popularly known as "Z-grams" in the fleet, which covered a wide range of personnel policies. Some officers, particularly senior officers and senior enlisted men, viewed the Z-grams with suspicion and sometimes with downright hostility. As the 1970-1971 academic year progressed at Newport, the Z-grams received close scrutiny. Officers returning to command and executive billets realized that changes were being made within the Navy, which, for better or worse, would affect their work afloat or ashore in the immediate future. In seminars and student offices, the new directives were discussed and debated in detail.

Colbert had continued the tradition of the president's hour, started under Admiral Austin in 1962. Periodically, the president met with students and responded to any questions or comments they might have. At a president's hour with the command and staff students, one officer suggested that middle-grade officers be given a chance to express opinions on the entire Z-gram effort directly to Admiral Zumwalt.

After Colbert passed this suggestion on to him, Zumwalt issued Z-gram 62. Pursuant to this order, a forum was set up in both classes at the War College to discuss means to improve the Navy. Twelve students summarized the results of the forum and made a 25-minute briefing to the Secretary of the Navy, Zumwalt, and other flag officers in February 1971. The presentation stressed the importance and the need for personnel stability to increase the combat readiness of the fleet.[30]

Another 1971 Z-gram (Z-41) instituted an academic chair in surface strike warfare to be filled by a commander or captain with a record of outstanding performance in command. In the same Z-gram, Zumwalt established a command excellence forum at the Naval War College "to identify, discuss, and promulgate the ideas and command leadership qualities of our most successful commanding officers and thus enhance overall common excellence."[31] The forum met during the period 26-30 April 1971, led by Captain J. E. McQueston, the first holder of the military chair of surface strike warfare. One of the 16 participants, Captain C. S. Christensen, Jr., summed up the forum succinctly:

> The quintessence of the Forum, to this participant at least, was the conviction that bureaucratic practices are eviscerating Navy management effectiveness. In a bureaucratic Navy, it is hard to attract and keep the best men in the fleet once they discover that the real "action" is in the bureaucracy ashore. We found this frightening, because when the chips are down, naval battles are won or lost at sea.[32]

Vice Admiral Semmes at the Helm

In April 1971, largely through Colbert's efforts and contacts at the Norfolk Virginia headquarters of the Supreme Allied Commander, Atlantic, (SACLANT), 42 naval warfare students made a three-day field trip to the United Kingdom, hosted by the Royal Navy. Each National War College class made a longer field trip, with sections going to different areas. Budget considerations precluded the naval warfare trip from becoming a regular part of each curriculum, as Colbert had hoped.

Soon thereafter, Secretary Chafee announced that Colbert, after three years at the college, would become Chief of Staff to SACLANT, Admiral Charles K. Duncan. The new college president would be Vice Admiral Benedict J. Semmes, then serving on Admiral Zumwalt's staff as Deputy Chief of Naval Operations for Operations (Op-03).

The new president, "B. J." as he was known throughout the fleet, was in his thirteenth year as a flag officer at the age of 58. A National War College graduate, his career afloat had been primarily with cruisers and destroyers. Ashore, he had emphasized personnel planning and administration. He was no stranger to the Naval War College with almost five years of fleet duty in Newport. He had been chief of staff to the Commander, Destroyer Force, when Colbert had led the first naval command class in 1956 and 1957, providing from the force staff lecturers and other assistance for the foreign officers. In 1963 and 1964, he had commanded the Cruiser-Destroyer Force at Newport, had lectured to naval warfare and command and staff, and as senior officer afloat had worked closely with Vice Admiral Austin, the college president at that time. His duty in the Bureau of Personnel, first as a detail officer, then as deputy for plans, and finally four years as Chief of Naval Personnel, had given him a continuing view of problems of student and faculty qualifications and student loading at Newport. In his last tour afloat as Commander, Second Fleet, and Commander, NATO Striking Fleet, Atlantic, he was well known by our allies with forces committed to the Atlantic area.

When Semmes arrived at the college, the curriculum for the coming academic year was set. Still, he saw that one of his tasks was to preside over some degree of shift in its emphasis, away from foreign and international affairs to management concepts—which would be more in keeping with the prevailing notions in Washington.

A few months after Semmes arrived, a second sea power symposium was held at the college. Vice Admiral Colbert, who was largely responsible for the extensive organization and plans for this gathering, returned to the college to attend it. At the conference, the Chief of Naval Operations, Admiral Zumwalt, in an informal conversation with Admiral Sudomo, head of the Indonesian Navy, made a commitment to help the Indonesians in their transition from Soviet to Western advisors. As a result of this commitment, Semmes and Captain Walter B. Woodson, director of the naval command and staff course, went to Indonesia in early 1972 to advise the Indonesians on instituting professional education in the Indonesian Navy. Semmes and Woodson were excellent choices for what was essentially a diplomatic mission.

Planning for the Naval Staff Course

During the 1971-1972 academic year, final plans were put together for a new course at the college, setting a convening date for the first class in mid-July. At the first international sea power symposium, interest in a junior course, complementing the naval command course, had been expressed. Such a course would parallel much of the regular command and staff curriculum. In order to accommodate more students and curb individual student expenses, the course would last for five months, as did the Armed Forces Staff College in Norfolk. There would be two classes each year for officers in the grade of lieutenant commander and lieutenant. It would include junior officers of navies already represented in the naval command classes and officers from smaller navies of Third World countries friendly to the United States. Semmes picked Captain Jack Quinn, an experienced naval aviator in the 1972 naval warfare class, to organize and head the first naval staff course. Quinn faced many of the problems that Colbert had faced 16

years earlier with the command course, but as a talented and innovative officer, Quinn established a strong beginning for the course, and
the first students quickly created an enviable spirit of their own. Quinn
remained the head of the naval staff course for eight years. At the time
of his retirement in 1980, he had led 16 groups through the five-month
curriculum complementing the naval command course.

Changes at Top and at the College

In late 1970, the office of Naval Education and Training was
established in Pensacola, Florida, to coordinate educational policy and
planning within the Navy. Its first chief, Vice Admiral Malcolm Cagle,
was also the Director of Naval Education and Training on the staff of
the Chief of Naval Operations (OP-099). With the establishment of this
office, the administrative chain of command for the War College was
altered and the president of the Naval War College reported directly to
the Chief of Naval Education and Training along with superintendents
of the Naval Postgraduate School and the Naval Academy.

While this administrative change was being made, names and faces
were changing in high positions. At the beginning of President Nixon's
second term in 1972, Secretary of Defense Melvin Laird resigned and, in
May, Secretary of the Navy John Chafee resigned to reenter politics in
his native state of Rhode Island. Chafee's successor, Under Secretary of
the Navy John Warner of Virginia, was already indoctrinated in the
ways of the Department and had a reputation for disagreeing with
Zumwalt, Chafee, and Laird over Zumwalt's personnel policies.

Shortly after Semmes returned from Indonesia, he announced that he
would retire at the end of June. Both Semmes and the college staff had
been surprised to learn that he would not be allowed to continue to fill
out two years at the college. Under Semmes' guidance, the faculty and
staff had already prepared plans for the forthcoming academic year, but
the announcement of Semmes' retirement was a clear sign that major
changes were in store for the Naval War Colleges. Semmes, the senior
vice admiral in the Navy, retired after 38 years of naval service, on 30
June 1972. In the ceremony which marked this occasion in Pringle Hall,
Vice Admiral Stansfield Turner relieved Semmes.

There had been significant gains at the college since 1966. The
curriculum had been improved, firm plans had been laid to expand the
physical plant and increase the student body, a means had been
established to maintain continuity in academic policy through the
long term appointment of a civilian academic advisor, and important
innovations had been made in establishing international naval
contacts. Yet the college had neither a stable faculty nor a large,
stringently selected student body. The college's expansion into a

number of special activities, supporting conferences and symposia, produced benefits for the Navy by establishing contacts and promoting a greater understanding of the U.S. Navy, but at the same time, it greatly increased the administrative staff and distracted officers assigned to those portions from academic work. By 1972, the college faculty and staff were proud of their accomplishments in rectifying the weaknesses in the college curriculum which had been attacked in the 1960s, but, at the same time, the college's reputation within the Navy had not changed significantly.

Notes

1. Deputy Secretary of Defense Paul H. Nitze to LCDR D. S. Strole, 7 December 1968, quoted in D. S.Strole, "Professional Excellence and National Security: The Educational Philosophy of Vice Admiral John T. Hayward," Naval War College School of Command and Staff. Thesis prepared for the George Washington University degree, Master of Science in International Affairs, 1967, p. 39.

2. Paul Gallico, "The Dropout Who Made It To The Top," Off print from Readers Digest, November 1966.

3. NWC Archives, R63, Box 124: File 5400 Mission and Tasks: Book Two: Hayward to Baldwin, 6 April 1966.

4. Loc. cit., Hayward to T. H. Moorer, 7 July 1969.

5. Loc. cit., Hayward to Baldwin, 6 April 1966.

6. Loc. cit., Box 123, File: Mission, VCNO Horacio Rivero to President, NWC, Op-10 C2 serial 87PO1B of 26 May 1965, approving President, NWC letter serial 714 of 26 March 1965.

7. Loc. cit., Memo: Assistant Chief of Staff for Plans to Staff, 1 Nov. 1966.

8. J. T. Hayward, "The Second-Class Military Advisor: His Cause and Cure," Armed Forces Management (November 1968), p. 68.

9. Ibid., p. 69.

10. Ibid., p. 67.

11. J. T. Hayward, "Challenge," Naval War College Review (September 1978), p. 1.

12. NWC Archives, R63, Box 124. File 5400: Mission: Hayward to Rivero, serial 1754 of 27 July 1966.

13. Loc. cit., Rivero to Hayward, 12 Oct 1966.

14. Loc. cit., Hayward to B. J. Semmes, ser 890 of 22 April 1966.

15. Neil Ulman, "School for Admirals," The Wall Street Journal, 28 June 1977, p. 1.

16. Ibid.

17. NWC Archives, R63, Box 123. File 5400 Mission and Basics. DCNO Manpower to PresiDent, NWC, Op-10 serial 11401P10 of 20 August 1967.

18. President, NWC to CNO, serial 3208 of 7 December 1966, quoted in Nepier Smith, "Historical Analysis of the Organizational Success of the Naval War College During the Twenty-Five Years Following the Second World War," NWC Advanced Research Project, 1974, pp. 131-33.

19. NWC Archives, R63. Box 123. File 5400: President, NWC, to CNO, serial 1275 of 3 June 1966.

20. Loc. cit., Chief, Bureau of Personnel to President, NWC, Pers E23 of 9 August 1966.

21. J. K. McDonald, "Thomas Hinman Moorer" in Robert W. Love, Jr., ed., *The Chiefs of Naval Operations* (Annapolis, 1980), p. 354.

22. Moorer personal letter to VADM Hayward, 17 January 1968 quoted in Nepier Smith, op. cit., 134.

23. NWC Archives, RG3. Box 123. File 5400: CNO memo to VCNO, Op 00 Memo 301-68 of 6 May 1968; VCNO Memo to Director, Navy Program Planning, Op-09 ser 240P09 of 5 May 1968.

24. Loc. cit., CNO memo serial 2500P09B33 of 28 November 1968.

25. Loc. cit., RADM Roy Benson to Hayward, 24 June 1968.

26. J. T. Hayward, "I Had A Dream," *Shipmate* (October 1975), p. 19.

27. Quoted in "Admiral R. G. Colbert, 1915-1973" *Naval War College Review* (May-June 1974), p. 4.

28. Ibid., p. 5.

29. NHC Ms. Coll. 30 Colbert Papers, Series 2, Box 18 Folder 20 Colbert to CNP, Serial 2579 of 29 Aug 1969.

30. Loc. cit., Box 19, Folder 66.

31. Loc. cit., CNO Message 121935Z Oct 70 (NAVOP Z-41) in Ms. Coll 30. Series 2, Box 29, Folder 67.

32. Loc. cit., Capt. C. S. Christensen, Jr., to CNO, 25 July 1971.

CHAPTER 11

THE BEGINNING OF A NEW CURRICULUM, 1972-1977

Admiral Elmo Zumwalt reached the mid-point in his four-year term of office as Chief of Naval Operations before his fundamental policy changes for the Navy had a direct and substantive effect on the Naval War College. Throughout his tenure, Zumwalt stressed radical and forceful change, rather than gradual evolution, as the best means to reshape underlying trends in naval policy and thought.[1] The changes which occurred at the Naval War College in 1972-1974 were no exception.

Zumwalt's policies were based on his perception that he had become CNO at a time of great military and naval crisis for the United States. While a large proportion of the defense budget was being spent on the Vietnam war, he believed that the United States was not matching the growth of Soviet military power. In particular, he pointed to the rapid increase in the size and sophistication of the Soviet Navy at a time when the U.S. Navy was shrinking. Further, Zumwalt felt increasingly frustrated that naval officers generally failed to break away from their orientation toward a particular type of naval activity, whether it was surface, submarine, or air, in addition to their failure to understand clearly the Navy's overall mission.[3]

In order to establish a clear general understanding of the Navy's broad mission, Zumwalt took several steps. He established the Navy Net Assessment Group to create a gauge by which the U.S. Navy could measure its likely effectiveness against the Soviets; he sponsored

Project 2000 to give a new long-range review of policy beyond the five-year planning cycles established by Secretary McNamara, and he sought to broaden naval thinking by revising the curriculum at the Naval War College. Although Zumwalt had considerable experience as a systems analyst, he believed that the college had strayed from its proper role in studying tactics and strategy by allowing too much emphasis on defense management. A graduate of both the Naval War College in 1953 and the National War College in 1962, he believed that the Naval War College course of instruction was neither rigorous nor challenging. As he looked back over his career, he believed his college days in Washington had been far more important than those in Newport.[4]

To carry out that part of his broad vision that applied to the Naval War College, Zumwalt chose Stansfield Turner, then a relatively junior rear admiral, to be the college's president, a position which for the previous 20 years had been held by a senior vice admiral. Turner wanted very much to be involved in naval education, and Zumwalt had planned to appoint him Superintendent of the Naval Academy. When opposition arose to Turner's appointment there, Zumwalt suggested to him that he go to the Naval War College for a year prior to taking command of the Sixth Fleet. Assuming that he would have only a year to make changes at Newport, Turner had to act quickly.[5]

Promoted to vice admiral upon taking up the Naval War College presidency, Turner was given full freedom to devise a new curriculum and to make whatever changes he saw fit at the college. Turner proceeded with Zumwalt's full support and with no policy guidance other than the CNO's express desire that the college accomplish two things: broaden officers who are often preoccupied with their area of specialty; and help them to learn to analyze problems.[6]

Turner's Concept for the Naval War College

In order to achieve these two basic goals, Turner wanted immediate results, not gradual evolution. Like Zumwalt, Turner believed that radical and dramatic change was essential not only to focus attention on his goals and to sharpen the difference between his approach and previous practice. He believed it essential to eliminate the restrictions on intellectual development which he perceived to be at the Naval War College.

A Rhodes scholar at Oxford University, Turner had never attended any war college course even though, in the early 1960s, as a commander, he had been selected to attend the Naval War College. When he heard the news of his selection, he recalled, his only thought had been "How can I get out of it?"[7] Instead of attending what he believed to be a poor institution, Turner wanted a more valuable experience. Avoiding the Naval War College, he went to the Harvard Business School and became involved in systems analysis work in the office of the Secretary of Defense.

A firm believer in preparing for his next assignment before reporting, Turner wanted to have a concept and a general plan before he came to Newport. He did not wish to interfere with the college's operations before taking command. Turner made a particular point of avoiding contact with officers then at Newport, largely because he thought they would represent "vested interests" at the college. Instead, he sought articulate people who knew the college and would be willing to give him their frank views. Representative of those who answered Turner's requirement was Commander James A. Barber, then commanding USS *Schofield* (DEG-3). Barber had been plans officer at the college and, later, Stephen B. Luce Professor of Naval Science. Turner asked Captain Hugh G. Nott of his Washington staff to go to Newport to discuss the current college curriculum. Although Turner was unaware of the reforms that had been made since 1966, the college's general reputation led him to conclude that the curriculum was of little value. He decided that he would examine independently what the purpose and focus of the college should be, and then proceed to use the resources at Newport as appropriate to his newly developed concepts.[8]

While he was still Director of the System Analysis Division in OPNAV (OP-96), Turner began to form his own ideas. In late January and February 1972, he started discussions on the new directions for the college with members of his Washington staff, three of whom would later come with him to Newport: Captain Nott, Lieutenant Commander David G. Clark, and Robert D. (Rusty) Williams. In March 1972, he convened a formal conference at the Center for Naval Analyses in Rosslyn, Virginia, which brought together some 20 selected War College graduates, businessmen, senior officers, academics, and defense analysts, including, among others, Commander Barber, Professors Philip A. Crowl of the University of Nebraska, Robert Osgood of Johns Hopkins University, Robert Bowie of Harvard, Alfred Kiel of the Massachusetts Institute of Technology, Dr. William R. Emerson of the National Endowment of the Humanities, Thomas Phillips of Raytheon, and L. C. Ackerman of the Newport News Shipbuilding and Dry Dock Company. Admiral Zumwalt attended part of the meeting, making a short address.

This meeting suggested to Turner that the academic needs of naval officers were wide, too wide in fact to be met in a single year's course of study. What was important in education, the conference suggested, was not to accumulate facts, but to learn the process to best go about one's profession.[9] As Turner emphasized, "With an infinite number of requirements it was important to be sure that they learned to know something, not just give them breadth."[10]

Although this conference and other early discussions with a cross section of specialists did not provide any explicit answers, they confirmed Turner's impression that since 1945 the selection of students for the Naval War College had had little or no relationship to a candidate's potential for flag rank. Moreover, he concluded, as Edward Katzenbach had in 1965, that the college's curriculum had little depth. Worse, it was largely a passive experience for the students as they listened to lectures, rather than engaged their minds in rigorous study.

Turner believed that officer-students needed to learn to reason through problems and to see that there was more than one answer to any problem. He wanted to teach them to deal with uncertainty. And he believed that if students, curricula, and faculty met uncompromising standards of excellence, Naval War College graduates would be regarded, assigned, and promoted as top-notch, professionally educated officers. In this way, the college could establish itself within the Department of Defense, by virtue of its academic excellence and the quality of its products, rather than by a bureaucratic directive that stated its position in service education.

In searching for a solution, Turner was much influenced by his days as a Rhodes scholar at Oxford University in 1947-1949. He remembered particularly the beneficial academic shock he had experienced as an American in Oxford. Unlike at an American university, lectures often had little direct relationship to the student's work. What mattered most at Oxford was a student's ability to explore intellectual issues on his own initiative and to develop his individual skills through writing essays and defending them in discussions with his teacher in weekly tutorials. Turner explained his vision in 1973 to fellow Oxford graduates and Rhodes scholars when he wrote,

> As Oxford tried to teach us to look beyond the shrinking boundaries of right and wrong answers, so my staff and I hoped to raise questions in the minds of our students which could never be resolved by the neat formulae for a shore bombardment or a submarine search pattern. As Oxford thrust upon us roles as philosophers and historians for which we may have been ill-prepared, so we hoped to encourage new dimensions of thought upon our students. In order to deal effectively with the protean conditions of war and peace, an officer must possess a negative capability whereby he can abandon his prejudices at will and look upon the problems confronting him with an eye forever new.[11]

To apply this idea to the Naval War College, Turner gathered around him a second group of key advisors. This time, most of them were former Rhodes scholars and Oxford-educated men who, despite varied professional experience and education in America, shared a similar reaction to their Oxford experience. Prominent among them was Dr. William R. Emerson, a 1948 Rhodes scholar and military historian, who had been Ernest J. King professor of maritime history at the Naval War College in 1963-1964. Since 1969, Emerson had been in Washington as director of the office of research grants of the National Endowment for the Humanities.

Soon after Turner learned about his appointment to Newport, he asked Emerson, as one well-acquainted with the Naval War College, what he could do to improve it. Emerson replied that for a start, he could assign Thucydides, *The Peloponnesian War*. Turner took up the idea and later asked Emerson to join him for further discussions. In a series of meetings, Emerson, Turner, and members of Turner's staff examined possibilities for the course.[12]

By late March, after about three weeks of meetings, Emerson was able to distill their initial discussions, based on a nearly unspoken appreciation of their common Oxford experience, into a basic curriculum concept for the Naval War College. Proposing to divide the curriculum into three basic sections, strategy, management, and tactics, each to be taught intensively, and to be followed by a period of research seminars, Emerson wrote that their concept was

> based on the conviction that naval commanders must deal with problems arising partly from history, in the sense that the large forces and fixed interests and concerns which influence policy and strategy stem from the past, and partly from current technology (naval and otherwise) which shapes the ways in which such permanent historical factors manifest themselves at any given point in time.
>
> Central to this concept is the parallel conviction that sound pedagogy at any level (but especially in dealing with officers of mature years) consists in involving the student most actively in the educational process and at the furthest level of particularity which time and circumstance permit . . . . Where a choice must be made, the proposed curriculum rests on the assumption that it is always best to teach what is *teachable*, which promises to develop the student's own powers of analysis, of synthesis, and of discrimination rather than subjects which, while of great significance at the moment, do not easily lend themselves to the educational process and to actual discussion in the seminar format, which *is* the Naval War College's basic teaching mechanism.[13]

Emerson's distillation of Turner's discussions with his staff and advisors became a seminal document. It was distributed within Turner's circle as they planned the specifics of the curriculum over the next three months, and was jocularly described among them as "one of the most widely xeroxed documents in history."[14] In the initial discussions, an unexpected displacement of viewpoints occurred. Emerson, the academic historian, stressed the importance of tactics and naval operations in the curriculum, and Turner, the professional officer, stressed the value of historical study.[15] Despite this apparent incongruity, Turner emphasized the study of strategy over other areas. He believed that naval officers knew most about tactics and had some understanding of defense management, but the area in which they were weakest was in understanding the purposes of their profession.[16]

The prospective president believed that the War College courses he was developing should be so demanding that students could not do justice to both college courses and the George Washington University cooperative degree program in international affairs at the college. He objected to the failure of students to give their full allegiance to the Naval War College course and was determined to make it challenging and all-absorbing. He wanted to excite them about their profession, not the academic study of history or political science. Suspecting that War College students were using the George Washington degree program mainly for retirement employment opportunities, Turner did not care that the program at Newport had been the best of the George Washington University's Master's degree courses at the various service colleges and that the college had the most cordial relationship of any of them with the University.[17] Turner advised Dean Burton M. Sapin of the University's School of Public and International Affairs that he intended to terminate the program for the naval warfare students immediately upon taking command at the War College and that he would make a decision on continuing it for the command and staff students in January 1973.[18]

Turner also concluded that the expensive field trips to the United Nations, London, and other places, which War College students had made, should be eliminated, because they detracted from the serious academic reading and individual thought required by the new curriculum. Moreover, he wanted to use the money that had been spent on these trips to supply students with the basic books of the curriculum, with which they could go back and restudy in future years.

Having made these initial decisions before he assumed the presidency of the college, Turner proceeded to gather together the people who could put the ideas into effect and to teach the new courses.

Implementing the Concept

The academic year was scheduled to begin in August, and a great deal of preparation was necessary in the few remaining months. Rejecting recommendations that the new program be delayed for a year until it could be fully prepared in all respects, Turner chose to implement it immediately. While gradual evolution might be appropriate in a university environment, he believed there was little to gain from a prolonged effort to gain consensus among the staff and faculty of the college and that no speedy agreement would be found, given the natural tendency of bureaucracies to resist change. He planned to institute the new concept immediately in the naval warfare course; the command and staff course would continue temporarily on its previous lines. Because the three new courses would be taught one after the other, the immediate problem was the strategy and policy course that opened the academic year for the senior-level course.

Through Emerson's academic contacts, Turner recruited J. Kenneth McDonald, a George Washington professor and former director of the George Washington University's program at the Naval War College, who was completing his doctorate in history at Oxford, along with military historian Philip A. Crowl, and James E. King, Jr., a 1937 Rhodes scholar and political scientist specializing in nuclear warfare. Casting around for other military historians, Turner asked friends at West Point and Annapolis to suggest names from their history faculties. Through these connections, he recruited Josiah Bunting, III, a 1963 Rhodes scholar and Army major, who resigned his commission in June 1972 following publication of *The Lionheads,* his novel about the Army in Vietnam, and Richard Megargee, a volunteer from the Naval Academy history department. Together, this new group of civilian academics joined those who had already been on the faculty at Newport: Martin Blumenson, Robert Delaney, and Frederick Hartmann. Together, they became the long awaited civilian strategy faculty.

The final syllabus in strategy was developed in June and July 1972, first by Bunting and McDonald, then refined and completed by Crowl, who served as Ernest J. King professor and permanent head of the strategy department until 1980. As it finally emerged, the strategy course stressed readings of about 1,000 pages per week, and tried to develop deep investigations of carefully selected historical case studies that illustrated recurring and major problems in the formulation and execution of foreign policy and military strategy. The emphasis, as Crowl pointed out in his introductory lecture, was on the word "and." As he told the students,

> We are concerned with military strategy *and* foreign policy, with the inter-relationships *between* them, with the *political* uses of military power—or, to use the phrase coined by the great German strategic thinker, Karl von Clausewitz, with 'war as an extension of politics by other means.'[19]

In selecting the readings, whole books were favored rather than short articles and excerpts. In lieu of the previous parade of visiting lecturers, only one academic expert was invited each week to lecture, attend seminars, and be available for discussions.

During their two and a half day working visits, these visiting lecturers faced a rigorous schedule, which Turner hoped would force the maximum number of students into a direct, intellectual encounter. In support of the visitor's theme, one faculty member delivered a complementary lecture. The remainder of the week was used by the student for in-depth reading in assigned and recommended works, for writing an assigned essay, and for attending one three-hour seminar. Using a system that had worked successfully at Swarthmore College and later in graduate seminars at the University of Nebraska, Crowl instituted procedures by which student essays were circulated in advance to each member of a small seminar group numbering 10 to 12 students. These essays, presented by the author and critiqued by a fellow student, sparked general discussion of the issues in a three-hour seminar. Later, the instructors returned the students' papers, fully marked and graded.[20]

With Turner's concept for a new curriculum already far advanced, the college president, Vice Admiral Semmes, designated his special academic advisor, Professor Hartmann, to go to Washington and establish liaison with Turner to facilitate the transition. Meanwhile, several civilian and military staff members established direct contact with Turner, providing personal and unofficial recommendations. Among them were Lieutenant Commander B. M. Simpson, III, Colonel John Keeley and Professor Robert Delaney.[21]

By the time Turner had relieved Semmes in June, he was already the center of controversy. While he wanted to be discreet and not interfere with the college before he assumed official responsibility, Turner had relied on advice from outside the college, and developed a radical plan. His concept meant totally scrapping the detailed program that the college staff under Semmes had carefully prepared for the year, hiring new civilian faculty members who would outnumber those already in Newport, reassigning military officers to newly formed military-civilian teaching teams, instituting a new curriculum, establishing the basis for what would become three new academic departments, ordering new books and reading materials, arranging for visiting lecturers, and creating the need for a fundamental reorganization of the college's administration. Wherever possible, qualified military staff members were to be diverted from administrative duties and paired with civilian professors to form teaching teams.

In short, his concept rejected much of what the college had stood for in recent years. Those who were closely associated with it and had devoted great effort to its improvement were offended. In this situation, the difficult and unenviable task of handling the vast array of administrative details to put Turner's concepts into effect was given to the college's new chief of staff, Captain Nott, and two successive deputies, Rear Admirals William L. Harris and Charles S. Williams, Jr.

When the college opened on 24 August 1972, the 467 new students and the staff expected change, but many were unprepared for the convocation ceremony and Turner's address. To stress the academic nature of the college, Turner directed that the opening ceremony would include an academic procession with the entire staff and faculty in appropriate academic robes.

Following the example of two previous War College presidents, Mahan and Sims, both of whom had received honorary degrees from Oxford while wearing academic regalia over their naval uniforms, Turner ordered that the same combination be followed in the ceremony held on Dewey Field, south of Luce Hall. The combination of academic and military insignia created difficulty in establishing seniority. Some senior officers with only bachelor's degrees were offended at the thought of some of their juniors with doctorates preceding them. At the same time, doubt arose as to whether it was appropriate to wear service dress or tropical white uniforms under the academic robes. The most difficult problem was whether to wear an academic cap or a uniform cap. In the end, no caps were worn.

The long academic column formed in the shaded roadway between Luce, Mahan, and Pringle Halls and then made its way out into the blazing August sun to Dewey Field, where all 467 new students and another 500 guests witnessed the ceremony. As college president, Turner came at the rear of the procession. He made an imposing figure, his service dress white uniform contrasting with his black, short-sleeved and open gown with the crimson hood of an Oxford Master of Arts askew on his shoulders. As he came onto the field, the Navy band finished Elgar's "Pomp and Circumstance," and struck up the "Grand March" from Verdi's *Aida*.

Turner's address to the students was as blunt and articulate as any delivered by Luce or Sims in their time at the college. To a surprised audience, he explained his new curriculum and his reasons for adopting it.

> This year's shift of emphasis toward a deeper study of strategy on the one hand and toward more attention to management and tactics on the other is really not something new at the Naval War College. They represent a return to our great traditions—to the strategic and historical contribution of men like Mahan; to the tactical and operational studies of men like William Sims, Raymond Spruance, Kelly Turner who were the experts in naval warfare in their day.[22]

Turner expressed particular alarm over what he called the "creeping intellectual devitalization in all war colleges since World War II." He said that prolonged briefings had been substituted for rigorous intellectual development. Intimating that the college had become only a gentleman's club where students could relax between demanding assignments, he noted, "It appears that no student in recent years has ever flunked." Although none would flunk out under his command, the assembled student body was appropriately impressed by his further observation, "As of this moment, those who do not perform have no guarantee of a full year at the Naval War College." Starting with the current year, students would be graded in order to assess more accurately their performance. The course of instruction would be rigorous, and "we will expect lots of individual effort in reading, in writing, and in solving case problems."

These statements were startling enough. But the real blockbuster, as far as many students were concerned, came when Turner announced that because the new course would be so time consuming, students in the senior course would not be allowed to participate in the George Washington University master's degree program. Returning to his basic point, Turner declared:

> You can run the risk of abusing your freedom, or you can use it for self-development. You are on your own to get your higher education in military decision making during these next ten months. My basic premise is that if we point you in a reasonable direction and just turn you loose, you will conquer every height ahead of you on your own. Always keep in mind that the product which the country desperately needs is military men with the capability of solving complex problems and of executing their decisions. Scholarship for scholarship's sake is of no importance to us. You must keep your sights on decision making or problem solving as your objective. Problems are not solved by standard or pat solutions, especially not in times of such rapid change as we are experiencing . . . .
>
> Mainly, though, I adjure you to take advantage of this opportunity. If you find yourself taxed hard, overtaxed in cases, do not let that discourage you. If we tailored a course to the average student, we would fail to tax those who are most ready to proceed. Remember the related point that course content is secondary. It is the development of habits of thinking that counts. If you cannot cover everything that is assigned, do what you do accomplish well, so that you think creatively. Ploughing through a wealth of material just to absorb it is not what we want or what you need. A modicum of excellence and understanding will far outbalance a plethora of mediocrity and superficiality.[23]

The final point in his address was the announcement that the first meeting to discuss Thucydides' *The Peloponnesian War* would take place that day immediately after lunch. For many students, that was an unknown book about an apparently irrelevant war by an author with an unpronounceable name. Yet to Turner it was the essence of his approach. "This was absolutely the best example of how you could use historical case studies to teach contemporary or strategic problems," Turner recalled. The story of the Athenian government's attempt to conduct an ever more expensive, protracted, overseas war in the face of political disaffection at home had broad similarities to the United States in Vietnam. By 1972 many students had served in Vietnam and held passionate views about the war. "To get them in a room and try to dispassionately talk about whether we should or should not have been in Vietnam and what were the strategic implications of a sea power going into a prolonged engagement overseas would have been impossible. Yet they talked about Vietnam when they talked about the Peloponnesian Wars, and they understood."[24] With the idea of getting at basic and recurring problems in strategy while avoiding the passions of current political views and personal experience, Turner's course stopped at the end of World War II.

Turner's speech was the keynote of his term as college president. A clarion call for reform, progress, and high intellectual standards, it also had some unsought effects. By throwing out a challenge as he did, he drew down a storm of protest from graduates, senior officers, and staff members who interpreted his comments as a direct attack on their own personal achievements and values. The other service colleges objected strenuously that Turner had tarred them with the same brush when he declared that "our increasing reliance on civilians and on 'think tanks' to do our thinking for us" reflected a failure of war colleges in general. Many officers resented the implication of a lack of quality and innovation in current military and naval thought when Turner said, "We must be able to produce military men who are a match for the best of the civilian strategists or we will abdicate control of our profession. Moreover, I am persuaded that we can be a profession only as long as we ourselves are pushing the frontiers of knowledge in our field."[25]

The reaction of students was typified by a resentful officer who told a professor in the strategy department,

> You are a professional historian. Suppose that in the middle of your career, say in your early forties, you had been told that you would have to take an advanced, graduate-level course in aero-dynamics, graded, and that you might even flunk. And suppose that you knew, or even suspected, that if you flunked, your career as a historian and teacher would be finished. What would have been your reaction?"[26]

The idea of grading at the Naval War College was not new. Luce had proposed in 1884 that the successful passing of academic examinations should be a prerequisite to attendance at the college. Most recently in

1966, Hayward had briefly used a grading system before he found it too cumbersome to administer with a small academic staff. Turner had the large teaching staff necessary to evaluate student performance carefully. Moreover, he believed that because officers were marked and graded all through their careers there was every reason to grade their academic performance in the Navy's highest professional course of study.

Although there were inherent difficulties and although it took several years before the idea and practice of grading became standardized, it succeeded immediately in focusing student attention on academic work, making them take it seriously, and giving them a yardstick to evaluate their own performance in dealing with varying types of strategic and tactical problems. The course required carefully thought-out essays; mid-term and final examinations; and spontaneous discussion in seminar. But the students were not the only ones to object. The manager of the officers' club reported that the profits of his bar were down by two thirds from the previous year,[27] and a Newport clergyman blamed Turner's new academic program for the decline in attendance at his church services.[28]

With the strategy course well under way, Turner saw the newly created management and tactics departments begin to develop their courses, which would follow on from strategy. The management course was first headed by Professor Robert D. Williams, who was followed a year later by Warren F. Rogers. Emerson had been the key person behind the ideas for the strategy department, and Williams provided the inspiration for the management department. Turner's concept for this course stressed systems analysis in making "choices between weapon characteristics, choices between weapons; choices between weapons and other necessary elements of military power such as personnel; and choices of how to procure and manage military forces."[29]

As in the strategy course, Turner used case studies, but instead of history, the management course used largely theoretical and hypothetical examples, even taking a case study from the Harvard Business School syllabus about street lighting.[30] After the first year, the course was renamed "Defense Economics and Decision Making" to reflect more precisely its content. It, too, used a blend of military and civilian faculty, with two civilians already on the staff, Philip L. Gamble and Felix Moos, joined by new faculty members, Jacques Naar, Charles Shirkey, J. Sweeney, and Francis J. West, Jr., to form the nucleus of a long-term civilian teaching faculty in the subject.

The third phase of the curriculum was tactics. Its "object was to teach people to understand the principles behind what you can do with weapons and sensors,"[31] as Turner explained. The tactics course, as initially planned, was divided into seven studies: the military planning process, fundamentals of naval weapons systems, engagement analyses, sea control, projection, presence, and strategic nuclear deterrence. As a whole, the course was designed to acquaint students with the technical, operational, environmental, legal, and political elements that directly affect a tactical commander's decisions.[32]   In order to provide the viewpoint and expertise of an important naval ally on the teaching staff of the tactics department, Turner proposed, in January 1972, to establish an exchange of officers between the Naval War College and the Royal Naval College, Greenwich, England. The exchange was approved in July 1973.[33] Captain Edward M. C. Walker, RN, having just completed the naval command course, became the first officer of another navy to serve on the faculty of the Naval War College. Walker was followed successively in this position over the next decade by Royal Navy commanders M. G. M. W. Ellis, E. M. England, Noel Unsworth, and Brian Needham. Largely staffed by active duty officers on two- or three-year assignments to the Naval War College, the department was chaired first by Captain W. K. Yates, followed by Captain E. C. Kenyon.

In a related area, Turner was particularly opposed to the way in which naval war games were being played at the college. He thought that war games should be used primarily for teaching individual students. The games involved the writing of complex operation orders and allowed only a few to play decision-making roles, but Turner wanted every student to have the opportunity to play an admiral's role. In order to do this, he ordered changes in plans for the computerized war gaming center that had been envisaged by previous presidents, and delayed its completion by two years in order to modify the equipment. As Turner explained his purpose,

> I wanted it so that they could actually see on a screen how their sonar beam went out. Then they would see the submarine closing and, as the beam would cross the submarine, the dice roll. On the screen you would see that you had a 50% probability and you did or didn't make it that time. That would let them understand what probability means. It would let them see what would have happened if they had used their sonar in a different way. You could run the action over and over again and let the man go back and make a different decision.[34]

Turner stressed simplified war games by students instead of encouraging fleet use of the war gaming center. With the assistance of Professor Jacques Naar, the first occupant of the McCarty Little chair of gaming and research techniques, tabletop war games were developed that gave as many students as possible an opportunity to play decision-making roles.

Additional Changes and Modifications

Before coming to Newport, Turner had envisaged that the three-part curriculum would be instituted for both junior and senior courses. But it was logistically impossible to change both courses simultaneously, so Turner moved ahead first with the senior course and followed up with the junior course later.

Additional modifications were involved. As the courses were actually put into operation, Turner began to expand his original concept. First, he decided to integrate the senior foreign officers' course, putting the naval command college students into the naval warfare course. Recognizing that the naval command college is the counterpart of the senior course for United States officers, Turner included the foreign officers in the new curriculum, beginning with the management course in February 1973. Taking the advice of two foreign-born faculty members, Jacques Naar and Felix Moos, Turner decided that part of the challenge for foreign officers should be direct participation in the college's courses on an equal basis alongside U.S. students. Moreover, he believed that U.S. students would gain immeasurably from hearing the viewpoints and perspectives of the foreign students as they worked side by side.[35] Despite the deep concern of Admiral Richard G. Colbert, then Commander-in-Chief, Allied Forces, Southern Europe, who feared that this change might destroy the international bond which the course had developed in the years since he had founded it, Turner proceeded with the change.

Bearing the brunt of the new curricular changes, the students in the senior course were unhappy and restive. They failed that year to produce the *Gaities*, the theatrical parody on college life which had been annually produced by students for many years. At the same time, the students in the junior course were listening to Turner's rhetoric on the new senior course curriculum. Part way through the first year, a delegation of students in the college of command and staff persuaded Turner to implement the new curriculum for the junior course sooner than he had planned.

For many years, the college had promoted the idea that the senior or naval warfare curriculum should be built on the academic foundation the students had acquired in the college of command and staff. Although the idea had been under consideration in the Navy Department since 1919, the bureau responsible for officer assignments had never been able to carry out this goal. In 1973, only 15 percent of the college of naval warfare students were graduates of any command and staff course.[36] In a reversal of the viewpoint expressed by previous college presidents, Turner concluded

> The Navy's policy of sending very few people to both courses is basically sound. It is doubtful that the Navy, with its relatively few

> homogeneous sea units, requires the same sort of exacting junior
> officer staff work as is required by the Army ... there is not the same
> distinction between the body of material required at the command
> and staff and senior levels in the Navy as in the Army.[37]

Although naval officers might well have only one opportunity in their careers to attend a war college, Turner opposed the idea of integrating the two groups into a single course. "There are some pedagogical differences in teaching two groups of students when one of them has a significantly greater depth of experience,"[38] he said,

> The officers in the junior course were generally more willing to
> accept new ideas and concepts. They proved they could handle the
> curriculum as well as—and in many cases better than—officers one
> or two ranks superior. They were intellectually more curious, more
> involved, more receptive, less conscious of minor prerogatives.
> They were also less mature and more hasty in reaching conclusions.
> On the other hand, the exceptional officer—the top ten percent or
> so—came from the ranks of the senior course.[39]

In February 1973, the command and staff students were phased into a program similar to that of the senior course, beginning with strategy in the second term and management in the third term. The two courses sought the same goal of expanding "logical reasoning capacity and analysis of the elements of choice rather than familiarization with factual material."[40] The two courses were to achieve these identical goals, with the senior one having only a slightly longer period in which to study policy and strategy and the junior course having a slightly longer period with tactics.

The implementation of the new curriculum in the junior class had several implications. First, it allowed the same faculty to teach similar courses to both senior and junior classes. But it meant also that the junior students would not be allowed to continue with their participation in the George Washington University program. Accordingly, Turner completely discontinued the program at the college at the end of the 1972-1973 academic year.

Unlike the senior class, however, the junior class could not easily incorporate its international counterpart, the naval staff course. Initiated as a result of Admiral Colbert's proposals in 1970, its first class met in July 1972. This course was designed to parallel the command and staff college. Unlike the others, it was a short course of only five months' duration and with two sessions annually. Because there was so little time, the curriculum changes that Turner was making did not easily fit in. The naval staff course, therefore, under its first director, Captain Jack Q. Quinn and his staff, more or less followed the earlier command and staff syllabus. Through Quinn's efforts, the students rapidly developed their own esprit d'corps, giving the course a life of its own.

In other areas important to the intellectual life of the college, the plans for new building construction were modified. Turner dispensed with the office space planned for Hewitt Hall and installed instead student carrels which he hoped would promote closer intellectual contact among the students. A lack of funds prevented him from carrying out his original intention of locating the carrels in the new Hewitt Hall library book stacks, which would have allowed students a greater opportunity to become more familiar with books and interested in ideas.[41] The carrels were placed on the upper floors, and the basement and first floor provided a much needed modern and functional library under its director, Earl R. Schwass. Turner decided that the old library building, Mahan Hall, should house the recently established Naval Historical Collection. Under its director, Anthony S. Nicolosi, this collection became the college's depository for archives, manuscripts, and original historical materials relating to the history of the college and naval warfare in general. At the same time, Turner instituted a series of historical monographs published by the newly established Naval War College Press, which he hoped would also publish a wide range of books on professional naval subjects. The first volume in the historical series was *The Writings of Stephen B. Luce* (1975), edited by John D. Hayes and John B. Hattendorf, followed by studies in other areas, including *The Development of Naval Thought: Essays by Herbert Rosinski* (1977), edited by B. Mitchell Simpson, III; *Understanding the Soviet Navy* (1979) by Robert B. Bathurst; and *Military Power in A Free Society* (1979) by Henry E. Eccles.

Turner took another important step forward by implementing plans developed with the University of Rhode Island to open a branch bookstore at the college. The store was to stock texts and to encourage students to buy their own books. In addition, he gave each student the textbooks and readings that he used during the year as the basis for a personal professional library.

Turner established the "contemporary civilization" lecture series, specifically to stimulate widening intellectual interests in areas outside the college curriculum. The first speaker in that series was Herbert Nicholas, Rhodes professor of American History and Institutions at Oxford University, who had been Turner's tutor. His address on DeTocqueville was followed in later months by an illustrated lecture on Matisse by the art critic and writer, Rosamond Bernier. The first annual Spruance lecture was given at Turner's invitation by the novelist Herman Wouk the day before the new Spruance Auditorium was dedicated on 7 December 1972. "When the creator of Captain Queeg addresses the Naval War College, a smoky trace of revolution already is in the air," Wouk remarked.

Evidently you have decided to overlook that well-known aphorism, 'the Navy is a master plan designed by geniuses for execution by idiots.' Of course I never said this; Lieutenant Keefer of the U.S.S. *Caine* said it. Much like a flesh-and-blood parent, an author has limited control over the utterances of his phantom offspring. I suppose forgiveness comes the more easily here at the Naval War College, where obviously I address only the geniuses.[42]

For Wouk, the building of great and costly weapons at a time when many lacked food, clothing and shelter approached the most disgusting of absurdities. "Yet, you must go on serving in such a military system," Wouk declared, "and not only that, you must recruit clear-eyed, free, critical young men in great numbers or the U.S. Navy will wither." The task of the naval officer in an age of revolution, he declared, is

> not to solve the great ongoing problems of social stress nor to despair at the immensity and complexity of these problems outside our country and inside, but to stand and to serve. To improvise, to make do with what we have; to serve in still another kind of revolutionary warfare, a contest which one wins only if no weapon is ever fired; to do battle against great odds of political trouble within and without our land, odds of events running almost out of human control; and with this fight, and with this service, to give freedom one more chance for one more generation.[43]

Such lectures were a hallmark of Turner's presidency: an insistence upon sponsoring the widest variety of viewpoints, bringing to the fore jarring, responsible viewpoints which challenged the common perceptions naval officers had of themselves and demanded that they develop their own well-thought-out philosophies. He brought to the college the widest cross section of opinion he could find, from critical newspaper correspondents to John William Ward, an anti-military activist and president of Amherst College.

While trying to broaden the perspectives of resident students in extracurricular activities, Turner took steps to widen contacts of the college both within the Navy community and the academic world. Formal ties were established when the college joined the Association of American State Colleges and Universities and the Rhode Island Council on Higher Education. Through these connections, he participated in conferences with local university educators and brought them to the Naval War College to hear special lectures and join in academic ceremonies. Within the Navy, he sought to increase student and faculty contributions to the *Naval War College Review*, making it a bimonthly journal with an increased emphasis on work produced at the college. At the same time, he widened circulation by allowing naval lieutenants and above to obtain personal subscriptions. For officers who could not attend the War College resident program, Turner initiated plans for students taking correspondence courses through the Center for Continuing Education to participate in off-campus seminars for their courses. Turner's initiative here was to apply an approach already in use for inactive naval reserve officers and to use it for active duty officers with a modified version of the new curriculum he had implemented for the resident course.

He opened a course for Naval War College student wives at Newport in "an effort to get them to feel what their husbands were doing was worthwhile for the sacrifice they were both making" as the student demanded peace and quiet at home for his studies. While Turner hoped that he might even have saved some marriages, it did not entirely succeed intellectually. One of the 110 wives who attended the specially designed wives' strategy course reportedly exclaimed to him, "Oh Admiral, my husband and I are enjoying the course so much. We are absolutely thrilled with Thuckadee and the Polynesian Wars."

Continuing Problems

The new curriculum that Turner established rapidly shifted the focus at the college from breadth of knowledge in numerous areas to depth in a few select areas. Coupled with the decision to discontinue the George Washington University degree program, it raised several issues which continued to be a matter of serious concern both to Turner and his successors. First, students no longer had an opportunity to gain an academic master's degree, an achievement which many officers argued had great significance when they were being considered for promotion and assignment. Second, there was a need to provide more extensive advanced work for the 10 or 15 percent of the students who were being sent to their second war college course. Third, the fact that the Naval War College had independently developed a curriculum quite different from other service colleges caused difficulties in coordination, implicitly questioning the other colleges' way of doing a similar job.

In order to meet the first issue, the college explored an idea that had been under consideration for many years, the possibility of awarding its own academic degree. In order to do this, the college courses would require formal accreditation by national educational authorities and the program would have to meet requirements of academic disciplines. Many hurdles would need to be cleared, including the passing of an act by Congress and coordinating the program with other war colleges. A serious potential difficulty was raised by the thought that if the college were to award a master's degree, it might have to compromise meeting the needs of the naval profession so as to meet the demands of academic accreditation committees. The academic subjects which interested the War College were quite different from the technical areas in which the Naval Postgraduate School met specific and clearly defined professional needs. At the same time, the purpose of the Naval War College has always been different and has been devoted to enhancing the ability of naval officers to make command decisions in their professional world.

While borrowing much from the academic world, Turner believed that the college would not be able to meet fully the professional needs of officers if it were forced to accept all the criteria for awarding a university degree. To make the best of the situation, the college continued its practice of obtaining current evaluations of its courses from the American Council on Education, thus enabling individual students to transfer credits to other universities. On the professional side, however, the college could authoritatively state on both the students' fitness report and diploma that the graduate level curriculum was recognized by both the Chief of Naval Operations and the Chief of Naval Personnel "as the professional military counterpart of an academic master's degree."[44]

As for the small percentage of naval officers who were able to attend both war college courses in their careers, Turner hoped that the newly established advanced research department would allow them to opt out of any portion of the basic curriculum that seemed repetitive in order to do individual research.

When Turner brought Professor James E. King, Jr. to the college, it was primarily to establish that advanced research department. As a one-man operation at the outset, King established the outlines of an organization that would provide for student research, encourage faculty research, and give assistance to outside scholars in projects relating to the Navy and to national security studies. Through it, a wide variety of work was undertaken by outsiders, ranging from the work of mature scholars to students undertaking doctoral work at universities such as Johns Hopkins, Yale and Oxford.

The third problem, that of a different method of teaching and different course content from the other service colleges, was serious, especially in regard to the command and staff level of education. The basic issue here was that the Navy, unlike the other services, did not regard the command and staff course as a prerequisite to a more advanced professional course. The issue was not solved for several years; its resolution involved a fundamental change in educational policy by the Bureau of Naval Personnel.

"The Turner Revolution"

Stansfield Turner's presidency at the Naval War College has often been called the "Turner Revolution," and in some respects it was revolutionary. Sharing with Mahan and Zumwalt a distrust of any bureaucratic organization's ability to reform itself, Turner forced reform on the college. He did it rapidly and with advice and assistance from outside, almost completely disregarding that from the resident staff until after the basic decisions for reform had been made. For the strategy department, he prepared an entirely new and unique syllabus, hired a faculty and ordered a wide range of books in less than three months, perhaps a record in academic course planning. The odd thing about it was that it worked and the students acknowledged appreciation of it in the course critiques after the first term.[45]

The subject matter of the curriculum did not change radically from what it had been before Turner's time, although there was a definite change in emphasis from current data and contemporary international relations to historical case studies that raised and illustrated recurring issues in the study of strategy. The most significant change was in establishing a teaching methodology which demanded more individual effort from the students. This was created by hiring a permanent civilian faculty, eliminating a large number of visiting lecturers, instituting a long and required reading list, setting aside large amounts of time for individual student reading and writing, requiring term papers and frequent written papers, making examinations mandatory, establishing highly structured seminars led by faculty members, and grading students on their written work and oral performance in seminar.[46]

These far-reaching innovations were accompanied by a strong reaction against them. In pursuit of his program, through radical and forceful change, many thought that Turner had overstated his case, that he had been unjustifiably rude and needlessly tactless. Knowing little about the history of the college, and indeed little was available, he was not interested in relating his innovations to it. Ironically, he gave the appearance of a revolutionary, but he was actually a reactionary to the extent that he introduced concepts and pedagogical techniques that were consistent with those of Luce, Mahan, and Sims. Those men would have wholeheartedly subscribed to Turner's view that the problems facing a naval commander arose from historic interests and political factors and that a proper understanding of history was indispensable to understand contemporary and future problems.

Mistakes and shortcomings were balanced by substantial and noteworthy achievements. Turner succeeded where his predecessors had not in establishing a faculty of professional teachers and scholars. Thanks to funds from both the usual and unorthodox sources within the Navy, Turner was able to pay civilian professors generous, even handsome, salaries. Skillful use of the techniques of public relations and his own indefatigable efforts and numerous public appearances in Rhode Island and around the country produced an external impression of academic rigor. Perhaps even more important was a slow but increasing groundswell of grudging approval among more senior officers for his program. In this respect, he contributed to the upgrading of the student body in terms of enhanced rates of selection for promotion.

Among his predecessors, Turner may be compared most readily with William S. Sims who left the college in the year before Turner was born, half a century before Turner became college president. Each held values in professional education similar to the other's and each had an exceptionally strong personality. Both were controversial; both had devoted admirers and ardent detractors; both were abrasive in doing exactly what they thought was right; both equated opposition to their positions with error; both thought their opponents were hopelessly wrong and misguided. Each left the college a very different place from what it was when he arrived. And they both set it on a course that continued for many years after their departure.

Having stayed twice as long as he originally expected, Turner had fulfilled most of his plans for the college when he was relieved as president by Vice Admiral Julian J. LeBourgeois on 9 August 1974. Turner went on first to command the Second Fleet, then as a four-star admiral to be Commander-in-Chief, Allied Forces, Southern Europe, and subsequently Director of Central Intelligence.

LeBourgeois at the Helm

As president of the Naval War College from 1974 to 1977, LeBourgeois faced a difficult problem. Well aware that neither the Navy nor the college could afford more radical changes in the college curriculum, he announced that he would devote his tenure to "consolidating and refining the innovations" that Turner had made.[47] He encouraged the further refinement of the three basic courses and expanded the initiative Turner had taken in the off-campus program through the Center for Continuing Education. Under its director, Vice Admiral Thomas R. Weschler, USN (ret.), the entire correspondence curriculum was rewritten to reflect more accurately the courses taught to resident students. Several experiments were conducted with off-campus services at a variety of bases. The most successful of these was that run by Dr. Charles Chadbourn in Washington, D.C.

LeBourgeois began quietly to reassess the curriculum. He soon expanded the elective program, giving it academic credit, where Turner had allowed it only as an extracurricular activity. LeBourgeois dropped the requirement for a term paper, and in its place reintroduced the staff study prepared by a committee of students. Most important, the process of differentiating between the junior and senior level courses was begun again. Coming to the college after four years in various flag billets associated with NATO, LeBourgeois was keenly interested in the two courses for officers from other navies. Well aware of the long-range problems posed by the newly expanded civilian faculty, he devoted much time and effort to selection of new professors who would continue the development and refinement of the curriculum and teach the students, who were being chosen for the Naval War College on a more careful basis by the Bureau of Personnel. At the end of his term, he could declare

> The faculty is two-thirds military and one-third civilian academicians. Almost all have advanced degrees—and today all but two civilian faculty members have doctorates from great universities. The military faculty members have excelled in their professional specialities and they are mainly concentrated in the areas of instruction relating to naval operations. The American Council on Education has evaluated the faculty as being comparable with the better faculties teaching similar work in civilian institutions.[48]

Bringing a sense of stability to the institution after a period of sudden change, LeBourgeois initiated other important changes, as we will see, but carefully avoided drawing attention to them or creating controversy.

In 1974, the Naval War College reacquired the building that had been its first home 90 years before. Following the removal of the Cruiser-Destroyer Force from Newport and the subsequent disestablishment of the naval base that had used the building as its administrative headquarters, the college took over the building it had last used in 1889. Renamed Founder's Hall, it housed college administrative offices until 1976, when Admiral LeBourgeois announced that it would become the Naval War College Museum. A museum had been established in 1952 by Admiral Conolly, but for nearly a quarter of a century no suitable space had been found to exhibit the historical materials that had been collected. Developed by its director, A. S. Nicolosi, the museum was devoted to the history of naval warfare and the history of the Navy in Narragansett Bay.

On 28 April 1976, LeBourgeois dedicated the final element in the college's building program, Hewitt Hall, housing the new library, as well as more classrooms and student study areas.

As a follow-up to Turner's advanced research department, LeBourgeois obtained official recognition from both the Secretary of the Navy and the Chief of Naval Operations that advanced research was an important part of the college's mission. In a letter to the Secretary written in December 1974, LeBourgeois sent a detailed plan to establish a Center of Advanced Research, as an extension of the college's work. "The needs of the Navy for clear conceptual thought and tough-minded research are particularly pressing," the plan stated, "as we move into the area of a smaller but vastly more modern Navy with substantial problems not fully defined."[49] Citing the incomplete understanding of future naval roles, missions, and tasks, LeBourgeois made it clear that the college offered an appropriate place for careful professional thought away from the day-to-day pressure of Washington life. To carry on from the beginning made in 1972, the college needed to centralize its research activity, and devote more money and faculty effort toward it. Looking back over the research works that had been supported, the college believed that several civilian academians had produced respectable, and, in some cases, highly original work, such as W. R. Louis's *Imperialism at Bay: The United States and the Decolonization of the British Empire* and Williamson Murray's *The Change in the European Balance of Power 1938-39*. Other studies, such as Richard Burt's *"SALT and Naval Force Capabilities;"* Mark Janis's on *"The Law of the Sea;"* James A Nathan and James K. Oliver on *The Future of U.S. Naval Power* and Edward Luttwak on *"American Naval Power in the Mediterranean,"* excited more interest within the Navy and the Defense Department. In order to stimulate more work of direct value to policymakers, both the Secretary of the Navy, J. William Middendorf II, and the Chief of Naval Operations, Admiral James L. Holloway III, endorsed the LeBourgeois proposal in early 1975. Echoing the original conception of the college envisioned by Luce, they approved an addition to the formal statement defining the college's mission:

> To conduct research leading to the development of advanced strategic and tactical concepts for the future employment of naval forces.[50]

With this mandate, the college established the "Center for Advanced Research" under its first dean, Captain Hugh G. Nott, USN (ret.), who held the position until December 1980.

Opening in March 1975, the center, or CAR as it became known, became a useful place for both students and resident scholars to pursue their research. Selection of students to work in the center was restricted to only the most promising. One of the first projects undertaken was a study of the potential uses for, and tactics of, the new Harpoon missile which would soon enter the fleet. This was followed in the years up to 1981 with a variety of projects, including a plan for the size and shape of the Navy in the year 2000, several studies on Soviet military aviation, an examination of potential operations in the Norwegian Sea, a concept of operations for the Marines, an attempt to delineate Soviet vulnerabilities, and a study on synthetic fuels.

With the establishment of CAR, LeBourgeois included the *Naval War College Review* as one of its activities. The policy of restricting articles to locally produced research in the *Review* had proved largely unsuccessful. Much of the work submitted to the *Review* for publication was of low quality, and by 1975 the *Review* had been forced to reduce publication, going from a bimonthly to a quarterly. In attempting revive the *Review*, LeBourgeois established a basic policy, creating a clear chain of command for the editor, from the director of CAR to the president of the Naval War College. LeBourgeois also wanted to emphasize strategic and tactical issues with "strong student/faculty input leavened with external source material." If we had to choose between two superb articles, LeBourgeois told the editor, Lieutenant Commander B. M. Simpson, "one student/one external, take the student paper. However, whatever the source, quality is first."[51]

It took nearly four years to attract a sufficient number of quality articles from academics for the *Review* to increase its number of issues. In February 1979, Commander W. R. Pettyjohn edited the first in the new series of bimonthly issues.

The most significant development in the LeBourgeois period stemmed from the great interest shown toward the college by the Chief of Naval Personnel, Vice Admiral James D. Watkins. In July 1975, Watkins and Vice Admiral James B. Wilson, Chief of Naval Education and Training, began a joint effort to define their function, responsibilities, and inter-relationships as they related to naval education and training. The two men agreed that Watkins, in his dual role as Deputy CNO for Manpower (OP-01) and as Chief of Naval Personnel, had overall responsibility under the CNO for all facets of personnel policy, including the determination of the nature and extent of education that must be provided at proper times to officers. Wilson, in his dual role as Director of Naval Education and Training (OP-099) and as Chief of Naval Education and Training, had responsibility under the CNO for the entire education and training establishment of the Navy, conforming to the broad policy set by the Chief of Naval Personnel. With this basic agreement made, the mission statements defining the function of their positions were rewritten.[52]

Following this agreement, Wilson and Watkins issued a joint education and training memorandum in March 1976, which related this agreement to the specific responsibilities that each undertook for the intermediate and senior level service colleges.[53] These broad policies were formulated without the knowledge of the Naval War College president or his staff. When this fact came to the attention of Wilson and Watkins, they took immediate steps to ensure that any future important policy statement on professional military education be coordinated with LeBourgeois and other commanders who had a principal interest in the issues.[54]

Following this, LeBourgeois and his staff were asked to make their recommendation for a revised statement on professional military education. First, the college objected to the statement in the Watkins-

Wilson joint memorandum that would limit cooperative degree programs with civilian universities to meeting the specific requirements of officer subspecialties, rather than allowing them to perform a broader educational purpose. The college also objected to the move lengthening the chain of command between the CNO and the War College. Historically, the college had always had a close and direct link to the Navy's top leader, but the plan put forward by Wilson and Watkins placed both the Chief of Naval Personnel and the Chief of Naval Education and Training above the War College president. While this would improve the coordination of educational policy within the Navy, it obscured the direct link to the Chief of Naval Operations which ensured that the college was at the forefront of professional development.

In order to resolve this issue and to draft a policy statement on senior college education for the Chief of Naval Operations, Admiral James L. Holloway III, representatives from the staffs of the War College, Chief of Naval Education and Training, and Chief of Naval Personnel began a series of meetings in early 1977. The Naval War College representatives were Captain William A. Platte, deputy to the president; Captain Huntington Hardisty, dean of academics; and Professor Frederick Hartmann, special academic advisor.

Following these discussions, Wilson, Watkins, and LeBourgeois agreed on most issues. However, Watkins and LeBourgeois came to an impasse on one fundamental issue, which was referred to Holloway for decision. The issue was the concept and context of the command and staff course. Before any decision or policy could be established on this point, however, LeBourgeois reached the end of his term as president. He retired in April 1977, but the decisions that emerged from the exchange of views initiated by Watkins, LeBourgeois, and their staffs established a firm high-level policy in making further refinements and changes to the Naval War College curriculum, setting the tone for the remaining years of the college's first century.

Notes
1. Norman Friedman, "Elmo Russell Zumwalt, Jr.," in R. L. Love, Jr., ed., *The Chiefs of Naval Operations* (Annapolis, 1980), p. 365.
2. Ibid., p. 368.
3. Ibid., p. 369.
4. Ibid., p. 370; Elmo R. Zumwalt, Jr., *On Watch: A Memo* (New York: Quadrangle, 1976), pp. 27-29. This and the views cited above confirmed by conversation, 4 May 1984: Hattendorf-Zumwalt.
5. Stansfield Turner, draft of portions from *Oral History* conducted by John T. Mason, U.S. Naval Institute, provided to the authors by Admiral Turner.
6. NWC Archives, R6.28: President's File: S. Turner; postscript on Turner letter to F. H. Hartmann, 1 June 1972.
7. Conversation, 13 April 1984: Hattendorf-Turner.

8. Stansfield Turner, draft *Oral History*; conversations, 5 March 1984: Hattendorf - Emerson; 7 March 1984: Hattendorf-Barber.

9. Ibid.

10. Conversation, 13 April 1984: Hattendorf-Turner.

11. Stansfield Turner, "The Role of Higher Education in Today's Navy," *The American-Oxonian*, Vol. LX, No. 4 (October 1973) pp. 186-192.

12. Turner, *Oral History*.

13. NWC Archives, Staff-Student File, W. R. Emerson, memorandum: Curriculum Concept for the Naval War College, 24 March 1972.

14. Loc. cit., W. R. Emerson lecture, "Strategy and History Discussions: Phase I -Strategy (The New Approach)," 2 August 1972, p. 2.

15. Conversation, 5 March 1984: Hattendorf-Emerson.

16. Conversation, 13 April 1984: Hattendorf-Turner.

17. Ibid.

18. Robert C. Burns, *George Washington University Program in International Affairs at the War College* (Washington, 1982), p. 48.

19. Quote provided by P. A. Crowl, 9 April 1984.

20. Conversation, 9 March 1984: Hattendorf-Crowl.

21. NWC Archives, Staff-Student File: B. M. Simpson III: Turner-Simpson correspondence.

22. NWC Archives RG28, President's File: Turner: "Convocation Address by President of the Naval War College, 24 August 1972."

23. Ibid.; see also the description of the address in NWC Archives, Staff-Student file, McDonald: Philip A. Crowl, and J. Kenneth McDonald, "New Courses at the Naval War College," paper presented at the Inter-University Seminar on Armed Forces and Society, 1973 annual conference, University of Chicago. Third Seminar (I), 12 October 1973, p. 11.

24. Turner, *Oral History*.

25. Quoted from Convocation address in Brooke Nihart, "Revitalization of the War Colleges: Intellectual Wasteland...or Challenge," *Armed Forced Journal* (March 1973), pp. 26-32.

26. Quoted in Crowl and McDonald, op. cit., p. 12.

27. NWC Archives, RG 28, President's File: Stansfield Turner, "The Time for Thinkers Has Come," address in Philadelphia, 27 October 1972, p. 11.

28. Turner, *Oral History*.

29. Turner, "Convocation Address."

30. Turner, *Oral History*.

31. Ibid.

32. "Annual Report of the President, Naval War College, 1972-73," *Naval War College Review* (Sept-Oct 1973), p. 44.

33. NWC Archives, RG3 1973 Records Box 9, File 5400: "Students at Foreign War College," RADM C. A. Hill, Jr. to RADM W. D. S. Scott, RN, 11 Jan 1973.

34. Turner, *Oral History*.

35. Conversation, 13 April 1984: Hattendorf-Turner.

36. "Annual Report." 1973, p. 15.

37. Naval War College. *Second Annual Report of the President*, 9 August 1974, p. 11.

38. Ibid.

39. "Annual Report," 1973, p. 15.

40. Ibid., frontispiece: "Mission of the Naval War College."

41. Conversation, 13 April 1984: Hattendorf-Turner.

42. Herman Wouk, "The Naval Officer in an Age of Revolution," *Naval War College Review* (March-April 1973), p. 4.

43. Ibid., pp. 8-9, 10.

44. "Annual Report," 1973, pp. 12-13. The 1973 wording of the diploma stated "Chief of Naval Personnel," but this was changed to "Chief of Naval Operations" in 1983.

45. Crowl to Hattendorf, 9 April 1984.

46. Ibid.

47. President Naval War College, *Report to the Leadership of the Navy Past, Present, and Future,* 1977, p. 1.

48. Ibid., p. 8.

49. NWC Archives, RG3, 1975 Records Box 6; File 5400: Missions and Tasks:" President, NWC, to SECNAV, letter serial 2130 of 11 December 1974. See also NWC Archives, RG28: Subject file "Advanced Research" and H. G. Nott, *U.S. Naval War College Center for Advanced Research General Concept Plan 1976 to 1979.* Report prepared by Ketron, Inc., under Office of Naval Research Contract dated 12 February 1976.

50. Ibid. The CNO's endorsement was dated 27 Jan 1975, and the Secretary's approval, 27 February 1975.

51. NWC Review Files: "Operating Directives": Memo: Simpson to LeBourgeois, 12 August 1975, annotated by LeBourgeois, 21 August 1975.

52. NWC Archives RG 27: Subject File "Professional Military Education, BUPERS/CNET NOTE 5430 Pers-1 of 16 July 1975.

53. Loc.cit., Joint Education and Training Memorandum (JEM-10) of 29 March 1976: "Officer Professional Military Education."

54. Loc.cit., CNET Memo for 01, Code 00 15 April 1976. July: JEM 10-76.

CHAPTER 12

TOWARD A SECOND
CENTURY, 1977-1984

In July 1977, Admiral James L. Holloway III, the Chief of Naval Operations, issued a statement on service college education which became a turning point in the development of the Naval War College. Holloway's was the first high-level statement of policy that defined the college's goals, functions and curricula. Moreover, it placed them within the bounds of a practical personnel policy and established procedures that could coordinate the needs of the various institutions and commands dealing with naval education.

The announcement of this policy came after Admiral Le Bourgeois had been succeeded in April 1977 by the newly promoted dean of academics, Rear Admiral Huntington Hardisty.

When Hardisty, who had come to the college as a captain in the summer of 1976 to be dean of academics, was selected for flag rank while serving in that position, it was the second time in three years that a serving dean of academics was selected for promotion to the rank of rear admiral. Charles Williams had been selected in 1974. Two years later, Joseph Ekelund was selected from the same position that Williams and Hardisty had held. These selections went far to announce to the Navy that not only was it possible to make flag rank at the college but also that the college might be a good place to make it. As a newly promoted flag officer, Hardisty, although he would have liked a full term, knew he would probably be replaced by a more senior officer, designated for promotion to vice admiral. His half-year tenure was too brief for a lasting impact or for real contributions. He was popular with the faculty and students, spending more time listening and learning than in demanding, and he possessed a fine sense of balance.

CNO's Policy for the Naval War College

As president of the Naval War College, Hardisty had the immediate responsibility of carrying out the policy that had resulted from Le Bourgeois' discussions with Rear Admiral James L. Watkins, the Chief of Naval Personnel, in developing Admiral Holloway's service college education policy. The major point that had not been resolved at the time of Le Bourgeois' retirement centered on the curriculum for the command and staff course. Le Bourgeois believed that the course structure had to take account of the fact that less than 10 percent of the Naval War College command and staff graduates could be expected to return to Newport for the senior course. For that reason, Le Bourgeois believed that the curriculum should go a substantial way in preparing a student for the full range of future assignments, rather than be merely an intermediate course concentrating on the naval operations and planning segments of the curriculum, which would be most immediately useful to an intermediate grade officer. Therefore, Le Bourgeois agreed that it made sense to expand the naval operations segment of the command and staff course, but he did not want to do so at the expense of shortening the strategy and policy segment.

Watkins argued that "our first priority in a command and staff course must be to ensure that the graduates possess a level of competence in naval operations and planning commensurate with the duties to which they will be assigned."[1]Having received reports that there was a significant weakness in these areas among officers at sea, Watkins believed that the Navy was not preparing mid-career officers properly to discharge their responsibilities at sea and on fleet and shore staffs. The senior level course at the War College was fulfilling its objectives, Watkins believed, but the command and staff course should not be allowed to continue with a significant overlap in its curriculum. "While I firmly believe a fundamental shift in the focus of the command and staff course is called for," Watkins wrote, "I do not think an abrupt change is necessary. The intent is not to be disruptive but to migrate through an evolutionary reorientation back to a course that fulfills Navy needs."[2]

When the two contrasting viewpoints were presented to the CNO, Holloway decided in favor of Watkins' view. In his policy statement in July 1977, Holloway declared, "The Naval War College plays the preeminent role in the professional development program for prospective naval leaders."[3]

Holloway went on to establish a firm policy on the number of officers who would attend service colleges. He directed that 30 to 35 percent of all unrestricted line captains and 25 to 35 percent of all unrestricted line lieutenant commanders should be graduates of a service college. Of these, at least 50 percent should have attended the Naval War College. To carry out this policy,

> The Naval War College will offer two major resident courses in the college of naval warfare and the college of naval command and staff, respectively, each at the graduate level of intellectual challenge but differing in subject focus. The senior-level course for selected captains and commanders will provide emphasis on strategy and policy. The intermediate-level course for selected mid-career officers will stress naval operations and planning and provide the opportunity to increase the professional competence associated with those areas. These two courses shall cover the broad spectrum of knowledge and expertise required to command forces in a combat environment and to assume positions of increasing responsibility in the Navy, the Department of Defense, and the highest levels of government.[4]

Stressing that college courses should cultivate individual capacities for logical reasoning, decision making, innovative thought, and articulate expression, Holloway encouraged advanced research in strategic and tactical concepts. In addition, he reflected the guidance of the 1975 Defense Department Committee on Excellence in Education headed by Under Secretary of Defense W. P. Clements, Jr., by defining three components: (1) a common core useful to all officers on strategy and policy, management and decision-making techniques and staff procedures; (2) a specific mission related to naval warfare, current naval technology, policies, and future capabilities; and (3) an elective program to permit students to enhance their knowledge in specific subjects of high interest to the Navy.

Establishing a clear policy on these issues, Holloway went on to clarify the command relationship of the college, giving it the clear direction it had lacked earlier. He preserved a clear link to the CNO by directing that authority and responsibility for command and support of the Naval War College was assigned to the Chief of Naval Education and Training to be exercised through the president of the Naval War College. Delegating responsibility to the president to carry out the CNO's policy, Holloway also named the Deputy CNO for Manpower and the Director, Naval Education and Training, to act as his principal agents in coordinating his policy for the college. In addition, Holloway established the Policy Advisory Board for Service College Education, chaired by the CNO, to develop future policy on the Naval Postgraduate School, the Naval War College, and on the Navy's participation at other U.S. and foreign armed forces service colleges.

Following on from Holloway's policy statement, Hardisty developed an action plan to change the curriculum over three academic years. On forwarding the plan to Holloway, Rear Admiral W. L. Harris, Deputy Director, Naval Education and Training, stressed that it "details the evolutionary (vice revolutionary) curricular changes"[6] designed for the Naval War College. By June 1979, Hardisty's plan called for the curricula of the college of naval warfare course and the college of command and staff course to be altered to "reduce the percent of commonality between the two courses from 78 percent to about 62 percent."[7] This meant that at the end of the three-year period, the command and staff students would devote about 50 percent of their time to naval operations, 25 percent to defense economics, and 20 percent to strategy. This contrasted with the college of naval warfare students who would devote 30 percent of their time to naval operations, 32 percent to defense economics, and 38 percent to strategy.

With the implementation of these policies during Hardisty's short tenure, the college was placed firmly on a well-coordinated plan to refine its curriculum, meeting a Navy policy for service education. At the same time that these changes were taking place, the faculties of the three departments were refining and improving their syllabi.

Trends in Syllabus Revision

Continuing on from modifications begun under Le Bourgeois, some clear trends were evident in the way in which the faculty was dealing with the curriculum. The 1972-1974 changes had emphasized the importance of a large teaching faculty. Many of the changes and modifications that were made in the following years resulted from the collective experience and knowledge of the faculty. The mixture of long-term and visiting faculty members began to make an enduring contribution to the curriculum. This was not possible in the early years when presidents, staff members, and faculty all rotated on short-term assignments, leaving no one in an influential position to nurture the gradual growth of an intellectual enterprise. Unlike so many earlier curricular revisions, the enduring changes that took place after 1972-1974 involved many individuals.

In the strategy department, the basic idea of using historical case studies has been retained to examine recurring themes involved in the interaction between military power and the political process, between strategy and policy. It has been faithful to the notion that Secretary of Defense James R. Schlesinger expressed in his 30 May 1975 address to the college:

> One of the things I hope would be accomplished in a year at the Naval War College is that the mind is stretched and this larger compass of the relevancy of military power is understood . . . . The purpose of military power . . . is the extension of policy by other means. You've

got to understand military policy in relation to national policy if
you are to fully understand how military power can best be
utilized . . . . [8]

Indicative of the changes in the strategy department was the fact that
after the first year the title of the course changed from strategy and
history to strategy and policy. Very quickly the content began to shift
toward more concern with the present than in its original version. By
the time Professor P. A. Crowl retired as head of the strategy department
in 1980, fully a third of the course dealt with post-World War II matters,
such as the Cold War, Vietnam, and nuclear strategy. Under Crowl's
successor, Professor Robert S. Wood, a political scientist who was
chairman 1980-1983, and Professor Alvin H. Bernstein, a classicist who
became chairman in 1984, the balance was maintained between the
political and military on the one hand, and the diplomatic on the other.

While they increased emphasis on the analytical themes that run
through the course, strategy faculty members made plain the way in
which the various elements in strategy change character and importance from one set of historical circumstances to another. In this way,
the strategy faculty sought to avoid false analogies between history and
contemporary affairs. At the same time, the strategy course benefited
from an additional case study in classical history on the Second Punic
War, complementing the study of the Peloponnesian Wars, as well as an
increased emphasis on naval history in the course.

Throughout, the strategy faculty has taken care to teach with the
idea that it is developing a basis for strategic thinking rather than
simply broadening a student's understanding of international relations.[9] A number of eminent scholars came for one-year appointments
in the strategy department. Long-term teaching contributions were
made in the period up to 1984 by Professors Jerome K. Holloway,
Richard Megargee, and Steven T. Ross.

The management course, established in 1972-1974, has changed
substantially in its approach, but has probably met more closely the
original role envisaged for it. Under its new name, defense economics
and decision making, the department has been chaired since 1975 by
Professor William G. Turcotte. During that period, the course has
moved away from emphasizing systems analysis to the broader basis
of developing and exercising a framework for choosing and supporting future forces under the constraints posed by national finance.
The faculty over the years has developed an extensive set of
theoretical readings, which in all teaching sessions are applied to a
wide variety of faculty-developed cases dealing with critical national
defense situations. As it evolved, the course and its faculty have
divided into three segments that focus on choosing future forces:
defense analysis, non-quantitative factors in defense decision

making, and defense economics. The department examines the conflicting viewpoints and interests confronting fundamental defense resource allocation issues that face senior defense officers.

As the course evolved, Dr. George Brown, who has since become vice president of Data Resources, made original and basic contributions to its development. Professor Richmond Lloyd initiated and developed the force planning aspects of the course, which became its dominant theme. Lawrence Korb, who taught at the college for five years and who in 1981 became Assistant Secretary of Defense for Manpower, Reserve Affairs, and Logistics, was responsible for much of the original development of the non-quantitative issues in defense resource allocation.[10]

Like defense economics and decision making, the tactics course has taken a number of years to develop and has seen significant shifts in emphasis. Renamed the naval operations department in 1975, it has been staffed largely by active duty officers on two- or three-year assignments to the Naval War College. During the chairmanship of Vice Admiral Thomas R. Weschler (ret.), 1977-1981, the course was substantially modified to stress a joint force approach and decision making at the fleet and task force level rather than individual or small unit tactics. The naval operations course for the college of naval warfare and the college of command and staff were differentiated by the distinction that the senior-level course was built around a four-star admiral's point of view, and the junior-level course, a two-star admiral's point of view. As developed by Weschler, the course was multi-faceted, building on concepts from history, strategy, physics, logic, and fleet and personal experience. The pervasive theme throughout the course was decision making, both to make optimum use of resources in developing tactics and to choose optimum tactics in achieving a strategy. Using case studies, the principal method of learning was in seminar groups, supported by lectures and war games. In the course, the capabilities of both U.S. naval forces and possible enemy forces were considered while concentrating on tactics and principles of war, operational planning and staff procedures, total force and the character of possible aggressors, international law and controls on the application of power, and decision making through historical analysis and war gaming practice.[11]

In 1977, a "total forces week" was added to the naval operations curriculum in order to provide a basic introduction to all the services. Following the distinction between an admiral's and a rear admiral's point of view, a greater separation was drawn between the junior and senior courses by emphasizing the employment of naval forces in the junior course and the selection and application of forces in the senior course. In later changes, the senior course moved to emphasize the unified command level in place of the previous emphasis at the fleet command level.

In October 1980, the naval operations department held the first of several tactical symposia. Developed from an idea presented by Professor Lawrence E. Brumbach in 1979, the symposium brought together fleet representatives, flag officers on duty in Washington, and War College students to exchange ideas, promote respect for the benefit of reflective thinking on modern tactical questions, and to stimulate students into examining areas that require innovative thought. From this introduction, each student in the naval operations course prepared a research paper on a selected tactical subject. After evaluation by the faculty, the best papers were circulated to fleet commanders and Navy Department officers for consideration and possible use in developing experimental tactics.[12]

The two international courses were also affected by these developments in the curriculum. The naval command college course was affected the most because it was almost entirely integrated into the academic course followed by the college of naval warfare. While the college continued to emphasize academic concerns over the professional contacts that develop naturally in this international group, it was faced with an increasing problem in the naval operations part of the curriculum. The growing emphasis on classified information and current, state-of-the-art data posed a problem for a class of foreign officers. In the academic year 1983-1984, the naval command college developed a separate course for the naval operations phase of the curriculum. Developed by Commander Brian Needham, Royal Navy, a member of the naval operations department faculty, it followed the course given to U.S. students, stressing the same aspects and using the same lecturers, but at a lower level of classification. In addition, foreign students were encouraged to use their own expertise in composing and contrasting U.S. practice with that of their own navies, and in providing knowledge in areas that were not common in the U.S. Navy.[13] This new course marked a return to the pre-1972 curriculum.

In 1979, the intermediate course for officers from foreign navies was renamed the naval staff college to reflect more accurately the rigorous nature of its course and the breadth of the material covered. In January 1981, the naval staff college moved to Pringle Hall in closer proximity to the other resident academic programs. At the same time, Commander Keith Robinson made a number of innovations as the naval staff college's academic coordinator, making greater use of the faculty from the strategy, defense economics and naval operations departments, and structuring the course to follow an abbreviated version of the course followed in the other colleges. In addition to the required reading, research paper, country presentation, and graded examinations, the naval staff students were then given an increasing amount of contact with U.S. students and resident faculty members, several combined seminars with command and staff students, and participation in the electives program. Each student has a sponsor from the Naval War College student body or staff. In addition, the students participate in a wide variety of athletic activities with their U.S. counterparts.[14]

The trends traceable to the syllabus changes that took place in the period between 1977 and 1984 were paralleled in other developments during the tenure of each president of the college.

Growth and Change

Soon after the 1977 graduation, Rear Admiral Hardisty received his orders to go to the Philippine Islands as Commander, U.S. Naval Forces, Philippines, and as Commander, U.S. Naval Base, Subic Bay. Later, he became Commander, Battle Force, Seventh Fleet, Deputy for Operations on the Staff of Commander, U.S. Pacific Fleet, and a Vice Admiral, Director for Operations (J-3) on the Joint Staff. Hardisty turned the War College presidency over to Vice Admiral James B. Stockdale on 13 October 1977.

Stockdale came to the Naval War College after serving as Director of Strategic Plans in the Navy Department. In 1965, Stockdale had commanded Carrier Air Wing 16 and had been shot down and taken prisoner by the North Vietnamese. Upon his release from captivity nearly eight years later, in 1973, Stockdale had been promoted to rear admiral and awarded the Congressional Medal of Honor for the valor and heroism of his leadership while senior officer in prison camp. During his captivity, his wife Sybil had become a leader among the POW wives at home and an articulate spokeswoman in reminding the American public of those in enemy hands in Southeast Asia. Stockdale was not a War College graduate, but he had earned a master's degree from Stanford University in 1962. These two different aspects in his background, his experiences as a prisoner of war and as a graduate student, played an important role in the way in which he perceived and sought to add to the college's curriculum. Its three subject focus he thought was too narrow.

While basically accepting the general thrust of the program that had been developing since 1972, Stockdale remembered that in his years at Stanford he had benefited from the wide range of courses he had been allowed to take. It was those courses, particularly one called the "Problem of Good and Evil," given by Professor Philip Rhinelander, which helped him to develop fortitude during the long years of his imprisonment. As he told the Naval War College community when he took up the college's presidency, "If I can firmly establish and illuminate to the students here the inevitable blindnesses of these particularized specialties of disciplines in which we must work—blindness to the psychological and subjective, as well as to the objective totality of the human experience we call war—I think I will have done something for my country."[15] Stockdale wanted officers to understand the irrationality and unpredictability of war. "War is a serious business," Stockdale stressed. "People get mad in war, and...the laws of logic are valueless in bargaining under such conditions."[16]

Stockdale thought that to some extent War College students had too much of "a lock-step curriculum," and he asked his special academic advisor, Professor Frederick H. Hartmann, to plan a comprehensive electives program outside of the three departments. The free choice a student was offered to add one course each trimester to the required course, gave students the opportunity to choose whatever they felt was needed to round out their education. Stockdale's proposals were based on his own experiences and they were backed by the words of John Ruskin, "The education which makes men happiest in themselves also makes them most serviceable to others."[17] During Turner's presidency a few electives had been available, but no academic credit was given for them. These had been expanded by Le Bourgeois to about 20 topics as extensions of departmental topics for extra credit study by students. But in the military-civilian staff and faculty of more than 80 people, Stockdale was sure there was undoubtedly much untapped knowledge and talent in additional subjects that could be made available to interested students. At a staff-faculty meeting in early February 1978, Stockdale told the assembly,

> If you have something to say and it can be taught within the bounds of an academic discipline—that is to say it has boundaries, it has unique assumptions, it has a literature, it has established authorities (and often a special vocabulary)—and if you can assemble a creditable reading list and lesson plans of the sort that our academic review committee would recommend as appropriate for academic credit, and further if you can draw a crowd, then I say 'Let a hundred flowers bloom, let a hundred thoughts contend.'[18]

Response from the faculty was excellent: seventeen electives were planned for the first trimester of the forthcoming year. The core curriculum was planned to continue to occupy 80 percent of the students' time, and electives would take the remaining 20 percent.

The electives covered a wide variety of topics and included a course taught by Stockdale, "Fundamentals of Moral Obligation." As a prisoner of war, Stockdale had vowed to himself that if he ever got out alive, he would teach a course in moral philosophy. After his release, he explained, "When I ejected from that airplane in 1965, I left my world of technology and entered the world of Epictetus. I was alone and crippled: self reliance was the basis for daily life."[19]

With the background of his Stanford years coupled with the experience of his long imprisonment, Stockdale went on to establish his course. With Joseph G. Brennan, professor emeritus of philosophy at Barnard College of Columbia University, Stockdale devised a course that began with his own reflections on Epictetus' *The Enchiridion*,[20] the little book his Stanford professor had given him as a parting gift, that had sustained him during his imprisonment. From that, the course went on to readings and discussion of the Book of Job, the Socratic dialogues of Plato, Aristotle's *Nichomachean Ethics*, Kant's *Foundations of the Principles of the Metaphysics of Words*, and Mill *On Liberty* and *Utilitarianism*. Supplemented with selections from Camus, Conrad, Dostoyevsky, Solzhenitsyn, and others, it ended with a careful examination of *The Enchiridion*.[21]

For Stockdale, a War College course in moral philosophy did not need to be organized directly around military ideas or on military writing. Classical philosophy and modern literature expressed the essential ideas better than writings in social science, Stockdale believed. At the same time, reading philosophy books would benefit War College students as human beings as well as military officers. Behind this belief lay Stockdale's conviction that individual character, freedom, and personal responsibility were more important than rules in moral life. But as Stockdale stressed,

> The important thing, of course, is not that all our charges [i.e., students] come to the same conclusions on these issues, but that each think out how his particular assumptions on the nature of the universe and man logically lead to his ideas of the proper norms of behavior... that man, each man, sort his system out in a consistent manner.[22]

The students responded eagerly to Stockdale's course and the the variety of other subjects offered, including such technical matters as "Advanced Electronic Warfare" and "Application of Ocean Research." Staff and faculty sorted out their talents for a full schedule in the year commencing in August 1978, and in the years following, some 20 courses were usually offered each trimester. Some feared initially that students would take electives in which they were already proficient. Stockdale's reply was based on a comment a retired flag officer made to him,

> Jim, when you go up there to Newport, don't spend all your time trying to box in the dope-offs. The few you'll get are not worth it, and they won't be kidding anybody. Spend your time doing the best you can to inspire those tigers at the other end of the spectrum. That's where the long-run payoff of your institution resides.[23]

It was natural that Stockdale, looking ahead toward retirement from the Navy, leaned toward further work in the educational field. In the spring of 1979, the trustees of The Citadel, a private military college, offered him its presidency. On 1 July 1979, the Navy Department announced that Stockdale would retire two months later to accept the Citadel position, becoming its fifteenth president and the first naval officer to head it.

Stockdale, noting with regret that he was retiring early and somewhat suddenly, stated, "But when the train stops for you, it is better to get aboard. There may not be another train coming."[24] This early retirement left a three-star billet available at a time of reductions in the numbers of flag and general officers in the armed services. With brief interludes, the Naval War College had been headed by a vice admiral since 1948. Despite greater visibility in the past two years and many supporters at various levels in Washington, the three star billet was lost. In early August, the Navy Department announced that Rear Admiral Edward F. Welch would become the fortieth president of the Naval War College.

Pointing Toward Fleet Operations

Rear Admiral Welch was relatively unknown to the college when his orders were announced. A submariner, a National War College graduate, and former dean of academic affairs at the National War College, Welch was an expert in the complex business of disarmament negotiations. In his opening statement, Welch emphasized that the Naval War College must point toward the fleet. Therefore, he placed continued emphasis on courses having to do with operational matters coupled with use of the improved naval war gaming facilities. For three academic years under Welch, this trend continued.

An important innovation begun in these years was the global war game. These were begun in 1979 by Captain Hugh Nott, Commander J. Hurlburt, and Professor Francis J. West, Jr., who in 1981-83 served as Assistant Secretary of Defense for International Security Affairs. The global war game was created to identify issues that required attention in planning global strategy. Like no other war game in use in the United States, it involves all aspects for worldwide military operations including logistics, strategy, and tactics in an effort to explore changing options within the matrix of policy, strategy, and technical capabilities.[25]

This emphasis on combined areas was reflected in another development at the college in 1981.

Center for Naval Warfare Studies

At the Current Strategy Forum in April 1981, the Chief of Naval

Operations, Admiral Thomas Hayward, in the final address of the forum announced that a Center for Naval Warfare would soon be established at the War College. The center would be staffed by "the best strategic thinkers in the world."[26] Within the audience of staff, students, and civilian guests, knowledgeable in college affairs, this statement provoked more than a few looks, whispers, and winks. Many thought that once again Washington was passing the ball back to Newport for planning support. That ball had been passed before, beginning in the days of Luce and Mahan when strategical concepts originated in the writings of Mahan. From time to time the War College had been called on for assistance in Navy planning. On other occasions War College presidents had been told that planning was exclusively a function of the Navy Department and later of the Office of Naval Operations. Through the years, what the college sent to Washington formally or informally had been used or ignored, depending on such factors as the personalities involved, timing, the problem at hand, and the organization of the Navy Department. Many wondered whether the CNO's announcement in Newport and the follow-up directives from his headquarters would change the position of the college in the strategic thinking and planning of the Navy.

In July 1981, Welch announced that the new Center for Naval Warfare Studies would be headed by former Under Secretary of the Navy Robert J. Murray. As Murray recalled,

> In July 1981, nobody knew what the Center for Naval Warfare Studies was to be, including me. It grew out of conversations I had with flag and general officers in the Navy and Marine Corps, including the CNO and the Commandant. We saw we did not have enough naval officers who were thinking broadly enough about war-fighting issues. And we certainly had nothing that we could call naval strategy. There were lots of ideas, but there was nothing that we could call all-encompassing as to how the Navy would operate in war. We didn't even have a system for producing such a concept. In other words, naval strategy was a mystery for many folks—certainly for most defense civilians.
>
> So Admiral Hayward decided that we ought to have such a place as the Center for Naval Warfare Studies, and Secretary of the Navy John Lehman said it was something he believed worth doing and would support. So I went to figure out what a Center for Naval Warfare Studies should be.[27]

As established, the center brought together under one structure these organizations which already existed at the college: the center for advanced research, the center for war gaming, and the naval war college press. To this, Murray added as the centerpiece the strategic studies group, comprising eight officers, six Navy captains (or commanders) and two Marine colonels chosen by the CNO and the Commandant of the Marine Corps. All were men of considerable operational experience, drawn from all the warfare communities, and assigned to the center for a year to help develop better ways for the Navy to contribute to national strategy. "One year is not a long time to do this," Murray explained, "but I wasn't interested in building career strategists; I wanted to give naval officers a chance to think through war-fighting issues and then go back to the fleet to spread the word."[28]

With Welch's support and insistence that war gaming be an important part of the center, Murray developed it in 1981-1983 with the help of key staff members: Commander Kenneth McGruther and Dr. Thomas Etzold, and Lieutenant Colonel O. E. Hay. Murray brought Frank Uhlig, formerly senior editor at the Naval Institute, to serve as editor of the Naval War College Press, which published the *Naval War College Review* and a small number of monographs dealing with strategy and naval history.

After two years at the center, Murray concluded,

> I think, frankly, you first have to discard the term *naval strategy*, and even its slightly more modern variant, *maritime strategy*, and talk instead about the naval contribution to national strategy. So what we need is neither a maritime strategy nor a continental strategy but a national strategy that has ample and balanced proportions of naval, land, and air forces, organized so that it can achieve national objectives, or more accurately, alliance objectives.[29]

Going further, he maintained that the center's studies had supported the conclusion that naval forces still contribute in their three traditional ways: "by establishing a military and naval presence in areas of interest, by responding to crises, and by helping deter or if necessary fight a general war."[30]

In Murray's vision, at its core, the center was an intellectually dynamic group of officers and civilians with access to everyone, no matter at what level, in the Navy and Marine Corps, anywhere in the world. Arguing real-life questions of strategy and tactics, testing real war plans, and developing new concepts of operation, the center in fact soon won widespread respect within the Navy. By concentrating on the uses of naval forces rather than entering the debate about specific budget programs, the center helped the college in its old task of building the foundations for better decisions. At the same time, the experience of broadly based advanced research, war gaming and highly experienced officers doing broad Navy thinking provided stimulus to both students and teaching faculty. The center was not the Navy's war planning agency; it was the place where new ideas were examined and tested for possible incorporation into war plans. The war gaming center at the college was the heart of all Navy war gaming at the battlegroup level and above. As Murray explained, "it is the place where the Navy is asking itself, how do the forces fit together—first at the tactical level, then at the theater level, and then worldwide."[31] As a result of these efforts, the Center for Naval Warfare Studies strengthened the link between the college and the fleet.

Cooperative Degree Program

The establishment of a cooperative degree program was the product of a long development under many presidents. This was the search for a means for students to obtain an advanced academic degree in conjunction with their War College studies.

Within a few years after the George Washington University cooperative degree program had been terminated in 1973, the War College was searching for alternative methods for its students to obtain degrees. Because it was the only war college not to offer a cooperative degree program, some officers were reluctant to accept their orders to Newport when they perceived that greater advantage and recognition could be obtained elsewhere. With this problem in mind, Admiral Le Bourgeois had obtained approval in 1975 for a joint program to be offered with the Naval Postgraduate School for Naval War College graduates in the Washington, D.C., area. However, an insufficient number of students applied to make it a practicable effort.

In March 1981, Admiral Welch's attention was drawn to the statistic that more than 90 percent of the students at the Air War College had an advanced degree while at the Naval War College, with a similar student population, less than 50 percent of the Navy and Marine Corps officers had more than a bachelor's degree. Welch was concerned that in recent years naval officers had been unsuccessful in obtaining key Defense Department, Joint Staff, and NATO billets because they lacked the necessary advanced academic degrees.[32] To remedy this situation, he recommended to the Chief of Naval Operations, Admiral Thomas B. Hayward, that the college establish a master's degree program. After considering of the pros and cons of the issue, Hayward approved the recommendation on the conditions that the program be voluntary, that it not detract from the Naval War College curriculum, and that it be given "off-hours" for those willing to spend the extra time in pursuit of a graduate degree.[33]

The college staff entered into extensive negotiations with a number of neighboring colleges and universities, including Boston University, the University of Rhode Island, Providence College and Salve Regina College, in order to find an institution that would be able to meet the needs of the Naval War College. Some of the proposed courses of study suggested by these institutions had such extensive requirements for additional work beyond the college's courses that those programs would have provided too much competition for the college's curriculum, thereby detracting from it.

Salve Regina, a Catholic community college located in Newport, offered an attractive program which, by granting the full academic credits which the American Council on Education recommended for the Naval War College's basic courses, would require only three additional courses to earn a master of arts degree in international relations or a master of science degree in management. In addition, the fees for the courses would be amply covered by each student's entitlement to educational benefits from the Veteran's Administration.

After obtaining confirmation of approval from the new Chief of Naval Operations, James D. Watkins, the course was begun on a trial basis 16 October 1982 with 110 students, 44 of whom were naval officers.[34] Since its first year, the course has been expanded. Located at the Salve Regina campus in Newport, the course was opened to students of both institutions but, after the trial run, had no official administrative link with the Naval War College.

Admiral Watkins Appoints Service from the Sixth Fleet

When Admiral Watkins became Chief of Naval Operations in the summer of 1982, he started with what, from the standpoint of the Naval War College, were two priceless assets: he knew the War College's curriculum thoroughly from his days as Chief of Naval Personnel, and he knew how to carry out his ideas as CNO in terms of ensuring the necessary changes in the personnel assignment area.

Admiral Watkins moved quickly to give greater prominence to the Naval War College. One of his first concerns was the flag appointments which would be made in the fall of 1982. In mid-July Watkins sent a personal message to Rear Admiral James E. Service, then commanding Carrier Group Two with the Sixth Fleet in the Mediterranean telling him, Jim,

> My initial attack on the fall slate is complete, and the Secretary has concurred in your assignment as the President, Naval War College. My decision follows a careful examination of the increasing role of the War College in the enhancement of tactical competence and professionalism in our officer corps. As you are aware, NWC is being assigned additional Navywide responsibilities in the areas of wargaming, tactical development and formulation of concepts of maritime operations at the battle group, theater and global levels.

For obvious reasons, I want a borad-based, operationally oriented president with extensive experience as an OIC afloat.[35]

In August 1982, Welch retired and was relieved by the War College deputy, Captain David Self, as interim president, until Rear Admiral James E. Service could take command in October. Service had become a naval aviation cadet while attending Pennsylvania State University early in the Korean war. Having flown combat missions in both Korea, and in Vietnam, Service was unusual in that he had served tours in fighter, attack and reconnaissance aircraft. In addition, he had been a test pilot and instructor and had also commanded two squadrons and two ships, USS *Independence* (CV-62) and USS *Sacramento* (AOE-1). Service earned his bachelor's degree in political science from the Naval Postgraduate School. He was a student at the Army War College in 1972-1973, and he also earned a master of science degree in communications at Shippensburg State College. Service came to the Naval War College after serving as Commander, Battle Force, Sixth Fleet. While in that position, F-14 fighters from his battle force shot down two Libyan aircraft during operations in the Gulf of Sidra.

With his extensive operational experience, Service's appointment as president of the Naval War College reflected Admiral Watkins' belief that the college was the proper place for capable fighting leaders and the place for innovative thought on future naval tactics and strategy. His presidency was marked throughout by emphasis on those areas.

During his initial speech as CNO at the college in August 1982, Watkins said, "We look to [the] War College to play a leading role in inculating into our professional officer corps a larger grasp of strategy and integrated tactics."[36] To emphasize Watkins' initiative in this area, Service came all the way from the Mediterranean to be present at Watkins' speech during the combined convocation and retirement ceremony for Rear Admiral Welch.

With the intent of revitalizing the naval operations and tactical aspects of the college's curriculum, Watkins declared in a message to senior naval commanders that the college would be the "crucible for strategic and tactical thinking."[37] Significantly, Watkins also announced how this would be achieved: through the infusion into the student body of high quality officers who had recently completed duty *in command*. This highly motivated student body would be guided by an operationally oriented faculty, be given extensive war gaming experience and have appropriate interaction with the strategic studies group. With this in mind, Watkins declared, "We will be able to test and harmonize our tactical thinking in a wide variety of strategic applications. At the same time these students will develop a solid base of strategic thought as they prepare for important and demanding follow-on assignments at sea and shore."[38]

To allow more officers to come to the Naval War College, Watkins ordered a more effective use of technical training time elsewhere through compressing some courses and eliminating others. Simultaneously, he extended the length of command tours of duty, thus getting more effective use out of officers. Hoping to obtain close to a 30 percent reduction in time spent in officer training, Watkins specifically planned to assign to the Naval War College the officers made available in these ways.

Watkins' plan had both interim and long term aspects. For the long term, he planned an increase of post command officers in the 10-month college of naval warfare course. Starting with only 10 to 15 officers in March 1983, Watkins planned to increase this number five times by August 1984. This would significantly raise the percentage of unrestricted line captains who had attended the college of naval warfare course. Changing the percentage from Holloway's 25 to 35 percent, Watkins established the figure at 35 to 45 percent of line captains who would be graduates of a senior service college, with 50 percent of those from the Naval War College.

As an interim measure, Watkins established a short post command course, to begin in February 1983. This course met for six weeks of seminars and war gaming with emphasis on the tactical and strategic aspects of naval operations at the theater and local level. With the idea of giving 60 to 80 officers per year an abbreviated and intensive course, Watkins began it with the initial intention of phasing it out as soon as attendance in the 10-month course could be substantially increased.[39] Following the success of the interim course, Watkins later directed that the course be continued on a permanent basis, but this in no way altered his earlier decision that the majority of successful commanding officers would attend the ten month senior course. Watkins insisted that both courses maintain the highest quality and that the personnel assignment system be strained to the limit in an attempt to ensure that as many potential flag officers as possible attend the Naval War College.[40]

Watkins also stressed the importance of the CNO Policy Advisory Board for Professional Military Education, which was established originally by Admiral Holloway in 1977. Watkins believed that the board's role should be institutionalized to ensure that the naval operations curriculum at Newport remain current and be in line with the latest concepts approved by the Office of the CNO and the Department of Defense.[41] With this in mind, he used the board to review the whole Naval War College curriculum in January 1983.

Watkins stressed these ideas to the naval commanders in chief at annual conferences he convened at the Naval War College in 1982 and 1983, using Newport rather than the usual location in Washington or Annapolis. These conferences were a significant signal by Watkins that

Newport had become a far more important place for professional thinking in the U.S. Navy.

Looking back on the record of war gaming at the Naval War College, Watkins underlined its use in connection with operational research and tactical analysis. As Rear Admiral William T. McCauley, Director of the Program Resource Appraisal division in the Office of the Chief of Naval Operations, commented,

> As we all know, war gaming has been practiced at the Naval War College for decades. The naval aspect of our current concept, though, is its ready applicability to tactical and strategic analysis and its acceptance by top Navy leadership (as demonstrated by recent CINC war games) as a valued and proven tool. Thus, naval analysts are beginning to make a new kind of impact by using analytical tools to support war gaming and drawing on war gaming results.[42]

A series of new war games incorporated many new concepts and helped to verify the best choice of fleet defenses as well as to test some of the issues raised in developing the Navy's Program Objective Memorandum (POM) for 1986. At the same time, Service increased the amount of student war gaming three-fold, using crisis action, theater and world-wide games.

Linked with his emphasis on an up-to-date naval operations curriculum and on experienced, high-quality students, Watkins now developed a direct link for the Naval War College with war gaming, fleet exercises, and operational planning. Using the strategic studies group and war gaming, in particular, the Center for Naval Warfare Studies at the Naval War College came to play an important role. Under Robert S. Wood, who became the director of the center in 1983, the four main elements of the center—war gaming, advanced research, the strategic studies group, and the press—were increasingly integrated to form a single entity, as the center became the CNO's "think-tank" of first resort. Thus, the center became the focus for a variety of studies and conferences on current issues, with topics ranging from terrorism to nuclear weapons problems and a host of political-military studies. For example, the first two strategic studies groups examined global warfare, and the third group in 1983-1984 looked at crises and contingencies short of general war.

As Chief of Naval Operations, Watkins thus implemented many of the same ideas that he had recommended to Admiral Holloway six years earlier. In his own statement on service college education policy, Watkins asserted, "The Naval War College does not prepare officers for their new assignment; it prepares them for the rest of their careers. The curriculum is designed to aid officers in meeting the intellectual demands of the second phase of their careers by fostering intellectual flexibility and rectitude essential for handling the unforeseen contingencies."[43]

An After Look-out Reports

Looking 100 years back, the Naval War College has left a discernible wake in the development of the naval profession in the United States. Defined by a continuing devotion to the education of naval officers for high command, it has stressed to its students an understanding of the fundamental ideas in the conduct of strategy and tactics, branching out from these basic concerns to related areas such as international law, logistics, management, and economics. The college has always sharply contrasted its approach with technological and scientific education, arguing consistently that its focus was on the highest professional aspects in understanding the nature and character of naval warfare, the purpose, function, and limitations of a Navy.

From the very beginning of the Naval War College, this view of education has consistently been opposed fiercely within the Navy. The college has had to battle all its life to obtain recognition and widespread appreciation for its goals from a service that has accepted much more easily the rationale for technological education, practical training at sea, and on-the-job training in staff positions.

Over the years, many of the dominating figures in the college's history have been reformers who have not always had a wide following among their colleagues. Men such as Luce, Mahan, Taylor, Sims, and Turner, strong-willed characters, not only criticized the Navy's system but tried to change it. Perhaps only naturally, those figures in the college's history who have been most widely accepted and played key roles in positions outside the college, men such as Pratt, Spruance, and Colbert, changed the college less dramatically during their presidencies. This very fact, however, has sometimes identified the Naval War College with reformers, rather than as the representative of the mainstream view. In many respects, this reputation has been unwarranted, yet more often than not it has taken the continuing personal and direct interest of the Secretary of the Navy, or in later years, the Chief of Naval Operations, to allow the college to achieve its long-standing goals in educating the most capable officers in the Navy. In this respect, Secretaries of the Navy William E. Chandler, B. F. Tracy, and Josephus Daniels, along with Chiefs of Naval Operations W. V. Pratt, Chester Nimitz, Robert F. Carney, Arleigh Burke, and the successive chiefs following Thomas Moorer, Elmo Zumwalt, James Holloway III, Thomas Hayward, and James Watkins, have played direct and key roles in bringing the college to the forefront of the naval profession in the United States.

The Naval War College's course was clearly charted by Stephen B. Luce a century ago, but like any course line it has been set by winds, currents, and helmsmanship over the years. While rarely straying far, the actual track suggests a sinuous course which at one time or another favors one set of elements among the larger number that make up the college's area of interest: national policy, maritime strategy, fleet tactics, operational planning, international law, management, economics, logistics, international relations, diplomatic, military, and naval history. Often, leaders have steered toward either practical application or theoretical research, rather than the direct relationship between them which Luce had envisaged. At times, there has been a tendency to promote either breadth or depth of thought in the curriculum, each at the expense of the other. An institution such as the Naval War College needs to remain responsive to the continually changing elements within the naval profession. The shifts in emphasis that have gone too far in either direction might well be attributed to the absence of a corporate memory and to a lack of continuity in policy, faculty, and staff, which did not begin to be rectified until the final chapters ending the story of the college's first century. Through much of its history, many naval officers have been reluctant to come to the Naval War College. Many have doubted that it could help their careers. Detailers in the Bureau of Personnel, and its predecessor, the Bureau of Navigation, have been reluctant to send "front runners," and students have at times suspected that only the second-rate officers were selected in the end. Although a pioneer in promoting advanced professional education along broad lines, the Naval War College has never achieved the full acceptance of its role that other service colleges in the United States have achieved in their own services. Ironically many of the other service colleges have adopted ideas first applied at Newport, as the Naval War College has also used concepts and approaches taken from its sister colleges. And non-naval students have often won from naval officers the Naval War College's own academic prizes and achieved its highest marks. Curiously, the Naval War College has at times been better regarded by officers from other services than by its own. Perhaps, in view of the significant changes of the last years, this will no longer be true in the future.

The nature of modern navies produces a natural conflict in outlook between the divergent views which stress extensive technological knowledge of equipment, practical experience at sea and on staffs, and broad understanding of the nature of warfare. Although the doubters and critics of the college might often stress one aspect over another, the challenge that Stephen B. Luce made to the Navy remains the continuing inspiration of the Naval War College in its work to lead officers to understand the total range of the naval profession as they prepare for high command. "One thing must be borne in mind," Luce reminded us:

> At the firing of the first gun proclaiming war, the so-called

'inspiration of genius' may be trusted only when it is the result of long and careful study and reflection.

Art is a jealous mistress; most of all so is the art of war.

If attendance here will serve, in any degree, to broaden an officer's views, extend his 'mental horizon on national and international questions, and give him a just appreciation of the great variety and extent of the requirements of his profession, the college will not have existed in vain.[44]

As the Naval War College ended its first century of service, it had clearly recovered from the long period of uncertainty that had followed World War II. Successive Chiefs of Naval Operations in the 1970s and 1980s established a degree of emphasis and interest in the college which had not been seen in 50 years. By 1984, the prime requisites to achieve fully the vision which Luce had proclaimed were finally in place: systematic guidance at the highest level within the Navy, carefully chosen college leadership, and increasingly more students selected on merit in courses taught by a first class, resident faculty. These permit the highest academic standards and the best available information to be used to engender innovative professional thinking while, at the same time, balancing a broad outlook with in-depth investigation.

At the beginning of its second century, the doors of the Naval War College remain open to the most capable officers as the only institution in the United States devoted to educating officers in the highest aspects of the naval profession, preparing them for the most responsible duties that can devolve upon them.

Notes

1. NWC Archives, RG3: 1977 Files 1500, Training and Education, NN-DEC: Watkins memo to CNO, Pers-40, serial 40 of 13 April 1977.
2. Ibid.
3. Loc. cit., Holloway memo to DCNO (Manpower), DNET, CNET, president, NWC, on Service Education Policy, Ser. 00/000315 of 11 July 1977.
4. Ibid.
5. Ibid.
6. Loc. cit., DNET memo for CNO, on Service College Education Policy, serial 099/142663 of 22 November 1977.
7. Ibid., and president, Naval War College, letter, serial 1866 of 8 September 1977.
8. NWC Archives, RG11: Syllabus: Strategy and Policy, November 1983-March 1984, p. 1.
9. Conversation, 19 April 1984: Hattendorf-Wood; A. H. Bernstein memo to strategy faculty, 27 February 1984.
10. Memorandum, Turcotte to Hattendorf, 10 April 1984.
11. NWC Archives, RG11: Syllabus: Naval Operations: Employment of Naval Forces Course, 1980-81.
12. Memorandum, Weschler to Hattendorf, 14 April 1984.
13. Conversation, 23 April 1984: Hattendorf-CDR J. J. Hinds, and Hattendorf-Needham.

14. NSC office files, "Naval Staff College Newsletter 1981-82," pp. 1-3.

15. NWC Archives, RG28: President's File: J. B. Stockdale, Change of Command address, 13 October 1977.

16. Ibid.

17. Quoted J. B. Stockdale, "The Problem of Ethical Brinkmanship," p.10. Talk given to the Third Taft Values Institute, 9-14 July 1978, Taft School. NWC Archives, RG28: President's File.

18. J. B. Stockdale, "Taking Stock," NWC Review (Summer 1978), p. 2.

19. Quoted in Joseph Gerard Brennan, "The Stockdale Course" in Michael J. Collins, ed., Teaching Values and Ethics in College (San Francisco: Jossey-Bass Inc.), 1983, p. 69, from New York Times, Sunday 1 April 1973.

20. J. B. Stockdale, "The Word of Epictetus," Atlantic Monthly (April 1978).

21. Brennan, op. cit., pp. 75-76.

22. Stockdale, "The Problem of Ethical Brinksmanship," p.9.

23. J. B. Stockdale, "Taking Stock," Naval War College Review (Summer 1978), p. 7.

24. J. R. Wadleigh notes on J. B. Stockdale, "Remarks to NWC Foundation," 23 June 1977.

25. NWC Archives, Subject File: Advanced Research. LTCOL D. E. Hay, USMC, presentation at Advanced Research Symposium, March 1984.

26. Hayward, Speech to Current Strategy Forum, 8 April 1981.

27. Robert J. Murray, "A War-fighting Perspective," USNI Proceedings (October 1983), p. 68.

28. Ibid.

29. Ibid., p. 70.

30. Ibid.

31. Ibid., p. 74.

32. NWC Central Files, File 1500, COOP DEGREE: Welch to Hayward, serial 598 of 18 March 1981.

33. Loc. cit. VADM Lando W. Zech memo to CNO, 23 April 1981, and CNO to president, NWC, serial 114H/371555 of 7 July 1981.

34. Loc. cit., J. E. Service to CNO Watkins, serial 2252 of 14 Oct 1982.

35. CNO message to ComCarGru Two 142053Z Jul 82.

36. Quoted in Rick Maze, "CNO Orders Cuts in Officer Training," Navy Times, 4 October 1982. See also James D. Watkins, "This Is Your Ticket to 'Compete' . . . ," Naval War College Review (Nov-Dec 1982), pp. 4-7.

37. CNO Message 221307Z, Sep 82, to NAVWARCOL.

38. Ibid.

39. CNO Message 151315Z, Nov 1982, NAVOP 125/82.

40. NWC Central Files, 5420 Boards: CNO Policy Board for Professional Military Education. Memorandum for the record. Memo 095/22-83 dated 26 Jan 1983.

41. Ibid.

42. RADM W. F. McCauley, "Fight Smart," PHALANX: Newsletter of Military Operations Research Society, Vol. 17, No. 1 (February 1984), p. 10.

43. NWC Central File, 1520 Training and Education: CNO Service College Education Policy, serial 00/3U448779 dated 12 December 1983.

44. John D. Hayes and John B. Hattendorf, The Writings of Stephen B. Luce (Newport: Naval War College Press, 1975), p. 44.

APPENDIX
CHRONOLOGY OF COURSES AND SIGNIFICANT EVENTS AT THE UNITED STATES NAVAL WAR COLLEGE 1884-1984

Year	Date	Event
1884	May 3	At suggestion of Commodore Stephen Luce, Secretary of the Navy W.E. Chandler appoints a board of three officers to report on the subject of postgraduate education for officers.
1884	June 13	Board headed by Luce recommends establishment of a war college.
	October 6	Navy Department General Order No. #325 establishes a Naval War College at Newport with Luce as "Superintendent."
1885	September 4	First course begins with 9 students. Ends September 30.
1886	June 22	Luce detached for sea duty without relief.
	August 26	Captain A.T. Mahan reports and assumes NWC presidency.
	September 6	Course begins with 21 students. Ends November 20. William McCarty-Little introduces first lecture on war gaming.
1888	August 6	Course begins with 14 students. Ends November 5.
1889	January 11	Navy Department orders consolidation of College with Torpedo Station. Mahan detached on temporary duty. Commander Caspar Goodrich assumes NWC presidency.
	August 5	Course begins with 12 students. Ends October 25.
1890		No course held.
	July 1	*Influence of Sea Power Upon History, 1660-1783*, by Mahan is published.
1891		No course held. Bureau of Navigation cites shortage of officers.
1892	May 28	First new building (present Luce Hall) completed.
	July 22	Mahan returns and assumes NWC presidency.
1893		No course held.
	May 10	Mahan detached for sea duty. Commander Charles Stockton, acting president.
	October 4	First visit by a Secretary of the Navy. Hilary Herbert inspects NWC.
	November 15	Commander Henry C. Taylor assumes NWC presidency.
1894	June 12	Course begins with 25 students, including first foreign officers, two from Royal Swedish Navy. Ends September 30.
1895	June	Course begins with 25 students. Mahan returns as lecturer. Ends October 15.
1896	June 1	Course begins with 27 students. Ends October 15.
	December 31	Captain Taylor detached for sea duty. Goodrich returns and assumes NWC presidency.
1897	June 1	Course begins with 22 students. Ends September 15.
1898	April 19	United States declares war on Spain. Staff including Goodrich ordered to sea. Planned course cancelled.

Year	Date	Event
	August 12	Cessation of hostilities between U.S. and Spain.
	November 2	Captain Stockton assumes NWC presidency.
1899	May 31	Course begins with four students. Others from fleet in bay attend part time. Ends October 1.
1900	March 12	General Order No. #544 constitutes Navy General Board. NWC president assigned as ex-officio member.
	June 1	Course begins with 30 students including 2 from Revenue Cutter Service. Ends September 30.
	October 25	Stockton detached for sea duty. Captain French E. Chadwick assumes NWC presidency.
1901	June 2	Course begins with 28 students including Rear Admiral Shepherd (first flag officer student). Ends October 1.
	November 27	U.S. Army War College established in Washington, D.C.
1902	June 2	Course begins with 25 students. Main problem plays a Russo-Japanese conflict in Far East. Ends October 1.
1903	June 2	Course begins with lecture by Stephen Luce to 21 students. Main problem, U.S.-German war in Far East. Ends October 1.
	November 16	Chadwick detached for sea duty. Captain Charles Sperry assumes NWC presidency.
1904	June 1	Course, redesignated "Summer conference," begins with 21 students. Nine flag officers attend on temporary duty. Ends October 1.
	June 17	New Library (present Mahan Hall) completed.
1905	March 3	First librarian, Frederick Hicks, appointed.
	June 1	Summer conference begins with 21 students. Ends September 30.
1906	May 24	Sperry promoted and detached for sea duty. Captain John P. Merrell assumes NWC presidency.
	June 1	Summer conference begins with 17 students including W.S. Benson, later first Chief of Naval Operations. Ends October 1.
1907	June 1	Summer conference begins with 15 students. Ends 1 October.
1908	June 1	Summer conference begins with 25 students. Ends October 1.
	July 8	Conference interrupted at direction of President Theodore Roosevelt. General Board and Dept. Bureau Chiefs join NWC staff and students in "Battleship Conference."
	July 22	President Roosevelt at NWC and chairs conference for the day.
	September 1	Secretary of the Navy Metcalf closes Battleship Conference.
1909	June 1	Summer conference begins with 26 students plus General Board in attendance on occasion. Ends September 30.
	October 1	Merrell retires from active duty. Rear Admiral Raymond P. Rodgers assumes NWC presidency.
1910	June 1	Summer conference begins with 26 students plus General Board in attendance on occasion. "Estimate of Situation and Formulation of Orders" introduced. Ends October 1.
1911	June 2	Summer conference begins with 28 students. Ends September 30.
	October 1	Long course begins with four students from summer conference; course ends September 30 1912.
	November 20	R.P. Rodgers retires from active duty. Captain William Ledyard Rodgers assumes NWC presidency.
1912	June 1	Summer conference begins with 28 students. Ends September 30.

Year	Date	Event
	October 1	Long course begins with six students from summer conference.
1913	February 1	U.S. Naval Postgraduate School established at Annapolis, Md.
	June 2	Summer conference begins with 26 students. Ends October 1 —last such course.
	October 1	1912 long course ends. Diplomas awarded to graduates of 1911 and 1912 long courses. 1913-14 long course begins with six students. Ends July 3, 1914.
	December 15	Rodgers detached for sea duty. Rear Admiral Austin Knight assumes NWC presidency.
1914	January 1	Long course begins with 13 students. Ends December 22.
	January 17	General order No. #70 establishes NWC curriculum at two long courses per year.
	April 1	General Order No. #89 establishes NWC correspondence courses.
	July 13	Long course begins with six students. Secretary of the Navy Josephus Daniels speaks. Ends June 26, 1915.
	December 1	Death of Alfred Thayer Mahan in Washington, D.C.
1915	January 1	Course begins with 14 students. Ends December 22.
	March 3	Formation of Office of Naval Operations in Navy Department.
	March 14	Death of William McCarty Little in Newport, R.I.
	July 5	Course begins with 20 students. Ends June 26, 1916.
1916	January 2	Course begins with 15 students. Ends December 15.
	May 31	Battle of Jutland between British Grand Fleet and German High Seas Fleet—most studied action at the NWC.
	July 5	Course begins with 19 students. Disbands in April 1917.
	October 7	German submarine U-53 at Newport. CO calls on NWC president.
1917	January 2	Course begins with 20 students. Course disbands in April.
	February 16	Knight detached for sea duty. Captain William Sims assumes NWC presidency.
	March 24	Rear Admiral Sims reports to Navy Department for duty.
	April 6	United States enters World War I. NWC closes except for Library.
	May 1	Commander C.P. Eaton (Ret.) assumes NWC presidency (acting).
	June 9	Sims detached from NWC.
	November 21	Commodore James Parker (Ret.) assumes NWC presidency (acting).
1918	November 11	Armistice Day, end of World War I hostilities.
1919	March 15	Captain Reginald Belknap assumes NWC presidency (acting).
	April 11	Sims returns to Newport and assumes NWC presidency.
	July 1	Course begins with 31 students. Ends June 2.
	December 2	Course begins with 30 students. Ends November 20.
1920	March 20	Sims in Washington to testify before Senate Naval Affairs Committee regarding World War I naval operations.
	July 1	Course begins with 30 students. Ends May 21, 1921.
	December 1	Secretary of the Navy in annual report recommends NWC be moved to Washington, D.C.
	December 28	Course begins with 45 students. Ends November 20, 1921.
1921	May 6	Approval by Bureau of Navigation to schedule one course per year.
	June 30	1922 class begins with 45 students. Ends May 20, 1922.

Year	Date	Event
1922	March 20	U.S. Senate ratifies Washington Treaty of Naval Limitations.
	April 18	Samuel Gompers, labor leader, addresses NWC.
	July 3	1923 class begins with 50 students including Chester W. Nimitz, Harold Stark, Thomas Hart. Ends May 20, 1923.
	October 14	Sims retires from active duty. Captain D. Blamer acting.
	November 3	Rear Admiral Clarence Williams assumes NWC presidency.
1923	March 6	General Order No. #48 establishes NWC junior course.
	July 7	1924 classes begin with 49 senior, 22 junior students. Graduation May 29, 1924.
1924	February 13	Japanese delegation visits NWC. Included is Captain I. Yamamoto IJN, later C-in-C Combined Fleet, 1940-43.
	February 21	U.S. Army Industrial College established in Washington, D.C.
	July 7	1925 classes begin with 46 senior, 25 junior students. Graduation May 29, 1925.
1925	January 24	NWC observes total eclipse of sun with temperature at 6°F.
	July 5	1926 classes begin with 43 senior, 25 junior students. Graduation May 27, 1926.
	September 5	Rear Admiral Williams detached for sea duty. Rear Admiral William Veazie Pratt assumes NWC presidency.
	September 25	Formation of "Kitten Ball league" (softball). First organized NWC athletics.
1926	July 1	Logistics division included in NWC staff.
	July 2	1927 classes begin with 44 senior, 26 junior students. Graduation May 27, 1927. Senior class includes Raymond Spruance.
1927	May 21	U.S. Fleet in Narragansett Bay after Army-Navy exercises off New England.
	May 24	Critique of exercises held at NWC by C-in-C, Admiral Charles Hughes.
	July 1	1928 classes begin with 40 senior, 38 junior students. Graduation May 29, 1928.
	September 17	Pratt detached for sea duty.
	September 19	Rear Admiral Joel Pringle assumes NWC presidency.
1928	May 31	NWC initiates correspondence courses for Naval Reserve officers.
	July 3	1929 classes begin with 48 senior, 52 junior students. Senior class includes H. Kent Hewitt. Graduation May 28, 1929.
1929	July 1	1930 classes begin with 48 senior, 35 junior students. Graduation May 26, 1930.
1930	January 27	Admiral H.K. Tu, Chinese Navy, visits NWC.
	May 30	Pringle detached for sea duty. Captain S.W. Bryant, acting.
	June 16	Rear Admiral Harris Laning assumes NWC presidency.
	July 1	1931 classes begin with 44 senior, 37 junior students. Graduation May 29, 1931.
	September 10	First America's Cup Races held off Newport.
1931	July 1	1932 classes begin with 42 senior, 37 junior students. Graduation May 27, 1932.
	July 21	U.S. Senate ratifies London Treaty of Naval Limitations.
	October 28	General of the Armies John Pershing and Marshal Petain of France visit NWC as part of Yorktown Sesquicentennial celebration.
1932	July 1	1933 classes begin with 48 senior and 48 junior students. Ernest J. King and William F. Halsey included in senior class. Graduation May 26, 1933.
1933	February 16	Marine Corps Schools team presents advanced base problem to NWC.

Year	Date	Event
	May 13	Laning detached for sea duty. Captain Adolphus Andrews, acting.
	June 3	Rear Admiral Luke McNamee assumes NWC presidency.
	July 6	1934 classes begin with 52 senior, 36 junior students. Graduation May 25, 1934.
	August 16	CNO approves advanced course at NWC.
1934	May 8	Pringle Hall dedicated.
	May 29	McNamee retires from active duty. Captain H.D. Cooke, acting.
	June 18	Rear Admiral Edward Kalbfus assumes NWC presidency.
	July 1	1935 classes begin with 11 advanced, 45 senior, 40 junior students. Graduation May 24, 1935.
	July 11	Admiral Joseph Reeves, C-in-C U.S. Fleet, addresses NWC.
	October 9	Change to Navy Regulations deletes NWC president from General Board membership and shifts NWC from CNO to Bunav direction.
1935	July 1	1936 classes begin with 11 advanced, 45 senior, 22 junior students. Graduation May 22, 1936.
1936	May 15	Colonel Robert McCormick, publisher of Chicago Tribune, addresses NWC.
	July 2	1937 classes begin with 12 advanced, 50 senior, 10 junior students. Graduation May 14, 1937.
	September 28	Death of William Sowden Sims in Boston, Mass.
	December 15	Kalbfus detached for sea duty. Captain H.D. Cooke acting.
1937	January 2	Rear Admiral Charles P. Snyder assumes NWC presidency.
	July 1	1938 classes begin with six advanced, 52 senior, 15 junior students. Graduation May 13, 1938.
1938	May 17	Congress passes Vinson-Trammell Act authorizing "Two Ocean" Navy.
	July 6	1939 classes begin with nine advanced, 53 senior, 17 junior students. Graduation May 27, 1939.
	September 21	Major hurricane strikes Narragansett Bay area.
	October 1	Addition to Mahan Hall completed to expand Library facilities.
1939	May 27	Snyder detached for sea duty. Captain J.W. Wilcox acting.
	June 30	Kalbfus returns and assumes NWC presidency.
	July 5	1940 classes begin with nine advanced, 53 senior, 17 junior students. Graduation May 26, 1940.
	September 1	Outbreak of World War II in Europe.
	September 8	President Roosevelt declares "limited national emergency."
1940	July 3	1941 classes begin with advanced, 28 senior, 5 junior students. Graduation May 15, 1941.
	September 18	President Roosevelt visits Narragansett Bay area including NWC.
1941	February 1	Formation of U.S. Atlantic Fleet under Admiral E.J. King
	March 25	Navy Department announces discontinuance of regular NWC courses for duration of national emergency. NWC to remain open for short courses as directed.
	June 10	First short courses begin with command class of 34 students, preparatory staff class of 18 students. Graduation December 2.
	December 1	Kalbfus retires from active duty and is recalled to duty as NWC president in rank of rear admiral (retired), raised to rank of admiral (ret.) in June, 1942.
	December 7	U.S. enters World War II.

Year	Date	Event
	December 30	U.S. Fleet reorganization effected with Admiral Ernest J. King as Commander-in-Chief (COMINCH) in Washington, D.C.
1942	January 9	Courses begin with 24 command, 9 preparatory staff students. Also special plotting course of eight. Graduation June 6.
	March 26	Duties of CNO and COMINCH combined under Admiral King.
	May 13	Bureau of Navigation redesignated Bureau of Personnel.
	July 1	Courses begin. 38 command, 56 preparatory staff students. Graduation December 18.
	November 2	Kalbfus detached to Navy Department Rear Admiral William S. Pye assumes NWC presidency.
1943	January 1	Courses begin with 32 command, 54 preparatory staff students. Graduation June 15.
	June 1	First Army-Navy staff college class arrives for month of study at NWC. Classes continue until end of war with 337 students in 12 classes.
	July 1	Courses begin with 28 command, 48 preparatory staff students. Graduation December 15.
1944	January 1	Courses begin with 29 command, 56 preparatory staff students. Graduation June 14.
	July 1	Rear Admiral Pye retires from active duty and is recalled to duty as NWC president in rank of vice admiral (ret.) Courses begin with 27 command, 58 preparatory staff students. Graduation December 16.
	July 15	Pye Board reports on postwar officer education.
1945	January 1	Courses begin with 27 command, 51 preparatory staff students. Graduation June 28.
	May 6	V-E Day. Germany surrenders.
	July 1	Courses begin with 32 command, 53 preparatory staff students. Graduation December 16.
	August 16	V-J Day. Japan surrenders.
	October 10	COMINCH headquarters in Washington dissolved.
1946	January 2	Course begins with 29 students in command and staff class. Graduation June 15, 1946.
	March 1	Pye retires. Admiral Raymond Spruance assumes NWC presidency.
	April 1	Army Industrial College redesignated Industrial College of the Armed Forces (ICAF).
	July 13	1947 classes begin with 65 senior, 36 junior students. First State Department attendee in senior class. Graduation May 25, 1947. Commodore Richard W. Bates begins work on World War II battle evaluation.
	August 1	National War College opens in Washington with 105 students.
	August 10	U.S. Navy General Line School opens at Newport with 600 students.
1947	January 20	First planning meeting for new NWC logistics course: Spruance, Vice Admiral R.B. Carney, and Captain H.E. Eccles.
	February 2	Armed Forces Staff College opens in Norfolk with 150 students.
	July 12	1948 classes begin with 69 senior, 34 junior, 46 logistics students. Graduation May 15, 1948.
	August	Logistics begins under Eccles.

Year	Date	Event
	September 18	Establishment of unified Military Establishment (NME) with Army, Navy, and Air Force, under Secretary of Defense.
	October 1	Air War College established at Montgomery, Ala.
1948	January 2	Navy opens Second General Line School at Monterey, Cal.
	May 22	Sims Hall (former Barracks C of Training Station) dedicated by NWC.
	June 10	First two-week Reserve Officer course begins at NWC.
	July 1	Spruance retires from active duty. Rear Admiral Allen Smith, Chief of Staff, assumes presidency.
	July 10	1949 classes begin with 65 senior, 52 logistics, 34 junior students. Graduation May 13, 1949.
	September 1	NWC starts publishing "Information Service for Officers."
	November 1	Smith detached for sea duty. Vice Admiral Donald Beary assumes NWC presidency.
1949	April 4	Formation of North Atlantic Treaty Organization (NATO).
	May 9	First "Round Table Discussions," forerunner of present Current Strategy Forum, begin.
	August 10	National Military Establishment becomes Department of Defense (DOD).
	August 12	1950 classes begin with 64 senior, 53 logistics, 36 junior students. Graduation June 16, 1950.
1950	February 10	New command & staff department organized within NWC staff.
	April 10	Admiral of the Fleet Lord Fraser of North Cape, RN, visits NWC.
	May 28	Beary hospitalized. Rear Admiral T. Ross Cooley, ComNavBase assumes additional duty as NWC president.
	June 25	Korean war begins.
	August 11	1951 classes begin. 56 strategy and tactics (S&T), 31 strategy and logistics (S&L), 31 command & staff (C&S) students. Graduation June 13, 1951.
	October 2	Army War College reopens after World War II closure.
	October 17	Cooley detached, Captain H.D. Felt acting.
	December 1	Vice Admiral Richard Conolly assumes NWC presidency.
1951	May 24	Financeer Bernard M. Baruch addresses NWC.
	August 10	1952 classes begin with 66 S&T, 47 S&L, 73 C&S students. Graduation June 14, 1952.
1952	June 9	First "Global Strategy Week" begins, replacing Round Table Discussions.
	July 14	CNO authorizes establishment of a Naval War College Museum.
	August 9	1953 classes begin with 4 S&S, 73 S&T, 56 S&L, 108 C&S students. New advanced class, strategy & seapower (S&S) included. Graduation June 10, 1953. First civilian academic chairs established.
	September 1	"Information Service for Officers" renamed *Naval War College Review*.
1953	July 27	Korean armistice effective.
	August 14	1954 classes begin with six S&S, 130 NW, 96 C&S students. S&T and S&L courses replaced by naval warfare (NW). Graduation June 16.
	November 2	Conolly retires from active duty. Rear Admiral Thomas Robbins, Chief of Staff, assumes NWC presidency.
1954	May 2	Vice Admiral Lynde McCormick assumes NWC presidency.
	August 23	1955 classes begin with 5 S&S, 67 NW2, 66 NW1, 114 C&S students. Naval warfare course split into first year

Year	Date	Event
		(NW1) and second year (NW2) sections. Graduation June 15, 1955.
1955	August 18	1956 classes begin with 2 S&S, 59 NW2, 72 NW1, 124 C&S students. Graduation June 12, 1956.
		NWC briefing team to indoctrinate Naval Reserve units formed.
1956	March 17	Major winter storm hits area, doing extensive damage to ships at recently completed Coddington Cove piers.
	April 19	CNO approves new naval command (international) course at NWC.
	August 16	McCormick dies suddenly at Newport. Rear Admiral Robbins, Chief of Staff, again assumes NWC presidency.
	August 17	1957 classes begin with 5 S&S, 59 NW2, 74 NW1, 132 C&S, and 23 naval command (NC) students. Graduation June 12, 1957.
1957	August 13	Robbins detached for duty in Washington. Vice Admiral Stuart Ingersoll assumes NWC presidency.
	August 14	1958 classes begin with 71 NW2, 95 NW1, 127 C&S, 28 NC students. Graduation June 11, 1958.
	September 5	President Eisenhower spends month vacationing on Naval Base. Meets with officers of new naval command course.
1958	May 29	Cardinal Francis Spellman addresses NWC.
	August 15	1959 classes begin with 156 NW, 111 C&S, 25 NCC students. NW1 and NW2 classes are combined in naval warfare (NW). Graduation June 10, 1959.
	August 15	Eisenhower again vacations in Newport, occupying quarters of NWC Chief of Staff at Fort Adams.
	November 7	Commissioning of Navy Electronic Warfare Simulator (NEWS) in Sims Hall.
	November 19	Madame Chiang Kai Shek addresses NWC.
1959	June 2	Separate war gaming department formed, removing NEWS from strategy department.
	August 21	1960 classes begin with 157 NW, 171 C&S, 25 NC students. Alexander Haig, Secretary of State in 1981-82, included in C&S class. Graduation June 15, 1960. Naval Long Range Studies Project established at NWC.
1960	February 12	NWC directed to provide NEWS time and instruction for fleet units.
	April 21	First military-media conference.
	June 30	Ingersoll retires from active duty. Vice Admiral Bernard Austin assumes NWC presidency.
	July	Eisenhower again vacations at Fort Adams.
	August 15	Correspondence Course Department redesignated Extension Education Department.
	August 19	1961 classes begin with 153 NW, 178 C&S, 24 NC students. Graduation June 14.
	November 6	NWC hosts first conference of heads of senior service colleges.
1961	February 2	Naval Long Range Studies Project becomes Institute Of Naval Studies (INS).
	June 19	INS conducts Limited War Symposium at NWC.
	August 18	1962 classes begin with 156 NW, 149 C&S, 26 NC students. Graduation June 20.
	September 27	President John F. Kennedy visits NWC.
	October 3	General of the Army Eisenhower addresses NWC.
	October 12	Fleet Admiral Chester Nimitz addresses NWC.

Year	Date	Event
1962	April 9	NWC hosts first conference of Heads of Naval War Colleges of the Americas.
	May 28	Two-week counterinsurgency course closes 1961-62 academic year at NWC.
	August 17	1963 classes begin with 150 NW, 175 C&S, 26 NC students. Graduation June 19, 1963.
	August 18	George Washington University graduate degree program begins with 180 enrollees.
	October 22	Cuban Missile Crisis—Newport based ships deploy to Caribbean.
1963	April 11	Austin on temporary duty for Court of Inquiry—loss of submarine USS Thresher.
	August 16	1964 classes begin with 159 NW, 160 C&S, 27 NC students. Graduation June 7.
	November 1	Institute of Naval Studies relocated to Cambridge, Mass. and becomes Center for Naval Analyses (CNA).
	November 22	Assassination of President Kennedy. Word passed at NWC during lecture by Chief of Naval Personnel.
1964	February 24	First George Washington University degrees presented to 16 students from NWC faculty and staff.
	April 10	Founders Hall, serving as Base Headquarters, becomes National Historic Landmark.
	June 8	Secretary of State Dean Rusk opens Global Strategy session.
	July 31	Austin retires, Vice Admiral Charles Melson assumes NWC presidency.
	August 14	1965 classes begin with 154 NW, 189 C&S, 24 NC students. Graduation June 16, 1965.
	September 10	Second extension to Mahan Hall for Library stack space approved.
	December 9	Former Secretary of State Dean Acheson addresses NWC.
1965	April 3	CNO approves reorganization of NWC built around school of naval warfare, school of command & staff, and correspondence school.
	May 18	NWC hosts meeting of Military Education Coordination Conference (MECC).
	August 13	1966 classes begin with 150 NW, 191 C&S, 22 NC students. Graduation June 15.
	December 1	Department of Defense team, led by Assistant Secretary of Defense Morris, visits NWC, first stop on inspection tour of senior military colleges.
1966	January 24	Melson retires from active duty. Rear Admiral Francis E. Neussle, Chief of Staff, assumes NWC presidency.
	February 15	Vice Admiral John T. Hayward assumes NWC presidency.
	March 29	General Earle Wheeler, Chairman, JCS, addresses NWC.
	June 10	Commander Rita Lenihan, NWC staff, selected as Director Waves, USN.
	August 12	1967 classes begin with 143 NW, 146 C&S, 21 NC students. Graduation June 14.
	November 23	Secretary of State Dean Rusk addresses NWC.
1967	April 1	Automatic data processing (ADP) introduced in NWC administrative work.
	May 5	First meeting of Naval War College Board of Advisors.
	July 1	NWC budgetary support shifted from Bupers to CNO (Op 09B).
	August 14	1968 classes begin with 95 NW, 117 C&S, 31 NC students. Graduation June 26. Interim C&S class commences two

Year	Date	Event
		weeks of NWC instruction with remainder of work through correspondence school.
1968	July 1	Position of Professor of Libraries established. Professor E. Schwass incumbent.
	July 14	First senior officers executive management course convenes, 40 attendees. Course primarily for flag and general officer selectees. Four-week duration.
	August 16	1969 classes begin with 143 NW, 152 C&S, 26 NC students. Graduation June 25.
	August 30	Hayward retires from active duty. Vice Admiral Richard G. Colbert assumes NWC presidency.
	November 28	CNO approves NWC plan to expand facilities for 700 students by 1980.
1969	January 1	NWC budgetary support returned to Bureau of Naval Personnel.
	February 1	Naval historical Collection established. A.S. Nicolosi, director.
	August 22	1970 classes begin with 169 NW, 190 C&S, 30 NC students. Graduation June 22.
	September 1	Chair of Air Strike Warfare, first military chair established.
	November 1	Chief of Naval Operations hosts First International Sea Power Symposium at NWC.
	November 28	Naval War College Foundation established under laws of Rhode Island. John Nicholas Brown first president. Rear Admiral Richard Bates, USN (Ret.), executive director.
1970	August 21	Classes of 1971 begin with 181 NW, 225 C&S, 30 NC students. Graduation June 21.
	November 9	Dedication of William McCarty-Little war gaming room in Sims Hall.
1971	February 1	Student team from C&S presents personnel study in Pentagon to SecNav and CNO.
	March 13	President Richard Nixon at NavBase for graduation of son-in-law, Ensign David Eisenhower from Officer Candidate School.
	April 27	Establishment of deputy to president billet. Rear Admiral G. Tahler reports.
	July 21	Establishment of Naval Education and Training Command at Pensacola, Fla.
	August 17	Colbert detached. Vice Admiral Benedict J. Semmes assumes NWC presidency.
	August 23	1972 classes begin with 202 NW, 244 C&S, 29 NC students. Graduation June 29.
1972	July 1	Semmes retires from active duty. Vice Admiral Stansfield Turner assumes NWC presidency.
	August 7	Naval staff course begins with 15 students. Graduation December 20.
	August 15	NWC bookstore opens in Navy Exchange Bldg. west of Sims Hall.
	August 24	1973 classes begin with 186 NW, 232 C&S, 32 NC students. Formal convocation and academic procession on Dewey Field. Graduation June 30, 1973. George Washington University courses end for naval warfare students.
	December 6	Author Herman Wouk gives first "Spruance Lecture" in auditorium of completed Spruance Hall. Building formally dedicated next day with Mrs. Spruance and Rear Admiral S.E. Morison, participating.

Year	Date	Event
1973	January 22	Second naval staff course begins with 16 students. Graduation June 30.
	April 17	DOD announces major shore reductions and fleet withdrawals from area.
	June 25	Global strategy discussions replaced by three-day Current Strategy Forum. Governor Jimmy Carter, USNA classmate of Turner, speaks to Forum.
	August 6	Third naval staff course begins with 14 students. Graduation December 21.
	August 30	1974 classes begin with 181 NW, 222 C&S, 31 NC students. Graduation June 28.
	October 23	NWC hosts visit Brazilian Naval War College staff and students.
	November 30	Death of Richard Colbert at Bethesda, Md.
	December 27	Death of Richard Bates in Newport, R.I.
1974	January 28	Fourth naval staff course begins with 17 students. ' Graduation June 14.
	March 1	Naval Base, Newport becomes Naval Education and Training Center (NETC).
	March 28	Dedication of Conolly Hall.
	June 25	Dedication of Colbert Plaza, seaward of new building complex.
	August 25	Fifth naval staff course begins with 18 students. Graduation December 20.
	August 9	Turner detached to sea duty. Vice Admiral Julien LeBourgeois assumes NWC presidency.
	August 28	1975 classes begin with 214 NW, 176 C&S, 38 NC students. Graduation July 1.
1975	January 20	Sixth naval staff course begins with 21 students. Graduation June 13.
	March 1	Opening of NWC Center for Advanced Research (CAR).
	May 8	Soviet officers from warships at Boston visit NWC.
	July 28	Seventh naval staff course begins with 17 students. Graduation December 19.
	August 29	1976 classes begin with 137 NW, 167 C&S, 32 NC students. Graduation June 17.
	October 13	The 200th Anniversary of U.S. Navy. NWC president reviews parade and speaks at Newport ceremonies.
	November 10	The 200th Anniversary of U.S. Marine Corps. Ceremonies on Dewey Field.
1976	January 13	Eighth naval staff course begins with 19 students. Graduation June 11.
	January 16	Formation of National Defense University (NDU) in Washington.
	April 28	Dedication of Hewitt Hall which includes new library.
	June 25	Tall ships visit Newport. Ships depart for N.Y. July 1.
	July 4	National Bicentennial Day. Full honors at noon by NETC and ships.
	July 8	NWC hosts Naval Command Course Conference celebrating 20th anniversary of founding of the international course.
	July 10	President Ford visits NWC and NETC to greet Queen Elizabeth and Prince Philip embarked in H.M.S. Britannia.
	July 13	Dedication of International Plaza, area between Spruance and Mahan Halls.
	July 26	Ninth naval staff course begins with 15 students. Graduation December 17.

Year	Date	Event
	August 25	1977 classes begin with 150 NW, 186 C&S, 32 NC students. Graduation June 30.
	October 1	Disestablishment of First Naval District. NWC now within Fourth District.
	November 29	Canadian Forces Staff College conducts exercise on NEWS.
1977	January 24	Tenth naval staff course begins with 16 students. Graduation June 17.
	April 1	LeBourgeois retires from active duty. Rear Admiral Huntington Hardisty assumes NWC presidency. NWC commences six-week extension course at New London Naval Base for Polaris-based officers.
	June 30	Rear Admiral Henry Eccles, USN (Ret.) completes 25 years' service on NWC staff since reporting upon his retirement from active duty 1952.
	July 18	Eleventh naval staff course begins with 13 students. Graduation December 16.
	August 15	1978 classes begin with 138 NW, 181 C&S, 39 NC students. Graduation June 27.
	October 13	Hardisty detached for overseas duty. Vice Admiral James B. Stockdale assumes NWC presidency.
1978	January 16	Twelfth naval staff course begins with 19 students. Graduation June 16.
	March 8	Former Secretary of State Henry Kissinger addresses NWC.
	May 26	Dedication of Founders Hall as NWC Museum.
	June 30	First NWC Alumni gathering addressed by Stockdale in Washington.
	November 16	Secretary of the Navy's Advisory Board on Education and Training meets at NWC.
	July 12	Thirteenth naval staff course begins with 18 students. Graduation December 15.
1979	January 15	Fourteenth naval staff college class begins with 22 students. Graduation June 15.
	April 20	The 105th annual meeting of U.S. Naval Institute (first ever held in Newport), held in Spruance Auditorium.
	July 15	Fifteenth naval staff college class convenes with 18 students. Graduation December 14.
	August 22	Stockdale retires from active duty. Rear Admiral Edward F. Welch assumes NWC presidency. 1980 classes begin with 127 NW, 156 C&S, 32 NC students. Graduation June 25.
1980	January 9	Sixteenth naval staff college class begins with 20 students. Graduation June 13.
	July 11	Bicentennial of arrival of Rochambeau's Army in Newport. NWC president is principal speaker at City of Newport ceremony in Eisenhower Square.
	July 16	Seventeenth naval staff college class begins with 21 students. Graduation Dec. 19
	August 20	1981 classes begin with 110 NW, 137 C&S, 31 NC students. Graduation June 24. 1980 classes begin with 127 NW, 156 C&S, 32 NC students. Graduation June 25.
1980	January 9	Sixteenth naval staff college class begins with 20 students. Graduation June 13.
	July 11	Bicentennial of arrival of Rochambeau's Army in Newport. NWC president is principal speaker at City of Newport ceremony in Eisenhower Square.

Year	Date	Event
	July 16	Seventeenth naval staff college class begins with 21 students. Graduation Dec. 19
	August 20	1981 classes begin with 110 NW, 137 C&S, 31 NC students. Graduation June 24.
	October 30	NWC hosts first Tactical Symposium.
1981	January 7	Eighteenth naval staff college class begins with 22 students. Graduation June 12.
	June 26	NWC International Park between Luce & Founders Halls dedicated.
	July 1	Center for Naval Warfare Studies (CNWS) established. Honorable R.J. Murray first director.
	July 15	Nineteenth naval staff college class begins with 26 students. Graduation Dec. 18.
	August 18	1982 classes begin with 162 NW, 147 C&S, 37 NC students. Graduation June 25.
	August 27	Humorist Art Buchwald lectures on Colbert Plaza to more than 1500 attendees.
1982	January 20	Twentieth naval staff college class begins with 26 students. Graduation June 25.
	July 21	Twenty-first naval staff college class begins with 17 students. Graduation December 17.
	August 17	Welch retires from active duty. Captain David Self, Deputy, assumes NWC presidency. 1983 classes begin with 141 NW, 148 C&S, 36 NC students. Graduation June 24.
	October 14	Rear Admiral James E. Service assumes NWC presidency.
	October 28	CNO hosts conference of Fleet Commanders-in-Chief at NWC. Updated Naval War Gaming System (NWGS) is used to show latest war gaming developments.
1983	January 19	Twenty-second naval staff college class begins with 20 students. Graduation June 24.
	February 7	First Post-Command class begins with 12 students. Graduation March 18. Courses continue through 1983 as follows: March 28-June 17, 12 students; May 9-June 17, 21 students; June 27-August 5, 23 students; September 12-October 14, 21 students.
	June 4	Centennial of Naval Training Station (presently NETC, Newport). Founded by Luce.
	July 18	Twenty-third naval staff college class begins with 17 students. Graduation December 1.
	August 16	1984 classes begin with 154 NW, 159 C&S, 34 NC students. Graduation June 22.
	September 24	U.S. loses "America's Cup" to Australia in seven race series off Newport.
	November 18	First formal graduation ceremony for phased-input naval warfare and command and staff college students.
1984	January 9	1984 Post-Command courses begin. Schedule as follows: January 9-March 2; March 26-June 15; June 9-August 31; and September 10-November 2. Total of 75 students in four courses anticipated.
	January 18	Twenty-fourth naval staff college class begins with 19 students. Graduation June 22.
	July 16	Twenty-fifth naval staff college class begins. Graduation December 1.
	August 21	1985 classes begin.
	October 1	Centennial Week at Naval War College ending on October 6. 100th anniversary of founding of the college.

INDEX